The Last Englishman
The Double Life of Arthur Ransome

~

ROLAND CHAMBERS

faber and faber

First published in 2009 by
Faber and Faber Ltd
Bloomsbury House
74–77 Great Russell Street
London WC1B 3DA
This paperback edition first published in 2010

Typeset by Faber and Faber Ltd
Printed and bound by CPI Group (UK) Ltd, Croydon, CRO 4YY

A CIP record for this book
is available from the British Library

ISBN 978–0–571–22262–9

MIX
Paper from
responsible sources
FSC® C013604

The Last Englishman

Roland Chambers studied film and literature in Poland and at New York University before returning to England in 1998. He has worked as a private investigator specialising in Russian politics and business. He lives in London. *The Last Englishman* is his first biography.

Praise for *The Last Englishman*:

Winner of the Biography Club's Prize for Best First Biography

'Fascinating.' Gabriel Weston, *Daily Telegraph* Books of the Year

'Deftly examines a murky career.' Ian Jack, *Guardian* Books of the Year

'Solidly researched [and] highly readable.' Ronald Frame, *Scotsman* Books of the Year

'A crackingly good book [and] a remarkable, gloriously well-written portrait.' Sam Leith, *Daily Mail* Book of the Week

'A riveting story.' A. N. Wilson, *Evening Standard*

'A fascinating study of a strange man.' **** Philip Womack, *Daily Telegraph*

'Chambers' achievement is remarkable . . . The historian's business is not to blame Arthur Ransome, or to apologise for him, but to understand him, as a means to understanding his times. To this necessary undertaking Chambers has undeniably made a large contribution.' Hugh Brogan, *Literary Review*

'Superb.' Richard Morrison, *The Times*

'Chambers brings the most extraordinary information to light in 'a biography which is as unexpected as it is gripping . . . Chambers approaches his subject with enthusiasm and seriousness, telling a great story along the way.' John Boyne, *Irish Times*

'You finish reading it with the sense that you've learned an enormous amount, and not only about Ransome but about the history of the early years of the century and the Russian Revolution.' Adèle Geras

'A fascinating biography . . . Does this book illuminate the man? As far as is possible.' Candida Clark, *Financial Times*

'Chambers neither whitewashes nor condemns . . . His Ransome is complex, contradictory and certainly not a cosy personality. This is good biography – and even better history . . . Chambers' triumph is to chronicle the crucial period of physical, emotional and intellectual exile through which Arthur Ransome finally came home.' *Guardian*

'Chambers' biography brings us nearer to Ransome than we have ever been before.' John Carey, *Sunday Times*

'Wonderful.' Roger Hutchinson, *Scotsman*

'Chambers' biography draws on information released since 2005 . . . Fascinating.' Caroline Moore, *Standpoint*

'An enjoyable yarn about a famous author's incongruous role in a murky, vitally important period of European history.' *The Economist*

'Chambers tells a rich story that will greatly surprise nostalgic readers.' *Saga*

'An engrossing story, and Chambers tells it superbly.' *Country Life*

'Absorbing and well written.' Piers Brendon, *Oldie*

For my mother and father

Contents

Illustrations

Ransome in 1932 with the Altounyan family.
The Shelepina sisters in Moscow, 1972.
Ransome the writer.

PHOTOGRAPH CREDITS

The photographs listed above are reproduced with the permission of Special Collections, Leeds University Library, Ransome Collection, with the exception of the following: Edward Thomas on page 2 is courtesy of Cardiff University Library; the Shelepina family in 1908 on page 5 and the Shelepina sisters in Moscow, 1972, on page 8 are courtesy of Gleb Drapkin.

Introduction

Five months after the close of the First World War, Arthur Ransome, returning from a 'fact-finding' expedition to Soviet Russia, cleared customs at Newcastle, boarded a train for London, and alighting at King's Cross station was politely informed by a plain-clothes detective that he should consider himself under arrest. There had been little fuss over the matter. Within twenty minutes he was sitting in Scotland Yard being cross-examined by one of the most powerful officials in the country: Sir Basil Thomson, head of Special Branch.

On the face of it, the position could not have been more serious. Thomson, also known as 'Spycatcher' Thomson, was a man of appropriately conservative convictions. As deputy prime minister of colonial Tonga, his closest friends had been cannibals, 'a far more estimable person', he claimed, 'than the town-bred missionary-educated native'. Later, as governor of a series of notorious British prisons, he had attended every hanging, and remained an enthusiastic proponent of the death penalty. Since 1914, under the Defence of the Realm Act, Thomson had enjoyed sweeping powers to arrest, interrogate and prosecute any person deemed a threat to national security, including German spies, pacifists, Irish revolutionaries, and in recent years, a species he viewed with special loathing, Bolshevik agitators. It was, therefore, unfortunate that amongst Ransome's papers was a letter signed personally by Lenin providing access to the entire Bolshevik administration, together with a diary detailing his recent trip to Russia in the most glowing terms.

As correspondent for the radical *Daily News*, Ransome had already established his reputation as one of the most notorious apologists for Bolshevism, both at home and in America, where his articles were printed with a health warning attached. Since the Bolshevik coup in 1917, he had applauded the suppression of Lenin's political opponents; condemned Britain's attempts, through military intervention, to remove the Soviet government by force; interviewed the founders of the Bolshevik secret police (original forerunner to the KGB) and found them to be men of unimpeachable integrity. It was a disgrace, Ransome had insisted, that others were not in Moscow at that very moment, taking the measure of 'the gigantic experiment' which Britain, as a nation, was permitting to pass 'abused but not examined'. On 4 March, he had been the only British correspondent to attend the inauguration of the Third International, the so-called 'Comintern', established by Lenin to foment revolution abroad.

In the early weeks of 1919, Britain had contended with a mutiny of sailors in Folkestone waiting to be demobbed, and in Scotland with a self-proclaimed council of workers, or 'Soviet', which briefly took control of Glasgow before 10,000 English troops were sent in to restore order. In Paris, at the Quai d'Orsay, the Allied leaders were hammering out a peace in the teeth of widespread revolution in central and eastern Europe. 'We are running a race with Bolshevism,' President Woodrow Wilson had declared, 'and the world is on fire.'

It was Thomson's own belief that communism threatened the very roots of Western civilization, and yet, seated in Scotland Yard with the evidence spread out before him, he saw no immediate grounds for prosecution. Ransome – very tall and thin, with an unruly red moustache and wire-framed spectacles – doubtless resembled a revolutionary. He certainly wrote like a revolutionary. In February, his name had been raised repeatedly during a senatorial investigation into Bolshevik propaganda in the States. In England, the Home Office had agonized as to whether to permit him back into the country at all. But Ransome did not *talk* like a revolutionary. His godfather was Sir Arthur Acland, former Minister of Education under Gladstone. His closest friends and family were Conservatives and Liberals. He was an ardent patriot, a keen sportsman who spent his weekends yachting and angling. He had never been, he assured Thomson, a communist, or even, in any practical sense, a socialist. If he admired Lenin, it was for reasons entirely consistent with his Rugby education. The Bolsheviks were the only viable government capable of preventing Russia from sliding into anarchy.

In short, after a frosty start, these two – both public schoolboys, both contemptuous of narrow bureaucracy, both men whose careers had materially benefited from the war – found themselves agreeing on almost every point. Thomson looked forward to Ransome's history of the Revolution, and particularly to his portraits of the Soviet leaders, of whom so little was known in England. He listened eagerly to his account of the inauguration of the Third International and thought it interesting, even funny. Within a few years of their interview, Thomson, knighted for his services to the empire, would be forced to resign his position over a nocturnal encounter with a prostitute in Hyde Park, subsequently turning his hand to detective novels. Ransome, in the meantime, went on to become one of the most famous authors in children's literature. Later, he would recall his arrest with bewildered amusement. When Thomson had asked him what his politics were, he had answered, 'Fishing.'

~

Today, Ransome is best known for *Swallows and Amazons* and eleven further stories written one after another on an almost yearly basis between 1930 and 1947. His name, and by extension his character, have become identified with a particular vision of England: a pastoral, old-fashioned utopia set in the Lake District sometime between the wars, with its roots in the Edwardian heyday of the British empire. One summer, with their father's permission, four Walker children set sail for a lonely island, pitched camp and proceeded to map a world; a world which expanded year after year, with new adventures, characters and discoveries. Five novels were set in the Lake District, two on the Norfolk Broads, two near Ipswich and one each in the Hebrides, the Caribbean and the South China Seas. The books could be read at random or consecutively as a series. They were usually published for Christmas, eagerly awaited by a growing horde of fanatics and filled with the practical details of Ransome's own passions: sailing, fishing, camping and the minute observation of animals and birds made on the long walks he delighted in throughout his life, until his legs could no longer support him and he subsided into the decidedly peevish fog that overtook him in old age. Collectively they founded a new genre: the holiday adventure.

Ransome joined the handful of writers who make up the British children's canon, but unlike authors such as Lewis Carroll, A. A. Milne, J. R. R. Tolkien and C. S. Lewis, who created separate universes, Ransome's world is a light-hearted fantasy sprinkled over a tangible, deeply experienced reality, one that can be visited and explored without the necessity of a wardrobe, a rabbit hole or a looking glass. As the popularity of the books grew, Ransome received hundreds of letters from children all over the world, begging for further details, asking for more stories, telling of their own Ransome-inspired adventures, and asking if it might be possible to come and visit the Walker children in person. Sorting through these letters the most common question is simply, 'Are they real?' more often than not followed by a confident, 'I think they are.' And this confidence was not entirely misplaced. The books, particularly those set in the Lake District, were drawn so closely from Ransome's own experiences that careful readers could spend weeks tracking down the real-life equivalents of places they had read about as a child: Wild Cat Island, Cormorant Island, Houseboat Bay. In doing so they would simply be reversing the process by which Ransome had conceived the stories in the first place. The world of *Swallows and Amazons* was created by flowing two lakes together: Windermere and Coniston Water. Ransome rearranged existing landmarks to create an ideal geography, and this geography became so familiar to him that when he visited the Lakes in old age, he was sometimes surprised by a brief sense of dislocation, as though an earthquake had happened while his back was turned.

Ransome's more literal-minded followers were not content simply to read his books. It was necessary to go out and perform them, to relive the adventures in practice. As an example, one might turn to Maurice Rowlandson, a man who had fallen in love with *Swallows and Amazons* as a child and later founded a cruising club on the Norfolk Broads where hundreds of school-children over the years experienced the joys of sailing, bird-watching, stargazing, fishing and exploring. 'John, Susan, Titty and Roger,' wrote Rowlandson,

Nancy and Peggy; Dick and Dorothea; Tom and the Coots; Squashy Hat and the Great Aunt to say nothing of Captain Flint himself are all very real people to me. I feel I almost know them. Mrs Blackett might call at any time; I am sure I would recognize her. As for Commander Walker and Mrs Walker, they are the world's most sensible and under-standing parents; may my wife and I be a little like them. I am 35 years of age now, but I will not outgrow these books. They have shaped my life . . .

Ransome preserved this letter carefully amongst his papers with a neat red tick in one corner, signifying his approval not only of a simple pleasure in reading, but the way in which Rowlandson had grasped a moral reality. Neither was Rowland-son alone. Halfway between two world wars there was good rea-son to welcome an author whose expectations were so modest, who preferred to dwell on the practical possibilities of life, to repair what could be repaired – torn sails, ruptured hulls, grazed knees – and quietly ignore the rest. The Great War had claimed 10 million lives; close to a million young men from Britain alone, many of them barely old enough to fight at all, machine-gunned, gassed, blown to bits or drowned in mud. Ransome's own brother was amongst them.

And yet Ransome's appeal was not universal. For every fresh convert that discovered in his stories a perfect England, there were others who found them flat, old-fashioned or too good to be true. William Trevor, the Irish novelist and short-story writer, recalled that as a boy he had been bewildered by the Walkers, later deciding that they were not children at all, but miniature adults, constructed according to a middle-class fantasy that he had little reason to identify with or admire. David Garnett, meanwhile, who had known Ransome for many years, regretted that in perpetuating this fantasy, his old friend had forgotten how strenuously he once opposed it. 'The weakness of contemporary children's books', Garnett complained,

is that the characters in them are almost always polite, rational and well-behaved citizens of a sensibly managed world. Strangely enough, this false picture is the work of a generation of violent rebels, who defied Victorian conventions and morality. Why don't they ever represent the grown-up world in its true light – with human children having to fight for their own hand?

It is often forgotten that Ransome was forty-five when he began writing his most famous books, and that the most interesting episode of his life, from a biographer's point of view, was already over. Between 1913 and 1924, he lived in Russia and the Baltic States, working as a correspondent first for the *Daily News* and then for the *Manchester Guardian*. The author of *Swallows and Amazons* had seen the March Revolution of 1917 with his own eyes, and following the Bolshevik coup in November, became one of a tiny number of foreign journalists granted access to the new Soviet government. During the first years of Bolshevik rule, he had retained close contact with the Kremlin, in spite of the liquidation of a British conspiracy headed by one of his closest associates, an Allied invasion, and a suspicion that Ransome himself was working as a British spy. In the aftermath of the Russian Civil War he had been in Egypt to cover the assassination of the British governor of Sudan, and in China to document a Soviet-backed nationalist revolution led by Chiang Kai-shek. By 1930, he had witnessed the most formative episodes of the twentieth century: the collapse of four empires, the emergence of modern Europe and the face-off between democratic and communist powers that laid the foundations for the Cold War. If he had ever finished his own history of the Revolution – a projected magnum opus sanctioned by Lenin himself – Ransome would be remembered very differently today. But instead he abandoned politics altogether, and with a sigh of relief embarked on the adventures of the Walker children and their friends. Very quickly his name became synonymous with an entirely different world.

Such has been the success of Ransome's books over the years that the details of his life, much like the real geography of the Lakes, have been subordinated to his fiction: an Edwardian idyll of bun loaf and pemmican, of butter and marmalade sandwiches, of cotton tents and grog and tea at four, and children who say 'jolly' and play by the rules; well-behaved children who rise early and know how to do things, tie knots and sail a boat, use a compass or flight an arrow with parrot feathers, who respect the enemy if he fights fair and happily share their chocolate when the battle is over. This was the world Ransome created, a world which expanded like a miniature, ideal empire, with new territories mapped and new skills acquired, with rival explorers, natives and savages, and all kinds of glory to be won. It was a world supervised by adults, but only at a distance, with Mrs Walker safely on shore, and far off on an obscure horizon, Commander Walker, the 'most sensible of parents', patrolling the limits of the real British empire in his Royal Navy destroyer. Nothing intruded into Ransome's paradise to interrupt the fun, either for the author or for his readers. It was as if the First World War and the Revolution in Russia had never happened at all.

Ransome's unfinished and posthumously published autobiography, designed to 'get down the quiet, dull truth' about his time in Russia, was greeted in 1976 with a mixture of scepticism and indulgence. The novelist Margaret Drabble suggested that he had treated the Revolution as a game, very much like his fictional characters had treated war as a game. William Golding, author of *Lord of the Flies*, defended Ransome's right to recall his life on his own terms: 'Ransome remains a private person still. As in his children, his dark or bright corners are cleaned up or concealed. What right have we to ask more about him than he chooses to tell us?' Tim Radford for the *Guardian*, by contrast, had visited the National Archive in Kew, where the Foreign Office wartime records are kept in their original wooden filing cabinets. Here he discovered that Ransome's correspondence was routinely intercepted by Britain's domestic counter-intelligence service, that the British ambassador in Sweden (whom Ransome counted as a friend) was convinced he was a Bolshevik agent; and that while married to an English woman named Ivy Walker, he had conducted a passionate love affair with Leon Trotsky's private secretary. And yet the nature of Ransome's allegiance remained obscure, and never more so than in 2005, when classified documents were finally released proving that at the height of his notoriety he had been recruited by his own government as an agent of the newly incorporated MI6.

~

My own book was intended initially as a brief and colourful *exposé*, a sharp adjustment to the whitewash that hitherto has screened Ransome from anything approaching a candid assessment. But very quickly I realized that his life, as well as the age that he lived through, offered something much richer. No other Englishman saw the war and Revolution from so many points of view. No other journalist so effectively blended the rhetoric of conventional democracy with the radical doctrines of Marxism–Leninism. As a struggling writer in pre-war London, Ransome had befriended strident nationalists and equally strident internationalists. In the same way, between 1914 and Lenin's death in 1924, he found himself on easy terms with arch-reactionaries and committed revolutionaries. Ransome was a bohemian and a conservative, a champion of self-determination and an imperialist, a man who cherished liberty but assumed, as a matter of course, that liberty depended on a successful negotiation with power. The fascination of his story consists in the ease with which he adopted all the competing ideals of his generation. Yet Ransome, who longed, above all, to be included, did not consider himself a controversial figure. On the contrary, while others had lost themselves in uncertainty, forgotten who they were or how to live, he had always, he insisted, been the simplest of men.

I

The Judgemental Professor

Ransome's conscious life began early, at the age of two, aboard the deck of a steamship after a night crossing, held high in his father's arms so that he could see pigs being loaded onto brightly painted schooners in Belfast harbour. He remembered how in Ireland he had slipped out of his mother's arms, through the tunnel of blankets he was swaddled in, and sat down hard in the road. He remembered snowdrops, and in the distance, across a wide stretch of grassland, a man riding a bicycle along an avenue of trees. Much later his father told him that he had imagined it, but he protested indignantly and described the place in such detail that it was eventually identified as the park of Sir Nathaniel Staples, near Cookstown in County Tyrone.

In 1887, when Ransome was three and a half years old, round-faced and heavy, he attended celebrations for Queen Victoria's Golden Jubilee at a tithe barn in Wold Newton in Yorkshire, where his uncle had a parish. He remembered the blue mug he had clutched in his hand on the way and the old ladies, who had seen the coronation half a century before, sitting on a raised platform in their smocks and linen sun bonnets. But when his father introduced him to a man who could remember Trafalgar and had been seventeen at the time of the Battle of Waterloo, he recollected the incident only to illustrate the difference between personal and borrowed memory. As an old man himself he concluded that it was not these 'chance touchings of the skirts of history' that formed the deepest impressions, but 'quite simple things, drifting snowflakes seen through a melted peephole in a frosted nursery window, the sun like a red-hot penny in the smoky Leeds sky, and the dreadful screaming of a wounded hare. That last I can never forget.'

Arthur Michell Ransome was born on 18 January 1884 at 6

Ash Grove in Leeds, where his father Cyril was Professor of History and Modern Literature at the newly instituted Yorkshire College. It was, according to Ransome, 'a mean, ugly little building', but his father's books were doing well, and over the next few years the family's situation improved rapidly. By 1890 they were in Balmoral Terrace, Headingley – a smart neighbourhood on the outskirts of town – and Ransome had a younger brother and two sisters, born conveniently in alphabetical order: Cecily, Geoffrey, and Joyce. They had a cook, a housemaid and a nurse, lived next door to the editor of the *Yorkshire Post*, who kept apples in his desk, and had long since taken their place amongst the small number of families who presided over the academic and public life of the city. Later, Professor Ransome would adopt Kitty Woodburne, the daughter of a wealthy, recently deceased local solicitor, whose governess, Mrs Sidgemore, or 'Sidgie', gave the youngest children their first lessons in French and arithmetic. But as the junior head of the household, Ransome grew up slightly apart, conscious that what was expected of him was expected of him alone.

At home his mother read to them: William Thackeray's *The Rose and the Ring*, Edward Lear, a good deal of Lewis Carroll, Charles Kingsley's *The Water-Babies* and all of Andrew Lang's fairy tales, which Ransome collected 'one by one at Christmas and on birthdays'. It was not an extensive library, but it was a good one. Edith Ransome never read her children a book she didn't like herself, and so she read well, with an enthusiasm that communicated itself to her children. 'We were never conscious that the bad was being withheld from us,' Ransome would remember, 'but in fact it was. I think our parents' principles in this matter were those of Tennyson's Northern Farmer who told his son "Doänt thou marry for money, but goä wheer money is." We did not know that we were forbidden to read rubbish but we were given every opportunity of reading the best.'

Professor Ransome started teaching his eldest son Latin when he was barely out of the cradle, with little success, later sharing the cost of tutors with another local solicitor, Octavius Eddison, whose coachman used to drive the young Ransome to his lessons every morning and enquire anxiously if he had eaten enough bacon for breakfast. Eddison's son, Ric, became his first close friend and made a powerful and lasting impression on Arthur – ever the hero worshipper – by fiercely resisting any attempt by adults to bully or patronize. Ric's uncle, by lucky coincidence, was Andrew Lang, whose fairy tales adorned the bookshelves in the Ransome nursery, while his next-door neighbour was Isabella Ford, a prominent Fabian, a pioneer of women's trade unions and a generous hostess, not only to young scholars tired of grammar and arithmetic, but also to political refugees from every corner of Europe. It was here, at Isabella's home at Adel Grange, that Ransome met his first revolutionary, the anarchist Prince Peter Kropotkin, who taught him how to skate on a frozen pond at the bottom of the garden.

Ransome understood from the earliest age that the world stretched a long way beyond his house between the Three Horse Shoes and the Skyrack Inn. Both his grandfathers married twice and left a great number of aunts, uncles and cousins. On the Ransome side was a line of Quakers stretching back to the Restoration, spawning parsons, teachers, doctors, industrialists, scientists, two missionary aunts and a family business, Ransome and Rapier of Ipswich, specializing in agricultural equipment. Ransome's paternal great-grandfather, who had founded the company, went on to become a famous surgeon, a friend to Brunel, and was commemorated with a bust by the Manchester School of Medicine. Ransome's autobiography contains several pages recounting his exploits and those of other relatives, including Edith's father, Edward Baker Boulton, who had a sheep farm in Australia and brought back emus' eggs, sharks' teeth, exotic shells and boomerangs, which Ransome stored lovingly in a small museum he had established in a bathroom washstand drawer. Collectively, these ancestors represented the solid backbone of Victorian middle-class society, and Ransome was proud of them. But his favourite grandfather was not the farmer but the wayward eccentric, Thomas Ransome, an ingenious inventor and natural scientist popular for his magic-lantern shows and

Professor Ransome started taking his family to the Swainsons at Nibthwaite the same year Arthur was born, 'a farmhouse at the foot of Coniston where we have spent some of our happiest hours and the children enjoyed an early taste of country life'. He fished and walked out with his pointer, Carlo, taught his children to row and hold a net, and on rainy days sat inside and wrote: a guide to Shakespeare, a book on the British colonies – *How We Got Them and Why We Keep Them* – an introduction to Thomas Carlyle's *Frederick the Great*, and a great deal more besides. Ransome recalled these holidays half a century later with a lucidity born of frequent repetition, losing any non-essential details that might obscure the ritual of an ideal return.

Long before they set out, Ransome's father prepared his fishing rods and tackle, laying the newly made casts over wooden candlesticks in his study. Meanwhile, Ransome's mother patched clothes, replenished watercolours and wrote long lists of necessities that finally found their way, on the day before departure, into a monstrous tin bath that doubled at Christmas as a present chest.

Then came the great day itself, and the railway journey, written up to match the rhythm of pistons and sleepers:

Through the outskirts of Leeds, through smoky Holbeck, past the level crossing on by Wharfedale to Hellifield, my father's guns and rods on the rack, ginger-nuts crunching in our mouths, noses pressed to the window to watch the dizzying rise and fall of the telegraph wires beside the track. By the time we reached Arkholme we could feel my father's mounting excitement. There were well-known landmarks as the train ran slowly round Morecambe Bay. There was the farmhouse that was built like a little fortress against invading Scots. There was Arnside Tower. There were our own Lake hills, and Coniston Old Man with a profile very different from the lofty one it showed us at Nibthwaite. Then at last we were at Greenodd, where the Crake and the Leven poured together to the sea not a stone's throw from the railway line. There would be John Swainson from Nibthwaite, or Edward his son, with a red farmcart and a well-beloved young lad with a wagonette.

The last leg of the journey was finished by cart: up the Crake valley, down by Lowick Green, over the river at Lowick Bridge, and finally, after a steep climb, 'there we were at the farm, being greeted by Mrs Swainson and her daughters, and getting our first proper sight of the lake itself – Coniston Water'.

After tea, the children – Arthur, Cecily, Geoffrey and Joyce – were released to explore, or rather to renew an acquaintance broken off the year before. But before joining his brother and sisters, Ransome liked to go down to the lake on his own.

'I had a private rite to perform,' he recalled.

Without letting the others know what I was doing, I had to dip my hand in the water, as a greeting to the beloved lake, or as a proof to myself that I had indeed come home. In later years, even as an old man, I have laughed at myself, resolved not to do it, and every time have done it again. If I were able to go back there today, I should feel some discomfort until after coming to the shores of the lake I had felt its coolness on my fingers.

~

Ransome felt more deeply than most that certain griefs and disappointments can only be resolved privately. When his brother Geoffrey died in the First World War, he never mentioned it in his letters or even his diary. When his mother Edith died in 1944, he regretted the many letters of condolence he received as well-meant intrusions. In the course of his life there would be many miseries, many anomalies, which he declined to explain, while deeply resenting those who attempted to explain them for him. But there was one loss that he went out of his way to understand, because it lay at the root of so much of the anxiety that dogged him throughout his life: the death of his father when he was thirteen years old. 'I have been learning ever since how much I lost in him. He had been disappointed in me, but I have often thought what friends we could have been had he not died so young.'

When Professor Ransome was courting Edith in 1882, he wrote her a series of letters declaring his love for her and advising her on every topic, from the composition of watercolours to politics, housekeeping, the history of British democracy and the merits and demerits of the Roman Catholic and Protestant Church. He himself was a Protestant and a Liberal, and was delighted to find Edith a Liberal too. 'I like you to be independent and think for yourself,' he told her. 'I know among weak conventional people it is assumed that wives think just like their husbands and it is thought so nice and so pretty, while I think it is simply degrading to one and demoralizing to the other.' Ransome's father went on to explain how at Oxford he had met his first Liberals and formed his views on class, the equality of 'men as men and women as women' and the importance, above all things, of moral character. 'The main thing that I learned is this,' he confided, 'that there are two great classes of people who pervade all sets, all politics, all religions, all ranks of society viz those who look at things from a high point of view, and those who look at things from a low point of view.'

Professor Ransome's career, since boyhood, had been a shining example of the 'high'. It was thought at first that he would be a clergyman, but instead he decided to be a teacher, a vocation that he pursued with all the zeal of his Quaker ancestors. As a scholar at Oxford, he studied mathematics, then history, and took his first teaching post at the Military College in Cowley, where he met Sir Arthur Acland, a 'truly great man'. Cowley, however, was run by philistines, and both men resigned soon afterwards. Acland – later Arthur's godfather – embarked on a career in politics, while Professor Ransome took an interim position at Rugby school as private tutor to Prince Alamayu, son and heir to the late Emperor Theodorus of Abyssinia. In 1878, he accepted his chair at the Yorkshire College, where, in addition to his other duties, he lectured at the working men's clubs, founded a reading society, and at the request of Queen Victoria's personal secretary, took Alamayu back into his care. But Alamayu was a reluctant student, and never more so than when, after falling asleep in the outdoor lavatory, he caught pneumonia, and refusing medication, died soon after. Recalling the incident in his memoirs, Professor Ransome confessed that he had found the boy 'a great nuisance', and regretted that he had shown so little gratitude for his Rugby education. Prince Theebaw of Burma proved far more satisfactory. At Nibthwaite, in 1892, he survived a midnight attack from Arthur's furry fox-moth caterpillars with admirable equanimity.

~

Ransome's autobiography, in so far as it deals with his father, is a mixture of calculated humility, nostalgia and bitter reproach. Professor Ransome had tried to teach his eldest son to swim by throwing him over the side of a boat, and had the pleasure of watching him sink like a stone. He had given him a copy of *Robinson Crusoe* at the age of four as a reward for having read the book from cover to cover, but found him tearing through Walter Scott's Waverley novels so fast that he insisted on quizzing him on each one before he was allowed the next. The boy had no ear for Latin, no appetite for serious study or reflection, and at home entertained himself with one futile project after another. Ransome later recalled:

I spent every penny I had on coloured paper, made spills for Leeds, for all Yorkshire, for all the world, and put the match factories out of business. In this my father saw at once something of a foreshadowing of my grandfather's disastrous venture as a manufacturing chemist. It seemed to him (and indeed it was) a miserable, mercenary ambition, and in a small boy of six or seven he saw already the man who threw away in exchange for empty husks the prospect, open before him, of a useful scientific career.

As a child, Ransome developed passions, in no particular order, for carpentry, drawing-room theatre, the breeding of Belgian hares, ventriloquism, mice, conjuring, photography, insects and, briefly, for William Gladstone, leader of the Liberal Party, who had infuriated his father by proposing Home Rule for Ireland. Professor Ransome encouraged him when he showed an early interest in rare hawk moths, but despaired when he revealed his intention to produce them 'on a monstrous scale and sell them sordidly to collectors'. Even the museum in the wash-stand drawer, containing treasures ranging from Aboriginal arte-facts to a seal from one of the first iron ships, met with censure when it emerged that it was intended as the nucleus of a much larger collection designed 'to fill a building something like the Leeds Town Hall, and attract pilgrims, at six pence a head, from all parts of the world'. Ransome acknowledged that his father was motivated only by the best of intentions, but revealed in one anecdote after another how his early development was impeded by an imagination so much less joyful and fertile than his own that rebellion was all but inevitable. Following the disastrous swimming lesson, he had taken himself, using his own pocket money, to the Leeds public baths, where he taught himself the backstroke in secret, only to be told when announcing the fact at breakfast that he was a liar. When the feat was eventually proved *in situ*, his father relented, but Ransome never truly forgave the accusation. He liked to remember the incident whenever any aspersion was cast on his honesty.

When Ransome was done with private tutors, he was sent to day school in Leeds, then to the Old College at Windermere – his first taste of boarding school and a rude awakening. The head-master, a friend of the family, liked to box, but Ransome was too short-sighted to defend himself and in consequence was called a coward. Neither was his performance in the classroom any con-solation. As the son of a professor whose books were becoming standard texts at schools and universities, great things were expected of him, but Ransome, made miserable by homesick-ness, struggled with the simplest lessons. He ran away, but hav-ing nowhere to run to, came back of his own accord, gaining some comfort at the weekends by visiting a nearby aunt. In the meantime, with awful tenacity, he petitioned his mother for pets.

'I am preparing a set of apparatus for Performing Mice,' reads one of his earliest letters to Edith.

It is a Race Course with hoops to go through and Hurdles to jump over. I wonder whether the children will like it. I have got a beautiful little cage made on purpose for rats here. Please will you tell the children

Habout the Rats and Mice and tell them that I am going to dress a rat up like an old Woman and Ventriloquize it. Please tell Mrs Sidgemore that I will write to her when I write to thank for the mice if they come. I am hoping for the mice.

Your loving son, Arthur.

As an adult, Ransome never shook off the bewilderment of being sent away or the tireless knack, when writing to his mother, of demanding what he wanted until he got it. But while he endured the taunts of his schoolmates and the contempt of his teachers, far worse was to come. When Ransome was barely ten years old, his father – of all men, the most solid, the least vulnerable, the least likely to confess weakness of any kind – came to grief quite unexpectedly. Late one night, returning from a trout-fishing expedition near the Swainsons' farm in Nibthwaite, he had tripped over an old grindstone in the dark and broken his ankle, but convinced it was only a wrench, forced himself to walk home with his catch so that it would not stiffen and ruin his holiday. 'For a long time', recalled Ransome,

he walked with crutches, the foot monstrously bandaged. The doctors were slow in finding what had happened, probably because my father was so sure himself. In the end they found that he had damaged a bone and that some form of tuberculosis had attacked the damaged place. His foot was cut off. Things grew no better and his leg was cut off at the knee. Even that was not enough and it was cut off at the thigh.

Ransome was still in his first years at the Old College when his father fell, and he returned home every holiday to find him visibly weaker. But Professor Ransome refused to give in. He bought an old tricycle and rigged a gun rest on the handlebars so that he could continue shooting. When his leg was replaced with a cork prosthetic, he continued to fish, balancing precariously in his waders. In the last year of his life he resigned his chair at Leeds and moved the family down to Rugby, where he intended to stand as a Conservative candidate in the general election, and as a Member of Parliament fight Gladstone's proposal for an independent Ireland. There was no talk of death in the Ransome household, nor any opportunity for the children to come to terms with what was about to happen. Professor Ransome's final contribution to Arthur's education was to enter him, against all the odds, for scholarships to Shrewsbury and Rugby.

Ransome was one of only two boys from the Old College who attempted scholarship examinations at all, and the consequences were predictable. At Shrewsbury he brought shame on the family by failing to decline *'parvus'*, but at Rugby his disgrace was complete. A few days after the exam, he went to read the results, which had been pinned to a public notice board on the school gates.

I began reading that list at the bottom, where I expected to find my name. It was not there. By the time I had come half way up the list and had not found it, an incredulous hope began to dawn. Could I, after all, have done better than I feared? I read on, higher and higher, name after name, until, in growing excitement, I had reached those names besides which were printed the scholarships that had been awarded to their owners. Hardly able to breathe I read on until I came to the top of the list and knew the dreadful truth. I had not won a scholarship. I was not even in the first one hundred but was either No. 101 or No. 102, one of the pair protected by a merciful anonymity from knowing who was last of all.

Ransome was enrolled at Rugby as an ordinary student, and returned to Windermere to complete his final term. A few weeks later, the headmaster's wife came to visit him in his dormitory. 'She sat down on my bed and told me that I should not see my father again. He was dead and I lay and wept with my head under the bedclothes.'

2

Education

Preparations for Professor Ransome's funeral coincided with Queen Victoria's Diamond Jubilee in the summer of 1897. One of Ransome's missionary aunts was staying with the family at the time and took the children out to the marketplace to see the decorations and wave their flags. For Joyce, Ransome's youngest sister, the jubilee celebrations, the death of her father and the death of Victoria at the turn of the century all blurred together into one uncomfortable dream:

It all became part of the aura which surrounded those last years of the Old Queen which made it seem quite natural that Mother should sit by the fire and cry on the day she died, the day when the newspapers were published with a black margin two inches deep on every page. By then Mother had struggled through three difficult years without her partner and some of the grief may have been for the passing of her own security.

Edith could not bring herself to attend her husband's funeral service, and so Ransome, thirteen years old, attended by himself.

I walked alone behind my father's coffin which, carried by six of his friends of unequal height, lurched horribly on its way. As the earth rattled on the lid of the coffin I stood horrified at myself, knowing that with my real sorrow, because I had liked and admired my father, was mixed a feeling of relief. This did not last. After the funeral more than one of my father's friends thought it well to remind me that I was now the head of the family with a heavy responsibility towards my mother and the younger ones. And my mother, feeling that she had to fill my father's place and determined to carry out his wishes now as when he was alive, told me (though I knew only too well already) of my father's fears for my character and her hopes that from now on I would remember to set a good example to my brothers and sisters.

The missionary aunt returned to China, leaving the family in a comfortable house on the Clifton Road, not far from the cemetery. Poverty was not an immediate concern owing to the professor's books, a stake in the family business, Ransome and Rapier of Ipswich, and a portfolio of railway shares. But money, in Cyril's absence, was never taken for granted, and it was possibly for this reason as much as any other that Edith, dressed in stiff mourning crêpe, now set about finishing her *First History of England*, a short summary of British kings and queens she had been encouraged to write by Professor Ransome as a primer for schoolchildren. 'I began this book', she wrote in the preface, 'in the hope and belief that I should have my husband's advice and help in the undertaking . . . I have done my best to finish it on the lines we planned together.' Meanwhile, Sidgie, as nurse, governess and playmate, consoled the 'babies', and Ransome entered Rugby as a day boy.

~

Several years ago, when I was gathering material for this book, a friend told me she had rescued hundreds of unsorted papers and photographs that were about to be tossed out of an attic. Amongst them was a picture of Ransome as a child, taken – judging from the bare trees in the background and the fact that he is not wearing glasses – at Rugby in early 1898, soon after his father's death. He is standing in a courtyard, wearing a striped school cap and holding something to his chest. It is not a good photo, but if one narrows one's eyes against the grain it is possible to make out some sort of dark animal: probably a cat. Ransome is clutching this animal as though he is afraid some harm will come to it. His chin is tucked down behind his scarf, his round face pinched into an anxious frown, while the shape of his mouth suggests he is trying to smile. One of the most arresting things about this photo is a curious optical illusion – the blot where the cat might have been, the way Ransome cradles his hands and hunches his shoulders – which makes him look as though he is hugging himself.

Thanks to Thomas Arnold, who in the early nineteenth century had served both as headmaster and school chaplain, Rugby encouraged scholarship grounded in godliness: the eradication of what was base – bullying, lying, cheating, ingratitude, boasting, blasphemy – and the perfection of what was noble – man in union with nature, reason and his Anglican Creator. 'Black' Arnold's example had helped inspire the widespread transformation of British public schools, which in turn supplied the engineers, scientists, politicians and entrepreneurs who drove the Industrial Revolution. Mechanization, education and the explosion of the middle class went hand in hand with social reform: a shift in power from the aristocracy to urban professionals – doctors, bankers, lawyers, businessmen – whose children, sixty years after Arnold's death, questioned not only the practical but the moral principles upon which British aspirations were based. This was why Professor Ransome, who had modelled his career on the Arnold philosophy, had entered his eldest son for the Rugby scholarship exam. Scarborough, the home of his own earliest childhood, was where he felt 'most natural', but Rugby was where his 'best self came forward'. Yet Arthur looked back on his time at the school with acute ambivalence.

Ransome's contemporaries at Rugby included Harry Ricardo, who during the First World War invented engines that powered the first British tanks; the artist and writer Wyndham Lewis, founder of vorticism and the modernist journal *Blast!*; and Ransome's 'fag-master' Richard H. Tawney, who went on to become a prominent Christian Socialist, fought in the war as an ordinary private, and as a professor at the London School of Economics helped craft the manifesto of the first Labour government in 1924. Other friends included Morgan Philips Price, who embraced communism during the Russian Revolution, and Ted Scott, son of C. P. Scott, who would eventually succeed his father as editor of the *Manchester Guardian*, the most powerful liberal newspaper in the country. But as Price and Scott leapt up the school, Ransome remained in the bottom division, where he found the first of a succession of father figures in the shape of W. H. D. Rouse.

Rouse was an eccentric of precisely the sort Ransome enjoyed most. During summer holidays he sailed in the Aegean with local fishermen, and in spare moments translated British sea shanties into Latin and ancient Greek. He had been born in India and was, in addition to his many other accomplishments, an expert in Sanskrit and 'a collector of Eastern folklore'. But by far his most important contribution to Ransome's career was his method of galvanizing students who, languishing in the depths of Lower Middle II, might otherwise have given up hope altogether. Every now and then, by way of relief from Tacitus or Thucydides, he would give his pupils a poem or a story in English and set them to write something in the same style – an exercise in pastiche which Ransome took to with extraordinary facility. Rouse was so astonished by a version of Percy's ballad of King John that he suspected foul play, but when the feat was repeated in a skit on the fourteenth-century travel writer Sir John Mandeville, he read Ransome's effort to the whole class, chuckling at the artful anachronisms. Ransome identified his ambition to be a writer with these early successes and the encouragement of a teacher who exhibited a confidence which his own parents had withheld. 'He saw nothing wrong in my determination some day to write books for myself, and to the dismay of my mother did everything he could to help me.'

Ransome's friendship with his mother – 'My Dear Maw', 'Old Girl', 'Dearest Ancient' – was the most important, the most familiar and trusting, of his life, evidenced by the hundreds of letters to her in his archive begging for favours, boasting of his most recent achievements or simply narrating, in an increasingly lucid, confident prose, the mundane details of his day. Edith was an energetic woman, tolerant and deeply supportive of her children, but at Rugby, in the immediate aftermath of her husband's death, had been anxious that her son should not be spoiled by the absence of a firm hand. Ransome's autobiography, in consequence, treats her influence as one of the many obstacles he was destined to overcome, while after the early years she fades quickly from the scene. Amongst his papers, none of her letters survive before 1924, when she wrote to his second wife, welcoming her into the family – a letter which reveals so much warmth and generosity that it is easy to understand why Ransome came to rely on her so heavily, and that much more difficult to accept the complacence with which, for the benefit of posterity, he reduced her to a fairy-tale Doubting Thomas.

Ransome spent four years at Rugby, and thanks to his first pair of spectacles (a blessing also dispensed by Rouse), went some way to dispelling his reputation for 'muffishness' on the sports field, took enthusiastically to billiards, joined the Natural History Society and started a literary magazine which he sold for tuppence in the school yard. But no amount of extracurricular activity, including a precocious fondness for Spenser, Shakespeare and Carlyle, could make up for the end-of-term reports, or the fact that, once out of Rouse's class, he showed no aptitude for any subject, including original English composition, save the sciences. When Queen Victoria died, Ransome published an 'earnest peace of doggerel' in a local newspaper, and had the pleasure of hearing it sung beneath his study window by an insensitive group of schoolfellows to the tune of 'We'll All Go A-Hunting To-day'.

Rouse had offered to train Ransome for Oxford, but Bob Whitelaw, whose house he had entered as a boarder in his second year, argued against it. From a strictly academic point of view, the boy had as little chance of winning a scholarship to his father's alma mater as he had had of winning a scholarship to Rugby, while he had no right to expect his widowed mother to pay for such an expensive education. Ransome's family had boasted scientists since the Restoration, and while he had as yet exhibited no particular brilliance in the field, he was, at least, competent. The upshot was that after struggling into the Lower Fifths – two years from the top of the school – he joined a small group of 'specialists', and under A. E. Donkin, 'a really fine mathematical teacher', was soon 'breathing the exhilarating mountain air of differential calculus and the binomial theorum'. In 1901, he sat the entrance exam for the Yorkshire College, passed in the first division, and within weeks was heading north again to the town of his birth, 'dear dirty smoky old Leeds'. He lasted exactly two terms.

~

The diffidence that had persuaded Ransome to pursue one family tradition – science – over another – the humanities – began to evaporate the moment he unpacked his trunk. One of the attractions of the Yorkshire College was its security, but another, far greater attraction was the freedom to swagger about town in the delightful knowledge that he need answer to no one and could do exactly as he liked. 'Going to the Yorkshire College in Leeds', he recalled, 'meant that for the first time in my life I was not conscious of a surrounding atmosphere of disapproval. This emancipation was immediate.' After a brief stay with a friend of the family, then a cousin who was also studying science, he took a room of his own, decorated it with portraits of some of his favourite authors – Browning, Carlyle, Tennyson, Hazlitt – and began laying the foundations of a personal library.

As a child, Ransome had given way to many passions, but none was so permanent or all-consuming as his passion for books: books as collections of words or as beautiful objects in their own right, to hold in his hand or prop up beside a candle in the evening and simply gape at. Books brought together the two strongest sides of his nature: the romantic dreamer and the scientist; the boy who loved fairy tales and the collector of seashells and caterpillars. In Leeds, the books that crowded his shelves, purchased at the cost of a lunch or a supper, reminded him that his project was worthwhile, furnishing physical, irrefutable proof of writing as an art, an assurance that was sorely needed in the early days when he threw away every scrap of his work as soon as it was done, while his landlady, as he fondly recalled, groaned at the frequency with which she was forced to empty his waste-paper basket. Surrounded by books, Ransome felt like an author. Hans Christian Andersen's tales, bound in green with gold letters down the spine, made him feel a little more like Hans Christian Andersen. William Hazlitt's *Table Talk* placed by his bed at night with his spectacles reverently folded on top made him feel as though he were living in Hazlitt's world even while he slept. For Ransome, books and a literary career were 'high' as opposed to 'low', and in this respect required as little explanation as the moral distinction by which Professor Ransome had divided the world into the saved and the damned. Later, when his library amounted to several thousand volumes, he identified with it so completely that without it he was firmly convinced he would not be capable of writing at all.

The decisive psychological break with the Bunsen burners, test tubes and retorts came one afternoon in the college library, when Ransome had lost himself amongst the 'M's looking for a book on magnetism or mensuration. Instead, he came across the *Life of William Morris* by J. W. Mackail, in two volumes, bound handsomely in brown leather.

I began dipping into one of them, sat down with it and never went back to the laboratory that day. I read entranced of the lives of William Morris and his friends, of lives in which nothing seemed to matter except the making of lovely things and the making of a world to match them . . . From that moment I suppose, my fate was decided, and any chance I had ever had of a smooth career in academic or applied science was gone forever.

Ransome's rejection of the expectations foisted upon him as the eldest child included a review of middle-class conventions in general. Henceforth he excused himself from church attendance or any denominational orthodoxy, and throughout his life revealed an equal aversion to political orthodoxy. Yet in choosing William Hazlitt and Morris as his earliest literary mentors, he had chosen two of the most aggressively political thinkers in the British canon: the first an ardent supporter of the French Revolution; the second one of the founding fathers of British socialism. Indeed, it was through Morris that Ransome, in the earliest stages of his personal epiphany, made the acquaintance of his first Russian Marxist, a fellow student named Zelda Kahan.

As one of Britain's most important industrial towns, Leeds was a natural focus for the labour movement and a popular destination for political refugees who hoped to pursue their livelihoods in England with greater freedom than they had enjoyed at home. Zelda Kahan was a Russian Jew whose parents had fled the vicious pogroms of the 1880s, and had approached Ransome in the chemistry laboratory because of a book laid beside him on the workbench: Morris's revolutionary daydream, *News from Nowhere*. Kahan had subsequently asked him round to tea, during which she discussed the possibility of establishing a forum for socialist debate, taking deep offence when Ransome appeared to pooh-pooh contemporary politics as superficial nonsense. Ransome had written to her shortly afterwards, apologizing for his behaviour but confessing that he could not commit himself to a cause he did not fully understand.

Perhaps it is because I have only heard the Conservative side of the question. I had hoped in this place to find people of all views so that I might hear the socialist side of the question. However I have been disappointed. The only question asked here is 'Lib or Conservative?' as if real things depended on minor matters such as present day politics. That is why I could not answer your question yesterday as to whether I was a socialist. I think I am, but I am not sure. I should very much have liked to help in your scheme but of course if you think me too utterly frivolous I will leave it alone. Please let me know.

Precisely what became of this 'scheme' remains unclear, but the meeting had definite consequences. Kahan went on to become an influential British socialist, working closely with her brother-in-law, another Jewish émigré named Theodore Rothstein. During the war, as a member of both the British Socialist Party and the Russian Social Democrats, Rothstein garnered funds for the Bolsheviks, and in 1917, following the November Revolution, provided Ransome with his first letter of introduction to the Soviet government. But in 1902, as Lenin penned his landmark thesis, *What Is to Be Done?*, Ransome had no intention of devoting his life to political reform, or indeed any sort of work not directly related to his 'beloved books'. Thus, in February, advising his mother of his intention to abandon his studies altogether, he headed down to London for an interview with the publishing company Grant Richards, who had advertised a position as an errand boy.

~

Grant Richards' offices stood opposite the Alhambra music hall in Leicester Square. The season's books, including a new edition of Hazlitt's *Table Talk*, were showcased in a broad latticed window beneath a handsome green tiled arch bearing the publisher's name written in gold. Grant Richards was twenty-nine years old, had entered the business as a publisher's clerk when he was sixteen, and was doing a brisk trade in children's fiction, costly editions of Shakespeare, and some of the rising talents of the day: George Bernard Shaw, G. K. Chesterton, John Masefield, A. E. Housman and Arnold Bennett. Ransome, meanwhile, had not applied for the position entirely without references. His first cousin, the poet Laurence Binyon, had recently published with the company, while the Macmillans – owners of perhaps the most powerful publishing business in Britain – were close friends of the family. In his memoirs, however, Ransome recalled his interview as a purely personal triumph. He had produced Hazlitt from the pocket of his best suit, then listened ecstatically as Richards explained that he would have to begin on the lowest rung of the ladder.

I was for accepting there and then, but he said that I must first consult my mother. I went back to Leeds in a whirl of enthusiasm. The critical step had been taken. My mother went to town to stay with friends. She called on Mr Richards and was charmed by him. His offer was accepted, and within a year of leaving Rugby, I had become a London office boy with a salary of eight shillings a week.

For Edith, maintaining sound relations with her son would always demand a degree of indulgent fatalism, but on this occasion she was not prepared to give him his head entirely. Thus, consulting with a selection of aunts and with Bob Whitelaw, who assured her that Ransome would never be happy in a job that did not allow him to 'elbow his way', she made arrangements to move the entire family down to the capital, the better to monitor proceedings.

3

The Collingwoods

There were still a few months to go on the lease in Rugby, and so Ransome arrived in London ahead of Edith, Sidgie and his younger sisters. The arrangement suited him perfectly. He took lodgings in a Clapham boarding house with six young professionals, rose early every morning, donned his bowler hat – 'the symbol of my calling' – took a horse-drawn omnibus to Chelsea Bridge, then a green Piccadilly or yellow Camden omnibus to the centre of town and arrived in Leicester Square at a run.

At Grant Richards', Ransome handled every sort of menial task: wrapping books, fetching staff lunches from the local public houses, filling in labels, checking invoices and saving on postage by delivering parcels on foot. Before he had been in London more than a few weeks he knew every bookshop in and around Soho, each one marking the heaving streets 'as the sea is marked with buoys'. Since Richards' business was overstretched and understaffed, he was soon given more responsible work: calling in sample bindings, ordering paper, learning the bibliographic language so essential to his trade. But Ransome was not content to remain at the manufacturing and distributive end of the industry. He wanted to be a writer, and his determination in this respect, not to mention his wide-eyed innocence, was illustrated by the enjoyment he took in collecting, by hand, the manuscripts of authors who were struggling to meet their deadlines. It was on an early mission of this kind that he met M. P. Shiel, a character who figured in his autobiography chiefly to demonstrate the sort of man a young adventurer might encounter if he took his life in his hands, stepped off the beaten track and ventured into the labyrinthine byways of bohemian London.

It was well known in literary circles that Matthew Phipps

Shiel, author of the *Purple Cloud* and *Prince Zaleski*, had been crowned king of the small Caribbean island of Redonda at the age of fifteen, spoke seven languages, had fathered an indeterminate number of illegitimate children and practised medicine, mountaineering and yoga. When H. P. Lovecraft reviewed Shiel's cult classic *The House of Sounds*, he hailed it as a masterpiece:

Yes! How can I describe its poison-grey 'insidious madness'? If I say that it is very like 'The Fall of the House of Usher', or that one feature mirrors my own 'Alchemist', I shall not even have suggested the utterly unique delirium of arctic wastes, titan seas, insane brazen towers, centigrade malignity, frenzied waves and cataracts, and above all, hideous, insistent, brain-petrifying, pan-accursed cosmic SOUND. God! But after that story I shall never try to write one of my own.

To wrest a manuscript from a man like Shiel, suggested Ransome, required some daring or lunacy in a boy barely out of school uniform. And yet he had not only survived the encounter, but was asked back for coffee. A little while later he was invited to supper, where he met Shiel's sister – 'a smiling Negress' – who gave him a painting of herself and her brother as children, sitting beneath a palm tree on their tiny island kingdom. Ransome was still being invited over in 1929, by which time Shiel had learned to take life a little more gently, had developed a taste for fly fishing and was living in a cottage on the Wey.

Shiel took to Ransome in the same way that many older writers took to Ransome. He enjoyed his vitality, the unfeigned hero worship, the diffidence clumsily concealed, especially at the age of eighteen, by a hearty, all-embracing bonhomie. Ransome could be gauche but retained, all the same, such a gift for making friends that at times it amounted to a kind of genius, so that however dubious his literary poses, however transparently he adopted, one after another, the manners and opinions of authors he admired, there was scarcely a person who knew him intimately that did not like him. In London, he charmed Shiel by sitting at his feet, dreaming of Balzac while the great man littered the floor with manuscript pages. He charmed his cousin,

Laurence Binyon, by standing beneath his window on cold nights, just to see the lamp guttering as he worked away at his poetry. In letters home to Edith, he held up each new encounter proudly, later recalling his lowly station as a badge of honour, proof of an authenticity denied his Rugby colleagues:

As a bowler-hatted office-boy laden with parcels, or sitting on the back of a van delivering books on publication day (which I much enjoyed), I used to see one or other of them on the London pavements, wearing school or college ties, going to Lords, perhaps, for the Rugby Marlborough match. None ever recognized me and I should not have known what to say to any who had.

Never far from the surface was the dead father, the bullying, the memory of sneering schoolteachers, but the glory of Ransome's profession was that all past slights were grist to the literary mill: the essential spurs (as Hazlitt had explained) to young genius. Meanwhile, class, vocation, even personal relationships were from the earliest stages of his career a form of fancy dress: attitudes to be discovered by consulting Schiller or Nietzsche, or by spending an entire week of suppers on Robert Burton's *The Anatomy of Melancholy*, which he had no intention of reading, or even sullying with a paper knife, but instead stared at where it lay on his desk, incredulous that he had been permitted to own such a thing at all. When Grant Richards closed his doors in the evening, Ransome would return to Clapham by omnibus, and sitting on the open top deck consider suitably poetic subjects for his evening writing exercises: sunset, dawn, pigeons, a tramp with his boots still muddy from the countryside striding through Trafalgar Square.

'One day, one of the young men, a clerk in a shipping office, asked to see what I was writing. He read it and looked at me with pity. "I say", he said, "if you think anybody is ever going to read this, you're mistaken. You'd much better chuck it. Why not do fretwork instead?"'

But Ransome did not doubt his talent. Instead, he tried his hand at every genre – essays, gothic horror, romantic novels, poetry and nursery rhymes – burning the evidence of his labours

34

at each volte-face. At eighteen years old, having only recently learned to smoke a pipe and with his moustache still in the awkward, downy stages of its first growth, nothing seemed beyond his grasp. Surrounded by books, steeped in books, spending the money he earned from selling books on buying books, the aim was not simply to own a library, but to become part of the library; to sit up one night, preferably in the not too distant future, and contemplate a book with his own name on it, neatly sewn and bound between cloth boards. It was not, he felt, too much to ask. It was only a question of practice and patience, and a refusal to accept defeat.

In pursuit of this end Ransome quit Grant Richards after six months. The long hours and heavy responsibilities were taking up valuable time that might have been spent writing – a consideration that Hazlitt would certainly have approved – but there was also the sordid matter of pay. As an office boy who had so rapidly acquired many of the duties of a clerk, Ransome felt he deserved a raise. Grant Richards, who was experiencing serious financial difficulties of his own, did not agree, and the result was that, through the kindly intercession of Laurence Binyon, he joined the Unicorn Press, a small publisher of beautifully illustrated art books and poetry offering one pound a week. So Ransome moved from Leicester Square to the little shop in Cecil Court, and by the time Edith and the rest of the family arrived, he had already taken up his station behind two red ledgers – one recording costs, the other profits – chronicling the rapid decline of the company.

~

Edith, of course, had already been consulted on the move to the Unicorn Press, and while voicing an initial surprise that Grant Richards' dazzling prospects no longer held any charms, allowed herself to be soothed by the reassurances of Binyon, whose good character was guaranteed by a steady job at the British Museum. As Geoffrey continued his career at Rugby, a house was taken in suburban Balham. Cecily was enrolled at art school, Joyce and Kitty continued their studies with Sidgie, and Ransome – who as writer-in-residence took the largest bedroom – proudly contributed half his wages to board and lodging.

In the brief interval before graduating to a decently bohemian establishment in Chelsea, Ransome spent more time with his family than he had done since he was a day boy at Rugby, and did not appear to resent the fact. The house, for all that it was a newly built, red-brick affair, identical to every other house in the row, was comfortable, and breakfast and dinner presented themselves regularly. He enjoyed late walks over Tooting Common, where 'lamplight through green leaves' joined other visible things he liked to remember. In the winter, when he came home from work, Sidgie – tiny and neat with her black hair done up in pins – would be waiting for him with nutmeg and a bottle of claret ready to mull in a saucepan. His only grief was a certain vulgar tendency on the part of his siblings to poke fun at his high calling, to lampoon him to his face and even, thanks to a family magazine edited by Joyce and Kitty, in writing. A caricature depicting the young poet 'discussing the relationship of art to literature' (placed by Geoffrey during the school holidays) caused enough offence to warrant a note in the 'stop press news' section of the *Huron Weekly*: 'Disgusted with our coloured plate by the anonymous artist, A M Ransome has failed to turn up to supper.'

Minor annoyances of this kind, however, were largely forgotten as Ransome's fortunes improved. Thanks to Binyon, Shiel and his work at the Unicorn Press, his circle of acquaintances was expanding rapidly, among them the Japanese writer Yone Noguchi; Cecil Chesterton, brother of G. K. Chesterton; and the future poet laureate John Masefield, who drank claret at teatime and sang sea shanties in Edith's kitchen. Noguchi led to Yoshio Markino, a popular illustrator, while the verse dramatist Gordon Bottomley – who had weak lungs and lived mostly with his parents in the Lake District – introduced him to Edward Thomas, a gifted critic and essayist, who described Ransome as a 'remarkable boy'.

My only fear for him is that he may become merely five years older than he actually is; that he may become merely old for his age. For he seems to be working, as hard as if he actually liked it, at pure journalism, though it is quite clear that he has in him things which can never be expressed in pure journalizing and may even be suppressed by it, at his age.

Ransome recalled all these friends fondly, each one of them an ally, each proving that he had not been mistaken in his chosen career. In 1903, he began supplementing his regular salary with reviews and articles – 'The Class System of Japan', co-authored by Yoshio Markino, is the earliest recorded with his byline – for the *Weekly Survey*, 'a good example of those obscure, high-hearted little rags that keep alive so many of the unknown writers, and help so many youthful critics to deceive themselves into self-congratulation at their own names in capital letters'. Before long he was contributing to every edition, and with the blessing of the editor, Paul Neumann, had joined what he called

the chosen band who met on Thursday morning, and, with paper and ink provided for free, lay prone on the back numbers in the long attic, and practically wrote the whole paper . . . and in their own special columns, over their own names, instructed the universe on everything under heaven, and sometimes made metaphysical excursions even there.

By May, it was clear that the Unicorn Press was not long for the world, but Ransome had enough freelance work to move out of the family home into lodgings of his own. Some time during the spring of 1903, he set off for a rented apartment in Chelsea, and courtesy of a horse-drawn cart and a local rag-and-bone man, was soon installed in a tiny flat in the Hollywood Road, where his library was laid out in grocery boxes.

Shortly afterwards, he rewarded himself with a visit to Bottomley in the Lake District, where he took a room at a bed and breakfast, and after dipping his fingers in Coniston Water, spent the afternoon writing poetry on a flat rock in the middle of Copper Mines Beck. Soon he was dozing so peacefully that when W. G. Collingwood – amongst the most venerable of local dignitaries – happened upon him in the evening, he mistook his motionless body for a corpse.

~

Ransome's family had been acquainted with the Collingwoods since 1895, when Professor Ransome wrote to congratulate Collingwood on *Thorstein of the Mere*, the adventures of a young Viking boy in the Lakeland of the Dark Ages. It had been one of the favourite novels of Ransome's childhood.

'Dear Collingwood,' Professor Ransome had written,

On behalf of four small children, Arthur, Cecily, Geoffrey and Joyce who have from their earliest recollections been accustomed to regard Nibthwaite and Coniston as a fairyland of pleasant memories and delightful holidays, I wish to thank you for your *Thorstein of the Mere*. Every member of the family old and young has read it with the utmost pleasure and interest, and we are looking forward to re-visiting all the scenes of his adventures with renewed enthusiasm next August which we generally spend with perhaps some of his descendants, the Swainsons of Nibthwaite.

Professor Ransome's thank you led to a picnic on Peel Island the following year, when Mrs Collingwood, as she later recalled, had been shocked to discover that such a pretty woman as Edith could have such ugly children. But Ransome claimed the meeting at Copper Mines Beck entirely for himself, laying it down in memory as a ritual baptism, the moment at which his own inclinations had been approved by an unquestionable authority. To be hailed from the shore of a fast-flowing stream by W. G. Collingwood – the secretary and biographer of the late John Ruskin; a man who had known William Morris, spoken to the Pre-Raphaelites and produced *Thorstein* from a horde of knowledge which surpassed that of any other scholar of the Lake District – was as close to a religious experience as he ever got until he witnessed the mass popular uprising of March 1917 in St Petersburg.

I got up and jumped ashore, because the noise of the rushing water was such that I could not hear what he was saying. He asked me what I was doing and I said that I had been trying to write poetry. Instead of laughing, he seemed to think it a reasonable occupation, and we walked down to the village together. Before we parted he asked me to come round the head of the lake to see him and told me his name.

Ransome was too shy to take Collingwood up on his invitation until the last evening of his holiday, but he received such a warm welcome at the Collingwoods' house at Lanehead that when he returned to the Lakes the following year, he dropped by at the earliest opportunity. Collingwood's eldest daughter, Dora, recorded in her diary on 3 June 1904:

Last Saturday Mr Ransome came to dinner. He is staying in the village and has been to dinner every day since. Today he has been on the water with us from 9 till 7 with an interval for lunch. This evening we stayed in the garden and he tried to make us see fairies. Last night we went on the water after dinner and two other nights we sat down in the wood on the railings til 10. He is coming to stay with us tomorrow.

'That first day,' recalled Ransome,

Mr Collingwood, though he was at work when I came, took me into his study. I can see it now, the books from floor to ceiling, the enormous table piled with books and manuscripts, the unfinished canvas on an easel, the small table at which he was writing and, over the fireplace, his lovely portrait of his wife, in a small boat with two of the children. He put me in one armchair, shifted his own from the table and asked about what I was doing. The miracle for me was the assumption that what I was trying to do was worth doing. Later in the morning room I met Mrs Collingwood who was soon, when he spoke of her to me, to become 'your aunt'.

Ransome stayed with the Collingwoods for three weeks, until Robin Collingwood, who would shortly join Geoffrey at Rugby, returned for the summer holidays. In the interim, Ransome slept in Robin's bed and set up his books in a spare study next to Collingwood's. In the morning Mrs Collingwood roused the family to breakfast with Beethoven sonatas on the piano. Then there was writing till lunchtime and in the afternoons, reading in the garden, posing for portraits amongst the lupins or sailing out to Peel Island in a dinghy owned by a friend of the family –

Ransome's first *Swallow* – for picnics or, when it was warm enough, to camp in the open air. Both Mr and Mrs Collingwood were gifted artists, as were their three girls, Dora, Barbara and Ursula, while Robin would become one of the best-known philosophers of his generation. Collectively, and to Ransome's lasting delight, they treated him as one of their own.

The Collingwoods did not replace Ransome's family. His relationship with his mother grew stronger as he grew older. Cecily, Geoffrey, Joyce and Kitty were always very dear to him, sent him letters often when he was away, and when they failed to do so, were reprimanded for their callousness. In the years to come, lonely and isolated in Moscow, Ransome would talk about them as his 'possessions' – querulously, waiting to be affirmed.

Meanwhile, he revisited the holidays of his childhood on his own terms. In London, Ransome would pack his boots, take a bus to Euston station, and eight hours later, collapsing in the chair specially reserved for him at the Collingwood dining table, discuss Wordsworth, Coleridge, Yeats and the Celtic Twilight, Icelandic sagas, the Norse and Roman digs which were Collingwood's particular passion; the whole heritage of England challenged daily by the incursions of science and industry – the factories, the bloated cities, the inanimate machines that took the place of skilful hands. There was no fear that W. G. Collingwood – whom Ransome christened 'the Skald' (ancient Norse for 'poet') – would judge him as harshly as he believed his own father had judged him. Nor was there any doubt, amongst his new friends, that an artist was justified in his calling simply because he was called. Lanehead meant community with nature and love of beauty for its own sake, in writing, in painting, in music, or simply in long tramps in the hills. 'We are *very* fond of him,' Mrs Collingwood would write to Edith. 'He is a dear, loveable boy, and I expect the reason of his being happy with us is just that he knows we are fond of him. I feel that he more or less belongs to us.'

On 24 June 1904, after a barren day with her sketch book, Dora wrote sadly in her diary, 'Yesterday morning Arthur went away. We went with him to the station and then we walked up to the copper mines. In the afternoon I looked for a subject but did not find one.' Twenty-five years later, her children – Taqui, Susan, Titty and Roger – set sail in another *Swallow*, and with minor adjustments for time and tide, became one of the most famous crews in British literature.

~

In 1903, Ransome had answered an advertisement in the *Daily News and Leader* (later the *Daily News*) – 'Journalist Wanted Temporarily. Good knowledge of football and athletics. Salary 20s' – and found himself ghostwriting 'books of practical instruction' and the autobiographies of 'well-known athletes' in a sitting room smelling of cats on the Brixton Road. This windfall led to a commission from Henry J. Drane of 'Drane's Well-Known ABC Handbooks', priced at one shilling apiece and including such diverse titles as *The ABC of Billiards*, *The ABC of Palmistry*, *The ABC of Cooking for Invalids* and *The ABC of Solo Whist*. Ransome's only known contribution appeared in August 1904 as *The ABC of Physical Culture*, and dealt with its subject in seven short chapters: 'Exercises for General Health', 'Muscular', 'Breathing', 'Smoking', 'Food', 'Drinking' and 'Sleep'. Appearing in August 1904, it was consigned to instant oblivion. Recalling his first published book, Ransome preferred to speak of another, far more welcome package, bound in mottled boards, that arrived at his new Chelsea digs (a larger establishment a few streets over from the Hollywood Road) towards the end of the month.

The previous summer, Gordon Bottomley had recommended Ransome as a consultant to a local printer in Ulverston, the Lanthorn Press, who were distributing young authors through a London publisher called Brown Langham. Ransome had naturally recommended himself and two of his closest friends: Cecil Chesterton and Edward Thomas. His own submission had been a slim volume of poetic essays entitled *The Souls of the Streets*:

'What memories would be lost if the ancient streets had no souls fit for dreaming? They have, and the lonely passer-by knows that they dream their stories to themselves, thrilling with their horror, throbbing softly with their tenderness.' It received reviews – some good – in periodicals, and Ransome was invited to tea by William Thackeray's eldest daughter, Lady Richmond Ritchie. Lady Richmond, a friend of the Macmillans, introduced him to Edith Sichel, the celebrated feminist critic, and the upshot was that he received his first column in a small newspaper, for which he received twelve shillings and sixpence a week and permission to write with precocious authority on anything that took his fancy. Edward Thomas – whose affection for Ransome was soon mingled with waspish exasperation – found little to celebrate.

'First, and before I forget it,' he wrote to Bottomley,

Mr Arthur M Ransome lives at 1 Gunter Grove, Chelsea, SW. He has quite a good room with a bed delicately suggested by a tapestry cover, and other things suggested by a Japanese screen . . . There are also three chairs, a table and a floor. Here smiles Ransome, whether in the company of his dreams or in the solitude created by visitors who do not always smile. Also he says 'Bother' and even 'Damn'. He gets younger every day and in September he produces a book – which you may have seen. I have seen it and have laughed and sighed and wondered. I suppose that if a man can write such things he should be encouraged to publish them. That he should want to publish them amazes me. In book form, I can only endure them when I think that he has made a tolerably good mould of a sentences &c into which he may some day find something to pour. I know something about sugar in prose, but this is prose in sugar . . . I am going to try to understand it before it is received by the *Chronicle*.

4

Bohemia

The first decade of the twentieth century saw the most influential writings of Freud, the introduction of the Nobel Prize, Einstein's first theories of relativity, the first aeroplanes, the first transatlantic radio signals, and a compensating craze for mysticism, seances and national mythologies. Every weekend the railway platforms swarmed with poets, off to find their roots in the countryside. Merry England and art nouveau were in, as were fairies, gypsies and the Celtic Twilight. For over half a century, Queen Victoria had been a symbol of stability and permanence. Now there was King Edward, gregarious, cosmopolitan and promiscuous. The Boer War had provoked a wave of unpatriotic pacifism. The Labour Party was on the rise, and with it, criticism of Britain's rigid class system. Key questions of the day included universal suffrage, the redistribution of wealth and the iniquitous powers wielded by the House of Lords. Nineteen hundred and three saw the first Tour de France, the first mixed-race unions in America, and in London, at the Second Congress of the Russian Social Democrats, a party schism that created the Bolsheviks and Mensheviks. In 1904, as Ransome published his first books, Kaiser Wilhelm recorded the first speech on Edison's marvellous phonograph, Britain and France signed the Entente Cordiale, and in Russia the outbreak of war with Japan nearly toppled the Tsar.

Ransome's autobiography, looking back on these years, records the long and supposedly tranquil Edwardian afternoon that preceded the Great War as a personal golden age – a period of cheerful, unattached self-discovery. *The Souls of the Streets* was swiftly followed by *The Stone Lady* and an invitation to edit the Macmillan family's fading literary journal, *Temple Bar*, which Ransome ran chiefly as a vehicle for his friends until it collapsed a few months later. By 1906, he had a host of articles and reviews to his name and seven books, including short stories, collections of essays and his first contribution to children's literature, *The Uncle and the Faeries*, published in a rattlebag along with works by Hilaire Belloc and Edith Nesbit. In London, he attended the theatre with Yeats, drank 'purple hush' and dined at home with the Chestertons, where Cecil's elder brother, author of *The Napoleon of Notting Hill*, laughed so hard at his own jokes that his eyes would disappear.

In 1905, Edith moved her family to Morningside in Edinburgh, where Geoffrey was apprenticed to a local printer, leaving Ransome to his own devices. Gunter Grove – where Edward Thomas had spent a raucous month as a lodger – was now abandoned in favour of Carlyle Studios, just off the King's Road. Here, Ransome, in addition to his ever-expanding library, enlarged his collection of contemporary artists, and when not entertaining at home, attended the salons of the celebrated Jamaican illustrator and writer Pixie Coleman Smith, where spirits were summoned to the Ouija board, Yeats and Bram Stoker read poems and stories, and where Pixie would round off the evening with the 'Anansi' tales she had learned as a child in Kingstown; always delivered in the same sing-song dialect, according to the same formula, so that those who listened could not help telling them in precisely the same way: 'In a long before time before Queen Victoria came to reign over we der lib in the bush one black fat hairy spider called Anansi . . .' or, 'Der lib in de bush one king an' dis king he was de most beautiful king dat eber was, but dis king he had one BEARD!'

With Cecil Chesterton, a convinced socialist, Ransome attended meetings of the Fabian Society, debates which stirred him so deeply that he took long night walks into the country to clear his head, returning to continue the conversation with the Collingwood girls, who wintered in Chelsea. But his interest in politics rarely extended beyond a fashionable contempt for the 'bourgeoisie'. In 1905, he visited Paris for the first time in the company of Clive Bell, the brother-in-law of Virginia Woolf, and instantly fell in love with the cradle of Western revolution. In Montmartre, he shopped for second-hand books: Victor Hugo, Balzac, Flaubert. At the Louvre, he dreamed of Hazlitt and differed sharply with Bell over the virtues of abstract art, which Ransome deplored. But while he wept over *Les Misérables*, he made no reference to the momentous events unfolding at the other end of Europe: the 'Bloody Sunday' massacre in St Petersburg, the strikes and demonstrations that swept the Russian empire, the arrest of the young Leon Trotsky, chairman of the first workers' council, or 'soviet'. Instead, he returned to London in a daze, devoted himself to learning French and continued his correspondence with Edith, to whom he had promised to write every Saturday.

Thanks awfully for the cushion. The colour doesn't fit the room, but I'm getting some one to put a new cover on it . . . I bless you exceedingly.

I left a guide to Coniston, a red paper book by Collingwood, in my room. Please send it. It contains a four-leafed clover. I want it.

My love to the kids and Company. Tell 'em to write me a letter and I'll send 'em a collective, individualistic, rhetorical imaginative, superlatively beautiful, impassioned and intellectual, little piece of four short verses . . .

In 1906, still only twenty-two years old, this monster of conceit – author of *Highways and Byways in Fairyland*, *The Child's Book of the Seasons* and *Pond and Stream* – was approached by Miss Stephana Stevens of the literary agent Curtis Brown, who declared that a book on the artistic scene in London was sorely needed, that Ransome was the man to write it, and that the publishers Chapman and Hall were waiting to get it. *Bohemia in London*, his most sustained effort to date, appeared in short order. It was nostalgically reviewed by Ransome himself in the *Onlooker* six years later, and even at the time was written in a style suggesting a fondness for days distilled and softened by the distant past:

My life will be happier, turn out what it may, for these friendships, these pot-house nights, these evenings in the firelight of a studio, and these walks, two or three of us together talking from our hearts, along the Embankment in the Chelsea evening, with the lamps sparkling above us in the leaves of the trees, the river moving with the sweet noise of waters, the wings of youth on our feet, and all the world before us.

~

After returning from his first trip to Paris, Ransome had met Lascelles Abercrombie in the Lake District, a verse dramatist whose poetry was so offensive to Ezra Pound that the impresario of modernism actually challenged him to a duel. Abercrombie would go on to found a poets' commune in the little village of Dymock in Gloucestershire. The result was an anthology titled *The Georgians*, published in 1912 and including work by John Masefield, Rupert Brooke, Walter de la Mare and W. H. Davies, a professional vagabond whose American wanderings, retold in *The Autobiography of a Supertramp*, had created a sensation in 1908. Today, the Georgians are frequently dismissed as a tired interlude between the great romantics of the nineteenth century and the more radical post-war experiments of poets such as Ezra Pound, T. S. Eliot and W. B. Yeats. Amongst their contemporaries, however, they were considered fresh and new, and during the war had a powerful influence on men like Wilfred Owen and Siegfried Sassoon. Later, Edward Thomas – the most gifted of Ransome's circle – would often be counted as one of their number, developing a lyric style that became one of the most distinctive and enduring voices of the twentieth century.

Ransome's association with the Georgians, almost as much as his association with the Collingwoods, encouraged the values that would later inform his own most significant contribution to literature: a series of children's books alive with natural details – weather, wildlife, land- and waterscapes – all bound by a fascination with the local, the joy of returning again and again to the same well-known landmarks, the same faces, the same rituals. But Ransome was never a poet, nor yet in 1907 a prose author of any note. Abercrombie, who wrote him long, high-spirited letters, was convinced that great things were in store for him. Edward Thomas, who described him as 'exuberant, rash and Protean', listened patiently as he explained his latest ideas. But for Ransome the consciousness of always being a junior partner rankled. In his letters to Edith, he dreamed of writing 'books for brats' or fairy tales, the only subject, he assured her, 'that it is possible to excel in without a degree'. Hitherto, however, Ransome's fairy tales had done very little business. Following the success of *Bohemia in London*, therefore, the challenge was to prove that he was no mere dabbler, to lay the foundations of a creditable living, and in doing so to find some suitable compromise between his peculiar genius and the all too practical demands of the industry. The result was a burgeoning career in literary criticism.

In 1908, Ransome visited his family in Edinburgh and met with the Scottish publishers T. C. & E. C. Jack, who commissioned a series of critical anthologies – *The World Story Tellers* – that would include his favourite authors, be prefaced with his own introductions and continue apparently indefinitely until he ran out of steam. Ransome produced eleven in two years, starting with a collection of short pieces by Théophile Gautier, and on the strength of the windfall, moved out of his Chelsea lodgings into rooms at Owen Mansions in Kensington, where there was plenty of shelf space for his library, a very sizeable study, a kitchen, an 'airy bedroom' and a maid to tidy up in the mornings. The only drawback, he recalled ruefully, was that so much opulence could not properly be enjoyed alone. 'Such a flat seems to be wasted on a mere bachelor, and before he knows what is happening nature is at her old business of abhorring vacuums and the bachelor is a bachelor no longer.'

~

Ransome had been flirting with the idea of marriage for some time, starting with Barbara Collingwood, who – possibly viewing him more as a playmate than a husband – turned him down twice, much to his own and her parents' disappointment. Next came her sister Dora, with equally painful results. In London, Ransome had proposed to Stephana Stevens over the kitchen sink, 'his forehead damp and reddened with the effort of explanation', and in Paris, to a Liverpudlian artist named Jessie Gavin.

'I am afraid it is too late to tell me not to fall in love with her,' he had written to Edith in 1907,

[but] I may leave Paris earlier than I otherwise should, because I think I shall be extremely unhappy. There is not the slightest chance that she will care for me. She is not at all the 'You love me and I love you kind of person.' She is much more like a kind of fairy that does not seem approachable at all. And yet she is as sweet and charming as she can be. What a cynic you are with your rubber heels. I'm ashamed of you and at your young age too.

So frequent and preposterous were Ransome's advances that they became a standing joke, figuring regularly in the Thomas–Bottomley correspondence and providing excellent material for a comic novel from Stevens in which Ransome appears as the shaggy, tweed-suited Matravers, a man 'with all the trappings of genius without the genius'.

He was very young, she discovered when she looked at him at her leisure, and he had a half-nervous, half-confident manner in playing the host which rather took her. He was so bursting with interests and enthusiasms and youthfulness that she almost forgave him his native egoism. It was the egoism of a big puppy that bounces up to you wagging his tail and jumping up to you as much as to say 'I *am* a jolly creature, am I not? Of course you'll make a fuss of me!' She felt the danger of intercourse with him would be that she might yield to the temptation of taking him at his own valuation just because he was such a happy, blundering piece of self-satisfaction.

By 1908, virtually every woman of Ransome's acquaintance had either laughed or sighed as he protested his devotion. Some were gratifyingly flustered; others offered him tea. No serious offence was taken. But it was inevitable that at some point or another somebody would take him seriously, and when it happened, no one was more astonished than Ransome himself. In 1909, he had started a diary, and amongst the first entries, drawn in the minuscule hand he reserved for events of monumental personal significance, wrote, 'See about licence,' followed five days later, on 8 March, by 'Get [or 'Got'] married.'

~

Ivy Constance Walker was the daughter of an English solicitor and a mother who claimed descent from the Portuguese aristocracy. She and Ransome had met via a mutual friend, Ralph Courtney, who worked with Stephana Stevens at Curtis Brown and who had brought Ivy with him one night to Owen Mansions. Ransome recalled the incident in his autobiography, under a chapter headed 'Disasters'.

She announced at once that she was not a barmaid, alluding, I suppose, to the impropriety of coming with young men to a young man's rooms. I should not have thought of it myself, for it had been perfectly natural that the Collingwood girls should visit Carlyle Studios or have tea with Chesterton and me in Gunter Grove. She had an extraordinary power of surrounding the simplest act with an air of conspiratorial secrecy and excitement.

Ransome could not remember exactly how it had happened, but before he knew it, he was engaged.

Ivy's father had initially forbidden the marriage altogether, claiming, according to Ransome, that it would be too expensive. He had suggested instead that the young couple pretend he knew nothing about the affair and elope to Gretna Green with his clandestine blessing. In the event, the marriage took place at Fulham church on 13 March and was blessed, after a few days' honeymoon in Paris, at a second church on April Fool's Day – possibly to allow Edith to witness the ceremony. No correspondence with Ransome's mother survives to illuminate her feelings at the time, while Ransome's diary offers only the barest details of time and place. Owen Mansions was sublet, and the couple took a cottage close to Edward Thomas in Froxfield, Hampshire, with a dizzying view over Petersfield Plain and beyond to the South Downs.

When Ransome wrote up his account of his first marriage, he described it as one might describe the onset of a dangerous fever. He had fallen in love, 'not happily, as with Barbara Colling-wood, but in a horribly puzzled manner', and was subsequently, he claimed, blackmailed to the altar. After the engagement, Ivy had revealed something of her 'inner life'. She was already betrothed to a cousin who lived abroad, and in this cousin's absence, was looking after his mistress and illegitimate child. Her mother was an unstable lunatic who believed the Sun God was in love with her, and had once allowed herself to be gar-landed with flowers to receive him, only to be terrified by a clap of thunder. Ivy – slim, brown-haired, with the figure and bearing of a Pre-Raphaelite ingénue – confided her father's passion for power and his habit, when she was a girl, of tying up her dog and beating it beneath her bedroom window. 'From all this fantastic horror,' Ransome recalled, 'I was to rescue her and I could see no other way before me.' Yet Ransome, who was editing an Edgar Allan Poe collection at the time, had in all probability delighted in such stories, including, shortly after their marriage, a sugges-tion that Ivy's jilted cousin and two former suitors were planning to abduct and detain her in a lighthouse. Ransome had actually purchased a revolver, cautiously noting in his diary his reasons for doing so: 'in case this melodrama should take a practical shape'.

During the first few months of the marriage Edward Thomas delivered news to Bottomley on a regular basis: 'in answer to Emily [Bottomley] I should say that Ransome is living emphati-cally with his wife – decidedly'; 'Perhaps you caught the smell of burning in the startled air – for I hear he is in Coniston. We see little of one another, as the Two rise for breakfast (when they do rise) between 1 and 5pm, while we are bourgeois in such mat-ters. Although he is a lightning author and transformationist there are not yet any small Electricians that I know of . . .'; 'They frequent Petersfield and other pubs, enlivening the countryside with song. We like the "painted lady" less and less and call her the Unicorn because she has a small ivory horn in the midst of her forehead. We feel very bourgeois beside them but deferentially expect *Bohemia in Froxfield*.'

When Ransome met Ivy, his star was rising fast. In the first year of his marriage, 1909, Jack would publish collections of Hawthorne, Mérimée, Chateaubriand, Balzac and Cervantes, along with *The History of Story Telling*, a collection of Ransome's own essays chronicling the development of narrative technique, from *The Romance of the Rose* to Flaubert and Maupassant. It would be dedicated to 'My Wife' and was completed in Paris, while on honeymoon. Returning to England, Ransome worked furiously on *The Book of Friendship*, which he dedicated to Lascelles Abercrombie and which advertised 'essays, poems, maxims & prose' from Cicero to Walt Whitman, revealing a depth of reading and a capacity for industry that flatly contradicts Thomas's portrait of sybaritic lassitude. On the other hand, Ransome's marriage was clearly not, as he later insisted, a calamity thrust upon him entirely against his own will. He had at first enjoyed Ivy's company, delighting in her appeal to other men and her very obvious devotion to himself. Alone together they were at first happy enough, but the social institution of marriage placed demands on Ransome he had not anticipated. Immediately after the church wedding, he visited Ivy's parents in Bournemouth, where Mr Walker coolly informed him that Mrs Walker was like a blowfly, 'depositing – is it five million or only five hundred thousand? – poison germs wherever she sets her foot'. On 20 April, Edith came to stay in Froxfield, and was succeeded by Mrs Walker a week later. 'Awful row,' records Ransome's diary, then, 'Exit of mother-in-law – Thank God!' Doubts set in early, leading to anxiety, fits of temper, and in the summer, to serious duodenal complaints, intensified by stress: 'Gut bad. Enema. Read Plato.'

In June, a trip to Coniston had not been a success. Ivy, possibly alarmed by Ransome's intimacy with the Collingwood girls, had found the north country crude, and according to Ransome, objected to the failure of country labourers to raise their hats to her when passing. But more serious matters were afoot. By early summer, it became clear that Ivy was pregnant, and in September, she left for Bournemouth to stay with her parents. Ransome remained in Froxfield to work on a sequel to *The Book of Friendship*, to walk to London (inflicting a hernia on himself in the process) and to consider his bills. Shortly afterwards, Jack informed him that his books were not selling, and his troubles began in earnest.

Faced with a complex problem and finding himself more than partly to blame, Ransome's instinctive reaction was to discover the root of the dilemma somewhere outside himself. Thus, while his autobiography contains a limited confession of youthful high spirits, he struggled to find any moderation in his condemnation of Ivy: her love of luxury, her snobbery, her addiction to melodrama, the insatiable hunger for attention which Ransome, increasingly, was unwilling to give. On one occasion, Ransome had been summoned to the bedroom simply to witness his wife empty a plate of poached eggs over her head.

Nothing could be too extravagant. Nor could I ever take any plain statement at its face value. I did not think she was to blame for all this. Brought up in a house where her father and mother competed for her affection, and accused each other of every kind of horror and depravity, she had had no chance of growing up a normal human being . . . With this nightmarish family background of mutual hate what could be expected?

It is worth remembering that none of Ivy's early letters survive to balance his account, while Ransome's notebooks, as well as the unfinished memoir of his daughter, suggest that his first wife was not quite the monster he painted. Ivy was a fine writer and helped Ransome with his research. She was entirely responsible for the everyday affairs of the house. She admired her husband intensely, and while suffering from jealousy, submitted to extended periods when, pleading work or exhaustion, he took himself off on visits to friends or on long solitary walks.

As for Ransome, he had married too young, and in choosing Ivy chose the most fantastical elements of his imagination over the deep-seated conservatism which underpinned so much of his character. Neither had he considered how the death of his father nor the effort he had already invested in retaining the happiest parts of his childhood would play out when he became a parent himself.

Ransome's first and only child was delivered in Bournemouth on 9 May 1910, three days after the coronation of King George V. 'My wife', he recalled sourly, 'had insisted that I should be in the room while my daughter was being born but, just before the delivery was complete, the doctor had the humanity to send me to his house for a bottle he pretended to have forgotten.' The baby was named Tabitha, courtesy of a joke Ivy had made when asked how she would cope with twins: 'Oh, drown the black one and keep the Tabby.'

~

In the immediate aftermath of Tabitha's birth, the couple went north to Edinburgh to visit Edith, Joyce, Kitty and Geoffrey, and to speak with Messrs Jack, who commissioned one final episode in *The World Story Tellers* series: *The Book of Love*, 'celebrating in all its forms the love between man and woman'. Ransome found his next publisher in Martin Secker, a newcomer to the industry who was building a promising list and who commissioned two further books: a critical biography of Edgar Allan Poe and a collection of original fairy tales called *The Hoofmarks of the Faun*.

By June, half of *Poe* – the first of Ransome's books to be personally typeset by Geoffrey – had been completed, and the family moved down to Milford in Surrey, near the River Wey, where in the company of a local postman Ransome discovered the delights of fishing. By August, the book was finished, and he went north again on his own to stay with the Collingwoods, sailing and camping with Robin and correcting proofs. In

October, the Collingwoods left for London, but Ransome stayed behind in Lanehead, and when Ivy joined him soon afterwards, he collaborated with her on *The Book of Love*, drawing from W. G. Collingwood's extensive library. On 7 November, shortly before its publication, Tabitha was christened in Coniston church. Both sets of in-laws attended, with predictable results: 'Evening spoiled by Ivy's mother. Night ditto; by the sheer ugliness of remembering her.'

In three years, Ransome had transformed himself into a serious man of letters. His critical anthologies had contained so much of the European and American literary canon that even Edith was impressed. *Poe*, however, did not sell, and at a time when Ransome was worrying constantly about money, Secker proved reluctant to take anything that would not guarantee a reasonable return. A biography of Hazlitt was turned down because Hazlitt, regardless of Ransome's protests to the contrary, was not read any more. An account of Robert Louis Stevenson, author of *Treasure Island*, was accepted, but then reconsidered. Secker proposed instead a subject that could not fail to attract both popular and literary interest: an author celebrated for his plays and yet so debased as a man that since his death in 1902 his name was rarely mentioned in dignified drawing rooms. It was a business, Secker stressed, that required the utmost tact. Would Ransome write a critical biography of Oscar Wilde?

Ransome and Ivy left Lanehead just before Christmas and spent January 1911 in Paris, speaking to some of the loyal few who had stuck by Wilde during his last years in exile: the critic Remy de Gourmont, Honoré Champion the famous bookseller, Stuart Merrill, Paul Forte and the socialist and Nobel Laureate Anatole France. They returned to London in February, taking rooms in Cheyne Walk by the river in Chelsea, and in May moved to permanent lodgings at Manor Farm, Hatch, a few miles from Salisbury. 'Thank you very much for the rent,' he had written to Edith on his second wedding anniversary. 'Highly needed because by a bother between England and

America, a ten guinea article of mine has been postponed by two months.' Ivy wrote a postscript: 'We send our love and thank-yous . . . Baby is vaccinated and well of it, and was never even restless or sleepless or with [more] appetite, though the arm "took" splendidly.'

~

Gathered in her unfinished autobiography, Tabitha's earliest memories describe the brief interval between her dawning self-awareness and the time her father vanished himself like one of the shiny pennies in his own magic tricks. She recalled how Ransome's study was sacred, and that 'Dor-Dor' was never to be disturbed when he was working there; when Tabitha's maternal grandmother once tried, he had thrown a small wooden stool at her. This little office, with its bookshelves from floor to ceiling and its low window looking out onto the garden, housed his priceless library and his many pipes, hung on tiny brackets around the whitewashed fireplace. Ransome had remembered his childhood carpentry to make himself a table and a desk that he could work at while standing as well as sitting, thus extending his working hours and soothing his tender backside. When he was reading, he sat with his back to the fire at a baize-covered kitchen table, set with silver candlesticks.

Outside the study an entire room had been given over to Ransome's collection of mice, fed and cleaned by Ivy and housed in innumerable cages, bred, trained and exhibited on a scale Ransome could only have dreamed of as a schoolboy. Tabitha admired the prize certificates pinned to the walls of the 'Mouse House' and watched her father attentively: how he returned from fishing trips, stepped into his slipper bath 'surrounded by kettles and cauldrons and saucepans of boiling water', lit his pipe and settled back with a book of poems to regale the ladies. Dor-Dor was a big man with a red moustache; rather bony to sit upon, though he could eat a huge bowl of porridge for breakfast with thick cream and follow it down with scrambled eggs, tomatoes and coffee. When he moved into a different bedroom, he told Tabitha it was her job now to be a hot-water bottle and keep Mum-Mum's back warm. He was chivalrous in other ways too. When the new maid, Bulpit, came to him in tears to confess she had broken one of a pair of heavy crystal goblets, Ransome ordered her to bring him the survivor, took it from her and smashed it on the floor. 'Now, Bulpit,' he told her, 'don't worry. I've broken the other, so now we are quits.'

When she was eighteen and living alone with her mother, Tabitha would try to explain to her father the sort of person she had become, and why the old farmhouse, with its surrounding woods, the nearby monastery and the books she had lived with for so many years, was so dear to her that she could never imagine leaving it. But for Ransome, Hatch became synonymous first with anxiety, then with guilt and frustration. Invitations would arrive from anonymous well-wishers, offering suppers at expensive London restaurants. Ransome and Ivy would arrive to discover they were the only guests, with a table laid and a menu ordered and paid for on a scale he could not possibly afford. In April, as expected, *The Hoofmarks of the Faun* had fallen flat, ensuring that Ransome's income for 1911 would be his lowest in six years. For the first days of June, his diary makes sorry reading: 'Piles terrible'; 'Paid six pence for the ginger kitten – piles bad'; 'Nanny gave notice, paid six pence to have the kitten taken away again.'

The Wilde biography, at least, progressed smoothly. Ransome had approached his cousin, Laurence Binyon, for an introduction to Wilde's literary executor, Robert Ross, who had read and admired his *Poe* and provided much-needed encouragement: 'It will be the first serious study of Wilde that has yet appeared, and I want it to be recognized as such.' Over the following months, Ransome met Wilde's two sons and his bibliographer, Walter Ledger, a member of the Royal Yachting Association whose invitation to a cruise was declined following news that he suffered episodes of homicidal mania. With a view to achieving as wide a readership as possible, Ross arranged for the book to be translated into French and German – countries in which Wilde's fall from grace had not dimmed his reputation as one of the greatest playwrights of the nineteenth century. Ransome met with Michael Lykiardopoulos of the Moscow Arts Theatre, who had undertaken a Russian translation for the Scorpion Press and who, in time, would become one of his closest friends.

For the present, however, it was Ross himself who proved the most helpful of his advisors, allowing access not only to Wilde's literary estate, but also to his own private correspondence. Ransome had been entrusted with the rehabilitation of one of Britain's most controversial writers, and Ross was anxious to give him a free hand. But in hoping for the first serious 'critical' biography – one which would concentrate on Wilde's art rather than his life – neither Ross nor Ransome could resist the temptation to address the central crisis of Wilde's career, encapsulated in *De Profundis*, a letter written from the depths of Reading Jail to Wilde's lover, Lord Alfred Douglas, accusing him of vanity, treachery and cowardice. Ross now handed Ransome the complete, unabridged text, making him only the fourth person, including the author himself, to have read the letter in its entirety. It was a fatal mistake.

5

De Profundis

By August 1911, the final draft of the Wilde biography was nearly finished, but Ransome found little cause for rejoicing. Secker had made it clear that he was no longer open to any suggestion, however dear to Ransome's heart, that would not guarantee his investment: 'I am very depressed and pessimistic about the outlook everywhere, and after losing £50 on *Poe* and £25 on *The Hoofmarks*, I do not think it is worthwhile adding to my list any more books for which there is apparently so little demand.' Wilde, at least, might yield a profit, but shortly before Ransome sent his manuscript off to his brother Geoffrey to be typeset, an unwelcome obstacle presented itself. The publishing house, Methuen, which owned the copyright to most of Wilde's work, protested that Ransome's book consisted of too much unabridged, original material: 'The extracts appear so numerous that the work appears to us to be practically an anthology, and we cannot possibly consent.' Methuen demanded a drastic reduction in the number of quotations, and a fee for each individual quote that Secker considered 'extortionate'.

Secker wrote to Ransome, 'Will you please consider it a moment from my point of view? It seems rather hard that thinking out the idea and suggesting it to you, providing all the aid I could, and being out of pocket in cash for a considerable time, that there should be no possibility of my making any money out of this book.' He proposed sharing Methuen's fee between the two of them – a 'division of disappointment'. If Ransome agreed, his contribution would be deducted from the balance of his advance.

Ransome approached Robert Ross, hoping that his influence might resolve the situation. What should be done? Might Secker be persuaded to back down? Or perhaps another publisher could be found for the project. Methuen, for example, might take it on themselves, obviating the need to pay a copyright fee altogether. Ross responded kindly enough, but advised Ransome to pull in his horns: nothing could be achieved by direct confrontation. Secker's objection, after all, was perfectly reasonable; any publisher might be expected to feel the same. So Ransome capitulated and – with a helping hand from Ross – agreed to share the costs. But he did not forgive Secker. Money had become a serious issue since the demise of *The World Story Tellers*, and the blame could not be borne by Ransome himself. Ivy's retinue of servants, her taste for fine dresses and parasols, her demands for this kitten or that puppy – all were unconscionable. Now his own publisher was expecting him not only to write his books, but to pay for them too. It was manifestly and outrageously unjust, and something had to be done.

Help came via the Chesterton brothers, who had begun editing a literary periodical with Hilaire Belloc earlier in the year. The *Eye Witness* had a circulation of over 100,000, was Catholic, radical, political and literary, broadly tolerant of anything the chosen few cared to contribute. Thus, as Cecil Chesterton and Belloc concentrated on current affairs, Ransome wrote on the medievalism of William Morris, the plays and stories of August Strindberg (which he loathed), the history of folklore, and on one occasion – abandoning literature altogether – produced a double spread on the behaviour of juvenile mice. All this was very satisfactory. The *Eye Witness* provided a welcome supplement to his income, a reason to visit London and regular contact with his journalist friends. But with Secker demanding compensation for Wilde and refusing Ransome's most cherished inspirations, the real virtue of the *Eye Witness* was its owner: a wealthy entrepreneur and would-be poet called Charles Granville, who operated his publishing house under the romantic alias 'Stephen Swift'.

By coincidence, Granville's office was only a few doors down from Martin Secker on St John Street, but there could be no comparison between the two. Secker, it was true, was building a remarkable list. In addition to Abercrombie and Ransome, he was publishing D. H. Lawrence; later, he would be responsible for works by Vita Sackville-West, Henry James and Thomas Mann. But while Secker had admirable taste, he had no capital. Granville, on the other hand, had plenty, and a knack, besides, for making his authors feel that they were sitting at the centre of the universe. 'He had a magnificent way with him,' recalled Ransome:

He invited me to visit him at Bedford, to meet a much older Arthur Ransom (spelt without an 'e') who held that in the distant past our families must have been related. This modest and kindly old man spoke with enthusiasm of Granville's generosity. Granville had indeed been kind to him and he had delighted Granville by having a high opinion of his poems.

Granville, on the strength of Ransome's work to date (and a very kindly review of Granville's poetry which shortly appeared under Ransome's name in the *Eye Witness*), agreed to take on all his books both past and future, and on the strength of antici-pated royalties, to start him on a regular, generous retainer to commence on signature of the contract. Ransome need only write, which he did, beginning with a translation of Remy de Gourmont's *Un Nuit au Luxembourg*, followed by a collection of literary essays – *Portraits and Speculations* – that Secker would never have contemplated. For a young man with a family to support and a liking for long summer holidays, it seemed almost too good to be true. And, of course, it was.

～

Ransome's quarrel with Secker had inclined him more than ever to a view that his future depended on reliable connections. The past year had seen its ups and downs. Ivy – or 'Bébé', as Ransome now called her – announced a second pregnancy, which turned out to be phantom. One nanny had resigned, and a maid was fired for 'stupidity'. Replacements had to be found just as Ransome was writing possibly his most important critical article to date: 'Kinetic and Potential Speech' for Granville's *Oxford and Cambridge Review*. To top it all, the proximity of Hatch to Bournemouth had inevitably meant visits from Ransome's mother-in-law, who had thoroughly entrenched herself as the guardian of her daughter's happiness, and by extension, the enemy of Ransome's. Mrs Walker's egoism was at least a match for that of her opponent. On one occasion, after hearing Ransome play his favourite song on the piano – 'Summer Is Icumen In' – she announced that he had put 'real hatred' into the piece: 'hatred of me'.

'Long and intimate talk with Bébé,' Ransome wrote in his diary on 2 January 1912. 'Both very happy. Corrected proofs of *Wilde*. Bébé helped.'

The book was published on 12 February, while on 8 March the agreement with Granville was formally signed, with Secker releasing all rights to future editions of *Poe* and *Wilde* on the twelfth. Everything seemed set fair, and so it might have remained had Ransome listened when Secker advised against including any controversial material in the biography of a man so recently dead: 'I believe even if you do not agree with me now that you will do so in the future.'

The day after Secker had signed away his rights, Lord Alfred Douglas – still very much alive and famously litigious – filed an action for libel against Ransome, Secker and *The Times* Book Club, which had distributed the biography to its members. On 15 April, the *Titanic* met its iceberg, but Ransome made no mention of it. In the year 1912, dubbed retrospectively his 'Annus Horribilis', his own disasters eclipsed all others.

In the wake of Douglas's announcement, Ransome's friends leapt immediately to his defence. Lascelles Abercrombie, Cecil Chesterton and John Masefield all wrote letters of commiseration. Even Edward Thomas believed he was being 'victimized'. Meanwhile, Robin Collingwood – now a young don at Oxford – offered more substantial relief in the shape of his entire life's savings to foot the legal costs. In July, Secker informed Ransome that he had reached a private settlement with Douglas out of court: 'I do not think it prejudices your position in any way, and it is a satisfaction to me to be definitely out of the business.' Ransome was consequently left alone with *The Times* Book Club to defend what promised to be the most sensational literary case in history, barring Wilde's own. The only silver lining was that Robin Collingwood's meagre fortune would not be necessary. Ross, Wilde's first lover, rightly saw Douglas's action as an attack on himself, and provided Ransome with the finest legal team available.

If the Wilde case demonstrated nothing else, it revealed an essential difference between Ransome and Ivy. Ransome, who courted literary fame, recoiled in horror from direct public scrutiny. Ivy, on the other hand, embraced it. Her husband's north-country manners and Quaker ancestors were entirely alien to her. Here was Bohemia as she understood it, the Bohemia of the aristocracy: desperate love, hate, treachery, great talent bankrupted, power debased, exquisite beauty spoiled, the whole world dazzling and killing. The first thing she had done on hearing that Douglas had issued his writ was to send a telegram to Ransome's mother claiming that a warrant had been issued for her son's arrest and that he was 'hiding in London'. 'Fortunately,' remarked Ransome, 'my mother already knew enough of her informant to take these statements with a pinch of salt.'

The Wilde biography, at least in the short term, had proved a disaster, but Ransome took comfort from the fact that he had provided himself – via Charles Granville – with a degree of insurance. By October, his latest collection of essays, *Portraits and Speculations*, had gone to the printer. In addition, Granville, under his alias 'Stephen Swift', had advertised his own edition of *Poe* and an as yet unwritten treatise on *The Philosophy of the Grotesque* in his autumn list. A new edition of *Bohemia in London* was also in the pipeline, while Granville's edition of *Wilde* – in anticipation of the furore that would surround the trial – had already been printed. If only Ransome could pull through the libel suit, the collaboration promised a bright future. But at the beginning of October, calamity struck again, with extraordinary, almost laughable precision. Chesterton telegraphed Ransome in Hatch to announce that Granville had fled the country with his secretary. A large cheque from the *Oxford and Cambridge Review* had gone with him, and Granville's company, in the wake of the scandal, went into liquidation. 'Just as I had put all my eggs into one basket,' recalled Ransome ruefully, 'the bottom of that basket had fallen out.'

Many years later, when Ransome was inclined to take a more indulgent view of the affair, he heard the whole story at the Garrick Club.

Granville had been at a dinner party where one of the guests was a well known London magistrate who, after the ladies had left the dining room, called Granville apart and said to him, 'I never forget a face. You came up before me in such-and-such a year, accused of bigamy. You were given bail and absconded. I shall do nothing tonight because we are fellow guests in this house, but I shall make it my business first thing in the morning to let the authorities know I have seen you. And now, shall we join the ladies?' Granville left early that night, and next morning was on his way abroad with his secretary. They were traced, followed to Algiers and thence brought back to England on an embezzlement charge, with which the authorities did not proceed, being content to send poor Granville to prison for bigamy in spite of the willingness of his wives to give him testimonials as a good husband.

Meanwhile, in 1912, Granville's creditors closed in. Mustering his allies, Ransome abandoned Hatch, seated himself at the long table in Granville's office, and remained there until he had recovered every marketable title, a feat he attributed entirely to obstinacy. His father's publisher, Macmillan – for whom Ransome had edited the failing *Temple Bar* – took over *Portraits and Speculations*, which remained in print until 1923. Ross made arrangements for *Poe* and *Wilde* with Methuen, who, having provoked the trouble between Ransome and Secker, now showed admirable common sense in acquiring a book whose success was already assured.

~

Douglas v. Ransome was announced in March 1912, but was not scheduled to open until April the following year. In the meantime, Ransome had attempted to get on with his life, withdrawing, so far as was possible, into the world he understood. When he was not writing, he was fishing, playing cards with Ivy (a duty he resented) or catching up with friends. In late spring, he paid five pounds for a donkey and cart and rode with Ivar Campbell, an old flame of Ivy's, from the British Museum in Russell Square down to Hatch – a journey of ten days. The following month, he went bicycling in Dorset with Abercrombie, who had scarcely heard from him, let alone seen him, since the coronation of King George and had been sending reproachful letters: 'Lord! The heart-searchings your long and utterly unconscionable silence caused. Ah then, he loves us no more? We are deserted? Why not indeed? What is it in us that he should always love us? And yet, and yet, we did think he was of that noble nature which can forgive imperfection and never murder friendship.'

The spring trip in the donkey cart had proved so successful that a second was planned in July, and this time Ransome, Campbell and the donkey (christened 'Moab') were accompanied by Tabitha and Ivy. Tabitha, aged just two at the time and a precocious child, later recalled some details of the expedition. The cart, which was painted with yellow roses, was loaded high with tents, rugs, pots and pans and every other essential for a comfortable roadside camp. The grown-ups walked beside the cart, and since Moab was a proud donkey, Tabitha rode on Campbell's shoulders or in the cart when he tired. Just as before, they went slowly, idling, enjoying the sun, taking over a week from Hatch to Yeovil, and then – leaving Moab to mind the cart – boarding a train to London, where they stayed with Campbell's grandfather, the Duke of Argyll.

The romance of the journey never left Tabitha, and certainly affected Ivy. Shortly after returning to Yeovil to pick up the donkey, she declared that she and Campbell had been having an affair and was taken aback when her husband, seizing his opportunity, immediately suggested divorce. But Ransome was too eager. Having failed to inspire his jealousy, Ivy quickly recanted. Technically, there were no grounds for a separation; she had not slept with Campbell. At the last moment she had changed her mind and locked the door against her lover, only to find a note pushed under it in the morning, reading simply: 'I can't, because of Ransome.' It was very wonderful and strange and noble, and pathetic too, because poor Campbell could not have known the door was already barred against him.

Ransome privately concluded that the whole story was a pack of lies, but as the dismal party made its way back to Hatch, it was at least clear that a corner had been turned. Things had been said that could not be unsaid. Ivy's behaviour, so often antagonistic and demanding, now became increasingly desperate. As for Ransome, having articulated what he wanted, it was now only a question of preparing the ground. Over the next few months, Robin Collingwood, Lascelles Abercrombie, Ransome's brother Geoffrey and even Robert Ross were left in no doubt as to the impossibility of the marriage or its probable conclusion. In the aftermath of Granville's flight, and with the Wilde case drawing near, Ransome succeeded in reducing the entire complex muddle to a simple choice.

'Dec. 12 1912,' he wrote in his notebook:

This last year has been the worst of my life. On this date last year my Wilde was finished. Since then I have done nothing but the three essays on Nietzsche, Pater, and *Art for Life's Sake*. I have not been able to work. I have allowed myself to keep my wife's times rather than my own. I have found it increasingly difficult to filch or force time for study of any kind. I have risen late, too late for a morning's work, I have played cards after lunch till it was too late for an afternoon's work. In the evening, for fear of hearing my wife's complaint that I have been away from her all day and might at least spare her the evening, I have played cards again. Nor has there been any satisfaction in this, for an ill conscience has made me ill-tempered and my wife unhappy. I have been unhappy almost always myself.

If Ivy had ever laid her hands on this document, she might reasonably have objected that her husband had spent over three months of the year on holidays of his own choosing. In addition, he had published almost forty articles and reviews, besides writing *Portraits and Speculations* and the beginnings of *The Philosophy of the Grotesque* (which would never be published). But for Ransome, the dilemma, as stated, was purely rhetorical. He had already made up his mind.

~

In February 1913, Ransome came across a disturbing article in *The Times* and wrote post-haste to Edith, now moved back down to Leeds, enclosing a cutting. Douglas, it appeared, had been declared bankrupt, and his solicitor had informed the official receiver that damages were expected in a forthcoming libel suit to the tune of £2,500: a fortune.

'Look at this,' wrote Ransome anxiously. 'I don't think it very frightening because nobody would give him such a sum, even if they give him anything at all. But you can see what a beastly big business it is going to be.'

On 6 April, from lodgings at Beaufort Mansions in London, he wrote in the midst of hurried preparations for the case to let Edith know how matters stood. The trial would open in just over a week. He had met for a briefing with his counsel and everything seemed to be going smoothly. 'Meanwhile,' Ransome added on a brighter note, 'I am working as well as I can at a dialogue between a philosopher and a homunculus.'

On the great day itself, he managed one more quick letter before committing himself to the abyss: 'I am writing just before going into court to tell you that I am feeling very glad that the business is actually upon me, and that in two or three days it will be over. As soon as it is over I shall go and walk somewhere, in order to avoid either commiseration or congratulation.'

The case, so long anticipated, opened on 17 April in the King's Bench Division of the High Court, with Mr Justice Darling presiding. It was a historic occasion. Ransome's biography, as Ross had pointed out, was the first serious appraisal of Wilde's entire opus since his death. But much to Ransome's chagrin, neither the court nor the public were concerned with the literary merits of *Wilde: A Critical Study*. It was the details of Wilde's life that drew the crowds, and particularly the details of his relationship with the plaintiff: the 'Dear Bosie' of *De Profundis*, the gilded boy who had once goaded Wilde into his fatal action against the Marquess of Queensbury and who now sat just yards away from Ransome, seething with righteous indignation and thirsting for revenge. Ransome could scarcely understand how he had come to be associated with the scandal in the first place. Throughout the trial, his chief concern was that his counsel, J. H. Campbell KC (later Lord Chief Justice of Ireland), should make a clear distinction between Douglas's feud with Ross and his own modest work of 'non-sensational literary criticism'. This, in his own view, was his proper defence, but Campbell would not stick to it. Indeed, as the trial progressed, Ransome became convinced that Campbell had not read his book at all, and grew increasingly alarmed at the 'dangerous irrelevance' of his questions.

Douglas had a strong case. Answering the charge that his client had ruined Wilde, the prosecution pointed out that Douglas was little more than a boy when Wilde first met him, whereas Wilde, almost twenty years his senior, had already written *The Picture of Dorian Gray*, a scandalous work sprung from a corner of life no proper gentleman ever visited, still less boasted of in print. If there had been any corruption, it had been Wilde's corruption of Douglas. As for the specific passages quoted from Ransome's book, Douglas had not, as Ransome claimed, destroyed Wilde's resolve to lead a better, cleaner life after his release from Reading Jail. Far from it, Wilde had begged Douglas to take him back. 'My own Darling Boy,' he had written from exile in Naples, '. . . I feel that it is only with you that I can do anything at all. Do remake my ruined life for me, and then our friendship and love will have a different meaning to the world.'

All this boded well for the plaintiff, but fortunately, while

Ross had furnished Ransome with the best representation money could buy, Douglas – now legally bankrupt – had to make do with Mr Hayes, an inexperienced junior barrister in awe of the heavy guns. Hayes shied away from documents that suggested any indecent intimacy between Douglas and Wilde that might reflect poorly on his client's character, significantly diminishing the impact of his central argument: that Wilde was a shameless predator who had deprived an innocent boy not only of his inheritance, but of his chastity. Campbell, by contrast, went for the jugular. He produced poems by Douglas clearly indicating his homosexuality, which Douglas furiously denied. Douglas was forced to admit that he had deserted Wilde before his original conviction and had not returned to England, let alone visited his friend in prison, in over two years. Letters proved that he had consorted with male prostitutes and leeched money from Wilde, not simply because he had none of his own, but because it gave him an erotic thrill: 'I remember the sweetness of asking Oscar for money. It was a sweet humiliation.'

Campbell drew Douglas out for the benefit of the jury, and having supplied evidence of his dishonesty, treachery, cowardice and rapacity, left his junior, Mr McCardie, to deliver the *coup de grâce*.

De Profundis was now produced, like a mummy's curse, from its box at the British Museum. 'My Dear Bosie,' it began, and proceeded, line by line, page by page, on the thinnest prison notepaper, to deliver the most devastating character assassination in the whole of literature. Nothing Campbell had contributed by way of indiscreet notes or invoices could touch the impact of *De Profundis*. Written in an agony of pride and self-reproach, it plotted the history of Wilde's relationship with Douglas from the moment they had met to Wilde's incarceration. Douglas's insatiable appetite, vanity and ingratitude were responsible for every catastrophe. His conscious failings were only surpassed by his spiritual ignorance, a lack of personal insight that set no limit to his depravity. 'But most of all,' confessed Wilde with homicidal candour,

I blame myself for the entire ethical degradation I allowed you to bring on me. The basis of character is will power, and my will became utterly subject to yours. It sounds a grotesque thing to say, but it is none the less true. It was the triumph of the smaller over the bigger nature. It was the case of that tyranny of the weak over the strong which somewhere in one of my plays I describe as being 'the only tyranny that lasts'.

Douglas, who claimed never to have read the letter, found the contents so upsetting he left the witness box, only to be called back and reprimanded by Judge Darling. The members of the jury themselves finally rebelled and protested they had heard enough. The defence rested its case, and after a brief appearance by F. E. Smith KC for *The Times* Book Club (who gratified Ransome by dwelling at some length on the merits of his biography as a critical work of unimpeachable integrity), the court was adjourned. After a three-day trial, the jury took just over two hours to return its verdict.

For Ransome, such a dramatic and well-publicized victory offered not only personal exoneration, but also the promise of financial security. All that remained was to exploit his sudden fame, get squarely behind his book and write another, preferably at least as controversial as the first. The ball, as one reporter observed, was at his feet. What was he going to do with it?

'Get rid of it,' replied Ransome, 'as quickly as I can.'

He did not give a single interview. For thirteen months Douglas's suit had meant nothing but wretchedness, while the dishonesty and spleen exhibited during the hearing had appalled him. In spite of the ruling in his favour, Ransome insisted that the offending passages be deleted from every future edition of the book. Henceforth, the less he heard about the case the better, as several of Wilde's future biographers discovered to their cost. Now the entire sordid business was at a close, and he was free to go. The only question was, how far, and for how long?

There is a photograph – possibly the last taken before their separation – of Ransome and Ivy standing side by side outside the High Court amid a crowd of journalists, pedestrians and spectators. Ransome is dressed in a three-piece suit and trilby, bending a little forward over his walking stick. He is only twenty-nine, but he looks forty. Ivy is standing beside him, very sober in a long skirt and tightly buttoned tweed jacket, with her handbag clutched nervously in one gloved hand. Both are smiling shyly at the camera as a gentleman dressed in spats, tails and a silk top hat ambles by, apparently oblivious to the gravity of the situation.

Shortly after the picture was taken, Ransome visited his mother in Leeds and had a long talk, touching on the difficulties of his marriage, the weakness of his health and the benefits of a proper holiday – a walking holiday in France, Sweden or Denmark, where Hans Christian Andersen had written his wonderful fairy tales. From Leeds he went north to Edinburgh, where he had a frank discussion about his marriage with Geoffrey and visited Messrs Jack, who commissioned the book on Robert Louis Stevenson that Secker had turned down. While he was away, a 'mutual friend' persuaded Ivy to meet with Ransome's solicitor, Sir George Lewis, to discuss the possibility of a separation. Ransome himself did not attend, but claims Ivy swept in with a bold statement already prepared: 'Tell me what he wants me to do,' she had declared. 'If he wants me to go and be a prostitute in Piccadilly Circus I will do it for his sake.' But the interview proved inconclusive, and Ransome took matters into his own hands.

In early May, Ransome secretly procured a passport. Shortly afterwards, bidding goodbye to Tabitha and Ivy as he had so often done when spending a few days away on business, he took the train from Petersfield to London and boarded a cargo boat bound for Copenhagen, pausing just long enough to post a hasty note to his mother from the quayside:

Dear Maw

I am going on a short holiday to Stockholm, address, *Poste Restante, Stockholm, Sweden.*

No time for more before going on board. Please write to me at Stockholm. I wish I had a letter from you that I could send Ivy, saying that you thought I ought to stay away 2 or 3 months for the good of my health and work.

As it is I am only going for 3 weeks which is useless.

Dear Maw you have my love. I am now going on board.

Goodbye,

Arthur

6

Escape

Arriving in Copenhagen in the last week of May, the fugitive was greeted by an offshore breeze carrying the smell of spring lilacs.

As we passed Elsinore the mist stirred for a moment, and showed the green copper roofs of the castle. That smell of lilac and that lovely sight on a misty morning of early summer come often to mind forty years later, seeming not to mark so much a beginning as a re-opening of the life I had known at Coniston and at Cartmel, the life I had thought ended for ever in 1909. Pervading everything, like that scent of lilac over the sea, was the pious memory of Hans Christian Andersen. Some day I might yet learn to write tales that English children might overhear with pleasure, or had those days since 1909 put that kind of writing for ever out of my reach?

Ransome took the ferry to Sweden, landing in Malmö on *Barnen's Dag*, or Children's Day, which he took as a good omen. But he did not stay for long, and had never, one assumes, intended to do so. In his suitcase was a passport, and in 1913 there was only one country in Europe that required tourists to carry one. Two weeks later, he was on a ship bound for St Petersburg, the capital of the Russian empire, with a letter of introduction to an Anglo-Russian family – the Gellibrands, friends of a 'Chelsea and Paris' acquaintance. Over the next few years, Ransome would sail the same route many times: out of Stockholm and across the Gulf of Finland (then a semi-autonomous province of Russia) to the twin mouths of the River Neva, where Peter the Great had raised his magnificent 'Window on the West' on a swamp, paying, as legend had it, a life for every block of granite required to build it.

Ransome watched the rocky coast of Finland sliding by to the north. In the Åland Islands, at Hago or at Mariehamm (he could never remember which), he saw his first Russian policemen, 'with their gigantic belts, boots and whiskers', and was informed by a fellow passenger that when a sudden silence fell at a dinner party, whereas the English would say 'An Angel has passed,' the Russians said, 'A policeman is being born.' At the Kronstadt Fortress, which guarded the sea approach to St Petersburg, he had his bags searched and his passport stamped, sucking in his breath as the gorgeous spires and facades of the city, gold, white and green, rose above the water. But much as he might have liked to linger, there was no tour of the capital. His hosts met him at the quay and hurried him away through the cobbled streets in a horse-drawn droshky, with his typewriter bouncing on his knees, to the Finland railway station.

After a brief, astonished glance at the Orthodox icons and devotional candles in the ticket office, he was on a train heading north-west, back across the Finnish border, rattling towards a country house set deep in the pine trees, where he was received with warm hospitality by the entire Gellibrand family. He arrived just in time for the children's holidays and the famous 'white nights': a solstice to balance the interminable darkness of winter.

~

When Ransome recalled his escape from England to Russia, he compared it to a story by Daniel Defoe in which a traveller journeys to the moon. Defoe realized that nobody would believe it was possible to fly to the moon directly from Fleet Street, so instead he set out to produce 'an effect of truth' by having his hero make the trip in incremental stages: first to Germany; then to Russia, 'where anything might happen'; and finally to China, which was so far away, and so fabulously exotic, that a jump to the moon seemed 'little more than a crossing of the street'.

Sitting beneath the pine trees in Terioki, Ransome may have considered the possibility that flight, however colourfully framed, had become an endemic feature of his personality. As a small boy, he had run away from the bullies at the Windermere College. Leaving Rugby early, he had next abandoned his studies at the Yorkshire College in favour of a career as a publisher's errand boy, which he had relinquished inside a year. As an author he had switched between half a dozen separate genres, adopting the costumes, one after another, of the hard-bitten journalist, the scholar, the poet, the well-to-do child of the middle classes, the tramp, the gypsy and the travelling minstrel. Now, facing the first major crisis in a marriage which had itself been an impulsive leap, his instinct was to get as far away from the cause of his anxiety as possible. And yet, having established himself at the opposite end of Europe, his most serious difficulty still lay ahead of him. In Wiltshire he had left behind not only his wife, but his three-year-old daughter. He had lied to his mother because he knew that Edith – a conservative woman devoted to the memory of her husband – would feel strongly that the vows he had made in church were binding vows, given of his own free will. The difficulty was how to set things straight without condemning himself absolutely; how to confess the full extent of his truancy while shifting the blame, so far as possible, onto Ivy.

Shortly after his arrival in Finland, Ransome drafted three letters: two for Ivy, which he sent through his solicitor, Sir George Lewis, and a third to Edith. Lewis replied on 25 June, advising that on consideration he had forwarded the shorter letter, and suggesting that Ivy come round to his London offices to discuss the matter. 'It is better that the request should come from you than from me. If you like to write that you are changing your address and that any further letters are to be sent care of my office as you wish you can do so.'

The letter to Edith went out on 30 June. 'Dear Mother,' Ransome began,

I had just settled down to hard work here on my book on Stevenson, the Gellibrands having made everything awfully nice for me, when Ivy sent a wild and furious letter telling me to leave at once. I sent the letter to Sir George Lewis with a letter from me to her refusing to change my obviously sensible arrangements. She telegraphs and writes with great violence, and I have written asking her to go and talk things out with Lewis.

I do not think I told you that three days before I left, in one of her terrific scenes (in this case because of a mistake I made in the name of a servant, a mistake I instantly admitted) she took up the two lighted lamps from the dinner table and beat them to pieces, narrowly escaping setting the house on fire.

I told this to Lewis before I left, and he agreed that it was more than unwise to remain in the house, as in another such scene she might, without meaning to, go a little further. He is going to try to arrange a peaceable separation, at least for some months so that I can have a chance of getting some work done . . .

Well: I did not want to worry you with all this: but remembering what you told me about her absolutely untrue letters and telegrams on a former occasion, and her hatred of you, it occurred to me that she may try and get at you in some way now: so that it is better for you to know all about it beforehand.

If she does ask you to do anything, or if she sends you violent letters, send them on to Sir George Lewis . . . with a letter saying that you are my mother, and do not want to do anything without his knowledge. He will tell you what to do or what to write in reply.

In any case, do nothing to help her to come out here in pursuit of me. Do not hesitate to write to Lewis if anything happens in which you need advice . . .

My dear Mother, when I think of Ivy's deliberate efforts to separate me from my own family, the censorship of my letters, and all the rest, I am surprised that I am fairly sane . . . If only Lewis can arrange a peaceable separation, I do hope that in a calmer life you and I will be able to be the friends we used to be before that unfortunate marriage. I am so glad we had that talk in Leeds before I left England . . .

This is a beautiful place, and when my worry and anxiety allow it, I lay the foundations for Stevenson at a wooden table under tall pine trees, close to the Gulf of Finland, now and then hearing the guns from the fortress of Kronstadt far away. It is a great relief to be able to write to you without the fear that Ivy will condemn the letter.

Your affectionate son,
Arthur

～

Had Ransome arrived in Russia four months earlier, he would have witnessed the entire nation converge on St Petersburg to celebrate the third centenary of the Romanov dynasty: a momentous occasion, designed to confirm Nicholas II, after a turbulent decade, not only as Russia's present monarch, but as the immortal incarnation of the history of Russia itself. Huge portraits of Tsar Michael I, crowned in 1613, hung above shopfronts and the pillared porticos of the city banks. Fairy lights had been strung along the tramways spelling 'God save the Tsar'. More lights spangled the palaces and public monuments, surrounded by pilgrims from every corner of Russia's vast territory, stretching from Poland to Vladivostok, from the Arctic Circle to Persia. St Petersburg had never seen such magnificent parties, such opulent processions, such crowds, such traffic jams. Taking to his carriage with the imperial family, Tsar Nicholas rode through the streets escorted by Cossack cavalry and His Majesty's Own Imperial Guard, all sumptuously uniformed, to receive a blessing from the three metropolitans of the Orthodox Church at Kazan Cathedral. Lining the road, dipping in waves as his carriage passed, were courtiers, soldiers, priests, merchants, workers in cloth caps and rural peasants in their red-belted smocks and best boots. Outside the factories, long queues formed at soup kitchens handing out free meals. 'In every soul there is something Romanov,' announced one of the nation's most reliable newspapers, 'something from the soul and spirit of the House that has reigned for 300 years.' It was the first time the Tsar had been seen in public since the failed revolution of 1905.

In May, as Ransome sailed into Copenhagen, the Tsar and a select group of courtiers had set off on a royal tour of ancient Muscovy, travelling now by train, now by motor cavalcade, sending up clouds of dust and terrified chickens as they swept through villages, where peasants, crossing themselves in the exhaust fumes of their divine ruler, knelt before little tables decked with icons and flowers. Pausing to have his photograph taken with the descendants of the boyars who had elected Michael to the throne, Nicholas – destined to be the last ruling monarch of his line – concluded with a triumphal entry into Moscow. Here, after a further round of costumed balls, parades and banquets, he turned to his Tsarina and declared, with the boyish naivety that so endeared him to his admirers: 'The people love me.'

From February 1913, the tercentenary festivities had been covered by the London *Times* in three special editions, examining Anglo-Russian relations since the Crimean War, Russia's former alliance with Turkey and the 'Great Game' played out for colonial India. Russia, noted *The Times*, was the most backward empire in Europe. Its harvests, almost without exception, were reaped by hand. Its roads were muddy tracks. Four fifths of its population were recently emancipated slaves. Russia was inward looking, superstitious, despotic, anarchic. And yet it was also, indisputably, amongst the greatest and most influential cultures in the world: the cradle of Pushkin, Turgenev, Tolstoy, Dostoyevsky; of the Bolshoi ballet, of Tchaikovsky and Mussorgsky. Its capital – Tsar Peter's 'Window on the West' – was one of the busiest trading ports in Europe. Along the Nevsky Prospekt, Paris vied with Savile Row to dress diplomats, businessmen, lawyers and accountants. Opposite the Admiralty, an entire quarter of the city – the 'English Quarter' – was inhabited by British émigrés who considered Russia a second home. While Tsar Nicholas favoured Moscow and the old Russia, it was with this new Russia that Britain and France, in 1907, had forged the historic 'Triple Entente', to balance the peace of Europe against Germany, Austria and Italy. In 1913, nobody liked to recall that Tsar Nicholas was married to Kaiser Wilhelm's first cousin, only that the Tsarina – an unbending autocrat – was the granddaughter of Queen Victoria. Monarchy, pageantry, national unity and continuity, viewed through the appropriate lens, were all tremendous things. Following an edition of commemorative stamps, noted *The Times*, it had proven impossible to send any letters in Russia, because patriotic postal clerks refused to frank the face of a Romanov: 'These loyal and eminently practical scruples are typical of the mind of the vast masses of the Russian people.'

For Ransome, Russia held several attractions. It was, for one thing, the furthest country in Europe from England. It had also, for many years, been a major client of the family company, Ransome and Rapier, which supplied Russian farmers with ploughs forged from the finest British steel. Ransome's hosts, the Gellibrands, had made their fortune exporting Russian timber, were members of the 'English Club' which convened at the Astoria Hotel, and in addition to their dacha in Finland, had a large town house in the capital. Amongst Ransome's literary circle in England were several Russophiles, including Lascelles Abercrombie, and more recently, Robert Ross, who, following the Douglas trial, had travelled to Moscow to see a performance of *Salome* at the Moscow Art Theatre. Ransome's *The World Story Tellers* series included an essay by Turgenev and work by Tolstoy, while in recent years the Chesterton brothers had developed a theory of benign anarchy – 'Distributism' – that bore a striking resemblance to Prince Kropotkin's analysis of Russian peasant communes. There were many reasons, in short, why Ransome should consider Russia, amongst all other possible destinations, a suitable and interesting asylum. But when he came to write his autobiography, he recalled only that he had stumbled across an edition of W. R. S. Ralston's *Russian Folk Tales* in the London Library.

I had made up my mind to learn Russian to be able to read Russian folklore in the original and to tell those stories in the simple language they seemed to need. For ten years I had been repeating to the children of my friends (and to grown-up friends) the Jamaican stories that I had learned from Pixie Colman Smith and I believed that in so doing I had learned a method that could be applied to quite another material.

In Finland, with the enthusiastic encouragement of the Gellibrand family, Ransome soon abandoned Robert Louis Stevenson in favour of a crash course in the Russian language. When pure grammar became too dry, he practised his reading, starting with children's primers and promoting himself by one year every week. Within a month, with a dictionary and willing helpers, he was attempting rough translations of fairy tales gleaned from second-hand bookshops on the Nevsky Prospekt. In August, he travelled overland to Estonia, on the southern shore of the Gulf of Finland, and lived for some weeks in the house of the owners of an English firm of flax makers. The family – friends of the Gellibrands – were away, and the business was being managed by Norman Whishaw, who delighted Ransome by taking him on long journeys to outlying factories. Together they rode by carriage day and night through the forests, stopping occasionally to change horses, on and on, without a change in the landscape, so that travel itself became a sensation without meaning; a static procession of the same trees, the same sky, the same creak and jingle of harness mixed with the thudding of the horses' hooves. Often they would wake to be told by their driver that they had covered many miles, and Ransome, looking foggily at the trees, would find himself astonished they had moved at all.

How long Ransome had planned to stay in Russia when he sailed from Sweden, or exactly how many letters and telegrams had been exchanged with his mother, his solicitor, his wife, his friends, is impossible to say; just as one can only guess that the original excitement of escape – now identified permanently with Russia and its culture – had acquired a more seasonal quality as summer faded and the long, bitter winter approached. In July, he had written to Abercrombie, who replied that he had guessed what was afoot and could find no 'blame at all' in his old friend. On the whole he was glad it had happened, since had it not, 'it would have meant the destruction of you as a writer. And that would have been more damnable to me than I can say conveniently.'

~

Ransome's return to Hatch was a lot like Defoe in reverse. Travelling back this time by train via Riga and Berlin, he arrived in London on 30 September, and went to stay with Abercrombie at the Gallows in Dymock, where he discussed his problems in depth. Abercrombie advised him to be frank with Ivy, pointing out that if there was no hope for the marriage, he should make the break as cleanly as possible, leaving no room for doubt. Ransome accepted this advice and set off north to visit his mother in Leeds, the Collingwoods in the Lake District and Geoffrey in Edinburgh. But returning south to meet Ivy for the fatal conversation in London, his resolve crumbled and he agreed to return with her to Wiltshire. Once in Hatch, he found Tabitha, three years old now and full of stories, and the idea of leaving her for good was more than he could bear. Inch by inch – unpacking his bags, emerging in the morning for breakfast, sitting down in his study surrounded by his pipes and books – he began to feel at home again, and Ivy was quite convinced she could make him stay.

For the present, and for several years to come, Ransome's approach to his marriage was to make no choice at all. He and Ivy fished together and visited the family in Edinburgh. The following spring, leaving Tabitha with Edith, they holidayed together in France. But while Ivy took this as a good sign, Ransome had by no means given up on Russia or the inviting prospect of a fresh start to his career. He would become a Russian expert, and at the other end of Europe, continue the life he had once lived before his marriage, transposed but in essence much the same: St Petersburg and Moscow, the libraries, the theatres, the chatter in coffee shops and peaceful country weekends. He would learn the language fluently and become a 'specialist' in all Russia's ways. He would become a historian, an essayist and a writer of folk tales, and in the bleak Russian winters, return to England to sign contracts, write articles for a hungry public and catch up with family and friends. The only immediate obstacle was money.

In Edinburgh, Ransome persuaded the Jacks to allow him to set Robert Louis Stevenson aside, but his first collection of Caucasian fairy tales was regretfully declined. Income from *Wilde* and the books he had managed to salvage from the Granville fiasco (all sold at fire-sale prices) did not meet the family's living expenses, so that Edith – whose reaction to his truancy can only be inferred – was obliged to bankroll not only the rent, but also a set of false teeth: 'I chew now with quite an air.' Through the winter of 1913–14, he had been working on an original fairy tale, which found no buyers, and a verse adaptation of *Aladdin and His Wonderful Lamp*, which he eventually sold to Nisbet & Co. but which was only published after the war. Cecil Chesterton, always ready to help, had repackaged the *Eye Witness* as the *New Witness* and took several articles on folklore, along with a dissertation on William Morris, a scathing critique of cubism and a brace of fairy tales 'translated from the Russian'. In early spring, growing increasingly impatient, Ransome rushed back from his Parisian holiday to cover the Oxford–Cambridge boat race, breaking his duck as a news correspondent. But it was not until 12 April that he finally garnered the contract required to justify another season in Russia: a travel guide to St Petersburg commissioned by the publishers of *Tramp* magazine. In addition, a 'daring publisher' had offered £40 if, by the end of the summer, he could bring back a 'fairy romance – a sort of *Hoofmarks* on a grand scale'. It would be a 'nice lump', he assured Edith, to have in hand when he returned the following autumn.

Tabitha, in the meantime, consoled herself with the story Ransome dedicated to her in February. *The Blue Treacle: The Story of an Escape* tells of a little girl, Tabitha, who so irritates her father with questions that she is swept away by a sticky haze, and in the company of a pair of woolly sofa cushions, endeavours to return to the comfort of her sitting room and the protection of her parents by following 'Dor-Dor's' dimly remembered instructions. This curiously tortured metaphor was deciphered by Ransome in a short explanatory preface. The blue treacle, he explained, stood for the 'general stream of unrealized experience which is the greater part of our life', while Tabitha's escape from the treacle and her eventual return to her family was 'merely the story of an escape from this unconscious living – a realization of a moment of experience'. The guiding 'Woolly Beasts' or sofa

cushions were instincts, while the Bald Headed One who invol-
untarily accompanies Tabitha on her odyssey was the 'scientific,
anti-poetical critic, who ends by being incapable of life . . .'
Tabitha was 'the poet in us', while a ladder of animated syllo-
gisms, which Tabitha climbs at the end of the story, stood for the
'chain of argument' that a poet constructs as a framework for his
story but by no means as an explanation as to how that story
might have occurred to him in the first place. Only imagination,
defined by Ransome as the incarnation of truth and freedom,
proves sufficient to restore his daughter to grace.

At the age of three, Tabitha was unlikely to have gathered
much beyond the simple fact of her abandonment or the omi-
nous repetition of a single word: 'escape'. Ransome packed his
bags and left the day after her fourth birthday.

7

War

My Dear Mother,
I have finally started to Russia, and prepare to beguile the appalling tedium of the way by writing to my family. It is not easy to deal with the machine, because of the jerking of the train. However, with a pen or pencil, I could not write at all. We have just passed the Belgian frontier at Erquitelines. I get to Cologne a little after four, and wait there some hours, when I hope to dine. Then I have a ticket for a bed in the second-class sleeper from Cologne to Berlin where we arrive tomorrow morning. I get to Wirballen, the Russian frontier, tomorrow night, where there is the perfectly horrible business of Russian customs. They go through everything, and sometimes even your pockets.

On his second trip to Russia, no longer possessing the advantage of surprise, Ransome had needed to negotiate terms for his release. It was not, in Ivy's view, a fair division of labour that he should spend all their money on summer holidays and leave her at home to look after the baby. In consequence, it was agreed that Tabitha would stay with Edith in Leeds, and Ivy would join her husband in St Petersburg once he had arranged comfortable quarters.

Ransome had left London on 10 May 1914 and spent a day in Paris, where an illustration by his old flame, Jessie King, for one of his fairy tales was hanging in an exhibition of decorative art at the Louvre. Afterwards, he heard all about her motoring tour of Morocco before dropping by at the studio of another illustrator to discuss possible etchings for his dialogue between a philosopher and a homunculus. The following morning, he continued his journey through Belgium, whose invasion in four months' time by the German army would provoke Britain to war.

'Belgium is a loathsome place of cranes, canals and rubbish heaps,' confided Ransome.

I keep remembering with diminution of horror the last time I came by here, at the end of four days infernal travelling in a third class carriage. At least this is quicker. But I do wish I was on a boat. We have now passed Namur, and I am going to open a tin of pate de foie that I have with me and feed.

Cocooned in the moment, tapping away at his typewriter or spooning foie gras as the train ploughed on, Ransome remained as oblivious as the rest of Europe to the coming conflict. He changed trains at Cologne and slept until Berlin. In Berlin, he took another train across German Poland to Wirballen – where the following October German machine guns would scythe down the Russian infantry – arriving in St Petersburg on the 13th. This time he did not stay with the Gellibrands. He had a guidebook to write, Ivy on the way and a growing network of friends of his own, so he booked comfortable rooms at the Hermitage Hotel on the Nevsky Prospekt and settled down to business.

Ransome's capacity for uninterrupted work when the mood took him was staggering. His plan was to have the guide finished in a month, before the museums and libraries closed for the summer holidays, and then to move out to the countryside in Finland, to the Gellibrands, or perhaps to a monastery, where he could recuperate and devote himself entirely to his fairy tales. To this end he established a strict regime. He got up early in the morning and worked through till lunch, then spent the afternoons gathering material, visiting the galleries and theatres, eating black bread in the buttery of the Metropolitan Hotel or watching with delighted astonishment as old ladies in head scarves abased themselves before a silver casket containing the remains of Alexander Nevsky, the patron saint of the city. In the evenings he returned to his room and worked on until bedtime, leaving a little window open in the small hours for a letter home to his mother. Within a week of his arrival he had already written 10,000 words out of a projected 60,000, and was chiding himself for laziness. Ten days later he could write to Edith boasting 41,000, and was in a position to give a complete résumé of the book's contents, which reflected both the demands of a practical reference manual and the idiosyncrasies of its author. There would be chapters on Peter the Great and the founding of the city; the Nevsky Prospekt; the Winter Palace; the people's market; the coastal islands; beggars; funerals; food and how to get it; the Alexander Nevsky Monument; advice on how to cope with customs officials; first aid; and at the back (and in the face of protests from his publisher), a brief history of Russia.

Ivy never did visit her husband in St Petersburg, either because Ransome had dissuaded her, or because, on further reflection, she had decided she had better things to do. Leaving Tabitha with Edith in Leeds, she announced that she was setting off on a European tour with friends. By June, she was in Monte Carlo and reluctant to come home. Ransome's relief, meanwhile, vied with an increasing fatigue. In June, the climate was humid and sticky. He suffered from coughs, colds, chest pains and chronic headaches. Some days he could not go out at all, and when he did, brightly coloured dragonflies hovering in the streets reminded him that the whole city had been built on a swamp. Poor health and exhaustion led to introspection, and his letters reflected a new mood. 'I do wish I did not feel so old and frightened!' he confessed. '. . . I do so violently wish for the old peaceful days.'

Writing to his mother, Ransome listed the number of pages he had pounded out on his typewriter, his ailments, his money troubles, the prospect of only a few brief weeks devoted to his fairy tales before the necessity of returning home. But folded into the humdrum of work were wishful thoughts, like photographs of a distant planet. Seated at his desk at midnight, with the sun dipping briefly to the horizon and a thousand words still to go before bedtime, he could see himself in another place: sharing a farmhouse, perhaps, with his sister, Joyce, or fishing for perch with Geoffrey by a river in the north country. Ivy had no place in Ransome's paradise; she simply ceased to exist. Only the good remained, warding off the anxiety – and accompanying stomach cramps – that nagged at him in idle moments.

'I was delighted to hear such good news of Tabitha,' he wrote, after learning that a spate of temper tantrums had finally subsided:

Please give her my love and kiss her on the 'pot from me. I am so glad to think of her at Leeds surrounded by such admirable sanity. I only wish she could come to the Lakes for a Ransomian holiday. Perhaps some day I shall make lots of money out of a book, and be able to take a whole crew of us up there, and have a boat, and everything as it used to be, without frenzy, and be just as jolly as jolly, and we would fish for perch, and get woolly bears, and let Tabitha have a bit of that to remember when she grew up. I remember it all about twice a day myself. Life is a terrific steam-roller. But I shall get woeful if I go on.

~

Ransome's guidebook was finished on 9 July, exactly two months and a day after it was started. It was never published. Within a few weeks the Teutonic-sounding St Petersburg would become Petrograd as Russia went to war with Germany. Three years later, in 1917, many of the streets would change their names to honour the dates and heroes of the Revolution. Ransome's book became redundant. Even the manuscript was destroyed. Retrieving it in 1919, the author burned it in a fit of pique, almost certainly because the views he had expressed before the war clashed so violently with his post-war sensibility. If so, one can only regret the impulse which deprived future readers of possibly the last detailed account of the Russian capital in the final days of the old world, when candles burned before icons of the Tsar, reluctant beggars blessed nobles in the streets, and in the department stores, English ladies mingled with the major-domos of Siberian khans.

The first bullets of the First World War were fired in Sarajevo on 28 June 1914. At the time Archduke Ferdinand, heir to the throne of Austria, had been visiting the Bosnian capital to direct military manoeuvres in the mountains. As his car drove slowly through the streets, a nineteen-year-old Bosnian Serb, trained by Serbian nationalists known as 'The Black Hand', stepped out of the crowd and fired two shots. The first hit the Archduke's pregnant wife in the stomach. The second struck the Archduke in the chest as he turned to help her. A few hours later, he died of his wounds.

In England, the assassination was initially treated as little more than a 'typical piece of Balkan savagery', but in Russia it caused serious alarm. As frantic diplomatic notes criss-crossed between at least a dozen governments, Ransome was dashing about in a tunic and crimson cummerbund, packing his bags for a richly deserved holiday with the Gellibrands. After a couple of days spent boating and sunbathing, he settled happily to his fairy tales, interspersed with a little tennis, fishing and conversations with the Gellibrands and their friends.

A month later, word of Austria's ultimatum to Serbia, and Russia's mobilization in defence of her fellow Slavs, reached Terioki with the morning papers. The news had momentous implications. In 1914, Serbia stood in relation to the great powers of Europe very much like a match next to a barrel packed with gunpowder. And yet the possibility that an obscure little kingdom in the Balkans could spark a world war seemed so farfetched that Ransome and his friends, peacefully ensconced in the countryside, could not bring themselves to take it seriously. 'Our talk', he recalled,

was like a novel by Mr [H. G.] Wells. We did not believe in it. In the evening we walked by the seashore and looking towards Kronstadt and down the Gulf, saw far away the searchlights of ships of war sweeping the quiet waters.

'What are they doing?' said one.

'Looking for Germans,' said another. And we all laughed.

Ransome was sitting with the same group on the veranda of the Gellibrands' dacha, scooping wasps out of honey, when the call-up papers arrived. The gramophone in the Gellibrands' sitting room stopped playing modern dance tunes, the fishing rods and tennis rackets were packed away, and Ransome found himself walking through the woods with one of his fellow guests, Nikolai Georgievitch, who was off to join his regiment in St

Petersburg. They discovered the Terioki railway station packed with conscripts.

'The train', wrote Ransome,

was several hours late, and so long that it had to stop twice at each station, once for the front carriage and once for those behind. It was full of Reservists. Some were alone, others came with their wives and mothers and children. At every station there were more of them. At every station there were weeping women, seeing perhaps the last of their men. There was an army doctor saying goodbye to his family, the servants kissing his hands and praying, his wife rubbing his wrist up and down mechanically. There was one man who talked, too gleefully, I thought, and too much. He was not going to war.

There had been disturbances in St Petersburg over the summer, and in July a general strike culminated in street fighting and barricades. Russian factory workers, tired of empty promises, wanted immediate concessions, and the militant leaders of the extreme Left were once again speaking openly against the Tsar. But war performed its age-old alchemy. With the mobilization of the army, anger against the state gave way to anger at Russia's enemies. German and Austrian nationals who had lived in the capital for generations were beaten up in the street. German shops were looted and torched, or else hastily changed their names. The German legation was sacked, and from the top storey of St Petersburg's premier department store came a sinister rain of German-made pianos.

Ransome recalled these acts of hooliganism with a shudder, but at the time he preferred to ignore them altogether. Instead, in the company of like-minded friends, he concentrated on what he admired: the willingness of the great mass of the Russian people to put aside their grievances, however serious, in the interest of something they loved better than themselves – their culture, their memories, the language they spoke, the integrity, even, of their domestic arguments. On the Sunday following his return, a huge crowd had gathered outside the Winter Palace, not to throw stones as they had in the summer, but to be blessed by the Tsar. In the streets peasants conscripted from their villages stood docilely outside public bathhouses, offices, riding schools or any other place that might expeditiously be used to vet and equip such a multitude. Many had brought their own kettles and were making tea or eating sunflower seeds. Days before, St Petersburg had been on the brink of revolution. Now, the city was swollen with millions of workers and peasants, taking orders without question, meekly bidding farewell to their families, accepting possible, even probable, death on the battlefield at the behest of the very men they had so recently been bent on deposing.

Just as the call to arms temporarily united a fractious Russia behind the Tsar, so it released Ransome – however briefly – from his private anxieties. His marriage, Tabitha, even his books seemed momentarily trivial by comparison. He was witnessing the birth of history and a great cause: love without reason, the almost bestial love of culture and country. Here, at last, the mystery of innocence was no longer obscure but easily identified, overwhelmingly present in the mighty tide of ordinary people flocking silently to the capital to demonstrate their helpless affinity to a place, an idea, a feeling, something that could only be described as 'home'.

Germany formally declared war on Russia on 1 August, and for three agonizing days Britain remained aloof. Crowds mobbed the British embassy, while the British ambassador, Sir George Buchanan, sat in conclave with one diplomat after another, including the German ambassador, Count Portales, who attempted to convince him that Britain could not afford to go to war without risking a revolution of its own. But on 3 August, Germany declared war on France, and the following day, after German troops swept through neutral Belgium, Britain honoured its contract. 'Heard England declared war on Germany,' Ransome wrote in his diary. 'Tremendous enthusiasm! Do not believe the news.'

Back in London, Lord Kitchener launched his 'Your Country Needs You!' campaign, and on the strength of a surge of anti-German patriotism, netted 33,000 volunteers a day, including Ransome's brother, Geoffrey. On 1 August, the British army stood at just 248,000 men, with only 120,000 stationed at home. By mid-September, half a million raw recruits were being trained up in barracks all over the country. But Ransome was not in England, and besides, considered himself a poor physical specimen: short-sighted, plagued with piles and duodenal cramps, and at thirty years old, just touching the maximum age limit for acceptable cannon fodder. So he decided to turn his hand to journalism.

~

When Ransome had arrived in Russia in 1913, he had known almost nobody, much like he had known almost nobody when he had arrived in London as an office boy at the tender age of eighteen. But just as he had found his milieu amongst the writers and artists of Bohemia, so in St Petersburg he had quickly identified the most interesting and useful men of the expatriate community. Amongst them was Harold Williams, the son of a British missionary, a gifted linguist and journalist whom Ransome looked up to as a second Collingwood.

Ransome had been introduced to Williams by a close friend of Lascelles Abercrombie, Bernard Pares, a professor of Russian studies at Liverpool University and former correspondent for the *Manchester Guardian*, currently living in Petrograd. Pares and Ransome would become friends, but Williams struck a far deeper chord: a shy, generous man a few years older than himself, with a pedagogic streak and a disarming stutter. Ransome benefited from Williams's encyclopedic knowledge of Russian history, his journalistic contacts (Williams was currently working for the British *Daily Chronicle*) and also from a friendship with Williams's wife, Ariadna Tyrkova, the first female representative elected to the Petrograd regional parliament, or City Duma, and a passionate advocate of constitutional reform. In Williams's company Ransome discussed not only politics, but philosophy, history and literature, sought out his advice on every subject and listened in amazement as he spoke in any one of the forty-two different languages used in Russia at that time. 'He opened doors for me that I might have been years in finding for myself [. . .] I owe him more than I can say.' To Tyrkova, meanwhile, he owed not only many pleasant weekends at the Tyrkov country estate, but a first-hand account of the deep internal divisions that would eventually tip the Russian empire into revolution and civil war.

By 1914, Tyrkova had passed through every shade of the political spectrum. In 1881, her elder brother, Arkady, had belonged to the People's Will, an organization of populist terrorists responsible for the assassination of Alexander II. As Arkady served his time in Siberia, Ariadna – then a schoolgirl – became a close friend of Lenin's future wife, Nadezhda Krupskaya, and by the time she graduated was already a seasoned revolutionary. Exiled from Russia in the 1890s for smuggling propaganda, she had lived for some time in Germany in a small commune gathered around Peter Struve, a Marxist lawyer responsible for the manifesto of the Russian Social Democratic Labour Party, of which Lenin, and later Trotsky and Stalin, were members. It was here, in Stuttgart, that she had met Williams, a former clergyman, Tolstoyan and pacifist then working as a correspondent for The Times. But as Lenin split the party in 1903, Struve and Tyrkova were already moving towards the liberal Right. Returning to Russia during the failed revolution of 1905, they had joined the central committee of the Constitutional Democrats, or 'Kadets', a group of middle-class professionals led by Pavel Miliukov, who in 1914, though an energetic proponent of parliamentary democracy, had announced his uncompromising support for the Tsar. Having abandoned socialism, Ariadna visited Krupskaya for the last time in 1908 in Geneva, where Lenin left her in no doubt as to her future should the Bolsheviks succeed to power. Strolling together to the tram stop, they had argued fiercely over Russia's national identity, the purpose and nature of reform. Tyrkova told Lenin she had no wish to live in a Russia ruled by illiterate factory workers. Lenin, smiling coldly, had told her this was exactly why, when the Revolution came, she would be amongst the first to hang from a lamp post. She did not forget the look on his face as he had said it, or the way he had savoured the French word *lanterne* – such a common practice under Robespierre that the noun had become a verb.

Among socialist wits, it was sometimes said that there was only one man among the Kadets, and she was a woman. Ransome would find out for himself what a formidable opponent Tyrkova could be, but in the first days of the Eastern Front, he aligned himself with her party: an organization that condemned social revolution, that squarely backed an imperialist war, and that based its reforming vision on a constitutional monarchy inspired by Britain. At Tyrkova's flat in Petrograd, both Miliukov and Struve were regular guests, as were British diplomats and journalists. Williams and Pares commuted daily to the British embassy, where Sir George Buchanan listened eagerly to their council. All this boded well for Ransome, and yet in 1914 he was neither a politician, nor a diplomat, nor a newspaperman. All his journalistic friends were running off to Galicia to watch the Russian army engage the Austrians, but he had no press pass and no newspaper to warrant one. The only solution, he decided, was to return home and look for work, in the meantime confining his commentary to private correspondence.

'The tennis court where I was playing a month ago,' he wrote to Mrs Collingwood on 12 August,

is a cavalry camp. The streets are full of soldiers. And, well, I always admired the Russians, but never so much as now. You know how our soldiers go off in pomp with flags and music. I have not heard a note of music since the declaration of war. They go off quite silently here in the middle of the night, carrying their little tin kettles, and for all the world like puzzled children going off to school for the first time. And the idea in all their heads is fine. They all say the same thing. 'We hate fighting. But if we can stop Germany then there will be peace for ever.'

On 18 August, Ransome joined a party bound for England via

neutral Sweden and Norway. The boat left from Raumo, far enough up the Finnish coast to avoid the German Baltic fleet, but he saw battleships to the south, and approaching Stockholm, torpedo boats hiding behind pinkish rocks that marked the seaway into the harbour and heavy guns 'almost indistinguishable from the stone'.

Swedish neutrality, as Ransome soon discovered, meant not only heavily armed borders, but a divided nation. On the coast the locals supported the Entente and saluted his passport, but the Swedish guard on the train which took his group from Stockholm to Norway favoured the Central Powers led by Germany, and found a dozen little ways to make his journey a misery. Nevertheless, he arrived safely in Christiania (modern Oslo), and finding an English vessel in dock due to sail for Hull, arrived at the mouth of the Humber on the evening of the 23rd. The following day, he woke to a view through his porthole of the estuary and four destroyers which appeared suddenly in a line, one after the other and low in the water, rushing past him to join the British blockade in the North Sea.

Ransome arrived at Hatch later that day and sat down immediately to the task at hand. Amongst his first contributions to the wartime press was a piece for Cecil Chesterton's repackaged *New Witness*, 'If Russia Wins', a meditation strongly influenced by his conversations with Harold Williams which analysed the probable effects of war on the Russian constitution and culture.

Ransome noted that, traditionally, Russian defeats had been followed by reforms, whereas victories had been followed by periods of harsh retrenchment. In the present case, however, he believed that the Tsar would be forced to allow constitutional reforms whether Russia won or lost. The reason was simple. Much of the war effort in Russia was already in the hands of 'revolutionaries' (Ransome placed all reformers in this category) who served cheek by jowl with 'reactionaries' in the army, the Red Cross and the domestic civil services. Once the conflict was over, it was inconceivable that the government would simply revert to the status quo: 'Men who have shown themselves able and willing to serve their country in her time of need can hardly be classed again among possible dangers to the state.' On the other hand, 'revolutionaries' who had worked side by side with 'reactionaries' would never again feel the 'uncompromising hostility' they had felt towards the Establishment before the war. Russia would become more liberal, less schismatic, and consequently 'less Russian'.

So much for politics: Russia, according to Ransome, was destined for a benign constitutional monarchy whether the Tsar (or the socialists) liked it or not. But the broader cultural landscape was a different matter. In this respect, he believed, Russia would become 'more Russian'. War would encourage nationalism, thus reversing the wholly deplorable collapse of indigenous culture owing to modern commerce – an excellent thing, not least because it would practically ensure a heightened demand for folklore. In short: 'England will be more English, France more French, and in the East, Russia will be more Russian and less inclined to suppose that civilization as well as the best of everything is made in Paris, London, Vienna and Berlin.'

'If Russia Wins' was published on 3 September, followed by 'Petrograd to Hull in Time of War' a month later. But the truth was that in these early days of national excitement, the only question was whether Britain would win. Ransome's diary, which includes places visited, number of manuscript pages completed and a fastidious account of perch and pike caught from rivers in Wiltshire and the north country, provides little insight into the prevailing mood during the first critical weeks: the strident patriotism, the unbounded optimism, the impatience with which schoolboys anticipated their eighteenth birthdays. All around him his countrymen were mobilizing, including his fellow writers. In September, John Masefield and G. K. Chesterton were invited to Waterloo House in London, where David Lloyd George, then Chancellor of the Exchequer, established a War Propaganda Bureau, to be headed by John Buchan and to include such household names as Thomas Hardy, Rudyard Kipling and H. G. Wells. The purpose of this bureau, the existence of which only became public knowledge in 1935, was to encourage, through novels, pamphlets, poems and articles discreetly placed in the mainstream press, the patriotic ardour so essential to the domestic war effort. Ransome's cousin, Laurence Binyon, had already written one of the most famous poems of the war, 'For the Fallen', which would be carved on a thousand memorials in Britain and France, while Lord Northcliffe's papers, *The Times* and the *Daily Mail*, printed leader after leader denouncing the 'Hun' for his perfidy, depravity and the insatiable greed for power that defined his race. But Ransome could find no place for himself. He did not want to fight, there was little demand for his writing, while Hatch held even fewer charms than it had in peacetime. In England, he felt himself almost a stranger, and dreaming only of Russia, noted Geoffrey's enrolment in the 23rd Yorkshire Regiment with a mixture of condescension and awkward approval.

'I doubt if he will ever be content to return to his printing,' he told W. G. Collingwood in a letter on 23 November:

If he gets a chance I expect he will stay in the army. He lived until recently in a tent, with a river running through the middle of it, and a leak over the place where he slept. He had no proper bed, and yet he emerged fitter than ever, without even a cold in the head. Also he gets on very well with his men, and when the regiment as a whole refused to go on parade, his platoon sent him a note to say they intended to turn up, and did so, to Geoffrey's lasting honour. They are mostly Northumberland miners, and he likes them very much . . .

I have heard one good joke about the war, which I will tell you, in case it hasn't been in *Punch*. It is a riddle. 'Why do the Germans spell Kultur with a K? Because Great Britain has command of all the seas.'

~

For the rest of the autumn and half the winter, Ransome devoted himself to translating fairy tales, hunting for a newspaper that might take him on as a Russian correspondent and attempting to persuade the Foreign Office to send him back to St Petersburg as a 'King's Messenger', one of the chosen few entrusted with the British diplomatic bag. Had he been successful, he would have travelled with a discreet silver greyhound attached to his lapel and a briefcase carrying all the new ciphers for the British embassy, as well as letters, official documents and any further miscellanea His Majesty's Government wished to shield from the prying eyes of Kronstadt customs officials. He had high hopes. His godfather's eldest son, Francis Acland, was currently serving as Permanent Undersecretary of State for Foreign Affairs, while Mrs Macmillan, of the Macmillan publishing company, enjoyed considerable political influence through her husband, and as a close family friend promised to lobby on his behalf. But King's Messengers, even in peacetime, were usually military men, and the 'glimmering chance' eluded him. So as Britain marshalled its reserves to reinforce the Western Front, Ransome divided his time between the Collingwoods and the Lakes, fishing and Hatch, where by October he had completed drafts for *Little Daughter of the Snow*, *The Coffin Maker of the Vosges* and *The Tsar of the Sea*.

He left for Russia in December with nothing but a few letters of introduction and a commission for a book of Caucasian folk-lore to be titled *Old Peter's Russian Tales*. Ivy received a fishing rod for Christmas, and a tackle bag to go with it. Barbara Collingwood got his last letter, posted from the Newcastle Station Hotel on the 22nd, shortly after the First Battle of Ypres wiped out Britain's entire standing army:

I sail by the *Venus* tomorrow morning from Bergen, and then go up the edge of the Gulf of Bothnia, to where the railway ends. Then sledge and then, if unfrozen, on by the Russian railway. The whole thing promises to be interesting but cold. I have been eating fish hard for the last three days, so as to have some sort of revenge, before the fact, in case a mine so contrives that fish shall eat me.

8

The Elixir of Life and *Old Peter*

Warmed by his chauffeur, who had kindly offered to sit on his stomach, Ransome crossed Lapland by sledge, reaching the Finnish border at Torino unscathed. 'There I felt myself all but home again, climbing into the Russian train that, it used to be said, started unwillingly and often stopped to look back, coming at last to the new-named city of Petrograd late at night on December 30, 1914.'

On 6 January, he met and talked with Henry Hamilton Fyfe, a correspondent for the *Daily Mail* who had been transferred to the Eastern Front following an overly frank account of the disastrous Battle of Mons, a debacle which he had witnessed under cover of the Red Cross. Hamilton Fyfe suggested that Ransome go to Warsaw and report on the fighting in Poland, but according to Ransome, the *Mail* was unenthusiastic, and besides, his diary recorded a bad cold: 'awfully sore throat'. On 10 January, he dined with Harold Williams who introduced him to Alexei Remizov, a Russian author known for his interest in fairy tales. The next day, he was on the train down to Moscow, the first seat of the Romanov tsars.

Ransome arrived at Moscow's Hotel Siberia on the 12th, with no proper winter coat and his moustache frozen into a solid block of ice. He did not stay long. An invasion of cockroaches, coupled with the iniquitous rates charged by the hotel's proprietors, forced him into cheaper rooms at a private house in Donskaya, where he practised his Russian with the widow of a senior civil servant and her many children. The cockroaches, however, were waiting for him, and when he protested to the housekeeper, a 'very handsome and filthy gypsy', he was told in no uncertain terms that his room never had and never would be cleaned. '. . . As for the unmentionable insects, God made them, so it was to be supposed that he intended them to live . . .' On the 14th, he dined at the Moscow Art Theatre with Michael Lykiardopoulos, who before the war had translated his *Wilde*, and another British author, Hugh Walpole, whom he had known in the old Chelsea days. By the end of the month, after visits to the Kremlin and St Basil's, he was beginning to find his feet.

Nineteen fifteen was not a good year for the Russian army, but just as Ransome had largely ignored the rampant militarism in England, so in Moscow, far behind the lines, he settled into a free-floating limbo, punctuated by anxiety over his haemorrhoids ('piles dreadfully bad – lost a lot of gore'), trips to the theatre, and thanks to Hugh Walpole, a sudden passion for Henry James. At the British Consulate he met Bruce Lockhart, the young Consul General, and no doubt discussed the war, but articles posted to his agent in London found no buyers. He read George Bernard Shaw's *Man and Superman* ('a very knowing bird'), took photography lessons, and concentrated on completing the manuscript for *Old Peter's Russian Tales*, until at some point in the middle of February his attention once again began to wander. Back in England his little sister, Joyce, was working on her first novel. Walpole, too, was working on a novel, *The Green Mirror,* which he completed – to Ransome's envious astonishment – by writing 'Chapter One' and continuing straight through to the end without revision or hesitation. Now Ransome, seemingly between one stride and the next, was struck by the most brilliant idea he felt he had ever had.

'My dear Dora,' he wrote in late February. 'This is merely a note of exclamation. I must boast to somebody . . . I am having the most exciting adventure of my life. I am – you need not believe it unless you want to, but it's perfectly true – writing a romance.'

~

If the writing of romances appeared, from any conventional point of view, a strange occupation for a prospective war correspondent, nobody was more aware of the fact than Ransome; and yet the chance, he believed, was simply too good to pass up. The very day the idea had occurred to him, he had the whole plot sketched out in twenty chapters. It would be called *The Elixir of Life* – a gothic homage to M. P. Shiel and to Balzac, who had written a short story with the same title. The book would be 60,000 words long; if he could get 40,000 done in a fortnight, he would write it through to the end. In the event, the whole project, from outline to final draft, was finished inside two months.

'The tale itself', Ransome informed Dora Collingwood,

seems to me prodigiously intriguing. I won't tell you the main idea . . . but it includes one murder, several attempted murders, the finest uncle that ever there was, a big Yorkshire cake, an alchemist, a housekeeper, a peddler with the voice and manner of Jeremiah the prophet, an old man, a weird and ancient house, six family portraits of horrible significance, and, of course, the prettiest heroine in the whole range of English fiction.

The Elixir of Life, Ransome's first published novel, was not a success, either commercially, technically or substantively, which may explain why it was his last before *Swallows and Amazons* appeared in 1930. It tells the story of a young wastrel, Richard Scarborough, who is offered the elixir; how Scarborough discovers that the mixture becomes potent only through murder; how he refuses to drink it, destroys the drug and its keeper, the unnatural Killigrew, and marries Rose, whom he rescues from bondage while angry villagers burn down the mansion which had been her prison. For a biographer, it makes extraordinarily interesting reading, and besides anticipating the fate of the Russian landowners, shows how Ransome, drifting through the war like a sleepwalker, instinctively translated the surrounding turmoil: the history of Russia transposed to the north country; the Romanov dynasty as a line of corrupt scholars, defeated by their own inherited evil; a dashing hero, closely resembling the author, forgiven his youthful misdemeanours and – after witnessing events too dreadful to speak of – permitted to return home with a beautiful bride.

Ransome returned to Petrograd in late March, and in April withdrew to rural Estonia, where he completed the final draft and plied the thawing rivers with his fly. The strain, however, inflamed his piles, so that as Killigrew approached his doom, the word 'gore' appeared with increasing frequency both in his manuscript and his diary. At the end of the month, he took the finished copy to Petrograd, where Walpole, who had now joined the Red Cross, gave it his approval, as did Williams. But then, in early May, news came from Ivy that Tabitha was sick – fighting for her life – and an entreaty that Ransome should return to England by the first available boat. He made no plans to leave, but for two weeks suffered an agony of suspense, provoking a violent resurgence of piles and an acute attack of facial neuralgia. One moment Tabitha was on the mend, the next she had suffered a relapse, but the worst of it was that Ivy had stopped telegramming altogether. Instead, Ransome was forced to deal directly with his mother-in-law: 'What an infernal lunatic the woman is!' ran his diary for the 14th. 'Why doesn't she say what the temperatures actually are? . . . Oh damn, either nothing to worry about or it is very bad.'

It was Edith who finally put him out of his misery: Tabitha, she wired on 20 May, was still weak but making a steady recovery – she had been suffering from whooping cough. Ransome replied on the same day:

I got your telegram . . . Thank you very much for being so quick . . . I've got no news because since I got that telegram from Mrs W[alker] I have done nothing and been nowhere and written nothing. My disease was alone in profiting, and now my head. Head is improved today, however. There are many places on it that I can touch with proud impunity. A couple more days and I ought to be fit to go out again, without exciting the ridicule and compassion of the crowd.

But Ransome was so weak he could scarcely crawl to his typewriter, and just as the summer heat threatened to finish him off, Harold Williams took pity, inviting him to stay at his wife's estate in Vergezha: a secluded and quintessentially Russian retreat ninety miles south-east of Petrograd on the banks of the River Volkhov.

~

Ransome left Petrograd with Williams at one in the morning, and three hours later exchanged a stuffy train for a small, comfortable steam boat, where a waiter brought tea on deck in a pot painted with roses. With every turn in the river, the scenery refreshed him: slender silver birches with bright green leaves; the thatched wooden huts of peasants; women with their hair tied up in kerchiefs; a cowherd driving his heavy, slow-moving charges into the shade of the forest. The final turn brought Vergezha itself into view, with its lake, brimming after the spring thaw, teeming with wild duck, snipe, geese and swans. The steamer stopped in front of the house, where six white columns and the green thickets of the garden were reflected in the still water. Ransome woke at noon to the smell of lime trees and apple blossom and the sound of the Tyrkov family going about their business.

'I love Russia more and more,' he wrote to his mother after a week spent alternately writing and fishing,

I know no place in the world except Coniston or Cartmel where I get the same gorgeous feeling of freedom and living with the whole of oneself. I am now able to talk to anybody, and understand pretty well everything, and I don't know which I like better, the people or the country.

Ransome had been ill one day in three ever since the beginning of the year, but the day after his arrival in Vergezha he settled again to *Old Peter* and wrote a steady ten pages a day: 'The Fool of the World and The Flying Ship'; 'Honesty and Dishonesty'; 'Little Master Misery'; 'The Fire-Bird, The Horse of Power, and the Princess Vasilissa'. He had been struggling with a form for the idea since 1913, at first attempting near-literal, word-for-word translations, but the effect had been clumsy and stilted.

Now, having lived with the stories for over two years, repeating them to himself as he walked, inwardly digesting them so they felt like his own, he developed a fluency and also a structure quite different from anything else he had yet written: simple, confident, spare in terms of its prose, and illuminated by a little of the magic he had found as a child in Andrew Lang and Hans Christian Andersen. *The Elixir of Life*, as a work of original fiction, had revealed how far, at the age of thirty-one, Ransome was from acquiring the stamina or technical understanding that informed his most famous books. But *Old Peter* already had the voice of *Swallows and Amazons*, the steady, almost metronomic incantation of places and things: trees laden with snow, a little hut in the forest, a warm stove and Old Peter, wise and patient, humouring two grandchildren with tales from long, long ago – a goat who sneezed gold, a witch with iron teeth, a village idiot who becomes Tsar of all Russia.

'My book is not for the learned,' Ransome had written in his introduction, 'or indeed for grown-up people at all. No people who really like fairy stories ever grow up altogether. This is a book written far away in Russia, for English children who play in deep lanes with wild roses above them in the high hedges, or by the small singing brooks that dance down the grey fells at home.'

The rough draft was finished on 15 June and was eventually illustrated by Dmitri Mitrokhin, who in Russia is now considered one of the most influential illustrators of the twentieth century. It was dedicated to Barbara Collingwood, and although its publication – much to Ransome's disappointment – was delayed by a year, it repaid his effort many times over. Besides the *Swallows and Amazons* adventures, it is his only book that has remained in print, virtually without interruption, since its first edition. He was, quite justifiably, immensely proud of it.

Ransome stayed with the Tyrkov family at Vergezha for most of the summer, punctuated by occasional excursions to the capital to pick up letters, meet with friends or post articles for

Harold Williams to the *Daily Chronicle*. When Williams was pressed for time, Ransome would occasionally write his articles for him, trimming sentences to save money at the post office: 'upfed' for 'fed up'; 'unwent' for 'did not go'. Later, Guy Berenger of Reuters would give Ransome his favourite example of 'telegraphese': 'UNCASH UNFED UPFED RESIGN.' But it was Williams who first introduced him to news journalism, and also to the intricacies of Russian politics: the narrow clique that surrounded the Tsar; the Imperial Cabinet; the lower parliament of elected representatives – or State Duma – to which Ariadna Tyrkova and so many of her friends belonged. During weekends in Petrograd, or over dinner in Vergezha, Ransome met the Duma president, Mikhail Rodzianko; the Octobrist Alexei Gutchkov; Peter Struve, the former socialist; and Professor Pavel Miliukov, the Kadet leader who in 1917 would announce the first Provisional Government from the steps of the Tauride Palace.

By 1915, the wild enthusiasm that had greeted the initial declaration of war was entirely spent, and had been replaced by anger. The Tsar was not his own master. The imperial household was run by the Tsarina, who, fearing for the life of her haemophiliac son, had become the slave of Rasputin, a lecherous holy man whom she believed possessed magical powers to quench the flow of blood when the sickly child was injured. The Tsarina and Rasputin viewed every public initiative, from the town councils to the Red Cross, as hotbeds of anti-tsarist sedition. The War Industry Committee, headed by Gutchkov, was denied funds to buy ammunition. On the Eastern Front, the Russians were facing the most disciplined and technically advanced army in Europe. German machine guns had the firepower of seventy ordinary rifles. German troop movements were co-ordinated with devastating efficiency owing to state-of-the-art field communication. German Zeppelins and aeroplanes dropped bombs deep into Russian territory. Poland had been lost. Galicia had been lost. In short, Tsar Nicholas's failure to modernize the Russian constitution was matched, all too evidently, by his failure to modernize the military. Yet as Ransome's friends condemned the Romanovs for their failure to prepare for the future, they also clung to the past. Miliukov did not preach revolution, while at Vergezha, where peasants reaped the harvest by hand, science was viewed with suspicion. Russia, after all, was not Germany. It valued life on a human scale.

Shortly before Ransome's arrival, Ariadna Tyrkova had visited retreating Russian troops on the banks of the River Ravka, where a factory had been turned into a field hospital. In her memoirs she recalled what she had found there:

. . . The huge factory building was full of human bodies. Dead and living lay behind the machines, under them, in the corridors, on the landings.

Blood was everywhere, precious human blood. Fresh and bright red or dark and congealed. It was on the floor, on the machines and on the men's overcoats, on their hands, their eyes, their faces. The reek of blood and decay seemed to enter one's brain. I walked in a nightmare. The wounded watched me with the set expression familiar to those who have seen soldiers after battle.

From all sides came whispers:

'Sister, water . . .'

'Sister, there is a dead man next to me, tell them to take him away.'

'Sister, there is a lad groaning pitifully behind that machine. Have a look at him.'

'Sister, sister . . .'

~

Far away from England, writing, fishing, adapting to a foreign culture, Ransome suffered from brief attacks of conscience. In April, Rupert Brooke, the most talented of the Georgian poets, had died on his way to Gallipoli. Geoffrey was now fighting in France and sent his brother letters describing – so far as the censor permitted – the boredom and terror that made up the average soldier's day. Many of Ransome's closest acquaintances had enlisted, including Edward Thomas, who, when asked by a friend what he was fighting for, had scooped up a handful of dirt and replied, 'Literally for this.' Meanwhile, during Tabitha's illness, Thomas's wife had visited Hatch to give Ivy a holiday.

'Helen', wrote Thomas to Gordon Bottomley, 'has just been staying a bit (with Baby) at the Ransomes'. A is away. She likes Mrs R very much indeed and consequently thinks even less of A than before. He has turned Superman.'

And yet Ransome felt his duty, both to his daughter and the war, very keenly. He considered Helen Thomas 'an ass', was incensed that Tabitha had been left in her care, and only wished that it was practical to take the 'little imptom' away from Ivy altogether. Geoffrey he admired and envied, but confessed that he, Ransome, had neither the temperament nor the constitution to follow his brother's example. Collingwood had attempted to comfort him about his not being a soldier, pointing out that good minds were required to promote understanding between Russia and Britain, to keep the Alliance strong; but Ransome had his doubts. Bernard Pares, in the meantime, was in England and had promised to secure him some sort of 'permanent position' courtesy of the Foreign Office. Ransome awaited results impatiently and toyed with joining the Red Cross. What he wanted most, he insisted, was to find some way, in all the mess, to be 'really useful'.

Three months into his holiday, however, Ransome had still not made up his mind to any practical course of action. Discussing Russian history with Williams, he had begun to hatch a plan for a new novel, this time set in the fifteenth century: *Lord Novgorod the Great*, the story of a young hero's battle against Ivan the Terrible, before the invention of mustard gas. 'The flowers are nearly out,' he told Edith the day the rough draft of *Old Peter* was finished. 'I have lilac, narcissus, and lilies of the valley on my table . . . I've visited several very interesting villages, and talked with peasants even more delightful and witty than north of Englanders.' He hunted butterflies, kept the kitchen well stocked with tench from the lake, played with Ariadna Tyrkova's nieces and their friends, and in the evenings, if Williams was away and there were no guests for dinner, played skittles or chess with the master of the house, the former revolutionary Arkady Tyrkov, whose political views had been softened by twenty years in Siberia and who now described himself modestly as a 'dairy farmer'. In the end, it was Ransome's 'disease' that forced the crisis.

On the opposite bank of the Volkhov, within view of the house, was a military colony of peasants, one of several instituted in the early nineteenth century to combine serf labour with a standing army on Russia's western frontier. In late July, at the height of the summer, the village caught fire, and everybody, including Ransome, rushed to help.

'The fire had its amusing points,' he wrote from his sickbed:

There was only one well in the village, and it was emptied in half an hour, and we had rough carts with barrels racing to the ponds by the river and back, with branches of trees shoved into the barrels to keep the water from splashing out. The charioteering was considerable fun, full lick over ruts and holes as deep as the dining room chairs, with herds of old women, children, pigs, hens, cattle, flying in all directions . . . If the wind had been a point or two different the whole village would have been burnt, but, as it was, they got off with a single hut.

Ransome was not so lucky. By the time the excitement was over, his piles were haemorrhaging so freely that he had been evacuated to Petrograd. Four days later, his fate was sealed:

Dear Maw, my health is finally smashed. I can't cross a room without nearly collapsing, and the day before yesterday I fainted in the street. I have seen a first rate doctor, and he said that I must be operated on at once . . .

DO NOT ON ANY ACCOUNT tell Ivy that I am having the operation or that my health has gone wrong. Nothing could be more awful than a sudden appearance of her over here.

~

Ransome was admitted to hospital by the famous surgeon Dr

Stuke, who had been recommended and paid for by Harold Williams. He found the place remarkably pleasant: 'V jolly nurses, everything as nice as could be. It's just like being in an unusually clean hotel.'

'First Act,' ran Ransome's diary for 7 August: '8 teaspoons of cod liver oil. Began writing the *Shepherd's Pipe*.'

'Second Act,' he noted on the 8th: 'Stubbly man gave me an enema. Read "Dawn of History".'

The day of the operation the diary remains a blank, but across the 10th and 11th, in bold block capitals covering the whole two pages, it reads 'VIOLENT AND ABOMINABLE PAIN'.

Ransome's ordeal on the operating table reflected the experience of millions of wounded Russian soldiers along the Eastern Front, where modern anaesthetics, previously imported from Germany, were all but unattainable. Under Dr Stuke's knife, he had been forced to make do with a cocaine paste followed by ether, neither of which had proved effective, and had gone without sleep for almost sixty hours after the operation. But in Petrograd there were at least friends to monitor his progress: Williams, Tyrkova and her nieces, Walpole and Hamilton Fyfe of the *Daily Mail*. Even Lascelles Abercrombie was by his bedside, in the shape of a wild effusion written on hearing that Ransome was desperately ill:

The symptoms sound most alarming. Do please, I beg you, by our friendship, which is the oldest and, I believe, the closest and dearest friendship I have or am ever likely to have – do please, I say, write or get someone to write *at once* to say how you are: a post card will do: a telegram would be best. I am too perturbed to write at length or in any entertaining vein: I want to know above everything how you do.

The only person who remained indifferent to Ransome's illness was, most uncharacteristically, Edith, who had sent no word since the beginning of the month. It was perplexing, and while Ransome blamed the incompetence of the post office, his anxiety was compounded by a chronic lack of funds. Whisked from the gates of the hospital to Harold Williams's flat, he had written to her two or three times a week to keep her abreast of the latest developments, including possible destinations for convalescence (should he remain in Russia, or return to her care in Leeds? If so, how should he pay the fare?), and most importantly, Dr Stuke's regimen for recovery.

My fair plans of Russian Red Cross work dished . . . I am to live in good air and to feed very well (pleasant advice to the penniless). I am to take, for the next six months at least, only very gentle exercise . . . I asked if I could fish? Yes. Excellent, so long as it means open air, sitting in a boat, or moving slowly. But wandering about in a rough stream, 'like your English', is absolutely forbidden. So I see myself solemnly watching a float and imbibing fresh air, and occasionally pulling out little perch. Pike I should think would be allowed . . .

Now. Don't lose this letter, because it represents the priceless advice of the best doctor in Petrograd, for which, as soon as money comes, I shall have to pay.

A cheque from Edith finally arrived at Crédit Lyonnais on 28 August, and Ransome went down again to Vergezha, where, for a few days, he followed Stuke's advice to the letter. But the respite was short-lived. In Petrograd, Frederick Rennet, foreign correspondent for the *Daily News*, had collapsed with locomotor ataxia, one of the more sinister symptoms of syphilis, and was no longer capable of fulfilling his duties. A. G. Gardiner, the editor, had approached Williams as a possible replacement, but Williams had demurred. Instead, he ventured to recommend a friend of his: a young writer with passable Russian, of a decidedly liberal, even radical character who would perfectly suit the politics of the paper. Ransome's first telegram was written on 2 September, inducing an instant, blinding headache. It was the beginning of a career in journalism that lasted over fifteen years.

For the next three weeks, the *Daily News* published articles from Russia under the old byline: 'From our Special Correspondent – Frederick Rennet'. But Rennet showed no sign of recovering, and Ransome was soon called to London. He sailed on 22 September, shortly after the Tsar, in an act of suicidal hubris, dissolved the Duma, sacked his commander-in-chief and took direct control of the Russian army.

~

On the very day Ransome arrived in England, Geoffrey was wounded in the heel at Loos, the first of three injuries sustained in the course of the war, each more serious than the last. Ransome heard about the business at Hatch, where he had gone directly after landing in Newcastle, and his feelings are probably best expressed by the fact that he made no comment at all. He stayed in Wiltshire for barely a week, interrupted by a day trip to London, where he visited the offices of the *Daily News*, met with Dora Collingwood and her new husband, an Armenian doctor named Ernest Altounyan, and was considerably heartened to see a copy of *The Elixir of Life* sitting in a bookshop window. It went with him to Leeds, then to the Lakes, where he showed it proudly to his old mentor at Lanehead. W. G. Collingwood had corrected the proofs in August.

For Ransome it was the briefest of north country holidays. He visited his family, saw Geoffrey in hospital and sailed a little on Coniston with Barbara. Halfway through October, he was down in London again to sign a formal contract with the *Daily News* and to visit the Foreign Office, where he chatted to Lord Robert Cecil, Francis Acland's successor as Undersecretary of State for Foreign Affairs. Bernard Pares' enquiries on his behalf appear to have born some meagre fruit at least, although there is no record of the conversation. He dropped in on his mother on the way to Newcastle and sailed on 27 October, arriving in Petrograd on 3 November.

Ransome had barely unpacked his suitcase when he received word from Frederick Rennet's secretary saying that the *Daily News* no longer required his services. Rennet, it appeared, had made a miraculous recovery. A brief investigation, however, revealed that Rennet was still at death's door, and that his secretary had hoped to take the position for herself. The *Daily*

News was cabled, Ransome's appointment reaffirmed, and once the post office agreed to accept his telegrams on account, he settled down to work. The first article under his byline appeared on 13 November on the front page:

SUCCESS ON
THE DVINA

———

IMPORTANT RUSSIAN CAPTURES

———

FIERCE BATTLES

———

FAILURE OF TEN GERMAN COUNTER-ATTACKS

———

From Our Special Correspondent,
ARTHUR RANSOME

9

The Anglo-Russian Bureau

As Ransome spoke of a bitter winter – of Germans frozen in their trenches, of wolves circling the villages, of the resilience and courage of the ordinary Russian soldier – Petrograd inched closer to revolution. Within the first five months of the war, Russian 'wastage' was estimated at 2 million men. In 1915, the humiliating and costly retreat from Poland had been blamed on chronic munitions shortages, the hopeless disorganization of the general staff, and the Tsar, who as the head of the army was presiding personally over a national catastrophe. On the Eastern Front desertion had become so widespread that untrained boys, often armed with cudgels or farming implements, were forced to advance at gunpoint. Collaboration with the enemy was commonplace. Officers were afraid of their men. In Petrograd, the Tsarina saw 'dark forces' everywhere, proudly suppressing every vehicle for reform, or any organization, however useful or patriotic, that dared to substitute itself for the power of the monarchy. 'I am your wall in the rear,' she wrote to her husband at his headquarters in Baranovichi, 'don't laugh at silly old wifey, but she has "trousers" on unseen.'

Dissatisfaction with the Romanovs expressed itself in many ways. By 1916, as bread queues lengthened, the extreme Left was extending its influence in the provinces and the urban factory unions. Strikes and demonstrations were growing more frequent, and were suppressed with increasing barbarity. In the country, peasants, deprived of vital hands to bring in the harvests, planted less grain and hoarded what remained. In the city, patriotism, which had once worked to the advantage of the autocracy, now worked actively against it. Russia, it was said, was no longer ruled by a Russian. The German-born Tsarina was in league with the Kaiser, while Rasputin was a slave to the

Jewish bankers who had most to gain from the war. With each humiliating defeat, the rumours became more vengeful: the Winter Palace was a brothel; Alexandra had sold the country to save the life of her weakling son and communicated with Berlin by carrier pigeon. And yet according to the British military attaché in Petrograd, Colonel Knox, the greatest difficulty facing the government was a wall of silence: a reluctance on behalf of ministers and officials not only to speak openly with the imperial family, but also to their allies in the West. Talking to Rodzianko, president of the now-liquidated Duma, he had expressed his astonishment that in the face of so much 'preventable suffering' the Russian people were not already 'breaking windows'. Rodzianko, sighing wearily, had observed only that Knox must have a 'hot head'. Russia would fight to the last drop of blood if only England would supply the money and arms.

For Ransome and his colleagues, regardless of the politics of their respective newspapers, the extremity of the situation was clear enough, but objective reporting was out of the question. *The Times* could not print a map of the Eastern Front without drawing an army of phantom reserves. Likewise, Ransome's articles for the *Daily News* – a paper founded by Charles Dickens as a lobby for social reform – avoided any suggestion that Russia was heading for a crisis. Censorship, both in Petrograd and London, limited his script to a monotonous litany of minor setbacks and resounding victories: 'Russians Turn the Tables'; 'No Change Does Not Spell Idleness'.

'At the beginning of the war,' Ransome assured his readers, 'each German was bigger than the one before, but now they are little ones, boys or old men with no muscles.'

In Russia, articles such as these were read, at best, with a knowing smile, but back home they encouraged morale. At the beginning of 1916, Herbert Asquith's Liberal government had introduced the first conscription laws in British democratic history. Behind the scenes, British generals, weighing their human resources, were planning a series of massive offensives, with a view to exhausting German reserves and bringing the war to an early end. The results, including the infamous Battle of the Somme, would be amongst the most futile and costly military catastrophes of the twentieth century. As trade unions went on strike to avoid the 'comb-outs' and a domestic revolution erupted in Ireland, very few in Britain cared if the Tsar was taking orders from his wife, if Rasputin was a visionary or a charlatan, or if their allies died like heroes or slaves. They only wanted to know that the Eastern Front would hold.

~

Long before Ransome wrote his first telegram for the *Daily News*, the excitement with which Russia had greeted Britain's initial declaration of war had given way to a dull resentment. Where was Britain's mighty navy? How many British soldiers, exactly, were fighting in France? How many dying? How was it that the most powerful empire in the world, in concert with France and Italy, could barely hold its own on the Western Front, while Russia was expected to hold the whole of eastern Europe, from the Baltic to the Black Sea, alone? In 1915, Bernard Pares had visited London to place a figure on Russian casualties – 4 million – and was immediately relieved of his salary as official 'monitor' of the Russian army. Plans, nevertheless, were set in train to improve Britain's image: a suitably trained army officer to give talks and show films of the British Tommy in action; 10,000 'cigarette cards' of British soldiers to be distributed amongst the Russian rank and file; an invitation to Russian officials to tour the British training facilities in Aldershot or the naval base at Portsmouth. All these schemes were implemented, but Pares – who had returned to Russia as correspondent for the *Daily Telegraph* – decided that a more fundamental solution was required. In Britain, a secret War Propaganda Bureau had been established in 1914. What was needed was a similar outfit in Russia, staffed by fluent Russian speakers; a centrally organized pool of talented expatriates to spread the word. Ransome's name was on a provisional short-list of five.

In mid-January, he travelled down to Moscow to talk the matter over with Bruce Lockhart, the young British Consul General, and Michael Lykiardopoulos of the Moscow Art Theatre. 'Lyki', disguised as a Greek tobacco merchant, had just completed a daring incursion behind enemy lines, and his stories of the desperate conditions in Austria and Germany had made him a national celebrity. In addition he spoke English like a native, had a natural flair for public relations and had friends in every newspaper office in Moscow. 'I felt sure', recalled Ransome, 'that if Lyki were well supplied with information from London the Russian editors would hang around him like hounds around a huntsman.' With Lockhart's enthusiastic approval, he returned to Petrograd, consulted with Harold Williams and submitted a written proposal, in person, to the British ambassador, Sir George Buchanan. The project was approved, and two days later handed over to Major Thornhill, chief of Military Intelligence in Russia, for execution.

The International News Agency, or the 'Anglo-Russian Bureau' as it became known, employed journalists and authors, encouraged co-operation between Russian politicians and British diplomats, and was doubtless seen by Military Intelligence (MI6) as a useful source of information. It placed pro-British stories in Russian papers, and as early as February was sending deputations of Russian writers to England, all of whom returned home to sing the praises of the British war effort. The Bureau was funded and supervised by the Foreign Office, and its activities, at least from Ransome's point of view (he adored secrecy), were intended to be strictly hush-hush. Lockhart organized the Moscow branch from the British Consulate, with Lykiardopoulos as a charismatic, well-connected linkman. Hugh Walpole, whose reputation as an author was already well established both in Britain and America, headed the Petrograd outfit, with Pares and Williams as his senior officers. A preliminary headquarters was established in a small hotel in Morskaya – 'the street of furriers, flower shops, jewellers, expensive dress-makers and pretty ladies'. Here, seated on a four-poster bed spread with a pink eiderdown, Ransome sipped tea with some of the founding members: Hamilton Fyfe of the *Daily Mail*, Guy Berenger of the Reuters news agency, Morgan Philips Price of the *Manchester Guardian*, Percival Gibbon, who knew Joseph Conrad, and of course Harold Williams, who knew everybody, spoke with the ambassador almost daily on the telephone, and who had attempted to console Ransome for being passed over for the top job. Ransome replied that he had not for a moment considered the possibility, though he thought it imprudent to have chosen such 'an obvious Englishman' as Walpole. In any case, he had plans of his own: he intended to join the army.

Ransome appears to have consulted widely on the subject, insisting that he would go to France not as an officer, but as a common private. His proposal for the Anglo-Russian Bureau had been submitted to Major Thornhill on 22 January. Two days later, learning that Walpole would be in charge, he visited the military hospital in Petrograd for a physical and was told that with the correct course of pills, he would be fit to fight in a matter of weeks. That very evening, Bernard Pares left a note in his hotel, explaining that he had visited the embassy and that Sir George Buchanan was adamant Ransome should stay exactly where he was. Neither, though the instinct was noble, was the government likely to meet his request for funds to travel back to England. He would have to pay his own way.

'May I add', entreated Pares, 'that I am strongly of the Ambassador's opinion. I even think that if you returned for military service you would be doing a wrong thing to your country. Surely public events and the call that has now been made to us by the Government itself for help with intelligence have shown this clearly . . .'

Two months later, Geoffrey chimed in from hospital. He had recovered from his wound at Loos and been wounded again, this time severely, on the French–Belgian border at Armentières.

My Dear Arthur . . . What you say about joining as a Private is absolute rot. Now that I have been wounded twice I am sure that our family has done enough, and you could not possibly join for months and months as you won't be fit enough for a long time yet. I know exactly what your training would entail by personal experience, and your health would not stand it, let alone your eyes. So you had better not go on bothering about it. You are doing very useful work where you are.

~

Towards the end of February, at last feeling confident that his new job was secure, Ransome had moved out of temporary rooms at the Continental Hotel and taken permanent lodgings in a much sought-after building on Glinka Street. From his study window he had a wonderful view of Theatre Square, the Mariinsky Theatre and the Litovsky Castle, the famous political prison soon to be liberated by crowds of excited revolutionaries. Near by were the coffee shops and galleries where local artists and poets gathered to discuss their work: Dmitri Mitrokhin, who had illustrated *Old Peter's Russian Tales*, Alexander Blok, Anna Akhmatova, the crowd of poets, painters and opera singers that clustered around Maxim Gorky. But one of the best things about Glinka Street was the fact that it was only ten minutes away from the post office, the shortest of dashes to wire an urgent telegram or post a letter to his editor, to his brother and sisters, to the Collingwoods, to Abercrombie, and most essentially, to his mother.

Writing to Edith, Ransome was speaking directly to 'Home'. She must on no account allow her cataracts to develop further: an operation was essential. Tabitha also required an operation. Her tonsils were to be cut out, and Ivy should not be permitted to put the business off. Ransome had sent a cheque to Hatch for the purpose. As for himself, things were going splendidly. He had met a brilliant young economist called Will Peters, who had useful things to say about Russian industry. The ambassador had allowed him to send the entire illustrated manuscript of *Old Peter's Russian Tales* back to Edinburgh in the diplomatic bag.

Bernard Pares was setting up funding for Russian departments at British universities after the war, and it seemed possible that Ransome might be offered Leeds, which would make him particularly proud 'because of Father'. Could Edith rally the troops? Meanwhile, although newspaper work was not as much fun as books, he was at last earning plenty of money. All debts would shortly be settled. He was becoming a genuine authority on the situation in Russia and had acquired a set of new and influential friends, and what with articles to write, Walpole's deficiencies at the Bureau to compensate for and *Lord Novgorod the Great* still vying for his attention, he was infernally but quite delightfully busy.

These jubilant moods, however, were apt to come and go. *Lord Novgorod* was never finished, and a small collection of Russian soldier songs Ransome had dedicated to his brother Geoffrey was not published. Macmillan had commissioned another edition of fairy tales, but Ransome did not complete the project. He considered a history of Russia for children, and later in the year, a third romance: a fishing adventure called *Piscator*, which he had high hopes for until Williams condemned the first few chapters. Ransome did not stop thinking about his own writing. On the contrary, literary writing joined England and the Lakes as a constant reminder of the pleasures that newspaper work denied him. But the reality was that from 1916, he had far less time to call his own. With the exception of *Aladdin* (already completed) and a few scattered fairy tales, he published nothing but journalism until 1923.

Ransome made three visits to the Eastern Front in 1916: first in April, then in August, and finally in October. Each time he took his camera, preparing slides for the magic-lantern shows that accompanied the Anglo-Russian propaganda initiative. The developed plates framed heartening scenes: soldiers sharing a brew of tea; a smiling, muddy group around a field gun; or a neatly turned-out division boarding one of the trains that shuttled troops up and down the line, patching the ragged holes left by German offensives. The first of these expeditions was made to Galicia, where the army was poised to launch the most brilliant Russian offensive of the war. Not even the Tsarina had been told the date of the attack, and journalists were carefully chaperoned.

Most observers had ridden horses, but the correspondent for the *Daily News*, owing to 'some affliction', sat in a cart lined with straw. From this vantage Ransome witnessed the rolling hills around Kiev and the local peasants tilling the fields, men who had little time for politics, and when asked who they were or where they came from, would invariably answer 'Greek Orthodox' or simply 'around here'. Otherwise, his memories of the trip were either vivid and isolated – a Russian observation post disguised as a muck heap; the sticky dirt roads made rotten by the spring thaw; a wrong and almost fatal turn taken close to the Austrian position at dead of night – or general and retrospective, written into his autobiography with the gloomy clarity of hindsight:

Looking back now I seem to have seen nothing, but I did in fact see a great deal of that long-drawn-out front, and of the men who, ill-armed, ill-supplied, were holding it against an enemy who, even if his anxiety to fight was not greater than the Russians', was infinitely better equipped. I came back to Petrograd full of admiration for the Russian soldiers who were holding the front without enough weapons to go round. I was much better able to understand the grimness with which those of my friends who knew Russia best were looking into the future.

~

General Alexei Brusilov's Galician offensive was launched in June, precisely co-ordinated to strike at three points simultaneously along the enemy lines. Two hundred thousand enemy troops were killed or taken prisoner within a fortnight, over half the entire Austrian force concentrated on the South-West Front. The number would rise to 450,000 by late July, as German reinforcements were hurried down from the north. Brusilov's achievement cut so sharply against the grain of the war that it made him an instant national hero and inspired the imagination not only of Russia, but the whole of Allied Europe. Collections of verse, cantatas and military marches were dedicated to his honour, while crowds in Italy, France and Britain flocked to see the silent film *Brusilov* just to gaze on his face. Ransome's headlines reflected the popular mood: 'A Farmer-General, the Russian Advance'; 'Austrian Losses Stated to Be Not Less than 100,000 Men'; 'Prisoners Now Total 166,000'; '600-Mile Front, Sure Development of the Russian Campaign.'

But in the sweltering summer fug that descended on Petrograd, the thread of his newspaper commentary was laced with personal grievances. In early June, Ransome's concerns regarding the Anglo-Russian Bureau erupted into the open. Transplanted from its discreet hideaway in Morskaya, the new headquarters on Fontanka employed a permanent staff of twelve, while telegrams from Russian soldiers who should not have known of its existence arrived with cheerful demands for a stout pair of English gloves or enquiries as to how many times George V had visited the Western Front. Since January, the whole arrangement (which Ransome increasingly viewed as his personal brainchild) had become a standing joke. It was neither a useful organ for the gathering of intelligence, nor an effective vehicle for the distribution of propaganda. Its so-called director did not even read Russian. Unable to keep his counsel any longer, Ransome had posted an article in the *Daily News* in which he made his feelings abundantly clear. Walpole had taken deep offence, and the rift was not healed until the publication of *Swallows and Amazons* in 1930.

The Russian chair at Leeds was endowed but still not filled, denying Ransome any prospect of post-war respectability the job had seemed to offer. Then, towards the end of July, Pares overlooked him when gathering a team of expatriate and Russian 'experts' to deliver a series of talks at Cambridge. Ransome was not at all mollified when Williams, who had been invited as a matter of course, asked him to lend a hand in preparing material for his own contribution – a lecture on Russian linguistics.

'I've refused,' Ransome wrote to Edith:

No power on earth is going to turn me into a philologist whatever other metamorphoses fate may have in store. Its odd enough to be turned into a war-correspondent. And I shall be jolly glad to turn out of that into being a writer again, as soon as the war is over, though I begin to see that I shall probably never escape altogether from newspapers having got my foot in the mud.

I've had no letters for ages. Even Barbara has failed me.

In Russia, as the summer dragged on, so, inevitably, did the scandals: the firing of reputable ministers in favour of disreputable ones; the ongoing battle between the War Industry Committee (full of reformers and revolutionaries) and the Artillery Department (full of offended noblemen); Rasputin's priapic exhibitions in Petrograd clubs and the impotence of the chief of police to do anything about them. In England, Pares and Williams had spoken to Lord Robert Cecil, Permanent Undersecretary of State for Foreign Affairs, and a raft of academics, army officers and domestic journalists who in the wake of the Somme, where 60,000 British troops were lost in a single day, wanted nothing but the very best of news. Ariadna Tyrkova recalled her husband returning from this expedition:

Harold's general impression of England was disquieting. From a distance he had not been able to see the full force of the strain of war upon the country. He was disconcerted by the mass enthusiasm for everything Russian. He wanted to see a real rapprochement between our two nations, but what he found in England was blind infatuation, not with Russia nor with the Russian people, but with the imaginary 'steam roller,' the mythical Cossacks, the fantastic wooden soldiers who might any day make a triumphal entry into Berlin. He knew that such morbid enthusiasm might disappear at once like a soap bubble. Unfortunately he proved to be right.

~

For Britain and France, the immediate results of Brusilov's June campaign had been entirely positive. The Romanians, witnessing its initial success, had finally been persuaded to join the Allies. In the west, Austria-Hungary (with the exception of the Italian Front) was almost completely knocked out of the war, relieving pressure on the French at Verdun. And yet Russia gained nothing. Brusilov, the most gifted of all Russia's generals, had intended the Galician offensive as a prelude to two devastating strikes against the German lines to the north in East Prussia. But the strikes never came. Generals Evert and Kuropatkin, both members of the Tsar's inner circle, ignored Brusilov's frantic telegrams and sent reinforcements to hang onto the coat tails of the popular southern advance. The Germans, blessing their luck, arrived in Galicia first, and by August the entire initiative had collapsed. Russia lost 750,000 men, including the elite Imperial Guard, strafed by German aircraft as they waded chest deep across a swamp in their green and gold parade uniforms. Colonel Knox had watched dolefully as 'the wounded sank slowly into the marsh', and with them the last glimmer of hope for the old regime.

On 8 August, shortly after this calamity, Ransome's second trip to the front took him to Belorussia, to a place equidistant between Evert and Kuropatkin's northern headquarters. He returned to Petrograd tired, depressed and feeling that his annual holiday to England was long overdue, but for weeks the *Daily News* kept him in suspense. The newspaper had no journalist to cover Romania's first forays into Hungary. The only question was whether Ransome or some other luckless stringer would be assigned to cover the business on the spot. On 30 August, he announced to Edith that he was coming home immediately. Hours later, he begged her to imagine the 'deluge of woe' when his editor, A. G. Gardiner, changed his mind: 'Cancel earlier telegram today and postpone your holiday trip.' Inside a week he was on a train to the Russian–Romanian frontier, banging away at little sheets torn out of his notebook with his typewriter balanced on his knees:

In another six hours I shall be a lone and helpless creature in a country whose language, so far as I can judge from my urgent efforts to acquire it, is one of the most difficult on earth. I have been at it hard on the journey, and can now read it with some difficulty, but enough, I think, to tell the head from the tail of a newspaper.

The trip, nevertheless, had proved surprisingly enjoyable. Autumn had set in early in Petrograd, but the southern sun was bright and hot. And whereas Ransome's colleagues at the Anglo-Russian Bureau had tried his patience, Romania was full of new faces, fresh perspectives, and on the train down to Bucharest, a tribe of attentive, energetic children and friendly soldiers who fed him sweets, melons, cheese, cold chicken, hard-boiled eggs and yellow wine. 'MY STOMACH STOOD IT!' wrote Ransome triumphantly. 'Think of that!'

In total he stayed in Romania for six weeks and treated the entire excursion as an Indian summer holiday, returning just ahead of the invading German army (Romania would play no further part in the war) in 'hot gorgeous weather . . . as happy as a bird and as burnt as a brick', clutching a Turkish coffee mill he had bought for twelve lei in a street market on the Black Sea coast. In Petrograd – 'full of the usual filth and snow of winter' – he stopped just long enough to speak to Will Peters about the economy, and thanks to an intercession on his behalf by Harold Williams, to pick up a letter from Major Thornhill at the British embassy, explicitly exempting him from military service. He arrived in Newcastle on 3 November, lunching shortly afterwards with Francis Acland and Lord Crawford of the Ministry of Agriculture and Fisheries. Russia, he told them, was expecting a revolution. Not one, but two.

10

Revolution

Thoroughly briefed by Will Peters, Ransome explained to Acland and Crawford that bread riots could be expected in March and October to coincide with the most serious food shortages. 'But that's rubbish,' Crawford had replied. 'Russia is one of the greatest food-producing countries in the world.' Ransome endeavoured to describe the difficulties in conveying grain to the cities – the trains diverted to the front to carry troops, the need for engines and wagons from England – but again, as Acland looked on, was rudely rebuffed.

He should not have been surprised. Britain had been experiencing difficulties of its own – the Irish Easter Rising in April, German submarines decimating the merchant navy, intrigues in the government that would shortly lead to Asquith's removal – all of which had exacerbated a general reluctance to look east with any real curiosity. Barely four months before the March Revolution, *The Times* would argue that the ordinary Russian soldier ('the Russian Tommy') was 'the simplest human animal that has survived the process of civilization', docile as his own cattle, childish in his 'unquestioning obedience and unreasoning reverence to the Tsar', incapable, even under the most trying circumstances, of expressing his own will because 'the spirit of revolt is not in him'. Ransome's own newspaper was banned in English barracks as unsuitable reading for the military, but in practice rarely deviated from the official record. Yet his first encounter with the obstinacy of British officials – Acland's treachery was especially wounding – had left his feelings painfully bruised. He set off back to Hatch in a dark mood for his annual ordeal with Ivy.

If Crawford's sin had been to make Ransome feel redundant, Ivy offended just as grievously by insisting he was indispensable.

She looked forward to his holidays with a theatrical ardour, petitioned him constantly to allow her to join him in Russia, and the previous Christmas had rebelled against her isolation by answering an advertisement in a lonely hearts column, forwarding a copy of her letter for Ransome's approval. He had not forgiven her, and remained just long enough to collect a few books from his library and to see Tabitha, who was now six years old. After one night he continued north, alone, and spent three weeks sailing, reading, fishing and conversing with the noble few who, over the years, had proved invaluable to his peace of mind.

'Left Coniston on the afternoon train after the happiest days of my life,' he wrote in his diary on 25 November, 'thanks to the Collingwoods and B.'

'B' was Barbara Collingwood, to whom Ransome had first proposed in 1905 and who had become, in the interim between his first and second marriage, his closest female confidante, save Edith. Ivy, however, was not prepared to allow her husband simply to drift away. She demanded his return to Hatch, where she argued with him, and when he fled, followed him up to London with Tabitha, sleeping at a separate address. They dined, argued again, and the following day (almost certainly at Ransome's suggestion), Ivy spoke with Gardiner at the *Daily News*, where, instead of listening patiently to the duty Ransome owed his country, she angrily disputed his right to desert his obligations as husband. He left for Russia soon after, so upset that he did not even find the time to drop by in Leeds on the way to Newcastle.

'You are wrong, of course,' he wrote to Edith, 'about my affairs ever sorting themselves and becoming happy. However, there's no good being bluer than one can help, and I see so much work ahead that I shall beat some sort of content out of that.' Ransome's diary records a splitting headache from the moment his ship sailed on 2 December to his arrival on the 11th. The situation in Petrograd offered little relief.

~

In Ransome's absence, the State Duma, dissolved in September 1915, was grudgingly permitted to return to business, but held out little hope of compromise with the Imperial Cabinet. In January 1916, the roles of prime minister, Minister of the Interior, Minister of State and Minister of Foreign Affairs had been collapsed into the person of one man: Boris Stürmer, whose German name, coupled with his extreme incompetence, fuelled rumours that he was deliberately starving the peasants on the Kaiser's orders. Towards the end of the year, the Tsar's own brother begged him to appoint a government that enjoyed the confidence of the people, but the Tsar had stubbornly refused: 'What you ask is impossible. On the day of my coronation I swore to preserve the autocracy. I must keep that oath intact for my son.' At the front it was said that the Tsarina was sharing her bed with Rasputin, and occasionally with Rasputin and her husband, who in idle moments wired Russian troop movements to his first cousin in Berlin. Morale had never been lower, either in the trenches or in the cities, so that when the Duma finally reopened on 14 November, even Pavel Miliukov, the Kadet leader, could no longer restrain himself. Addressing the assembled delegates he listed every abuse, demanding each time with a rhetorical flourish: 'Is this folly or treason?' Treason was the almost unanimous conclusion.

Ransome had written to Edith on Christmas Day, wondering if Geoffrey had played his bagpipes and if the rum had burned brightly round the plum pudding. On Boxing Day, he left for Pskov, and was with Russian troops in Estonia, covering the effects of the third and coldest winter of the war, when General Radko-Dmitriev summoned him to an interview. Presenting himself at field headquarters on 31 December, he was accosted by a 'short, stocky little elephant of a man', pacing up and down in the throes of an exultant fever. 'General Radko-Dmitriev came up to me, shaking his fist as if it were a dagger. "Rasputin was killed last night and I wish this hand had been in it."' Ransome returned to Petrograd on New Year's Day to find the city 'like a pot of porridge coming slowly to the boil, with bubbles, now here now there, rising to burst on the surface'.

Rasputin, the most hated man in Russia, had been killed in the Yusupov Palace, just around the corner from Glinka Street: poisoned with arsenic, shot three times and dropped through the ice into the freezing waters of the Neva. His assassins included members of the Tsar's own family, two grand dukes and the husband of a grand duchess. Recent evidence suggests that a British agent was responsible for the third and decisive bullet: an unjacketed 'dumdum' to the centre of the forehead. Back in Britain, *The Times* hailed it as a victory for the war effort. The whole of Russia, it proclaimed, breathed more freely for the removal of 'one of the pivots of Germanophile forces'. Now that the 'hideous mediaeval nightmare' was over, loyal citizens could only marvel at the power wielded by an 'uneducated Siberian peasant' whose 'baleful influence' was generally ascribed to hypnotism. Ransome's own telegrams declared Rasputin an improbable figure from Russian folklore whose orders, though badly spelled and scarcely legible, were 'invariably obeyed'. 'His social advancement in no way checked the licentiousness of his private life and both shared in preparing the dramatic, bloody finish to this almost incredible story.'

In practice, Rasputin's murder benefited neither Britain nor the Tsar. As Prince Yusupov was quietly exiled to his country estate, his co-conspirator, the Grand Duke Dmitri, was given a standing ovation as he entered his box at the Mikhailovsky Theatre. Nothing could have illustrated more plainly the gulf that separated the autocracy from both the nobles and the masses, or the helplessness of the Tsarina as she mourned 'our Friend'. In the Duma, Miliukov, whose incendiary speech in November had been printed cheaply and distributed by the thousand in pamphlet form, called perversely for moderation. Others called for revolution, including Alexander Kerensky, who spoke more directly to the mood on the streets. The appeasers, he jeered, were men of straw. They wanted peace merely as an excuse to remain comfortably seated in their 'warm armchairs'.

In January, Ransome reported demonstrations to mark the anniversary of the Bloody Sunday massacre in 1905. In mid-February – as the correspondent of a radical newspaper – he was approached by a representative of the Central Workers' Group, an organization of powerful trade unionists interned for agitation in the munitions factories. Ransome delivered their petition to the British embassy and wired a telegram on the subject to the *Daily News*: 'Arrests in Petrograd. Working men's aim to "turn Russia into a Social Democratic Republic."' But as the future of the empire hung in the balance, he was careful to keep his options open. Within days of Rasputin's murder, he had accepted an offer from the conservative *Observer* to post weekly articles. Russian politics, he warned, were becoming dangerously polarized. There were 'disturbances' on the front, while the scarcity of food was exacerbated by the transport union's decision to strike. In the company of Williams and Tyrkova, Ransome listened to Miliukov describe his vision of a constitution based on 'democratic England'. In the coffee shops and restaurants around Theatre Square he listened to the gossip of Russian artists and writers. Everywhere, speculation was rife. Would the revolution come from above or below, by way of a palace coup or a popular upheaval? Would the Tsar, as the Kadets hoped, finally see reason, or would he deliberately provoke an uprising, with a view to suppressing it with exemplary force? Would there be any revolution at all? In the brief time span remaining to the Romanovs, all these things seemed possible, and Ransome accommodated them as best he could.

'I spend most of my spare time at present sweating up Russian Constitutional law,' he wrote to Edith at the end of February:

It's interesting, but only like chess, and I'd give anything to have another of my own books ahead. Never mind. Some day or other, regardless of the advantages of a settled income, I shall fling my typewriter over the moon, catch it on the other side with a joyful yell, and spend three years in pouring out novels – at least romances – in collaboration with Joyce, and a mass of fairy tales in collaboration with myself . . . But when is this time coming? . . . I expect when it's all over

I shall be a dry political old oracular idiot with no power whatever of playing with imps and other merry devilments through the jolly forests of fairy books. I shall be bald, 'orrid serious, and altogether contemptible.

~

For weeks, Ransome had been telegramming the *Daily News* so frequently, and at such length, that at the beginning of March his editor, A. G. Gardiner, had commanded tersely that he confine himself 'to vital matter and the shortest possible form'. Shortly afterwards, his diary records 'rows on bread', but Ransome saw no serious cause for alarm. He reassured his readers that both the Duma and the public were anxious to avoid any civil disturbance that might 'play into the hands of their political enemies'. The Tsar and his police would be provided with no excuse for a crackdown or any pretext to avoid the constitutional concessions that Miliukov and his fellow reformers had worked so hard to obtain. This was the game of chess that Ransome had alluded to in his letter to his mother. But in spite of the warning he had delivered to Crawford and Acland back in London, neither he nor his political informants appear to have guessed how few moves were left to play. 'A long expected event', he explained, 'may yet take by surprise those who have been long expecting it.'

Ransome witnessed the first serious demonstration on International Women's Day, Friday, 8 March, when hard-pressed Russian matriarchs took to the streets to protest against the lack of bread and were joined by thousands of angry strikers from the Putilov munitions factory. He had spent the morning at the Anglo-Russian Bureau, drawing a map for the British embassy, and was heading back to Glinka Street when he encountered a group of British officers. 'Rioters!' ejaculated one of them. 'They ought to be put up against a wall and shot!'

Ransome walked on and shortly found himself on Nevsky Prospekt, in a milling crowd, hemmed in by mounted Cossacks armed with whips and sabres. But no violent suppression was attempted. The Cossacks were smiling, and when a woman shouted, 'Go for the police, not us!' one of them replied, 'We shall settle accounts with the police later.' Ransome had been struck, chiefly, by the good humour of these rioters, made up not simply of workers, but of men and women from every class, most of them, he thought, only curious to see what was going on: 'Women and girls, mostly well dressed, were enjoying the excitement. It was like a bank holiday, with thunder in the air.'

By Friday evening, over 200,000 demonstrators had taken to the street. On Saturday, Ransome stayed at home and wrote a rough draft for an article on 'crowds'. A few trams were running, 'but these were brought to a standstill by bands of small boys, who, unmolested by police, turned everybody off the cars'. Order, he expected, would be restored shortly. On Sunday, however, Harold Williams phoned with news that troops had confronted rioters at Moscow station but had refused to fire, only to be tricked by agents provocateurs.

'Police agents opened fire on the soldiers, and shooting became general,' reported Ransome, 'though I believe the soldiers mostly used blank cartridges.'

On the same day, a massacre of civilians by loyal troops in Znamenskaya Square transformed a loosely co-ordinated bread riot into a mass movement. Ringleaders began to emerge, and red flags and political slogans appeared above hastily erected barricades.

The Revolution proper began on Monday the 12th. The Duma was officially dissolved but defied the edict and instead formed a temporary committee made up of representatives of all parties save the extreme Right. Meanwhile, the absent Tsar, distracted by an outbreak of measles amongst his children, commanded that the disturbance be put down with all necessary force. The decision proved catastrophic. Soldiers who had fired on the crowds in the morning were overcome with remorse and by evening were mutinying in large numbers, often killing their officers. The city arsenal was ransacked, the Peter and Paul Fortress liberated, and siege was laid to the Admiralty – Petrograd's vast naval headquarters on the banks of the Neva – where thirteen generals of the old guard had locked themselves up with a printing press and were issuing pamphlets ordering people to 'go home'.

'Saw a great deal,' wrote Ransome in his diary, but what he recorded for the *Daily News* – 'orderly battle for Petrograd' – bore little relation to his immediate experience at the time: the feeling of sudden submersion, then levitation; of terror, exhilaration, fascination and occasional surreal amusement as, ducking behind a corner to avoid a hail of machine-gun bullets, he discovered a line of elderly women calmly scraping ice off the pavement, or, standing suddenly alone and exposed in an open space, he watched a horseman gallop up, point a pistol in his face and demand, 'For or against the people?'

'I am English,' replied Ransome, helplessly.

'Long live the English!' shouted the horseman, and galloped away.

Ransome's chief concern in the early stages of the revolution was to gather news without finding himself on the wrong side of the fence. On that crucial Monday, he followed a large detachment of loyal troops to the Tauride Palace and witnessed a salutary conversion as they handed their rifles to the crowd. But he did not linger. Instead, he spent the greater part of the day hunting for friends. Ariadna Tyrkova and Harold Williams were with the Duma, which was wondering how to cope with 140,000 hungry troops who refused to return to their barracks. Will Peters, unbeknownst to Ransome, was holed up with the thirteen loyal and indignant generals at the Admiralty. Otherwise, the entire city was in pandemonium, and Ransome simply followed his nose, trying, like everybody else, to piece together what was happening from snippets of breathless and often contradictory reports. That evening, he joined a crowd of British officers and expatriates at the Astoria Hotel, before setting out in the pitch darkness for the short walk home to Glinka Street, tailing a detachment of Russian soldiers under a young noncommissioned officer who charmed him by the sweetness with which he encouraged his men.

At street corners they hesitated.

'Come on, children', cried he. 'Nothing to be afraid of!'

And on they went. I joined them.

'Whither you?'

I told him 'Glinka Street'.

'Our road also,' said he, and I was thus adopted. What they were about I do not know, but I think he was shepherding his men back to barracks because just as we passed under the walls of the Commissariat a hand grenade was lobbed from the roof by someone who could not see us, but I suppose had heard the tramp of our feet. It made a hole in the pavement but damaged none of us.

'Devils!' ejaculated the young man, but continued instantly, 'Not our business. Forward *rebyata* ("lads")!' And on they went.

The following morning, now safely installed behind his desk, Ransome was afforded a ringside seat as armoured cars with mounted machine guns converged on the Litovsky Castle.

'Having moved across Petrograd with the revolutionaries I now need move no further as the battle has come to me and my windows have the best possible view of the preparations for the storm of the prison which is next door on my right . . .'

In the ensuing fight, what he noticed most were the visual analogies to ordinary life: the students who held ribbons of bullets for the guns like bridesmaids carrying bridal trains; the scattering bystanders, caught in the crossfire, running for cover with their arms flung across their faces, as if against a sudden shower of rain. Within an hour, the castle was in flames and the wall of Ransome's apartment building was pitted with bullet holes, though he was amazed to discover that his own windows remained unscathed. The only serious inconvenience was a stray shot which had severed his telephone connection, 'which hampered me considerably, as I did not hear as soon as I might of the re-opening of the telegraph office'.

Tuesday was the day the Petrograd garrison, the Tsar's praetorian guard, mutinied and placed themselves at the disposal of the people. Ransome spent the night with Will Peters, who had escaped from the Admiralty and ravenously devoured a mass of sticky halva procured by Ransome from one of the few shops courageous enough to stay open (or so he contended). Together they walked along the canal, where huge bonfires were being fed with records from captured police stations. By now, every prison in the city had been liberated, and the inmates, hailed indiscriminately as comrades of the Revolution, had joined the crowds which looted shops, smashed windows and cheered as police snipers were hurled down, one after another, from their hideaways on the rooftops.

But the most important prisoners to be released were the leaders of the Central Workers' Group, whose arrest Ransome had reported in February. While the Duma was forming its Temporary Committee for the Preservation of Order, it was the Central Workers' Group who had invited workers and soldiers to form the first elected body of the Revolution – the Soviet of Workers' and Soldiers' Deputies.

'Citizens!' ran their proclamation.

The representatives of the workmen, soldiers and population of Petrograd assembled in the Duma to announce that the first meeting of their representatives will take place at 7pm today in the Duma building. All military units that have come over to the side of the people must immediately select representatives in the proportion of one per company. Factories must choose their deputies – one for 1,000 employees. Factories with less than 1,000 workmen must choose one deputy each.

By Monday evening, they had installed themselves in the main hall of the Tauride Palace, and this was where Ransome found them on Wednesday, in a shambles of piled-up 'ammunition, sacks of flour, and machine-guns'.

Deep inside the building, seated on gilt-legged chairs beneath portraits of the imperial family, the temporary committee had been slower to act. Terrified of exceeding his authority, Mikhail Rodzianko, the Duma president, had telegraphed the Tsar to advise him that unless a government which 'enjoyed the confidence of the country' were appointed immediately, it would mean 'death'. 'Pray God that this may be our responsibility, and that it may not fall on a crowned head.' Receiving no reply, a second telegram had been sent: 'The situation is becoming worse. Measures must be taken immediately, for tomorrow it may be too late. The last hour has arrived when the fate of the country and the dynasty may be decided.' By Thursday, when Miliukov emerged from the Duma to declare a new Provisional Government, any chance of preserving the monarchy had been lost.

'Dynasty?' roared the crowd.

'You ask about dynasty,' replied Miliukov, who had waited half a lifetime to answer this precise question. 'I know beforehand that my answer will not please all of you. But I give it . . . We propose a Parliamentary Constitutional Monarchy. Perhaps others have different views, but if we stop to discuss instead of instantly deciding Russia will find herself in a state of civil war, and the destroyed regime will be reborn.'

Miliukov went on to announce the Provisional Cabinet – Prince Lvov as prime minister, Alexei Gutchkov as Minister of War, Alexander Kerensky as Minister of Justice, Miliukov himself as Foreign Secretary – but the putative figureheads of the constitutional monarchy quickly melted away. The Tsar, exhibiting a resignation that shocked and moved the generals who received his signature, abdicated on 15 March (a week after the first bread riot) in favour of his brother, the Grand Duke Michael, who wisely declined the throne and withdrew into private life. The news of Moscow's successful uprising reached Petrograd amidst scenes of riotous celebration, while Ransome recorded his own feelings on the front page of the *Daily News*.

Russia's Days of Joy: Men Call Each Other Comrade:
a War Dance of Jubilation

It is impossible for people who have not lived here to know with what joy we write of the new Russian Government. Only those who know how things were but a week ago can understand the enthusiasm of us who have seen the miracle take place before our eyes. We knew how

Russia worked for war in spite of her Government. We could not tell the truth. It is as if honesty had returned.

Today newspapers have reappeared, and their tone and even form are so joyful that it is hard to recognize them. They are so different from the censor-ridden mutes and unhappy things of a week ago. Every paper seems to be executing a war-dance of joy. The front pages bear such phrases as 'Long live the Republic,' and 'Long live free Russia'.

The organization of the gigantic general election which must take place later will naturally take time. Meanwhile Russia will find her own mind, and I have no doubt that the decision will be worthy of the revolution that made it possible.

With hindsight, each witness to the March 1917 Revolution projected back onto the chaos some sense of order and proportion according to their prejudice. Ariadna Tyrkova, whose fear of the mob was enlivened by her noble status, concentrated on the dignity with which the Provisional Government had assumed its role as regent of the new republic, laying the foundations for the Constituent Assembly which would provide Russia with its first truly democratic parliament in history. Colonel Knox, the British military attaché, striding to and fro between the British embassy and Russian government buildings, had grasped immediately the threat to the Eastern Front: the difference between Russian patriots and Russian 'internationalists', the so-called socialists who promoted class war. Ransome's own memoirs stressed the turbulence of events from the perspective of a newspaper reporter: the announcement that the Tsar was marching on Petrograd, received within minutes of news that he had been arrested; Miliukov's declaration on the steps of the Tauride Palace coinciding with an entirely separate declaration by the Council of Workers' and Soldiers' Deputies; the confident 'We' with which the Kadet leader had declared a constitutional monarchy dismissed instantly, without the need for any vote, by the angry roar of the crowd.

Ransome's earliest telegrams were a collage of ill-sorted

impressions designed to communicate the excitement of the Revolution, while placing British readers at their ease. Soldiers were shooting their officers, but showing admirable restraint. They had 'struck the fetters from their nation', proving themselves 'far stronger than their oppressors believed', but this strength was by no means hostile to the Allies or the war: 'Long Live England!' ran his headline on 16 March. The Revolution was not a 'revolt' or a 'rebellion' or a 'mutiny', but an intensely patriotic reaction against 'The German Gang'. Now that the press was free to speak its mind, it was possible to reveal that the riots themselves had been deliberately provoked by tsarist agents with a view to crushing reform, and in all probability, to brokering a separate peace with the Kaiser. Britain, in short, was witnessing 'far and away the greatest victory over Prussianism gained in this war'. And yet, shortly after Prince Lvov had been installed as the head of the new Provisional Cabinet, Ransome was announcing a fresh riot by soldiers, while readers of the *Daily News* discovered, for the first time, that Russia was ruled not by one government, but two.

In the right wing of the Tauride Palace sat the Duma, headed by Lvov's ministers: a parliament of conservative liberals which Britain, along with its allies, had formally recognized on 25 March. Even the American ambassador was quick to extend the congratulations of his president, although Woodrow Wilson would not join the war until April. But the question was, did Lvov's government speak for Russia? How long, indeed, would they continue to speak for anyone at all, when in the left wing of the palace, in a fog of cigarette smoke, amid a deafening hullabaloo, sat the Petrograd Soviet, whose flag was the red flag of the workers and who had wrested control of every significant lever of power before the Provisional Cabinet had announced its existence? According to 'Order Number One', the army and navy answered only to the Soviet. Soldiers were no longer required to salute their officers or to cringe and scrape in their presence. Formal terms of address – 'Your Honour', 'Your Excellency' – were dispensed with. Generals were now 'Mr General', colonels

'Mr Colonel'. Off-duty soldiers could drink, attend political demonstrations, and if they wished (and many did), abandon fighting altogether. The central tenets of Order Number One explicitly prohibited the removal of the Petrograd garrisons to the front or any surrender of arms or equipment to former officers. The authority of these officers was now replaced by the soldiers' committees, which, along with the sailors' committees and the workers' committees (and before long, the regional soviets), reported to the All-Russia Soviet, which was their official congress. As Foreign Minister in the Provisional Cabinet, Miliukov promised that the empire would stand firm by its allies. But the Soviet had no interest in extending the Russian empire or any other. What it wanted was peace, and preferably peace enforced from below. In March, the Soviet leaders issued an appeal to the international proletariat, imploring the workers of the world to take their future into their own hands. The only reason they did not seize power in Russia immediately was because the *Communist Manifesto* had told them not to. Karl Marx had said that the socialist revolution would be preceded by a bourgeois revolution: first democracy, then the dictatorship of the proletariat. Had Marx, a German, not laid this down as one of the cornerstones of his philosophy, it is possible that Germany would have won the war.

From the socialist camp, only Alexander Kerensky, after much public soul-searching, had joined Lvov's eminently bourgeois Cabinet, where he was the only man who enjoyed any real authority. As Minister of Justice and vice chairman of the Soviet he impressed everybody with his eloquence, fire and ability to appeal both to the Right and to the Left: to those who demanded a continuation of the struggle against the Kaiser, and to those who reached out in brotherhood to the international masses. When Miliukov supported a war which might win Russia Constantinople and the long-coveted Dardanelles, Kerensky was quick to contradict him. The Foreign Minister spoke only for himself, he assured the soldiers. And yet liberty, however noble, must be defended against its aggressors. The Revolution had delivered Russia from the Tsar, but who would deliver Russia from the Kaiser? The war must continue, if only in self-defence.

'Then, as on a dozen other occasions,' reported Ransome, 'Mr Kerensky saved the situation . . . It is no longer possible to accuse the Government of seeking Constantinople or, indeed, anything but the salvation and preservation of Russia and Russian freedom. For that purpose there is no party in the State unwilling to make the utmost effort.'

~

Ransome's earliest impressions of the Soviet reflected a conflict which had existed in his character ever since he was a boy. Culturally, in terms of his family background and education, he belonged to the class which dominated and was protected by the Provisional Government. His father might have made an excellent candidate for Prince Lvov's Cabinet. His masters at Rugby would have been Kadets to a man. In Russia most of his closest friends and associates – Harold Williams, Ariadna Tyrkova, Bernard Pares – were men and women of the liberal Right, highly educated imperialists, enlightened, confident, on easy terms with the ministers and ambassadors who sought them out for information and advice. Hitherto, most of Ransome's journalism had echoed their views, and he continued to echo them. He supported the war and the Provisional Government. He considered himself in every way a loyal British citizen.

But the very things that drew Ransome into the bourgeois fold also gave rise to mixed feelings. No doubt he had a strong emotional attachment to his class, but he also had good reasons to resent it, not least because he judged himself, often very painfully, by its standards. His father, he knew, had been disappointed in him. He had failed at Rugby, and after a brief spell in Leeds had abandoned formal education altogether. As a young author struggling to be noticed, no amount of reading or literary criticism had made up for the fact that the Oxbridge crowd made him feel ignorant and gauche. In Russia he had been passed over for the top job at the Anglo-Russian Bureau, taken to task by Hugh Walpole, and scoffed at back in London by Lord Crawford, who would now, he fervently hoped, be eating his hat.

When Ransome recalled the Revolution, he spoke of the giddy disbelief, the feeling of living through a miracle. Something had happened which eclipsed all expectation: three hundred years swept away in a matter of days. It was like living in a dream or a fairy tale. And yet when he wrote to his mother, he wanted to stress the importance not only of the dream, but also the distinction bestowed upon those who had been welcomed into that dream from the first moment of its inception. In February, as Harold Williams sat in conference with the Kadets, Ransome had been approached by the Central Workers' Group, whose predicament he had not only published in the *Daily News*, but communicated to the British embassy. Now the workers had approached him again, with a pass to attend meetings of the Soviet. 'It was the first proletariat parliament in the world,' he proudly informed Edith, 'and by Jove it was tremendous. They said very nice things when they asked me to come. It was because of the stuff I got through on their behalf before the revolution.'

On 12 April, he witnessed the return of one of the first political exiles: Madame Breshko-Breshkovskaya, a founding member of the Socialist Revolutionary Party, the party of the rural peasants to which Kerensky also belonged. Ransome was delighted to discover her almost indistinguishable from the peasant 'babushkas' who had kept the Russian family together for so many centuries.

'The whole conference,' he reported in the *Daily News* on 12 April,

stood and cheered while she came in on the arm of Kerensky, who looked very ill and trembled with excitement. He was followed by other leaders and representatives of the army and the fleet and spoke in greeting. Many broke down altogether. The Grandmother of the Revolution is a little kindly old lady with nearly white hair and pink cheeks who laughed and cried as she kissed them. At last she made a short speech urging that Hohenzollern [the Kaiser] should not be allowed to conquer what had been taken from the Romanovs. I have never seen such enthusiasm. Soldiers and sailors leapt from their places and rushed to the tribune, and in some cases kneeling before her cried, 'we have brought you from Siberia to Petrograd. Shall we not guard you? We have won freedom. We will keep it.' She gave away some roses from the bouquet with which she had been met at the station and I saw a soldier who had only secured two petals wrap them up in paper while tears of excitement ran down his face.

By the end of March, Ransome had already commissioned Dmitri Mitrokhin to illustrate the front cover of what he anticipated would be his magnum opus: a definitive account of the Revolution projected to end with the opening of the Constituent Assembly promised by Miliukov on the steps of the Duma. But the Revolution proved surprisingly difficult to pin down – took unexpected turns, threw up new heroes, stated new aims – so that within weeks Mitrokhin's portrait of the Litovsky Castle in flames began to feel redundant, a picture postcard of purely sentimental value. Over the next seven years, it was all Ransome could do to keep his own head above water. It would be thirty before he set down the story of his Russian adventures in a book, and another twenty before he realized he would never finish it.

11

Kerensky

Ransome was outside the Finland station in April when Vladimir Ilych Lenin, after ten years of unbroken exile in Europe, arrived in Russia to give his first speech of the Revolution. Two regiments of sailors had volunteered to provide the Bolshevik leader with a guard of honour, and though it was close to midnight, the crowd numbered in the thousands. Lenin, striding out into the glare of searchlights in his homburg and a Swiss wool coat, energetically mounted the bonnet of an armoured car and announced that the 'world wide revolution' had begun. The rest of his speech was lost in the answering roar, although a bystander recalled a few intelligible words – 'any part in the shameful imperial slaughter . . . liars and frauds . . . capitalist pirates'.

Lenin's famous 'April Theses' were delivered on 4 April to two separate meetings of the Bolshevik Party and, later, to the All-Russia Congress of Soviets of Workers' and Soldiers' Deputies. On these occasions Ransome was not present, but those who were could scarcely believe their ears. Lenin denounced collaboration not only with the Provisional Government, but also with the moderate majority within the Soviet itself, all of whom he condemned as 'counter-revolutionaries'. A far-reaching and systematic campaign of agitation must be undertaken immediately, targeting the workers in the cities, the peasants in the countryside, and most importantly, the soldiers in the barracks and at the front. The imperialist war could not continue. The Provisional Government must be removed by any available means. Only when the second phase of the Revolution – the complete transfer of power to the proletariat – had been accomplished could the Bolshevik programme begin in earnest: the nationalization of all commerce and industry, the abolition of private property, of class, of ethnic and religious distinctions, and the inception of a new 'revolutionary international' designed to establish a world commune and to bring down that most pernicious of bourgeois institutions, the nation state itself.

All this filtered out in a matter of days, provoking a furore within the political community. Amongst Ransome's friends on the Right, the Bolshevik philosophy amounted to treason, the betrayal of an entire culture. Ariadna Tyrkova, who knew Lenin personally, viewed him with something approaching religious loathing, while Harold Williams, though a journalist, would not even go to hear him speak and appears to have suffered a nervous breakdown shortly after his arrival. He spent the next few weeks recovering in the Caucasus.

From the Left the reaction was more nuanced, but only in so far as it reflected a long history of factionalism in which Lenin, almost without exception, had been the most extreme and divisive element. In 1903, it had been Lenin who had split the Russian Social Democrats into two factions: the Bolsheviks and the Mensheviks. In 1904, Leon Trotsky, choosing to join neither one side nor the other, had predicted that Lenin's appetite for rigid bureaucratic control would lead to tyranny. 'The organization of the party will take the place of the party; the Central Committee will take the place of the organization; and finally the dictator will take the place of the Central Committee.' During the following decade, Lenin – by way of bearing Trotsky out – had engaged in one feud after another, each ostensibly a challenge to a misguided interpretation of Marx, each designed to shore up Lenin's political control of the party which he intended to form the vanguard of social revolution: centrally organized, authoritarian, governed by his own iron discipline.

In 1914, the Bolshevik leader had been virtually alone amongst European socialist leaders in voting against the capitalist war, and had condemned all other parties, especially the German Social Democrats, as traitors to the cause. And yet Lenin, isolated in neutral Switzerland with only half a dozen loyal followers around him, had welcomed the ensuing holocaust. The war, he declared, was the final catastrophe of capitalism, the essential trigger, he hoped, for a global class war. In 1917, he had come into Russia on a 'sealed train' provided by the German high command (one more revolutionary, they had reasoned, to bring down the Eastern Front), and had amazed everybody by spitting on any compromise with the Provisional Government. The Mensheviks cried heresy. What about the fabled 'bourgeois revolution'? What about the period of parliamentary democracy that both Marx and Engels had insisted on as the essential prelude to pure socialism? Even those within his immediate circle shouted that Lenin had taken leave of his senses. In his absence, Joseph Stalin and Lev Kamenev, as editors of the Bolshevik newspaper *Pravda*, had already passed motions pledging the party's co-operation, both with the Provisional Government and with their rivals in the Soviet. Lenin had been away too long, they said. He no longer understood his own country. Any move against the Provisional Government would result in civil war. Only Madame Kollontai and Alexander Shlyapnikov stood by Lenin as he demanded out-and-out class war. And yet, within three months of the April Theses, he would find himself actually restraining his comrades, Trotsky now among them, beseeching them that the time was too soon, that the troops assembled in their thousands beneath his balcony should go home. First, he reasoned, the Bolsheviks must win control of the Soviet. Then they would settle their differences with the bourgeoisie.

Ransome's own immediate reaction to Lenin's arrival was to delete it from the record. There is no mention of the speech at the Finland station or the Theses in any of his articles, either for the *Daily News* or the *Observer* – though he had, on two occasions, visited the headquarters of *Pravda*. By April, he had formed a clear idea of the political spectrum that emerged from the March Revolution, and with regard to the radical Left, pursued, for as long as he was able, a policy of strategic evasion. Lenin's name did not figure in any of his telegrams for several weeks, while the Bolsheviks and anarchists were lumped together under the general heading 'Extremists'. In the meantime, as the Provisional

Government lurched from one crisis to another, he reserved his most stinging criticism for the Kadets, those who before the Revolution had been pleased to consider themselves liberals.

~

The critical difference between the Provisional Government and the Soviet, regardless of doctrinal distinctions between the Bolshevik 'hards' and their more liberal counterparts, was the notion of 'democracy from below' – a phrase which the Kadets interpreted as a thinly veiled euphemism for mob rule, and which the socialists embraced as the just and irresistible will of the people. Ransome, navigating carefully between the bourgeoisie and insurgent proletariat, never rigorously defined the term for himself or for his readers, but there is little doubt where his romantic sympathy lay. Amongst his most formative experiences was the occasion, pivotal to his childhood, on which his father, taking matters into his own hands, had thrown him over the side of a boat in the Lake District, expecting him to swim, spontaneously, like a tadpole. Ransome did not forget the unlooked-for humiliation of the experience, or later, the unforgivable charge of dishonesty. No anecdote could better illuminate his suspicion of authority or his still greater horror of rejection: the wonderful sense of vindication when he had proved his newly acquired skills at the Leeds public baths. 'I don't think I ever saw my father so pleased with me as he was that day.'

In 1914, Ransome had seen Russia plunged, without preparation, into a war which served the interests only of the patrician class, with catastrophic results. Three years later, the people had risen up on their own authority, taken their future into their own hands and created a system of government both original and entirely suited to their needs, being local, directly democratic and representative of all but a tiny minority of the population. It was not, in Ransome's own view, the duty of the Soviet to prove to the Provisional Government, or to England, that it had learned to swim the backstroke. The miracle had already been performed, a miracle that so far exceeded anything accomplished in the West that nothing remained but a humble act of obeisance. The manly thing was to recognize the courage and initiative whereby Russia, formerly the most primitive and oppressed nation in Europe, had suddenly become 'the freest country in the world'.

In his articles, Ransome played down the elation with which he had greeted the rise of the Soviet, presenting himself instead as an impartial observer acting as a vital mediator between the new Russia and Britain. But it was pleasant nevertheless for him to feel that from the very beginning – even before the abdication of the Tsar – his analysis of events had been borne out to the letter. On his last visit to London, he had predicted the Revolution, only to be told by Lord Crawford that he was talking 'rubbish'. Yet here was the Revolution all the same – 'I cannot help whispering "I told you so,"' he confided to his mother. Next, while friends of a less adventurous persuasion – Tyrkova, Williams, Pares – had snubbed the Soviet, Ransome had embraced it, with the result that no other English reporter was quoted so frequently in the left-wing press. Finally, and most importantly, he had warned England that the war would be fought on the Soviet's terms, and not on those of the Kadets. Before long he was proved right again, with the major villain of the piece being a man who bore a very striking resemblance to his father: a professor of history, a confirmed imperialist, a former liberal turned conservative destined for a mighty fall – Russia's present Minister of Foreign Affairs, Pavel Miliukov.

On May Day, the streets of Petrograd were packed with excited citizens marking the first official holiday of the Revolution. 'In all directions as far as I can see,' reported Ransome,

red flags are waving above the dense crowd, which leaves just room for the constantly passing processions. On either side of the processions, long strings of men and women walk along holding hands . . . the whole town is hung with flags, banners and inscriptions. A characteristic emblem, an enormous red and white banner, hangs over the granite front of the German embassy, which was sacked in 1914 and has stood empty ever since. The banner is inscribed, 'Proletariat of all lands unite.' That is the thought in the minds of the Russian workmen today. When will such a day be seen in Berlin?

While Ransome sat in his room, writing up his telegram for the *Daily News*, Professor Miliukov was drafting an entirely different document: a note to the Allies confirming that Russia, in spite of the Soviet 'defensist' policy agreed explicitly by the Provisional Government, remained committed to the war aims determined by the Tsar, specifically with regard to Miliukov's most treasured ambition, the annexation of Constantinople. When news of the 'Miliukov Note' leaked out, Bolshevik agitators in the barracks had a field day, and within hours 25,000 angry soldiers, armed to the teeth, had marched on the Mariinsky Palace where the Cabinet now sat, demanding the resignation of the 'ten bourgeois ministers'. Ransome condemned Miliukov in the most uncompromising terms, while introducing his audience for the first time to the novel idea of the fanatical 'Leninists'. One extreme, he urged, was just as bad as the other. The middle way lay with Kerensky, who alone enjoyed the confidence of the people, the moral authority to defend the Revolution and the power to prevent Russia tipping over into anarchy.

Within a fortnight, Miliukov had resigned, with Gutchkov ceding the Ministry of War to Kerensky. Meanwhile, Kerensky's Soviet comrades, arguing that the Provisional Government could not stand without their support, took the Ministries of Agriculture, Communication and Labour. In prospect, the new Coalition Government appeared to address the interests of all factions save the extreme Right and Left, but in practice served nobody but Lenin.

The interim period between the first 'bourgeois' uprising in March 1917 and the Bolshevik military coup that would take place in November was defined by a single, relatively straightforward principle. Each time a politician, however indirectly, identified himself with the war, so he identified himself with fear, hunger and disease. Each time he used the words 'freedom' or 'honour', so he reminded the majority how meaningless those words really were. While the moderate socialists agonized over Marxist doctrine, the soldiers at the front were routinely fraternizing with the enemy, murdering their officers (some were skinned alive) or deserting to the countryside, where they terrorized the gentry, cut down the forests and seized the farms they believed were theirs in all but name already. Workers in the cities quickly discovered that their rising wages still could not match the price of grain. In the absence of a proper police force, citizen 'militias' took the law into their own hands. Strikes, lynchings and random violence became routine. In this way Russia moved towards the Left, not as a determined effort towards the Marxist millennium, but through the rapid erosion of every ideal, until only three words really mattered at all: 'Land', 'Peace' and 'Bread'.

~

Towards the end of May, Ransome received word from Ivy that his old friend Edward Thomas had been killed in France, blown to bits in his observation post overlooking no-man's-land and leaving behind a widow and three children. Ransome's reaction reflected the coolness that had grown up between them since the happy days in Chelsea: 'It's pretty tough luck on poor, incompetent Helen,' he told his mother, 'but for Edward himself perhaps not. It's about four years or more since I saw him but I rather fancy he had a rotten time to look forward to after the war.'

In this brief interim, Thomas had earned his place in the British literary canon, thanks to over 140 poems written since 1914 which balanced nostalgia for the pre-war tranquillity of the British countryside against the empty horror of the trenches. But Ransome – possibly unaware that Thomas had published under the pseudonym Edward Eastaway – had nothing to say on the subject of his writing, and little on his death, which, in view of Thomas's frequent ideations of suicide, he took as a blessing. He was, in any case, completely absorbed by his own affairs.

I am afraid I've been rather bad about writing since the revolution, and probably some of the letters I've written have not reached you, but you will have seen from the D. News that I have been extremely busy and am so and will be. What you don't see probably in the D. News telegrams is that I am extremely worried about the development of things here, particularly with regard to a proper understanding between Russia and England. I wish to goodness I had Geoff out here, whose solid sense would be a mighty stand by . . . I wish to goodness I could come back and see people.

Edith must not suppose that the Revolution had in any way become a settled affair or that its various factions could be judged and arranged 'like a lot of Japanese boxes fitting smoothly into one another'. Ransome himself had seen 'the workings of the thing' much too closely to believe anything so foolish or to imagine that the Revolution would necessarily be confined to Russia alone. In 1918, he predicted, conditions all over Europe would match the conditions which in Russia had preceded the bread riots in March. The total food supply of the world was diminishing with each year the war continued. 'Wise men in England', he advised, 'ought to be jolly grateful to have been given so clear an illustration of what may be coming, and to be given this illustration at such a distance.'

Puzzling through these letters, Edith may reasonably have wondered what her son valued most highly: the savage joy with which Russia had claimed its liberty, or victory on the Eastern Front. In early May, he had explained in the *Daily News* that 'free Russia' criticized Britain on the basis of 'first principles'. Why did Britain, claiming to oppose the tyranny of the Kaiser, continue the war, if not for imperial gain? A week later, the Soviet proposed a peace conference, to be attended by all European socialist parties and convened in neutral Stockholm. But British delegates were denied visas to travel either to Sweden or Russia, where their comrades eagerly awaited them. Was this democratic? wondered Ransome. Was it surprising that in

Petrograd, England was accused of hypocrisy? And yet Edith's favourite paper, *The Times*, insisted that a meeting of socialists in Sweden would mean little more than a conference of revolutionaries, while Ransome – who abhorred the notion of revolution in England – continued to insist in his articles that Russia had never been fitter or more eager to fight the Germans. Only one thing was clear: a heavy burden rested on his shoulders.

'I am tired completely out,' he confessed,

and just get through from day to day, in a sort of hopeless effort to keep head above water in the rush and muddle of by no means cheering events. I see the Anglo-Russian friendship, everything I've ever sweated at all these years crumbling day by day, while Russia is being turned into a large helpless market ready for German goods and German influences and full of dull resentment against England. It is not a very cheerful prospect especially as it gives the Germans the East as well as the Balkans, and as far as I can judge from the newspapers that come out here nobody at home understands how very serious the position is. I suppose they've got enough to think of, poor things, but, as far as world politics goes, England is like a baby playing in a back garden. She is losing support here every day. Posters against her are distributed in the main streets, printed in Russian on one side and in German on the other. It looks as if the war may end with England an American island on the edge of Europe, a prospect horrible to contemplate.

Small wonder that headaches, stomach cramps and 'gore' once again become almost daily entries in his diary, or that Ransome consoled himself at night with a well-worn edition of Hans Christian Andersen. Two months after announcing Russia the 'freest country in the world', he was already demanding a summer holiday. He longed for the company of his family. He dreamed of the 'adorable penguins' in London Zoo.

~

In the wake of the Miliukov Note, Kerensky had two options. He could seek an immediate, separate peace with Germany, thus alienating the Allies but winning breathing space at home, or he could continue the war in the hope that the Russian army, inspired by the Revolution, would defend their liberty with a passion they had never found under the Tsar.

Convinced of his own heroic destiny as the 'saviour of Russia', Kerensky left Petrograd in May to tour the front. Dressed in an expensively tailored, semi-military uniform, he admonished the troops for their faint-heartedness. They were no longer 'mutinous slaves' or the citizens of an 'exhausted nation', but champions (so ran Ransome's quote) of the 'greatest movement for liberty the world has ever known'. Pursued by the cheers of his comrades and the gasps of love-sick noblewomen, it seemed that nothing was impossible for the young hero. In Petrograd, there was scarcely a mantelpiece that lacked his portrait. At the Mariinsky Theatre or the Tauride Palace, his speeches provoked mass hysteria. As a boy he had wanted to be an actor, and as an orator had the remarkable gift of fainting at climactic moments. Addressing the soldiers, he sometimes wore his arm in a sling, giving the impression that he not only understood, but had actually shared their suffering. As a politician, he offered Russia passage through the war and revolution with its identity intact: freedom for the people, honour for the nation. He was as adored as Rasputin had once been reviled, but he was not a general.

Russia's last great offensive of the war was launched in Galicia, following the pattern already established by General Brusilov. After subjecting the Germans to a three-day bombardment, the Russian infantry met with little resistance. Kerensky's adoring public was ecstatic. Champagne corks popped in every restaurant and private dining room from Petrograd to London; but the jubilation was short-lived. The advance was soon mired in disputes between officers and men, with entire regiments refusing to budge beyond the first enemy trenches, where vodka was discovered in abundant supply. As the Women's Battalion of Death fornicated with their comrades in shell craters, a decisive counter-attack caused an immediate stampede. Soldiers shot their officers rather than face the enemy. Deserters stormed every train going east, fighting for space on the roof, clinging to the window frames, tumbling off in villages to ransack cellars and rape the local girls. The first rumblings of the November Revolution came shortly afterwards.

In mid-July, the Kadets walked out of Lvov's Provisional Cabinet, leading to the immediate collapse of the First Coalition Government. While the politicians debated what should be done, Petrograd's most 'Bolshevized' garrisons – amongst them the sailors stationed at the Kronstadt Fortress and the First Machine Gun Regiment in the Vyborg District – poured out of their barracks, this time in vast numbers. Private and official motors were commandeered and raced around town bristling with bayonets. Armoured cars appeared at crossroads or sat in squares, swivelling their machine guns to terrorize the public. The Tauride Palace was besieged by over 50,000 soldiers chanting the Bolshevik slogan 'All Power to the Soviets!', and when Viktor Chernov, the Minister of Agriculture, attempted to reason with them, threatened him with a lynching. Over a period of seventy-two hours, Ransome sent up to six telegrams a day, combining political analysis and vivid discursive detail: bloody street battles between rebels and Cossacks; crowds moving nervously to and fro; the bewilderment and anxiety of the troops themselves, wandering sleepily smoking cigarettes, leaping into cars to arrest, unsuccessfully, Prince Lvov and his Cabinet (the assembled ministers had simply refused to come down from their sitting room), or posting themselves at strategic points to guard against a counter-attack from the Northern Front, an attack that never came. It was here, too, that Ransome first introduced a recurring motif, a wishful thought which he used in various guises to suggest peace vying with the prevailing anarchy: 'at the bridge over the Moika canal, two armed soldiers anxiously scanning approaches while a small boy on the bridge fished unconcernedly for stickleback'.

The 'July Days' did not, as the mutineers had hoped, lead to the immediate overthrow of the Provisional Government. Lenin's own carefully laid plans depended on the Bolsheviks gaining supremacy in the Soviet before taking control of the country. It was not enough to seize power if he saw no chance of keeping it, and without the popular authority of the Soviets, he saw no chance for the Bolsheviks at all. Consequently, when 20,000 Kronstadt sailors marched on the Bolshevik headquarters looking for direction, Lenin, stepping out onto his balcony, advised them to go home, which they did, reluctantly and much to the relief of his enemies on the Soviet Executive Committee. The uprising became a scattered riot and finally, lacking leadership, dispersed altogether. When Kerensky finally returned from the Baltic, he entered Petrograd with all the trappings of a military dictator, processing from the Warsaw Station to the Mariinsky Palace escorted by Cossacks and a regiment of Russian cavalry. Ransome welcomed him with open arms.

'Last night,' he informed the *Daily News*,

I saw the cavalry regiment just arrived from the front to support the Government riding from the station. Dusty, sunburnt, with full equipment and gas masks swinging in cases at their sides distinguishing them from the troops at the rear, they moved through the streets on little grey horses. One man with his reins loose on his horse's neck played the accordion accompanied by another who beat time on a tambourine. They brought with them into the hot, damp July evening in Petrograd something of the old vigour of the front; something of the vivid contrast there has always been between the front and the rear. I have never felt so strongly that Petrograd was a sick city as when I read the little dusty red flags fastened on their green lances. Here were the original watchwords of revolution: 'Long Live the Russian Republic,' 'Forward in the Name of Freedom,' 'Liberty or Death.'

Simultaneously, Petrograd learned the full scale of the Galician disaster. Half a million men had been lost in the German counter-attack, with twice as many deserting to the rear. The catastrophe only served to intensify the government's fury at the Bolsheviks. Trotsky, who had joined forces with his old political rival at the beginning of July, was arrested, along with ten other party leaders. The Bolshevik headquarters at the Kshesinskaya Palace was purged and *Pravda*, the party newspaper, closed down. Only Lenin and Grigory Zinoviev escaped, slipping away to Finland disguised in wigs and workers' caps, amidst widely publicized rumours that the Bolshevik leaders had been injected into Petrograd by the German high command, along with German funds for their political campaign. Few conservatives paused to reflect that Lenin – by whose standards the Kaiser and the Kadets were equally abhorrent – had always insisted that revolutionary morality transcended any petit-bourgeois notions of consistency. To the reactionary press in Russia and England (even Ransome toyed with the idea), the conclusion was obvious: the entire Bolshevik movement was composed of the Kaiser's agents, mostly Jews with no country of their own and therefore no dignity to defend. A vicious pogrom accompanied the backlash.

In Lenin's absence, the axis of power swung violently to the Right. Prince Lvov, exhausted and utterly disillusioned by the divisions within his Cabinet, resigned as prime minister in favour of Kerensky, who invited the Kadets to join a Second Coalition Government as the dominant party. Under their influence – and with the co-operation of the Socialist Revolutionaries and Mensheviks who retained a small number of ministries – the Soviet was removed from the Tauride Palace to the Smolny Institute, a neo-classical edifice on the outskirts of town which had formerly served as a boarding school for girls. General Brusilov was sacked as Supreme Commander of the army and replaced with General Lavr Kornilov, a staunch reactionary and disciplinarian who promptly reintroduced the death penalty. Kerensky himself, supposedly the popular champion of the Revolution, took Alexander III's former rooms at the Winter Palace, with a bust of Napoleon in his study and a bodyguard posted outside his bedroom door. When not weighed down with affairs of state, he reserved the Tsar's billiard table for his private entertainment.

But Kerensky's vanity was framed in a peculiar way. Though he slept in the Tsar's bed, used his desk and rode about town in his motor car, he still considered himself a man of the people, so that when the Soviet leaders argued that the incarceration of the Bolsheviks was an act of tyranny, he ordered their release. Many years later, sitting with Lord Beaverbrook at the Garrick Club in London, he would confess that his principal weakness as a statesman had been naivety.

~

Very few friends from Russia that Ransome described in his memoirs returned the compliment by providing him with more than a paragraph in their own; chiefly, one assumes, out of tact. Bernard Pares mentioned him fondly, but could only joke about his conflation of politics and folk tales (failing to notice that folk tales are usually dark affairs). Ariadna Tyrkova, on the other hand, felt too deeply betrayed by the Revolution and Ransome's later commentary on it to mention his name at all, observing only that when her husband felt morally let down by a friend, that person 'simply ceased to exist for him'. Hugh Walpole did not write a memoir, while Bruce Lockhart (who spent most of his time in Moscow) had been recalled to London on account of an adulterous affair. The result is a distressing dearth of information from anybody who could claim a real intimacy with or provide an impression of Ransome as he struggled through the events of 1917.

Fortunately, one source does describe him in some detail: the autobiography of a young woman named Lola Kinel, who before the Revolution had lived with relatives in America. Returning with her twin sister in 1916 (she was eighteen at the time), Lola had met Ransome on the train from Finland. She recalled 'an odd-looking man walking up and down the corridor and throwing occasional surreptitious glances in our direction. He was tall, dressed in a Russian military coat, though without insignia, and a fur cap. He had long red moustaches, completely concealing his mouth, and humorous, twinkling eyes . . .' Following an introduction during which Ransome had delighted both girls with his broken Russian, they spent the rest of the journey playing chess.

Shortly afterwards, Ransome offered Lola a job researching

the daily press, on which he based so many of his own articles. She accepted enthusiastically and became a regular visitor, continuing to place herself at his disposal even after she started working for Maxim Gorky's newspaper, *Novaya Zhizn*. In her memoirs she gives a vivid description of Ransome's room in Glinka Street:

It was the first bachelor room I had ever seen; it had a desk and typewriter in one corner, in another a bed, night table, and dresser all behind a screen; then a sort of social arrangement, consisting of an old sofa and a round table with some chairs around it in the centre.

And books. They were everywhere heaped on the sofa and even on the floor. Among these books I found occasionally torn socks. I used to pick them up gingerly in my gloved hand and wrap them in a piece of newspaper . . .

'Doesn't anyone ever mend your socks for you?' I asked one day.

'No. Don't bother to pick them up. I wear them and throw them away when they get torn. The maid forgot to take them away.'

'But then you must buy an awful lot of socks.'

'I do. These Russian *prachki* [laundresses] never bother to mend things. I live like a wild rabbit.'

'And look at your desk – look at all this dust. Doesn't the maid ever dust here?'

'I would wring her neck if she did. She daren't touch my desk,' he said with the air of a fanatic threatened with some danger.

In the first few weeks of their friendship, Ransome would often drop in to see Lola's parents, but after the Revolution these visits came to an abrupt halt. They were, Lola recalled, suddenly too 'bourgeois' for him. But she took no offence, and came trotting round as before.

'His own Bohemianism was not a pose,' she recalled,

but seemed real. He had, I remember, a thorough contempt for men who dressed well, or the least conventionally. He forgave women if they were pretty, but he preferred most Russian women, who do not pose and are simple, to English girls. For England he seemed to have a queer mixture of contempt, dislike, and love. He was clever, yet childish, very sincere and kind and romantic, and on the whole far more interesting than his books . . .

Lola Kinel's account of Ransome is unique in plotting his steady swing to the Left from the point of view of a close friend. There is, however, one other source, though scarcely as illuminating of his domestic habits, which sheds light on how this swing was viewed by the British authorities as Russia tottered between military dictatorship and social revolution.

During the war, British censorship of the press was carried out in Whitehall by the official censor. But running in parallel, and frequently at odds, were the activities of the domestic security service, MI5, whose 'Press Office' read not only telegrams, but all the correspondence of British nationals who were considered, for one reason or another, suspicious. Ransome had been of little interest to MI5 before the March Revolution. Following the inauguration of the Provisional Government, however, and the simultaneous creation of the Soviet, he had begun to attract more attention, particularly in the context of the Stockholm Peace Conference, proposed by the socialists, roundly supported by Ransome in the *Daily News* and a bone of severe contention within Lloyd George's Coalition War Cabinet.

Lloyd George's refusal to permit British socialists to attend the Stockholm Conference had provoked sharp criticism in the British liberal press and angry denunciations from the unions. As a concession, but by no means a surrender, Arthur Henderson, then Minister Without Portfolio and Secretary of the Labour Party, had been sent out to Russia in June 1917 to sound things out. Henderson, prior to departure, had voiced significant reservations about the conference, but to the horror of the prime minister, he returned a convert. In an open letter to *The Times* in August, Lloyd George accused his former minister of playing politics at a time of war, betraying the trust of the Cabinet, and most egregiously, of suppressing a vital note from Kerensky himself, indicating that the Russian government viewed the entire Stockholm business with as much suspicion as its allies in the West.

Henderson's enforced resignation, and the subsequent public scandal in Russia when Kerensky's 'secret diplomacy' was discovered, provided Ransome with his first real journalistic coup. In May, the Miliukov Note had provoked a riot by issuing a pledge to the Allies that flatly contradicted Soviet policy. Now Kerensky, who in addition to his duties as prime minister of the Provisional Government was still vice chairman of the Soviet, had made exactly the same mistake. What was needed was a friendly English journalist to explain the situation, and this was how Ransome – courtesy of an acquaintance he had made through the Gellibrands – snatched five minutes on 14 August with the busiest man in Russia.

'Important statement from Kerensky,' ran Ransome's telegram:

I was sitting with Sergei Feodorovitch Oldenburg, Minister for Education, when the door suddenly opened and Kerensky flung into the room, shook hands rapidly, sat down and immediately proceeded to business . . . He was dressed in a khaki uniform without epaulettes and brown leggings; a very different figure from the thin, young anxious looking Labour member I used to watch with interest in the Duma before the Revolution.

At the first mention of the Stockholm conference, Kerensky had 'fired up at once'. He had, he said, been appalled by misunderstandings arising from his note to the British government. He had merely intended to clarify that Russia's position regarding the war could not be determined by a single political group: the socialists. The Provisional Government naturally accepted the Stockholm conference in principle, but 'as a coalition we cannot be bound by its decisions'. The notion that he, Kerensky, was personally opposed to it was pure nonsense, while 'any opposition offered to it by Allied governments was simply playing into German hands'. Having handed Ransome a signed affidavit to this effect, Kerensky swept from the room, leaving the special correspondent of the *Daily News* feeling that he held in his hands a document that might alter the course of history.

There was no Stockholm conference, no negotiated peace, and before long, no Provisional Government. But Ransome had already been flagged as a man to watch. In 2005, almost forty years after his death, MI5 released a portion of their file on Ransome to the British National Archive, with the earliest significant entry appearing in the summer of 1917: a letter to Edith on the subject of the Stockholm conference, detailing 'a tremendous talk' he had enjoyed with the Soviet Executive Committee. Ransome claims to have 'dished' both extremists and moderates on the subject of England's brutal suppression of the Irish Easter Rising, but could find no excuse for Lloyd George's failure to conclude peace at the earliest opportunity. 'No power on Earth,' he told her,

will keep the Russian army in the trenches this winter . . . If England cares tuppence for Russia, if England does not want to see the whole of Europe and the whole of Central Asia up to Afghanistan and the *Indian borders* [Ransome's italics] under the moral dominion of Germany, she will conclude peace this year . . .

  Can you imagine that I am pretty well worried? . . . I don't think that it's possible for anybody who knows the truth to take a different view. Even men just out from England [i.e. Arthur Henderson] who start with the opposite prejudgments are, one after another, convinced in the face of the only too obvious facts. They start with the idea that 'we must count Russia out.' The next stage is reached when they realize that Russia can't be counted out, except by people incapable of looking ahead. You cannot count out the influence of over 180 million people.

This candid account of the Soviet's position, for Edith's eyes only, was written in July and intercepted on 1 August, the day Arthur Henderson sat in 10 Downing Street as his Cabinet colleagues decided his fate behind closed doors. There is a brief (and typically confused) summary appended by MI5's 'Press Office': 'Writer is, or was, correspondent for the *Observer*. Previous letters suggest that he is pessimistic by nature, and made more pessimistic by poor health.'

~

This final point, at least, was true. Ransome's 'pessimism' (an official term for 'defeatism') was exacerbated by ill health and a growing exasperation with politics in general. Leafing through similar letters, one sees how his mood had altered since March, when joyful crowds had swarmed outside his window to celebrate the end of tsarism and the birth of liberty. In those days, it seemed, elections for the Constituent Assembly were only weeks away. But each new crisis had seen it delayed, tarnished some of its glamour and exposed the frailty of its appointed guardians, both within the Provisional Government and the Soviet. Ransome's own health reflected the general malaise. He had suffered four bouts of dysentery in as many months, a vengeful resurgence of his piles, headaches, toothache and neuralgia. Every article he wrote provoked a streaming nosebleed, while in his letters to Edith he blamed England bitterly for Russia's misfortunes.

'It really was jolly hearing about Tabitha and you playing at retrieving grouse,' he wrote towards the end of July:

All that, however, seems so very far away, and every sentence in your letter which touched on Russia showed that people in England, even intelligent birds like yourself, have not the faintest notion of the condition of things here. I think of England as a sort of dream country, in the world and the war but not of it . . . You do not see the bones sticking through the skin of the horses in the street. You do not have your porter's wife beg you for a share in your bread allowance because she cannot get enough to feed her children . . . That is why these English newspapers who rail against the Russians are criminally wrong. It is because things are like that here that German agents and Extremists [Lenin and the Bolsheviks] who promise an immediate millennium do succeed in carrying away the absolutely simple minded Russian soldier whose poor head is cudgelled with long words till he does not know where he is, and does exactly what they tell him, even if it may be to his own ruin and to that of his country.

In this way Ransome explained the current state of the nation to his mother and, unwittingly, to the postal clerks at MI5. 'The time may come', he concluded, 'when England will be the most hated country in Russia, and that would be a German victory of the most real and valuable kind . . .'

Whatever Britain's crimes as a nation, however, Ransome

dreamed of the hills around Coniston all the time, and by September had convinced himself that his annual holiday could be combined with a vital diplomatic mission to Whitehall, where a firm hand was so clearly required. Edith, as always, was under strict instructions not to inform Ivy of his plans, but to send a letter to the *Daily News* 'to be called for' informing him of her own whereabouts and that of his most trusted friends. He would miss nothing in Russia, he assured her, by taking a holiday, which he considered an urgent necessity. He would refresh himself amongst the Lakes, take in a little fishing, deliver his verdict on the Anglo-Russian situation in person to the Foreign Office, and return much refreshed to witness the Constituent Assembly – now scheduled for October – which would supply the last, triumphant chapter in his history of the Revolution. It was therefore with a sinking heart that after announcing his imminent arrival in England, he was forced to report an unexpected delay. Civil war had broken out in Russia.

The rise and fall of Kerensky, the first great demagogue of the Revolution, was determined by his desire to appeal to all parties simultaneously. He had promised the Soviet he would end the war at the earliest opportunity. He had promised the Kadets that he would deliver them a decisive victory. He had promised every contradictory thing – freedom, security, honour in battle, relief from suffering – and had delivered nothing. Meanwhile, the July Days had effectively carved Russia in two, at the same time throwing up two new leaders, each possessing the ability to halt the country's rapid descent into anarchy. On the Left there was Lenin, whose support amongst the workers and soldiers had grown with every new proof that co-operation with the Provisional Government only weakened the Soviet and prolonged the war. But Lenin was still in hiding in Finland, convinced that any return to Petrograd would lead to his immediate arrest, and for the moment this made the Bolsheviks indecisive. On the Right there was General Kornilov, whom Kerensky had appointed as Supreme Commander of the army in July. Kornilov expressed himself in the simplest military language.

He blamed the deplorable state of the nation on a total collapse of discipline. He had reinstated the death penalty at the front and made no secret of his conviction that it should be instated in the rear. The Soviet must be stamped out altogether; the Bolshevik leaders hung; the soldiers' committees disbanded. What was needed was not a half-cocked democracy, but martial law.

On 28 August, Ransome had reported on the Moscow Conference, convened by Kerensky to heal the breach between Left and Right, thereby consolidating his own position. Ransome had not attended personally owing to dysentery, but had nevertheless reported its success. It had, in fact, been a disaster. Kerensky's speech convinced even his closest supporters that he had completely lost his way, while Kornilov's sudden arrival in the city had been greeted with rapturous cheers from the Kadets and cries of 'All power to the Soviets' from the Bolsheviks. A week later, the *Daily News* reported that Reval, the closest Baltic port to Petrograd, had been captured by the Germans. Ransome could not deny the 'strategic significance' of the victory, but would certainly not have allowed it to delay his holiday were it not for an accompanying catastrophe so serious that any mention of it in the press was banned until the dust had settled.

In early September, General Kornilov ordered troops stationed on the North-West Front to march on Petrograd, claiming that the Provisional Government had fallen under the influence of the Bolsheviks, who were themselves 'in full agreement with the plans of the German General Staff'. On hearing the news, Kerensky instantly dismissed Kornilov from his post, appointed himself Supreme Commander, and called on Petrograd to defend itself against the counter-revolution. Within hours, his Cabinet had resigned, ceding him all necessary power to deal with the crisis.

But as Kornilov's army continued to advance, Kerensky found that he had no troops to command, and was forced to appeal to those who did. The Smolny Institute, where the Soviet had languished since July, was now turned into a military headquarters, and a Committee for Struggle Against the Counter-Revolution established with representatives from each of the main socialist parties. Nobody, however, was in any doubt as to where the real power lay. The Socialist Revolutionaries and Mensheviks had collaborated with the government too long. Only the Bolsheviks had the authority to galvanize the city barracks and the workers' militias – the revolutionary Red Guard – into action. To press its advantage home, the party declared that it was prepared to defend the Revolution, but considered Kerensky as bad as Kornilov. If the masses were to shed their blood, it was to be for the Soviet alone.

No fighting, in the end, was necessary. While Petrograd was fortified by the same troops that had mobbed the streets during the July Days, the railway union held up trains carrying Kornilov's supplies. When the advance slowed, Bolshevik envoys were sent out to explain to the soldiers under Kornilov's command that the Provisional Government was not, as they had supposed, in any danger. The whole business had simply been a misunderstanding cooked up by two ambitious tyrants: the first being General Kornilov, the second already notorious for betraying every promise he had made to the people. For the moment, it would be in the Soviet's best interests if they simply laid down their arms.

'Failure of the Russian Revolt,' read Ransome's headline on 15 September. 'Kornilov's Cause Wrecked.'

With the collapse of the Kornilov offensive, the immediate threat from the Right had been removed. Kornilov's second-in-command – the man who had actually led the mutiny – committed suicide. Kornilov himself and twenty-three of his generals were arrested and incarcerated. But as Ransome himself hinted, much about the affair remained unclear. Had Kornilov really sent his troops against Petrograd on his own authority? Or had he been incited by an agent provocateur? Had Kerensky, in fact, deliberately exaggerated the Bolshevik threat with a view to removing his rival and installing himself as dictator, as *Pravda* insisted? Ransome would not go so far. Instead, in accordance with his own patriotic commitment to the war (he had chosen the word 'Revolt' carefully), he stressed the importance of restoring discipline at the front. Otherwise, he had little to say on the subject. His diary for September and October suggests he was concerned chiefly with getting his passport in order.

The Kornilov Affair, far from reinforcing Kerensky's authority, deprived him of any credibility remaining to him, either with the Left or the Right. Now officially dictator of all Russia, he withdrew into his quarters at the Winter Palace, with a private guard outside his suite that he liked to change every hour and a narrow clique of advisors known as the 'Council of Five'. The Bolsheviks, had they chosen, could have swept him away at any moment, but Lenin – returned from Finland to a secret location in Petrograd – was still in hiding, leaving it to Trotsky to organize and lead the final putsch.

~

The Bolshevik *coup d'état* took place on the eve of the Second All-Russian Congress of the Soviets, and was deliberately calculated to prevent any other party from diluting – through approval or disapproval – the initiative that Lenin reserved entirely for himself. The American revolutionary and journalist John Reed recorded how a date for the uprising was established.

Lenin spoke: 'November sixth will be too early. We must have an all-Russia basis for the rising; and on the sixth all the delegates to the Congress will not have arrived . . . On the other hand, November eighth will be too late. By that time the Congress will be organized, and it is difficult for a large organized body of people to take swift, decisive action. We must act on the seventh, the day the Congress meets, so that we may say to it, 'Here is the power! What are you going to do with it?'

In Room No. 10 at Smolny, on 5 November, the Military Revolutionary Committee, headed by Trotsky, heard that the

Peter and Paul Fortress was with the Bolsheviks, as was the regiment recalled by Kerensky from the front to guard Petrograd. Communication with the factories and barracks had been established via field telephone. A regular traffic of couriers and officials came and went. Everything was ready 'at the push of a button'.

Reed left Smolny at three in the morning, noticing that two machine guns had been mounted either side of the gates, while patrols stood on nearby street corners. Bill Shatov, a Russian-American, came bounding up the steps: 'Well,' he cried, 'we're off!' Kerensky, said Shatov, had suppressed all the Bolshevik newspapers, but the Bolsheviks had broken the government seals and sent troops to take control of the bourgeois papers.

On 6 November, the Council of Five decreed the arrest of the leaders of the Petrograd Soviet and the Military Revolutionary Committee, but the arrests were never made. Instead, Kerensky had gone to the Tauride Palace, where he announced to a gathering of Duma delegates that in the face of the Bolshevik insurrection, he was declaring martial law.

... The Provisional Government has never violated the liberty of all citizens of the State to use their political rights ... But now the Provisional Government declares: in this moment those elements of the Russian nation, those groups and parties who have dared to lift their hands against the free will of the Russian people, at the same time threatening to open the front to Germany, must be liquidated with decision!

But Kerensky had long since missed his chance. In the small hours of 7 November, shortly before the opening of the All-Russian Soviet Congress, the Petrograd Soviet held a meeting, permitting the Bolsheviks' mainstream opponents to express their horror at an unconstitutional revolt. Fedor Dan, the Menshevik, had condemned Lenin's plans in the most uncompromising terms, shouting above the jeers and wolf-whistles that a military coup was not a revolution but a hijacking: 'Those who are urging this are committing a crime!' But Trotsky, to tumultuous applause from his comrades, had only mocked him for his weakness. 'Dan tells you that you have no right to make an insurrection. Insurrection is the right of all revolutions! When the down-trodden masses revolt it is their right . . .'

Trotsky's troops, in any case, were already on the move. As Dan and his supporters walked out, protesting that they would make no decision under threat of arms, a Bolshevik regiment was marching on the Telephone Exchange, another on the Telegraph Agency, another on the State Bank . . .

'Behind us', recalled Reed, 'great Smolny, bright with lights, hummed like a gigantic bee hive . . .'

~

Reed's unabashedly partisan description of the November Revolution, *Ten Days that Shook the World*, became the definitive first-hand account not only for Western socialists, but also many Western liberals. As a detailed journalistic diary of his experience, taken day by day, it revealed how effortlessly the Provisional Government had been toppled, how weak it had become, how little it was mourned by the masses. The storming of the Winter Palace, according to the orthodox Soviet history that grew up under Lenin and then Stalin, was a momentous event, but in Reed's book it barely figures. Kerensky, an inveterate coward, had made his getaway before the first shell was fired by the battleship *Aurora*. The Council of Five were led away like lambs. When Reed woke up the following day, he had gone out onto the Nevsky Prospekt.

'What side do you belong to?' he had asked a group of soldiers outside the State Bank. 'The government?'

'No more government,' one answered with a grin. '*Slava Bogu!* Glory to God!'

As for Ransome, his own eye-witness account is conspicuously absent from the canon of revolutionary literature, for the simple reason that he never wrote one. Three weeks after Kornilov's defeat, he had packed his bags and left for England. As Lenin opened perhaps the most significant chapter in the history of twentieth-century politics, the Russian correspondent for the *Daily News* was at Fonthill, fishing for perch.

12

Interlude

Following the Kornilov Affair, every journalist in Russia realized that Lenin could seize power at any moment. And yet Ransome had convinced himself that he would have plenty of time to visit London, explain the idiocy of the British government's foreign policy and return to Petrograd in time for the opening of the Constituent Assembly, now scheduled for January. It had been, to say the least, a serious error of judgement, but he did not reproach himself too severely. In August, he had told his editors at the *Daily News* that if he was denied his holiday, he would be unfit for work of any kind. In his last letter to Edith before leaving Petrograd, he had not mentioned politics once, save by analogy to his own body. He was falling apart. What he needed most, he insisted, was absolute rest amongst the people and places he knew best: the north-country hills, his favourite rivers, his family, his closest friends. 'I don't think you can have any idea', he told his mother, 'how homesick I actually am.'

Had Ransome been motivated exclusively by his obligations to Anglo-Russian diplomacy, he would no doubt have rushed down to London and forced his way into the Foreign Office. Instead, after landing in Aberdeen on 17 October, waving his usual letter excusing him from military service, he stopped by in Edinburgh to discuss books with T. C. and E. C. Jack, who had published *Old Peter* the previous year. Next, having ascertained that Edith was not at home in Leeds, nor the Collingwoods in the Lake District, he continued south to Hatch, arriving on the 20th to an empty house. Ivy was with her parents in Bournemouth, but on receiving his telegram, joined him the next day with Tabitha.

It was, by all accounts, a remarkably happy interlude. Hatch was not the ideal sanctuary he had hoped for, but it was

England, and compared to the turmoil in Russia, seemed extraordinarily friendly and familiar. There is a photograph from this time of Ransome and Tabitha romping arm in arm down a lane. Ransome has his pipe stuck between his teeth and is lifting his knees up to his chest. Tabitha, now seven, in her white pinafore and stockings, is beaming back at him. A few days later, all three of them went to the nearby village of Fonthill, with its abbey and lakes, on a fishing expedition. Ivy mentioned no lonely hearts columns or phantom lovers and made no fuss when Ransome left Wiltshire at the end of October to see Edith and the Collingwoods in London. Two months of gorgeous telegram-free indulgence stretched ahead, and he showed no sign of applying himself to anything even glancingly related to politics until his peace was shattered by news that Kerensky's government had fallen. Ransome's first article on the Bolshevik coup appeared on 9 November, beneath an explanatory note: '*Mr Arthur Ransome, The Daily News's Special Correspondent in Petrograd, whose illuminating dispatches have for many months past been widely quoted in the British and Allied Press, is at present in England, and sends us the following comment on events in Russia.*'

'Extremist Power Due to Kadet Tactics,' Ransome declared.

The news from Russia means that the Extremist formula, 'All Power to the Soviets,' has now been put into effect, at any rate in Petrograd. This has long been expected by all who observed the increasing power of the Extremist party, which in the early days of the Revolution was insignificant, but gathered recruits with every move made against it – by the Kadets and by other parties on the right. Banners were in the streets proclaiming this formula on the occasion of Miliukov's Note to the Allies in May . . . In greater force they showed themselves once more during the great Bolshevik outbreak in July. The Extremists or Bolshevik Party gathered new impetus after Kornilov's mutiny, which swept into their ranks many who til then had supported the Moderate Party in the Soviet . . .

The lack of bloodshed during the Bolshevik *coup d'état* is due to two causes. First the comparative unanimity of the classes represented in the Soviet, and second to the fact that the large masses of the population increasingly despair of politics, and, though possibly disapproving, are willing to stand aside . . .

Beneath Ransome's summary ran a series of articles by other correspondents offering details to curious readers. They included the manifesto promise that had swept the Bolsheviks to power – 'Land, Peace and Bread' – an effort to interpret the significance of this promise, and biographies of the Bolshevik leaders:

The two chief personalities of the latest drama, Lenin and Trotsky, both have been prominent figures in the Russian Socialist movement for many years. Lenin (whose real name is Ulyanov) is of revolutionary stock, his brother having been hanged in 1887 for conspiring against the life of the Tsar. He is the leader of the Extreme Left of the Russian Social Democratic Party. He lived for some years abroad, and returned to Russia on the outbreak of the first revolution of 1905. In 1907 he attended the Russian Social Democratic Congress in London, and since then has never returned to Russia until the outbreak of the present revolution. During the war, he has taken an irreconcilable anti-war attitude, violently attacking both the French and the German Socialists, not sparing even the German minority. He returned to Russia in the early months of the Revolution, having crossed Germany in a sealed carriage, because, as he alleged, he had been unable to get the permission of the Allied Governments to proceed from Switzerland, where he had lived, through France and England.

Trotsky (real name Bronstein), a younger man, was deputy president of the [Petrograd Soviet] in the first Revolution, and following the suppression of that Revolution lived abroad. The outbreak of the war found him at Vienna, where he was editing a Socialist journal for smuggling into Russia, but he succeeded in escaping to Paris where he started an anti-war daily. Shortly before the Revolution he was expelled from France and went to America via Spain . . . He then set out for Russia, was detained at Halifax, released, and went on to Petrograd, where his considerable oratorical talents soon brought him into prominence.

～

While Ransome remained in Britain, he was in no position to provide day-by-day commentary on events in the Russian capital or to report the bloody street battles between Bolshevik troops and supporters of the Provisional Government which still raged in Moscow. But there were, all the same, compelling arguments for staying exactly where he was. One of Lenin's first acts as Chairman of the Council of People's Commissars, or 'Sovnarkom', as the new executive government of Russia was known, had been to close down virtually every hostile newspaper in Petrograd. With the telegraph office, the post office and the telephone exchange all in Bolshevik hands, the result was that in the first days of the coup, news arrived in unreliable fits and starts. Kerensky, it was announced, was leading 'loyal troops' against the capital. The civil service had refused to work for the Bolsheviks, and all the ministries had ground to a halt. Lenin's own party had turned against him, and half the Bolshevik Central Committee had resigned. Shortly afterwards, news arrived from neutral Copenhagen that Kerensky, his arch-rival Kornilov and the Cossack leader, General Alexei Kaledin, had retaken Petrograd and captured Lenin. But just as *The Times* and the *Morning Post* were claiming a resounding victory, the *Daily News* reported that Kerensky had, in fact, suffered a surprise defeat and disappeared into thin air.

There were advantages, then, for a foreign correspondent who found himself in London, far away from the confusion in Russia but armed with considerable first-hand knowledge of the immediate history of the Bolshevik coup. Lodging quietly at the Rembrandt Hotel in Knightsbridge, Ransome was ideally placed to bring his own experience to bear and to inform his readers as to the main causes of the current crisis, its character and its probable implications for Russia and the war. In the first two instances, at least, he could claim a virtually infallible record. As he had predicted, aggressive pursuit of the war against the wishes of the general populace had undermined the Provisional Government. Only peace could have frustrated Lenin's plans, and none had been forthcoming. The fact that Petrograd and Moscow were now in the hands of 'Extremists' was therefore entirely the fault of warmongers, both in Russia and in Britain, who had proven as greedy as their enemies in Berlin, and in view of Britain's constitution, vastly more hypocritical.

Addressing the all-important question of whether Russia would continue to fight or seek instead a separate peace with Germany, Ransome hastened to explain that only a failure on behalf of the Allies to learn from their recent mistakes would push Lenin into the arms of the Kaiser.

'As to the attitude of the Bolsheviks towards the war and towards the Allies,' he insisted,

it may be expressed in the formula (their own): 'We are opposed to separate peace with Imperialists of any nationality.' They do not want any peace which would leave Russia in the position of a sleeping partner of Germany. On the other hand, they are opposed to assisting what they regard as Imperialist war-aims on the part of ourselves. They will probably use their new position to press more insistently than their precursors for definition of Allied war-aims. If, however, we wish to force them into a more hostile attitude, and perhaps into a separate peace, we cannot do better than to follow the example of some of this morning's newspapers in loudly condemning what we do not understand.

Ransome did not waste time harking back to former articles in which, owing to circumstances beyond his control, he had painted the Bolsheviks blacker than they truly were. Now that the damage had been done, there was nothing to be gained by suggesting that the Soviet had been hijacked by paid-up German agents or that Russia's position would be substantially altered by Bolshevik rule. As word reached London of the collapse of Kerensky's offensive and the victory of the Red Guards in Moscow, he recommended caution. There could be no disputing that the Bolsheviks enjoyed a real majority, both in the most important regional Soviets and on the Central Committee of the All-Russian Soviet. Neither was it useful to place too much hope in the officer class and cavalry that might be rallied against them, since 'the bulk of the army is infantry, and the bulk of the infantry is Bolshevik'. Facts needed to be faced, and the fact was that the Bolsheviks were far stronger and better organized than reactionaries in England might hope. But while Ransome did not underestimate the new leaders of the Soviet, he would not allow them too much credit either. The Bolsheviks had come to power because Russia suffered. They had promised peace, land and bread, and if they failed to deliver these things they would be swept aside.

'The most important thing to be remembered in estimating the present situation in Russia,' he argued,

is that 'Bolshevism' is a tendency quite independent of the personality and doctrines of the Bolshevik leaders. When during the last few months in Petrograd we observed to each other that more and more people were turning Bolshevik, we meant not that they were embracing the principles of Socialism as expounded by Lenin, but simply that they were coming nearer to active and open hostility to the Government.

Ransome estimated the impact of the Bolsheviks in such a way as to leave the most important question firmly in the Allied court. Lenin's success had depended on Britain's failure to use its political influence to end the war. If the war continued, the situation could only deteriorate, with far-reaching consequences: anarchy in Russia, the collapse of the Eastern Front and a horde of German soldiers arriving shortly afterwards on England's doorstep. It was in Britain's interests, then, to step back from the brink, to abandon the propaganda of hypocrisy, hatred and revenge, and instead to broker a peace that would save all Europe from catastrophe. The only flaw in Ransome's argument was his failure to judge Lenin's determination to remove Russia from the war at the earliest opportunity or to gauge how the peace platform might be used by men dedicated not to national, but to international revolution.

Trotsky's first move as Commissar for Foreign Affairs had been to appeal to the masses for a general armistice, with or without the co-operation of their respective governments. Next, he published the secret treaties from the Tsar's imperial archives, signed by the Allies in 1915, carving up the territories which England, France, Russia and Italy – all capitalists, all oppressors – had hoped to colonize when Germany was defeated. Finally, as Lloyd George struggled to control the damage, it was announced in Ransome's own paper that negotiations with Berlin had already commenced. Nor did Trotsky envisage any obstacle in resolving them to his satisfaction. Diplomacy, he explained cheerfully to his comrades, was a vastly overrated profession. 'I shall issue a few revolutionary proclamations to the people of the world,' he had told them, 'then shut up shop.'

'If it is indeed true that the Bolshevik Soviet has offered peace to Germany,' Ransome mused,

it means that the Bolshevik leaders are themselves desperate. Up to a month ago the worst accusation which one Russian political party could throw at another was that it was in favour of a separate peace . . . It is, of course, hard to judge. Is it possible that the Soviet, in accordance with the Bolshevik public program, offered Germany and other Powers an armistice, and that Germany, with a view of dividing Russia from her Allies, has chosen to reply to an offer of peace which was never made?

~

Over the next four weeks, Ransome found no shortage of British liberals prepared to look on the Soviet government with a kindly eye, including Francis Hirst, whose magazine, *Common Sense*, would soon be publishing his views as definitive. Hirst, a fierce opponent of the war, was well connected with every mainstream party in Westminster, while his co-editor, Molly Hamilton, was a Fabian close to the Bloomsbury set. Ransome soon counted both as good friends, and it was possibly Hamilton who introduced him to Lenin's first unofficial representative in London, Maxim Litvinov, who ran his legation from a tiny office in Hampstead. Shortly afterwards, in late November, he met with Theodore Rothstein, brother-in-law to Zelda Kahan, who in 1902, when Ransome was eighteen years old, had attempted to convert him to socialism at the Yorkshire College in Leeds. By 1917, Rothstein, a close confidant of Lenin's, was both a senior executive of the British Socialist Party and a Bolshevik, which made it that much more astonishing that at present he was employed by the British War Office in the highly sensitive position of translator and interpreter. Ransome had sought him out with a view to gaining a letter of introduction to the Bolshevik leaders, and was not disappointed. 'Mr Ransome', Rothstein assured his comrades, 'is the only correspondent who has informed the English public of events in Russia *honestly*.'

Yet as rumours of separate peace talks with Germany began to harden, Ransome became increasingly reluctant to return to Russia at all. His entire family, with the exception of Geoffrey, had congregated at the Rembrandt Hotel. Relations had improved with Ivy. He had spent several happy weekends fishing, and thanks to strolls in Regent's Park, a healthy appetite and so many friendly, well-loved faces, had begun to feel his old self again. Set against this was the prospect of an indefinite period reporting a revolution which, according to any sensible appraisal of the situation, was heading rapidly towards a full-blown civil war. Why not, then, seek out alternative employment, something that would offer a steady income, security from conscription and a chance to influence Anglo-Russian affairs closer to home? A desk, for example, at the Foreign Office.

Much to Ransome's disappointment, no position was offered, but he had attempted, nonetheless, to make himself useful in other ways. Between 29 November and his departure for Russia a week later, he visited the Foreign Office on three separate occasions, and spoke at length with Lord Robert Cecil, Acland's successor as Permanent Undersecretary for Foreign Affairs. Recognizing that a return to Russia was now all but inevitable, he had suggested himself as unofficial envoy to the Soviet, or indeed to any other faction that might, given the extreme volatility of the present situation, come to power. Ransome was prepared to talk on behalf of England to the Bolsheviks, but as a promising leader for the counter-revolution, he recommended that Britain back General Kaledin, Ataman of the Don Cossacks, whom he had met and admired intensely. '. . . Mr Arthur Ransome gave me a very favourable account of him,' wrote Cecil in an internal memo on the 26th. 'He described him as a man of 48 of great energy and determination.'

Cecil approved of Kaledin, but after examining the relevant file, decided against Ransome as an envoy. 'If the long telegram to Petrograd of which the draft was approved today has not gone,' he told his secretary, 'please strike out the sentence referring to Mr Ransome. If it has gone please send an urgent telegram to Petrograd . . . In view of Athens telegram No. 2191 about Mr Ransome if the allegations made against him there are true he would obviously not be a suitable agent.'

Athens telegram No. 2191 has either been lost or is yet to be released, and so one can only conjecture that somebody – a fellow journalist or hostile Russian émigré – had already observed Ransome on friendlier terms with the 'Extremists' in Petrograd than he cared to admit. Over a year later, John Pollock of the *Morning Post* sent Whitehall a lengthy and damning description of Ransome's behaviour in the months before the coup. 'In the summer of 1917,' claimed Pollock, 'I met him in Petrograd, where he was publicly abusing the British government, and in particular Mr. Lloyd George, for setting up tyranny in England . . . In the Autumn of 1917 I heard that he was in close touch with the Bolshevik leaders.' Whether Pollock's statements were true or not, Ransome – armed with a pass to the Soviet Congress – had boasted to Edith of spirited conversations with the All-Russia Soviet Central Committee, where by August 1917 the Bolsheviks were well represented. Certainly he had been careful to prepare for every eventuality, and in London endeavoured to keep his options open. Speaking to Litvinov and Rothstein he had emphasized his sympathy for the Revolution, while at the Foreign Office he had offered General Kaledin as an avenging angel: a Bolshevik-hater who had promised his supporters a swift and savage purge of the entire Soviet establishment. Ransome's autobiography, meanwhile, records only his final interview with Lord Cecil, who addressed him on 3 December with almost paternal affection.

He stood in front of the fireplace, immensely tall, fantastically thin, his hawk-like head swinging forward at the end of a long arc formed by his body and legs. 'If you find, as you well may, that things have collapsed into chaos, what do you propose to do?' I told him that I should make no plans until I could see for myself what was happening, and that from London I could make no guess in all that fog of rumour where to look for the main thread of Russian history. He gave me his blessing, and made things easy for me, at least as far as Stockholm, by entrusting the diplomatic bag to me to deliver to the Legation there.

~

Tabitha remembered saying goodbye to her father at King's Cross on 5 December 1917. He was dressed in a Russian army great coat and an astrakhan hat, which made him look very serious and imposing. She was sad to see him go but recalled that Ransome himself seemed angry that Ivy had insisted on bidding farewell in person. Ransome remembered the scene very differently. The distress of leaving his daughter at the station had reduced him almost to tears, while the prospect of so much uncertainty ahead provided little comfort. It all contributed to a familiar state of mind in which England, of all the world, seemed much the best place to be.

'My Dear Mother,' he wrote from the train on his way up to Aberdeen,

... I am not at all keen on this trip this time, and if I had been offered a job would have been very glad to stay in England for a time. Russia is all very well, but too much Russia makes men mad, besides wearing them out.

So if Mrs Macmillan or anybody else does choose to exert themselves to get me into the FO, I'd be pleased and proud. Otherwise, I'll go on. Don't be worried and think I'm discontented. I am not. Only I would like a year in England. You see I've been away five years now pretty continually, pumping in Russia. And I'd like to be at home pumping out Russia for a bit.

Arriving in Stockholm on the 11th, Ransome delivered the diplomatic bag to the British embassy and accepted an invitation to lunch with the ambassador, Sir Esme Howard, whose children he enchanted with Russian fairy tales and Anansi stories. Howard warned that entry into Russia was at present impossible, and this view was seconded by Bernard Pares, who had also been in England, and arriving in Stockholm some days before Ransome, had unsuccessfully petitioned the head of the Bolshevik legation, Comrade Vorovsky, for a visa. The situation in Russia was deteriorating fast. Splinters of the old imperial army had formed themselves into counter-revolutionary factions, loosely termed the 'Whites', each under their own generals. On the Eastern Front, the Russian commander-in-chief, General Dukhonin, had been torn to pieces by his own men for refusing to implement an armistice with Germany, while Trotsky, it was whispered, had brought back the guillotine. With all this in mind, it was highly unlikely that the Bolsheviks would permit foreign journalists to stir up trouble when they extended so little freedom to their own.

Pares finally gave up on his visa and went back to England, travelling round the world to join the Whites in Siberia. But Ransome was not, like Pares, a correspondent for the right-wing *Telegraph*. He had no intention of stirring up trouble for the Bolsheviks, and besides, he had an ace up his sleeve: Rothstein's kindly letter of introduction. Ransome's full-length interview with Vorovsky was wired to the *Daily News* on 19 December, instantly establishing his reputation as a leading authority on the Soviet.

'You have lived in Russia long enough', Vorovsky reminded Ransome, 'to know that Russia is not in a condition to carry on a war. Russia must make peace. It is for the Allies to choose whether that peace is to be a separate or a general peace.'

Vorovsky declined to argue with England as a nation. National unity was a divisive fantasy of the bourgeoisie. Instead, he drew a careful distinction between the rulers and the oppressed masses. The Revolution's quarrel was not with the English working class, but only with the British government, which clung so obstinately to the destruction of

Germany. The Bolsheviks, claimed Vorovsky, did not wish to destroy anybody. Destruction was not in the interests of democracy. They sought peace with Germany because the English had forced them to do so, an irony he bitterly regretted. As for the death penalty, it was pure nonsense about the guillotine, but in view of the Dukhonin affair, some deterrent was necessary to 'prevent worse things'. 'Continual sabotage on the part of the bourgeoisie', Vorovsky offered sadly, 'may exasperate the mass of the people to such an extent as to carry them beyond the control of their leaders . . .'

Ransome, who had found Vorovsky well-educated, amiable and cosmopolitan, accepted these views without protest, just as he accepted the banning of the Kadet Party, thus effectively ending his friendship with Ariadna Tyrkova and Harold Williams. Tyrkova now lived under constant fear of arrest, while Williams had been blacklisted by the Bolshevik press bureau. Speaking to Bruce Lockhart, who would arrive in Petrograd in one month's time at the head of an unofficial British diplomatic mission, Williams warned that the Bolsheviks required peace in order to make war on their own people. But to Ransome, who had spent one of the happiest summers of his life at Vergezha in 1915, he offered no advice at all. He never spoke to him again.

~

Ransome picked up his visa from Vorovsky the morning after the interview, dined with Howard that evening and arrived in Petrograd on Christmas Day. In his articles he described a frozen city, choked with mounds of unswept snow 'as hard as ice bergs' and policed by armed patrols standing at street corners. Blaming reports of widespread disorder on the 'willful misrepresentations' of the bourgeois press, he assured nervous Englishmen that the Russian capital was more peaceful than it had been since the Tsar. 'For the first time since the Revolution the Government in Russia is based on real force. The people may not like the Bolsheviks, but they obey them with startling alacrity.'

Other sources suggest a less salutary picture: mass strikes both in the factories and the civil service; chronic food and fuel shortages; and following the creation of Felix Dzerzhinsky's 'Cheka' – forerunner to the KGB – a sharp increase in the use of state-sponsored terror to coerce civil obedience. Ransome, however, was determined to make the best of things, and having re-installed himself at Glinka Street, wasted no time in calling on the Bolshevik headquarters at Smolny, where within three days he had secured a second interview, this time with Leon Trotsky himself.

Today, the names of three Bolshevik leaders are familiar to anybody with the smallest knowledge of European history: Vladimir Lenin, Leon Trotsky and Joseph Stalin. But in late 1917, Lenin was still an obscure figure in the West, while Stalin, the future 'Red Tsar', though already a senior member of the Bolshevik Central Committee, was virtually unknown outside Russia. Trotsky, on the other hand, was notorious. As Commissar for Foreign Affairs, it was Trotsky who had published the secret treaties, called on the workers of the world to take democracy into their own hands, and who now supervised the Bolshevik diplomatic mission which, quartered in a small Belorussian town called Brest-Litovsk, was deciding Russia's future in the war. With no previous experience of diplomacy, it was Trotsky's belief that surrender to Germany would prove unnecessary. Properly handled, Brest-Litovsk would serve as a grandstand for propaganda: an opportunity to stir up mutiny amongst German troops and revolution in German cities. Once the Soviet was established in Berlin, the rest of Europe would fall like dominoes. Nothing seemed more probable. Nine months ago, the Revolution had been a dream, while Lenin could count his loyal supporters on his fingers. Trotsky himself still owed money on the furniture for his tiny apartment in the New York Bronx. Theatrical, ingenious and charismatic, he had already achieved the impossible and looked forward to running rings around the German high command. He welcomed Ransome with the utmost cordiality.

'I saw M. Trotsky by appointment today at Smolny Institute,' ran Ransome's article:

At the end of a long corridor of what was once a convent school for girls I found a door with a piece of paper fastened on it with the words, 'People's Commissary for Foreign Affairs'. Beside it stood a sentinel, who was a workman from the Red Guard in ordinary clothes, with a rifle and bandolier over his overcoat. In an anteroom one of Mr Trotsky's secretaries, a young officer, told me Mr Trotsky was expecting me.

Going into an inner room, unfurnished except for a writing table, two chairs and a telephone, I found the man who, in the name of the Proletariat, is practically the dictator of all Russia.

He has a striking head, a very broad, high forehead above lively eyes, a fine cut nose and a small cavalier beard. Though I had heard him speak before, this was the first time I had seen him face to face. I got an impression of extreme efficiency and definite purpose. In spite of all that is said against him by his enemies, I do not think that he is a man to do anything except from a conviction that it is the best thing to be done for the revolutionary cause that is in his heart. He showed considerable knowledge of English politics . . .

I asked him for an explanation of the belief in Russia's strength which led him to demand [of the Germans] in the name of the Russian Labour Government more generous terms than at the present moment any other Russian party would have dared to ask.

He said, 'Russia is strong in that her Revolution was the starting point of a peace movement in Europe. A year ago it seemed that only militarism could end the war. It is now clear that the war will be decided by social rather than political pressure. It is to the Russian Revolution that German democracy looks, and it is the recognition of that fact that compels the German Government to accept the Russian principles as a basis for negotiation.'

I asked whether then M. Trotsky considered the German offer as a joint victory of the Russian and German democracies.

He replied, 'Not of Russian and German democracy alone, but of the democratic movement generally. The movement is visible everywhere. Austria and Hungary are on the point of revolt, and not they alone. Every Government in Europe is feeling the pressure of democracy from below. The German attitude merely means that the German Government is wiser than most, and more realistic. It recognizes the real factors and is moved by them. The Germans have been forced by democratic pressure to throw aside their grandiose plans of conquest and to accept a peace in which there is neither conqueror nor conquered . . .'

~

Ransome's article, published on 31 December, made such a powerful impression in London that the Foreign Secretary, Arthur Balfour, telegrammed the embassy in Petrograd to enquire if its author might after all offer his services as an unofficial agent, communicating British views to the Soviet and vice versa. It was the beginning of a vexing relationship with the British authorities that would last, on and off, for over a decade. But Whitehall was not entirely to blame for the difficulty. As Ransome entrenched himself at Smolny and acquainted himself with other unofficial missions from the West, an unexpected complication arose: he fell in love.

The interview with Trotsky had taken place in Room 67 of the Smolny Institute, a building so vast that couriers ferried documents back and forth on bicycles. And yet Trotsky's office was an intimate affair. At one end, sectioned off by a screen, were his night quarters: an iron bed and side table; a wooden chair and a small bedside rug to save his feet from the chill of the bare boards. At the business end of the room stood his desk with a telephone, stenograph and two typewriters: the first was for the commissar; the second was for Evgenia Petrovna Shelepina, a young woman recently recruited from the Ministry of Labour as Trotsky's personal secretary.

Evgenia was taking minutes when Ransome interviewed Trotsky on 28 December, but they did not speak privately until that evening, when he visited the offices of the Commissariat of Foreign Affairs in a building facing the Winter Palace. Wandering unchallenged through the corridors, he had heard a distant, cheerful discussion, and following the sound of voices came at last to a room with people in it, one of them instantly recognizable. Ransome in turn was recognized, and when he explained that he was looking for a censor to stamp his telegram, instead of being chastised for the lateness of the hour he was offered a kindly greeting. 'This', he gratefully recalled, 'was Evgenia, the tall jolly girl whom later I was to marry and to whom I owe the happiest years of my life.'

Together, they had found the censor nodding off as a pot of potatoes, roaring away on a Primus, sent up a cloud of black smoke. Evgenia had been appalled, and scolding the man for his negligence, deftly emptied the contents onto a sheet of official Foreign Office paper.

'Thank goodness! They've only just begun to brown. They're still edible,' she said. 'You must try not to let the water boil right out or there will soon be a hole burned through the bottom of your pot.'

She introduced me to the old man and explained what I needed. He went off rather uncertainly to look for a rubber stamp with which to mark his willingness not to prevent the sending of my telegram, and we went back to wait for him. Her sister was there. The old man came in and stamped my telegram. The two girls asked me to stay and drink a glass of tea . . .

In this 'odd accidental manner', Ransome explained, he gained the confidence of his hosts and a view behind the scenes 'such as no other foreigner enjoyed'.

13

Bolsheviks

Sitting down on 30 December to write to his mother, Ransome hardly knew where to begin.

'Things here are such as to keep me most frantically busy. I wish to goodness I had been able to get here before. It's too late to do very much good now; but there is a lot that must be done unless we are to throw up our hands and leave Russia to the Germans.'

In the space of twenty-four hours, he had met with 'eighteen or nineteen folk, ranging from the current dictator of Russia [referring to Trotsky], to our ambassador through pretty much every shade of contradictory Russian opinion'. Amongst the foreign missions gathered in Petrograd, the French were taking the 'maddest because the angriest view', while the Americans were the most sympathetic. On the day after the Trotsky interview, Ransome had dined with Colonel Raymond Robins, head of the American Red Cross, and Edgar Sisson, former editor of the *Chicago Tribune*. Robins, he concluded, was by far the superior specimen. As an evangelical Christian, an Alaskan gold prospector and straight-talking Chicago progressive, his politics were no more compatible with Bolshevism than those of Woodrow Wilson, whom he counted amongst his personal friends. But Robins had seen the Bolsheviks at work in the regional soviets. No other government, he believed, was capable of maintaining order at home while opposing German interests. If the Allies wanted an Eastern Front, they should supply the money and arms. If they wanted peace, it would have to be a general peace. By the time Ransome returned to Petrograd, Robins was on excellent terms with Trotsky and Lenin, whom he considered men of courage and integrity. Brest-Litovsk was a crisis of the Allies' own making. If they wanted Russia to sign a separate treaty with the Kaiser, all they had to do was blow hot air.

Thanks to the Americans, Ransome's articles were soon appearing in the *New York Times*, substantially increasing his salary and providing him with millions of new readers across the Atlantic. At the British embassy, he reported directly to the ambassador, or to Major Thornhill of British intelligence. He became a regular fixture at Smolny and the Commissariat of Foreign Affairs, one of the privileged few permitted to witness the building of the new regime from the inside. Within two weeks of his arrival, he had interviewed Trotsky three times, was receiving daily bulletins from Evgenia and had become an intimate friend of Trotsky's number two at the commissariat, a Polish Jew named Karl Radek, recently installed as the Bolshevik chief of Western propaganda.

Born in Lvov, barely a year Ransome's junior, Radek had joined the Second International as a law student in Krakow and counted Felix Dzerzhinsky, founder of the Cheka, amongst his earliest political mentors. In 1913, he had been expelled from the German Social Democratic Party for libel and embezzlement, and in 1914, fled to Sweden to avoid conscription. Here, after considerable wrangling, he joined the Bolsheviks, and in April 1917, thanks to his contacts in Berlin, helped negotiate the so-called 'sealed train' that carried Lenin into Russia. However, as an Austro-Hungarian citizen, Radek had been permitted to travel only as far as Stockholm, and it was here, at Lenin's request, that he founded the 'International Bureau', the Bolshevik headquarters in western Europe. In December, handing over to Vorovsky, he had entered Russia for the first time, joined Lenin's Central Committee, and in addition to transforming the Commissariat of Foreign Affairs into a gigantic printing press, became a vital component in the diplomatic talks at Brest-Litovsk. There was no greater linguist in the party, and no sharper wit. Sly, ambitious and mercurial, he was the Bolshevik Puck or Rumpelstiltskin, a spirit of pure mischief, and Ransome adored him.

Ransome's autobiography recalls his first meeting with Radek as a complete coincidence. Expecting a difficult journey from Stockholm and deciding to travel light, he had left a box of non-essential miscellanea with Vorovsky in Sweden marked 'Ransome, *Daily News*' to be forwarded to the Press Bureau at the Commissariat of Foreign Affairs. Vorovsky had kindly complied, but when the package arrived, Radek, with typical lack of scruple, had torn it open, and finding inside 'a Shakespeare, a folding chessboard and chessmen, and a mixed collection of books on elementary navigation, fishing, chess and folklore', had instantly demanded to meet the correspondent 'who was interested in subjects that seemed incompatible'. Thanks to this 'bit of good fortune', Ransome was soon on tea-drinking terms with most of the Bolshevik leaders.

'Radek had been born in Poland', he recalled,

and spoke Polish (badly as his wife used to say, because he had talked too much German in exile), Russian (with a remarkably Polish accent) and French with the greatest difficulty. He always talked Russian with me but loved to drag in sentences from English books, which I sometimes annoyed him by being slow to recognize. 'Marley was as dead as a doornail' [*A Christmas Carol*] was one of his favourites and he loved to apply it to politicians and to political programmes that had been outstripped by events. He continually quoted from Shakespeare. He had an extraordinary memory and an astonishingly detailed knowledge of English politics . . . We fell easily into the habit of 'putting our cards on the table', inviting contradictions, and this, in 1917 and 1918 was a good way of clearing our heads.

In his letters and notebooks, Ransome boasted of his new friend as one might boast of a brilliant schoolmate. Here was Karl Radek, his pockets bursting with newspapers, reciting 'To be, or not to be' to a pair of illiterate Lettish riflemen. Here he was again, puffing on his pipe in a brand-new chocolate-coloured military uniform, distributing incendiary pamphlets to German soldiers right under the noses of their generals. In the game of diplomatic push-me pull-you at Smolny, Ransome supplied Radek with news from the British embassy and expatriate community, while Radek, switching his pipe dextrously from one corner of his mouth to the other, honoured Ransome with party gossip, merciless caricatures of every Bolshevik leader from Trotsky down and a fluent analysis of the current political situation.

In Radek, Ransome found an alter ego. They were like a pair of brothers, both writers, both voracious readers, both self-proclaimed bohemians with a mortal scorn for flat-footed bureaucracy. But if one were to ask who had the better of the relationship, one only has to observe that on Ransome's second visit to the British embassy, Colonel Knox – who made no distinction between Bolsheviks and Bolshevik apologists – had threatened to have him 'shot like a dog'. Ransome's articles reflected the party line so accurately that there was little to choose between them but style, while as his relationship with Evgenia deepened, so any change of heart or sudden epiphany became that much more improbable. In his autobiography, she is pictured either as a distant functionary, handing out official releases, or as guardian of his personal happiness; never both at the same time. They had grown together gradually, as ordinary people do, strolling in the evenings, taking supper at the rooms she shared with her sister at the commissariat's headquarters in the centre of town. Once, he recalled, she had slipped when boarding a tram, and clutching the rail, was dragged full length along the track, so that if her grip had failed she would have been cut in two.

'Those few horrible seconds during which she lay almost under the advancing wheel possibly determined both of our lives. But it was not until afterwards that we admitted anything of the kind to one another.'

Over forty years later, Ransome remembered the decisive moment at which he realized he was in love: a mixture of terror and relief over which he had no power whatsoever. But as he snatched his future wife from beneath the wheels of history – the war, the Revolution, the fatal passage of circumstance which Lenin had declared indifferent to the fate of any single individual – the possibility of separating his private from his professional affairs remained as remote as ever.

~

Evgenia was born on 10 April 1894 in the imperial town of Gatchina, about twenty-five miles south-west of Petrograd. Both her grandparents had been peasants, but her father, Pyotr Ivanovitch, though born a serf, had died a minor nobleman. Following emancipation in 1861, he trained as a scribe at the City Hospital in Vitebsk, before serving in the army and the St Petersburg police department, where he translated the dubious scrawl of his superiors into exquisite copperplate. By 1885, he had been promoted to assistant manager of the Imperial Hospital in Gatchina, with the title 'Office Clerk of the First Class' – the lowest tier in the bureaucratic table of ranks. From his study window he had looked over the beautiful grounds of the Imperial Palace, landscaped in the English style by Catherine the Great for her lover, Prince Orlov. He died in 1912, leaving his third wife, Maria Alexeevna, with a small state pension, a number of useful contacts and a financial struggle on her hands.

Evgenia was the eldest child of six, with two sisters and three brothers: Iroida, Serafima, Viktor, Roman and Gleb. The year after her father's death, at the age of nineteen, she had gone to Petrograd to study at the Stenography College on Nevsky Prospekt and was soon working as a typist at the Ministry of Transport. When the Bolsheviks took power in November, her colleagues had crowded the windows to watch the soldiers and workers pouring over the Liteiny Bridge, but when the ministry came out on strike against the Bolsheviks, Evgenia had refused to join their protest. Back in Gatchina, she and Iroida, the next eldest, had a friend called Mara, daughter of the local chief of police and secretary to the Gatchina branch of the Bolshevik Party. Through Mara they had gained an introduction to Karl Radek's wife, Rosa, and through Rosa to Trotsky. Over the following months, thanks to Rosa and her husband, most of

Evgenia's family would also find work with the party adminis-tration: Iroida as a secretary; Roman as a courier; Serafima as a journalist with the Press Bureau; and Evgenia's mother, Maria Alexeevna, as a 'linen keeper' at the Lux Hotel in Moscow. Co-operation of this kind offered protection from the police, the power to requisition goods from the bourgeoisie – food, cloth-ing, lodgings – and for Evgenia a heavy obligation to her spon-sors. Only Viktor would disgrace himself, joining the Whites in Siberia, so that for a few brief months in 1920, he and his brother would fight on opposite sides of the civil war.

When Evgenia first met Trotsky, she was so frightened she hardly knew how to speak to him. Under the old regime such a magnificent personage would have been addressed as 'Your High Excellency', but Trotsky had done away with the old regime for good. Evgenia tried 'Comrade Trotsky', but he laughed at her and called her 'Comrade Shelepina'. After that she always called him Lev Davidovitch, and settled in quite comfortably. One of her first tasks had been to organize his office and find him a type-writer that actually functioned. It pained her deeply that he should have to think of such things himself, and she had quickly taken him under her wing, arranging his furniture, chaperoning his sixteen-year-old daughter and relieving him of any visitors or paperwork she considered beneath his dignity. At twenty-three years old, standing well over six foot tall in her favourite pair of high-heeled shoes (shoes and taxis were her passion), Evgenia soon enjoyed an influence which she would never have believed possible as a humble typist at the Ministry of Transport. When she walked past, soldiers and sailors leapt to attention. When she went out on some official errand to deliver vital documents or a message by word of mouth, she was assigned a car with her own chauffeur. In the American camp, she was known as 'The Big Girl', because, as Edgar Sisson so acutely observed, 'she *was* a big girl'. But as assistant to a man whose reputation rivalled Lenin's as the governing genius of the Revolution, she was rarely taken for granted. She typed up most of Trotsky's private corre-spondence, including his internal memos and notes to foreign delegates. She organized his schedule. On any matter of urgent business, she could speak to him directly, and during the final stages of negotiations with the Germans, had made herself so indispensable that she was summoned to Brest-Litovsk.

Where Ivy was all whimsy, Evgenia was tough and literal-minded. Where Ivy, who boasted her descent from the Portuguese aristocracy, was bourgeois, Evgenia was descended from peasants. At Smolny, Ransome found a young woman who resembled, in many particulars, the ideal north-country house-wife, being shrewd, generous, quick to anger and impatient of all nonsense. When he had dared to raise the possibility that his regard for her might present a conflict of interest with his com-mitment to the British Foreign Secretary, she laughed him to scorn. The subject was rarely spoken of again.

Within days of Ransome's arrival in Petrograd, it was com-mon knowledge amongst the small and often eccentric commu-nity then doing the work of the Allied embassies that the correspondent for the *Daily News* had 'unusual channels of information', and his influence grew accordingly. In England his telegrams were read with interest by Lloyd George's War Cabinet, while in the States his articles made front-page news. Delighted with a series of scoops that had left every other corres-pondent standing, the *Daily News* rewarded him with fulsome praise, a sizeable cash bonus (£50) and a picnic hamper full of sugar, chocolate, tinned delicacies and his favourite navy plug tobacco, which Ransome distributed generously amongst his friends (Radek was naked without a pipe). Journalism allowed him to move with extraordinary facility between Smolny and the embassy, to conduct a passionate love affair and still have time to translate fairy tales: *The Little Cattle, The Two Brothers, The Holy Blacksmith*. But luck of this kind came at a price.

Before the November coup, Ransome had hung his hat almost daily at the Anglo-Russian Bureau, where Hugh Walpole, Bernard Pares and Harold Williams had attempted to build bridges between Britain and the Kerensky government. But the bureau had been funded by the British to serve British interests.

Karl Radek, by contrast, supervised two highly controversial organizations: the Press Bureau and the International Bureau for Revolutionary Propaganda. These curious institutions were funded by Smolny and were unequivocally devoted to Bolshevik interests, the fruit of twenty years underground in which the party had operated almost entirely through newspapers. Radek himself spoke a dozen languages, and as a journalist was surpassed only by Trotsky.

At the Commissariat of Foreign Affairs – the vast departmental headquarters just opposite the Winter Palace – brass-buttoned porters removed the galoshes of foreign correspondents with the same reverence they had once attended grand dukes and duchesses. Long tables on either side of the columned halls groaned beneath the weight of revolutionary pamphlets. Pro-Bolshevik articles were penned for the Allied press, while half a million copies a day of Radek's paper *The Torch* were printed and loaded onto Red Cross trains and distributed behind enemy lines like bundled sticks of dynamite. Ransome's acquaintances at the International Bureau included John Reed, author of *Ten Days that Shook the World*, Reed's wife, Louise Bryant, Boris Reinstein, who brought some of the refinement of American advertising to Bolshevik political slogans, and Ransome's only remaining colleague in the English camp, Morgan Philips Price of the *Manchester Guardian*, whom he had known at Rugby. Louise Bryant recalled the excitement of those first months in her memoir: 'What grand plans for a revolt in the Central Empires were hatched in those days! What magnificent hopes to end the war, to bring peace to the world by a rising of the workers.'

And yet while Price – who frankly declared himself a Bolshevik – spoke fondly of the good work he and Ransome had done together during the Revolution, Ransome erased any memory of the International Bureau. Karl Radek was a simple press officer, as well as a close and inspiring friend. Colonel Raymond Robins had fought tirelessly to counteract 'the stream of tendentious stories sent home by other Americans', and had set a magnificent example to his compatriots. Figuring his own relationship to the

Soviet government, Ransome claimed to have associated with the Bolsheviks in much the same way as he had once associated with artists in Paris: 'not as a rival painter but as a mere writer who was very much interested in what they were doing. My complete lack of any political past was a help, not a hindrance, and I was soon getting a view of what was happening from much nearer than any regular journalist or politician could approach.'

He celebrated the Russian New Year with the Trotsky children, the Shelepinas and the Radeks, noting with amusement that Trotsky's boy – barely ten years old and fully armed – had frightened his chauffeur half to death by firing off his pistol. Later, when the girls had gone to bed, he stayed up with Radek and a Kronstadt sailor, drinking and smoking. He had been treated almost as a member of the family.

Professor Cyril Ransome shortly before his death in 1897
Edith Ransome
Ransome's younger brother, Geoffrey, after enlisting in 1914
From left to right, Ransome's three sisters: Kitty, Cecily and Joyce

Ransome during his first year at Rugby, clutching a cat to his chest

Ransome in his Bohemian days, smoking a clay pipe on one of his country holidays

Edward Thomas, the most talented writer of Ransome's immediate circle, who died on active service in 1917

Lascelles Abercrombie, founder of the Dymock community of poets, whom Ezra Pound once challenged to a duel

W. G. Collingwood and Edith Collingwood, Ransome's surrogate parents
Dora and Barbara Collingwood. In 1929, Dora's children would inspire *Swallows and Amazons*

Ivy Walker around the time of her marriage to Ransome in 1909

Ransome and Tabitha dancing down a lane in 1917

Ransome and Ivy standing outside court following the Douglas trial in April 1913.
Ransome fled the country two weeks later

Ransome, 1916, in the press corps uniform required when visiting the Eastern Front

Evgenia Petrovna Shelepina in her winter furs

The Shelepina family in 1908. From top left: unknown, Evgenia, Elena (half-sister), Maria Alexeevna holding Seraphima, Pyotr Ivanovitch holding Gleb, Iroida holding Roman, Victor

Evgenia and her sister Iroida, with a grass snake

Evgenia, 'The Big Girl', with a Bolshevik officer at the Commissariat for Foreign Affairs

Harold Williams, husband of Ariadna Tyrkova and Ransome's first political mentor in Russia

Karl Radek, Lenin's propaganda chief and Ransome's closest friend amongst the Bolsheviks

Ransome dismounting a train in Soviet Russia

Three of Ransome's boats, anticlockwise from top: *Racundra*, *Slug* and *Swallow*

Ransome in 1932 with the Altounyan family. From top left: Susan, Taqui, Ransome, Roger, Barbara (the youngest), Evgenia

The Shelepina sisters in Moscow, 1972. From left: Evgenia, Seraphima, Iroida
Ransome the writer

14

Brest-Litovsk

On 1 January 1918, the *Daily News* published a scathing attack on British foreign policy entitled 'Mr Trotsky and the Germans – Words of Warning to the Allies.'

'I wonder', wrote Ransome,

whether the English people realize how great is the matter now at stake and how near we are to witnessing a separate peace between Russia and Germany, which would be a defeat for German democracy in its own country, besides ensuring the practical enslavement of all Russia.

A separate peace will be a victory, not for Germany, but for the military caste in Germany. It may mean much more than the neutrality of Russia. If we make no move it seems possible that the Germans will ask the Russians to help them in enforcing the Russian peace terms on the Allies . . .

Hours after Ransome had threatened England with a possible German–Soviet alliance, he was summoned to Smolny to hear that negotiations with Germany had, in fact, been broken off. The Kaiser's military representatives were demanding Poland, Lithuania, Courland and a huge treasure chest by way of reparations. The Revolution could not possibly concede to such terms and now waited to hear from its so-called allies. Would Britain and America listen to reason and join a general peace conference in Stockholm? Or would they permit Russia to be invaded, colonized and systematically ransacked, with calamitous consequences on the Western Front? Trotsky hoped that the bellicose capitalists of the Entente, though hardly likely to extend the hand of friendship to the Soviet, would at least act in their own best interests.

Thanks to Ransome and Colonel Robins, who had attended the same meeting, word of the Soviet rupture with Germany reached Britain and America within a matter of hours. In Washington, the news contributed to the timing of President

Wilson's Fourteen Points, which set out Allied war aims for the first time, laid the foundation for the future League of Nations and described Russia's situation as 'helpless, even hopeless'. In London, Lloyd George made an impassioned speech in the House of Commons, maintaining that he 'earnestly desired peace' and had no wish to destroy Germany or deprive her of her colonies. But no move was made to convene an international peace conference or to extend any practical help to the Soviet. Far from it. On 2 January, at a meeting of the British War Cabinet, it was noted that Ransome was 'in full sympathy with the Bolsheviks', while with regard to Trotsky, who had clearly painted himself into a corner, the British government had no intention of 'extricating him from his difficulties'.

Two days later, the *Daily News* published Trotsky's impassioned appeal to the German proletariat, titled 'The Mask Torn Off':

German soldiers and workmen, the world is with you. If you do not compel your government to renounce the peace proposals which it had the audacity to announce to the Russian Revolution, your own blood will be spent to an infinite extent! Up proletariats, up soldiers of Germany, and join the revolutionary struggle against the continuation of the war, and against the Governments which are betraying the masses . . . If you wish for a general peace, make the people listen to reason. Long live the international workers' and peasants' revolution!

On 7 January, the British ambassador, Sir George Buchanan, packed his bags and sailed for England, leaving only a skeleton staff at the embassy. Meanwhile, at an emergency meeting of the Bolshevik Central Committee, Lenin advocated unconditional surrender to the German terms, but met with stubborn opposition. In vain he explained that the Soviet was defenceless, that enemies threatened on every side: the Whites in newly independent Finland, the Cossacks in Rostov-on-Don, the Kadets and counter-revolutionaries agitating quite openly in Petrograd. 'The bourgeoisie has to be throttled,' he implored his comrades, 'and for that we need both hands free.' Only Stalin, Zinoviev and three others agreed with him. Most, including Radek, sided with

Nikolai Bukharin, a prominent internationalist who denounced the scheme as a betrayal of the Revolution, both in Russia and abroad. Indeed, Ransome's dream of a glorious Soviet offensive might very possibly have been realized had not Trotsky, fearing a mutiny within the army, suggested a third way. Scraping a majority with a reluctant Lenin, he proposed no war and no surrender. He would return to Brest-Litovsk and spin out the talks for as long as possible. The Soviet had not signed the Allied treaties binding Russia to war. If the Germans advanced against a peaceable country, they would lose all credibility in the eyes of their people and the world.

Ransome's articles over the next ten days read like a jigsaw puzzle drawn from two separate and ill-matched boxes: one picturing a pro-Allied effort against Germany; the other a thinly veiled translation of Trotsky's broader agenda. 'Democracy from below' became 'democracy'. Revolutionaries were 'idealists', while Soviet pacifism vied with hints of a Soviet–German alliance. To be so close to a gang of cut-throats who longed to save the world was so exciting that Ransome sometimes forgot he was writing news at all, confusing the Bolsheviks with *Treasure Island* pirates or knights of the round table. Indeed, between Marxist doctrine, patriotism and his growing fondness for Evgenia, Ransome found the international question so absorbing that it took a series of mass demonstrations to draw his attention back to immediate events unfolding in Petrograd, where the future of Russian democracy was about to be decided.

On 18 January, the Tauride Palace, former seat of the Provisional Government, was due to host the first meeting of the Constituent Assembly – the same Constituent Assembly which Ransome had originally planned as the final chapter in his grand history of the Revolution. Promised by Miliukov in March 1917, and delayed by each successive Provisional Cabinet, the Assembly offered Russia its first parliament based on direct, equal, universal and secret suffrage in its history. Elections had finally been held in November, giving the Socialist Revolutionaries, the party of the rural peasants, a majority of more than two to one over the Bolsheviks. But Lenin, who had considered it unwise to prevent the ballot, was quick to undo his error. The Soviet, declared the Bolshevik press, was already the longest-standing government since the abdication of the Tsar, and had moved decisively to place power in the hands of the people. The banks had been nationalized, as had the mining sector and the munitions factories. The bourgeoisie no longer lorded it over their servants but had themselves been set to work. At Brest-Litovsk, Trotsky was struggling to deliver peace in the teeth of opposition from every other party. Who, then, was now demonstrating for the right to a Constituent Assembly? Were the Socialist Revolutionaries not the party of Kerensky? And was Kerensky not the man who had betrayed every promise to the workers and the soldiers? What was the Constituent Assembly, in essence, but a Trojan Horse to reintroduce the Kerenskyites and the Kornilovites by the back door? It was a counter-revolutionary, German-backed conspiracy to defraud the proletariat, a transparent bid to resurrect the old regime. But the natural leaders of the Revolution would not stand idly by and watch the people robbed of their freedom. If the Constituent Assembly challenged the authority of the Soviet, it would discover who held the whip hand.

'In five days' time the Constituent Assembly meets,' wrote Ransome on 13 January:

It now seems probable that it will contain a majority against the Bolsheviks by some other necessarily weaker government [which] will offer the German generals an antagonist infinitely less dangerous to them than Trotsky. Efforts are being made to secure street demonstrations in the Constituent Assembly's favour. If these efforts are successful, the result will be anarchy, for which the Germans could wish nothing better.

~

By the beginning of 1918, the one-party state envisaged in Lenin's definitive 1902 manifesto *What Is to Be Done?* had already emerged in embryo. The November coup had removed Kerensky's enfeebled Cabinet by force. The bourgeois press had been gagged. Martial law had been imposed, and from within the Soviet, the Bolshevik-dominated Council of People's Commissars ruled Petrograd as virtual dictators. Only the Left Socialist Revolutionaries – a radical splinter of Kerensky's party – were included in the new Soviet executive and the Cheka, and then only as a fig leaf. In consequence, all that remained to Lenin's opponents was the sacred institution of the Constituent Assembly, with a clear democratic mandate to replace the Soviet as the universally elected government of Russia.

In the weeks running up to the Assembly's inauguration, the Right Socialist Revolutionaries had launched a frontal assault on Lenin's foreign policy, accusing the Bolsheviks of opening Russia's borders to the Germans and of preparing the ground for an international class war: 'a holy war, which prostrate Russia, deprived of her army by their very efforts, shall wage against the entire world'. By way of an answer, the Bolsheviks arrested virtually every member of the Committee for the Defence of the Assembly with the exception of those who had wisely gone into hiding. Meanwhile, the Bolshevik press issued proclamations against 'counter-revolutionary' demonstrations: 'Under the watchword, "All Power to the Constituent Assembly" is hidden the watchword, "Down with the Soviets". This will be a demonstration of strikers, the bourgeoisie and the servers of the bourgeoisie, who are hiding under the names of the Right Social Revolutionaries.'

As machine and field guns were set up at Smolny, Lenin drafted his own constitution, to be read as the first item on the Assembly's bill of fare. The 'Declaration of the Rights of the Working Man' demanded that all key points on the Bolshevik manifesto – the nationalization of land and of industry, labour conscription, the arming of the working class and the disarming of the bourgeoisie – be ratified without exception, including the supremacy of the Soviet itself. The Constituent Assembly, elected on the basis of 'party lists' drawn up before the November coup,

was obsolete and without real authority of its own. If it confessed this openly, it would be permitted to continue as a conven-
tion of harmless eccentrics. If not, the Soviet would know what
to do about it.

On the eve of the Assembly's opening, Ransome had celebrated his thirty-fourth birthday, and the next morning, in company with Edgar Sisson, dropped by at the Commissariat of
Foreign Affairs to pick up his pass to the Tauride Palace. The
marble halls, usually bustling with party officials and journalists,
were completely deserted, save for Evgenia and Rosa Radek,
huddled up in furs against the cold and taking their breakfast in
the magnificent apartment once inhabited by Miliukov. As
Ransome made them a fire, they tried to persuade him to stay
where he was. He and Sisson would have a dull day of it, they
said. The whole business, in any case, was a fait accompli.

Shortly after noon, a peaceful demonstration in favour of the
Assembly was fired on by Bolshevik snipers hiding on the
rooftops, killing fifteen and wounding over a hundred. It was the
first time such a thing had happened since the days of the Tsar,
and Maxim Gorky, writing for his paper *Novaya Zhizn*, did not
hesitate in comparing it to the Bloody Sunday massacre of 1905.

I ask the 'People's' Commissars, among whom there must be decent
and sensible people: Do they understand that . . . they will inevitably
end up strangling the entire Russian democracy and ruining all the con-
quests of the revolution? Do they understand this? Or do they think, on
the contrary, that 'either we have power or everyone and everything
will perish?'

Ransome had not witnessed the slaughter. When the shots
were fired, he had been taking his lunch with Karl Radek and
Evgenia in Trotsky's office in Smolny. He returned to the Tauride
Palace just before seven, threading his way through the ranks of
armed sailors, artillery and field kitchens to take his place in the
gallery set aside for foreign diplomats. Below him, the hall was
arranged in much the same way as the American House of
Representatives, with red leather chairs for the four hundred or
so delegates fanning out from the presidium. Red banners circled

the auditorium, which resounded to the tramp of booted feet. The congress would take place within a 'ring of steel'. Even the ushers were Red Guards.

Ransome never mentioned the dissolution of the Constituent Assembly in his autobiography, and as a journalist, devoted himself to justifying its demise. Aside from a regrettable clash with street demonstrators (they had been warned), there had been no violence or any serious interest shown by the general populace. The speeches of the Socialist Revolutionaries had, he insisted, been excessively dull, while the defeat of Lenin's 'Declaration' signified nothing at all. The Assembly had not met to decide *what* should be done in Russia, but 'who should have the doing', and since this question had already been decided, the whole business approached farce. The Bolsheviks had walked out of the Tauride Palace the moment Lenin's constitution was rejected, while Ransome followed at midnight, noting that the streets were quiet and littered with sledges: a good sign, since at the first hint of trouble 'they vanished like magic'.

In his absence, the debate continued until four o'clock in the morning, when the Red Guards, who had amused themselves by pointing their guns at the heads of the speakers, announced that they were sleepy and wanted to go home. When the SR delegates returned the next morning, they found the doors barred against them. Forty-eight hours later, two Kadet leaders were shot as they lay in hospital by a gang of Kronstadt sailors. For Harold Williams, who had for several months scarcely dared sleep at night out of fear for his wife's safety, it was the last straw.

'If you lived here,' he exhorted his readers,

you would feel in every bone of your body, in every fibre of your spirit, the bitterness of it . . .

I cannot tell you all the brutalities, the fierce excesses, that are ravaging Russia from end to end and more ruthlessly than any invading army. Horrors pall on us – robbery, plunder and the cruellest forms of murder are grown a part of the very atmosphere we live in. It is worse than Tsarism . . .

The Bolsheviks do not profess to encourage any illusions as to their real nature. They treat the bourgeoisie of all countries with equal contempt; they glory in all violence directed against the ruling classes, they despise laws and decencies that they consider effete, they trample on the arts and refinements of life. It is nothing to them if in the throes of the great upheaval the world relapses into barbarism.

Ransome angrily denied any suggestion that the killings had been carried out under direct orders. It had been, he said, a great embarrassment for the Bolshevik leaders and had naturally played directly into the hands of their enemies. Reminding his readers that British democracy, too, had sprung from civil war, he likened Lenin to Oliver Cromwell, and in the immediate aftermath of the Assembly's closure, drew on the lofty rhetoric of William Morris and John Ruskin: 'I tell you I walk these abominable, unswept, mountainously dirt-clogged, snow-clogged streets in exultation. It is like walking on Wetherlam or Dow Crag, with the future of mankind spreading before one like the foothills of the Lake Country, and the blue sea to the West.'

On 23 January, sitting once again at the Tauride Palace, Ransome witnessed the dissolution officially ratified by a packed house at the Third All-Russian Congress of Soviets, where Trotsky, freshly arrived from Brest-Litovsk, addressed the new Russia.

'My position', he reported,

was immediately behind and above the presidium, looking down on Trotsky's muscular shoulders and great head and the occasional gestures of his curiously small hands. Beyond him was that sea of men: soldiers in green and grey shirts, workers in collarless ones, or jerseys, others dressed very much like British workmen, peasants in belted red shirts and high top boots; all picked men, not elected for this assembly alone but proved and tested in the local soviets that had chosen them as delegates. And as I watched that amazing crowd, that filled the huge hall and packed the galleries, following point by point Trotsky's exposition of the international and inter-class situation and the policy of the Revolution, I felt I would willingly give the rest of my life if it could be divided into minutes and given to men in England and France so that those of little faith who say that the Russian Revolution is discredited, could share for one minute each that wonderful experience.

~

The closure of the Constituent Assembly brought Lenin's party one step closer to a socialist dictatorship in Russia, but the German threat remained. The governments of Finland, Poland, Latvia and Estonia – formerly provinces of the Russian empire – were all now looking to Germany for protection, and towards the end of January, Ukraine joined their number, handing over close to a quarter of Russia's grain reserves to the enemy. It was a devastating blow, but Trotsky still refused to admit defeat. His only concession to Lenin – now apoplectic with rage and demanding instant surrender – was to return to Brest-Litovsk, followed shortly by Evgenia.

For the Allies, Soviet talks with Germany were not only a betrayal of the treaties signed at the beginning of the war, but a breach of faith with ordinary soldiers then fighting on the Western Front. Stretched to the limit of its own resources, the British government pictured the grain which would nourish German cities, the oil which would fuel German military vehicles and the German troops who, released from duty in the east, would transfer to France for a potentially decisive offensive. It was for these reasons that Lord Northcliffe's papers continued to beat the same old drums: a German-Jewish conspiracy that would plunge the world into darkness; priests crucified before their congregations; and particularly offensive to the Archbishop of Canterbury, a Soviet initiative to nationalize women. But it was for these same reasons – an awareness that the Bolsheviks might hold the future of the Western Front in their hands – that Lloyd George was reluctant to alienate the Soviet altogether. Thus in December 1917, Bruce Lockhart, former British Consul General in Moscow, had found himself seated at a Lyons tea shop in London, negotiating an exchange of informal diplomatic privileges with two of Ransome's recent acquaintances, Theodore Rothstein and Maxim Litvinov. In January he sailed for Russia with instructions to make himself as friendly and as obstructive as possible.

Lockhart's mission arrived in Petrograd on 30 January, taking rooms in a large well-furnished palace endowed with an excellent wine cellar and facing the Peter and Paul Fortress. Amongst the guests at his house-warming, in addition to representatives from every Allied embassy, was Colonel Knox, the British military attaché, who made it clear that the proper policy regarding cowards and mutineers was to shoot them on the spot. The principal speaker, however, was Raymond Robins of the American Red Cross. Standing before the fire and smoothing his long black hair with a characteristic gesture (Robins admired the Inuit of Alaska), he made a moving appeal for Allied support, debunking the ridiculous and popular notion that the Bolsheviks were working towards a German victory. The Allies, he said, were fools if they hoped Russia's fighting spirit might be restored by the demoralized bourgeoisie, who wished for nothing better than German help in restoring their civil rights and property. Trotsky was a 'four times son of a bitch, but the greatest Jew since Jesus'. If the Germans thought they'd bought him, growled Robins, then they had 'bought a lemon'. Begging his audience to forget political prejudice, he reminded them what was at stake, concluding with Lieutenant Colonel John McCrae's famous call to arms, placed in the mouths of fallen heroes on the Western Front:

> We are the Dead. Short days ago
> We lived, felt dawn, saw sunset glow,
> Loved and were loved, and now we lie
> . . . In Flanders fields.
>
> Take up our quarrel with the foe:
> To you from failing hands we throw
> The Torch; be yours to hold it high.
> If ye break faith with us who die
> We shall not sleep, though Poppies grow
> . . . In Flanders fields.

With the exception of Colonel Knox, there was not a dry eye in the house.

Lockhart's memoirs provide several portraits of the key figures in Petrograd at that time, the most colourful being Karl Radek:

A Jew, whose real name is Sobelsohn, he was in some respects a grotesque figure. A little man with a huge head, protruding ears, clean shaven face (in those days he did not wear that awful fringe which now passes for a beard), with spectacles and a large mouth with yellow, tobacco stained teeth, from which a huge pipe or cigar was never absent, he was always dressed in a quaint drab-coloured Norfolk suit with knickers and leggings. He was a great friend of Ransome, and through Ransome we came to know him very well. Almost every day he would turn up in my rooms, an English cap stuck jauntily on his head, his pipe puffing fiercely, a bundle of books under his arm, and a huge revolver strapped to his side. He looked like a cross between a professor and a bandit. Of his intellectual brilliance, however, there was no doubt. He was the virtuoso of Bolshevik journalism, and his conversation was as sparkling as his leading articles.

As for Trotsky and Lenin, they furnished Lockhart with diametrically opposite examples of the revolutionary demagogue: Trotsky, proud, theatrical, furious at the humiliation the Germans had subjected him to at Brest-Litovsk and ready to die for the Revolution 'provided there was a large enough audience to see him do it'; Lenin, by contrast, apparently devoid of emotion altogether. When Lockhart first laid eyes on him, he took him for 'a provincial green grocer' rather than a leader of men, but this impression soon gave way to the deep-seated respect Lenin commanded in virtually all his acquaintances, friend and foe alike. 'Trotsky', recalled Lockhart,

was all temperament – an individualist and an artist, on whose vanity even I could play with some success. Lenin was impersonal and almost inhuman. His vanity was proof against all flattery. The only appeal that one could make to him was to his humour, which, if sardonic, was highly developed . . . In the Council of Commissars there was not a man who did not consider himself the equal of Trotsky. There was not a commissar who did not regard Lenin as a demi-god, whose decisions were to be accepted without question . . .

Ransome, to whom Lockhart owed so many of his contacts, makes his cameo as an eccentric go-between:

a Don Quixote with a walrus moustache, a sentimentalist, who could always be counted on to champion the underdog, and a visionary, whose imagination had been fired by the revolution. He was on excellent terms with the Bolsheviks and frequently brought us information of the greatest value. An incorrigible romanticist, who could spin a fairy-tale out of nothing, he was an amusing and good natured companion . . .

~

On the morning of 9 February, according to Ransome's diary, he translated three pages of *The Mouse and the Sparrow* and met with Chukovsky, the great Russian children's poet, to discuss an idea for a play based on Hans Christian Andersen to be staged at the Besarabskaya Theatre (there is no suggestion that anything ever came of the plan). In the afternoon, he lunched with Goldem, head of the Petrograd Union of Journalists, and borrowed a copy of Thomas Carlyle's *French Revolution*, which he promised to return the following Monday. The final entry for that day reads: 'Declaration at Brest, "War ended by peace on German terms will not be signed."'

On the same day, the Kaiser, exasperated by over two months of fruitless negotiations, had ordered his envoys to present the German demands as an ultimatum. If the treaty was not signed within twenty-four hours, the ceasefire would be at an end. Facing humiliation both at Smolny and abroad, Trotsky now played his final card. Russia, he declared, had no interest in fighting but refused to sign the brigand's peace. If the Germans chose to invade, they would expose themselves as murderers and bandits. 'No peace, no war!' was his slogan, and it had no precedent in the history of military diplomacy. For five days, the German delegation were thrown into complete confusion, but on 18 February the order was finally given to advance. 'It is the most comical war I have ever known,' wrote General Hoffman in his diary. 'It is waged almost exclusively in trains and automobiles. We put a handful of infantry men with machine-guns and one gun on to a train and push them off to the next station; they take it, make prisoners of the Bolsheviks, pick up a few more troops, and go on. The proceeding has, at any rate, the charm of novelty.'

On the afternoon of the 18th, a decisive meeting was held in Smolny, where Lenin, still facing opposition from Radek and Bukharin, threatened to resign unless the German terms, however iniquitous, were accepted without delay. The decisive vote was cast by Trotsky, who, fearing a split within the party, finally submitted to reason. At midnight, Lenin cabled Berlin, but receiving no reply, turned in desperation to Raymond Robins and Bruce Lockhart, both of whom sent urgent telegrams demanding military support. Both were treated to a deafening silence. As the remaining Allied ambassadors made plans to retreat to Vologda, several hundred miles along the Siberian railway to Russia's back door, Lenin announced the evacuation of the capital to Moscow, simultaneously demanding that the Russian army fight to the last man. On 22 February, at a meeting convened to discuss whether Allied aid – proffered or not – should be accepted, the motion was passed by the slenderest of margins. 'We are turning the Revolution into a dung heap,' Bukharin had shouted at Trotsky, and then burst into tears.

Ransome, meanwhile, was drafting a fond farewell to his mother:

I have only a few minutes to spare, not to write a letter, but to send you my love. This letter will be taken by those who are going home. I shall be stopping here though I hope as one of my American friends says, to get out six jumps ahead of the Germans and to make them good long jumps . . .

I am fairly well, tired of course, but very glad, whatever happens, that I came back to Russia. The one thing I am afraid of is getting copped by the Germans, but the chance of that simply may have to be taken. And it's terribly sickening having to sacrifice my entire collection of folklore, and all the notes of five years sweating at Russian fairy tales and similar things. Still, it's no good howling about that.

Please, in case I don't get time to write another letter or two convey the fact that cessation of telegrams does not necessarily mean misfortune to various persons who are good enough to be interested. Be good to Barbara [Collingwood].

Under no circumstances is my book about the revolution to be published without revisions by me.

Please send my love to Geoffrey, and give it to Cecily, Joyce, Kitty and everybody else . . . Goodnight my dear. I hope I shall see you again some time or other, though it looks as if I may have to go half way around the world to do it.

Ransome could not have known, when he wrote this letter, that his brother was already dead. Geoffrey – wounded three times in the course of the war – had been shot in the leg, and on 15 January, died of blood poisoning at the Casualty Clearing Station in Achiet-le-Petit. He would not in any case have lived much longer. In March 1918, his entire battalion was wiped out by Germany's huge March offensive, facilitated by Russia's exit from the war. Ransome received no word from Edith or any other member of his family until August. There are no letters nor any passage in his autobiography to articulate his feelings, though he and Geoffrey had always been friends. Joyce, who had adored her brother, remembered Edith's grief when she learned that on his deathbed her child had called out for a stranger – a girl she had never met.

~

Between the 26th and 27th of February, Ransome spent over twenty hours helping Rosa Radek, a Bolshevik historian named Professor Pokrovsky and Evgenia pack the Russian imperial archives – including the secret treaties and a sensational correspondence between the former Tsar and Tsarina – into wooden crates to be shipped down to Moscow. On the evening of the 27th, with Lenin's telegram of unconditional surrender still unacknowledged and the German armies barely a hundred miles from Petrograd, he was approached by Bruce Lockhart with an errand. Colonel Raymond Robins was going as far as Vologda with the American embassy. Would Ransome go with them and plant a Union Jack on any building suitable for a British legation?

'Very urgent!' read Lockhart's telegram. 'Ransome *Daily News* correspondent is remaining in Russia and will probably go with my party and Americans. He will not be attached to my mission, but his help and co-operation will be very useful [and] as he will not be able to obtain money from his paper, may I finance him according to my discretion?'

The Foreign Office consented immediately, and while observing that 'Mr Ransome is very much in sympathy with the Bolsheviks,' agreed that this was exactly why he would be so 'useful to Mr Lockhart'.

The removal of the Allied ambassadors 350 miles from the capital was an unpopular decision with the Bolsheviks, who regretted it much as a card player might regret the loss of so many aces, which may explain why, as the Americans installed themselves comfortably at a local monastery, the British would have to wait several weeks for a legation of their own. Ransome found no appropriate accommodation in Vologda for the legation, and over the next two days admired the sleepy little town – its churches with their colourful domes, its haphazard market squares – and waited for news to arrive from Petrograd.

Germany had finally acknowledged Russia's surrender on 28 February, but since Trotsky adamantly refused to humble himself further, it had fallen to Georgy Chicherin, recently released from Brixton prison, to go to Brest-Litovsk and sign the treaty. The German terms, which had grown harsher with every delay, deprived Russia of over half its industrial enterprises, 90 per cent of its coal and a third of its population and farmlands. As a European power, the Russian empire had been placed on a par with seventeenth-century Muscovy, but for Lenin – who had predicted the entire fiasco with painful clarity – the only question was, did the Bolshevik government have any future at all?

On 3 March, two telegrams were sent from Brest-Litovsk to Smolny, the first announcing the signature of the treaty, the second requiring a train to be sent 'with an adequate number of guards' to pick up the Soviet delegates. Unfortunately, the second telegram had arrived first, leaving Lenin with the impression that at the last minute, the deal had fallen through, meaning a continuation of the German invasion. Practical in times of crisis, he had decided that now, more than ever, he needed support from the Allies and had telegrammed his most sympathetic contacts in Vologda – Ransome and Robins – in the hope of them lobbying the ambassadors. Evgenia, charged with communicating this message, had supplied a postscript: 'As this means war, and consequently your immediately going further, I am sending my best wishes for a happy journey.' Assuming he would leave Russia with the Americans, she had sent Ransome her love, but by evening he was on his way back to Petrograd, meeting the remnants of the Russian army fleeing in the opposite direction.

Every station was like an opened hive of grey bees, all drones, swarming over the lines and the platforms, packing themselves again into cattle trucks, travelling on the buffers when there was no other room . . . every stopping place smells like a vast latrine. Meanwhile other traffic is almost impossible. I believe myself it may be years before this nomadic era ends and the de-mobilization of the Russian army is concluded, and the grey sediment of aimless migration subsides . . .

The Treaty of Brest-Litovsk marked a critical turning point. In the West, the Allies began seriously mooting hostile intervention in Russia, though the precise purpose of such an intervention – to prevent Allied equipment from falling into German hands, to install a pro-Allies government – or the scale of the putative invasion remained far from clear. Within Russia itself, the decision for peace had been greeted with horror by every other political faction, including the Left Socialist Revolutionaries, who now resigned their ministries and devoted themselves to 'terrorist' tactics. Lenin had sacrificed the international revolution for a local revolution and appropriated that revolution to a single party; a party torn by violent internal conflict. Nevertheless, the Revolution had survived, so that on 14 March, now safely removed to Moscow, he was in a position to address the Fourth All-Russian Soviet Congress as a saviour.

The previous day, Ransome had walked around the Kremlin wall, noting three men fishing in the Moscow River, blue-green reflections on drifting ice and crows 'behaving like seagulls' around the storm drains. In the evening, he attended a cabaret of gypsy singers and dancers with Evgenia at the Hotel Elite and was delighted to note that the only sign of the Revolution 'was that the whole staff of the kitchen came . . . to enjoy the fun, cooks in their white caps and aprons, and the kitchen maids with their shawls over their heads dressed for going home.' Later, he summed up Lenin's greatness for the *Daily News*:

He was the most Russian of them. Time and again, after listening to speeches which might have been made in any language in any country by men of any nationality I have suddenly, as it were, been brought back to Russia when this little urgent figure stepped to the tribune, stuck his thumbs in the armholes of his waistcoat, and mingled jest and argument in language that tasted of Russian tobacco and the life of the Russian peasantry. It was natural to hear him talk of the principle of his international revolution in the language of the Volga peasants, and in his mouth political theory seemed in no way out of tune with the peasant proverbs . . . At the Assembly which ratified peace, for example, he suppressed Steinberg by remarking to general delight, 'One fool can ask more questions than ten wise men can answer.'

15

The Fool of the World

Readers of *Old Peter's Russian Tales*, Ransome's first truly successful book for children, will recall 'The Fool of the World and the Flying Ship', the story of a young village idiot who brings the Tsar a magical ship that flies through the air as if it were water. Spurned at first for his lowly station, the fool nevertheless overcomes every obstacle with the greatest nonchalance and is rewarded with wealth, power and a beautiful bride. As peasant-Tsar of a grateful people, he becomes so clever that the whole court repeats everything he says.

Ransome attributed many of the qualities of the folkloric fool to the leaders of the Revolution he supported, and by extension to himself: tenacity, noble ideals, courage, the ability to champion the cause of the universal underdog. But the quality he valued most highly was the ability to acquire authority without the loss of innocence. Others, describing the rise of the Bolsheviks in Russia, would speak of mass terror, of an injunction to 'loot the looters', of the eradication of all political opposition. Ransome, concentrated on a very British commitment to liberty. Readers of the *Daily News* were not drilled in the harsh realities of class war, or asked to choose between the government appointed by King George V and a dictatorship of the proletariat. Neither did Ransome, whose career had been transformed by his intimacy with the Bolshevik leaders, have any intention of making such a choice for himself. It was not necessary, he argued, to be a socialist to respect the moral principles behind the Soviet. Indeed, had it not been for Evgenia, he might have enjoyed Radek's hospitality without a single qualm of conscience, but having fallen in love with the 'tall jolly girl' who had fed him potatoes over Christmas, he could not help hurting somebody's feelings, for the simple reason that he could not be married to two women at the same time.

Back in 1913, when Ransome had fled his first marriage, ostensibly for a health-giving 'walking holiday', he had approached his wife through a solicitor. This time he chose Tabitha as his intermediary, knowing that Ivy read all his letters to his eight-year-old daughter with the closest possible attention.

'My Dear Babba,' he wrote on 28 May,

at last Dor-Dor has a lot of green and purple ink and a little, a very little time, and so he can write a proper letter to his woolly Babba. All my beasts are well: the hen, the owl, the peacock and the elephant (although as you can see from the picture the elephant is very hungry and hangry from having had no dinner). Dor-Dor is very busy every day trying to make imperialists see sense [here Ransome has drawn a man with a pipe, cheerfully indicating a barn door to a scowling uniformed imperialist].

Dear Babba, you must ask Mum-Mum to explain this and she won't be able. Never mind. That is because she is a good Mum-Mum what knows all about witches and puddings and donkeys and Babbas and nothing whatever about politics. If you want to know what politics are, Dor-Dor can tell you. They are a kind of porridge, which Dor-Dor has to eat THREE WHOLE PLATESFUL EVERY DAY even when he'd like to be fishing or playing catch. Politics is what keeps Dor-Dor in Russia and makes him SICK [here Ransome supplies a sketch of a man vomiting copiously into a bowl]. Mum-mum will say this is a naughty Dor-Dor to make such a picture, but it is the truth, and Dor-Dor draws it with his whole heart . . . Dor-Dor wishes he and his Babba were lying in the long grass singing their songs and smoking. This is the long grass. The red is poppies. Or if only we was fishing.

On the final page of the letter is a further series of drawings: a Russian boy dressed for summer in his belted peasant smock, and the same boy in winter, in a sheepskin coat and hat. Ransome showed Tabitha how her name would look in Cyrillic if she were a Russian girl, and beneath it drew two frogs walking arm in arm, one in a waistcoat with a pipe and stick, the other holding a flower. Beside them is a pine tree with a mushroom growing beneath it. They are very obviously and sweetly in love.

'The drawing of the frogs', Ransome explained, 'is done for a Babba by a big girl as big as Dor-Dor who carries a revolver and a sword and is a fierce revolutionary. Dor-Dor must stop now because the messenger is going [a drawing of a messenger, a boat and Tabitha receiving her post].'

A few weeks later, Ivy was explaining to her terrified daughter what divorce meant, and wondering if Tabitha's father and mother ought to have one. Tabitha's answer, unsurprisingly, was an emphatic 'no'.

~

The evacuation of the Bolshevik government to Moscow was a strategic military retreat. On 2 March, the day before the Treaty of Brest-Litovsk was signed, German planes had bombed Petrograd. The railway stations and southern roads out of the city were clogged with refugees, and even Ransome, who had spent a whole day and night helping to pack the Russian imperial archives into wooden crates, was forced to leave most of his own effects – his notes, his extensive collection of Russian newspapers, his fishing rods and his favourite Turkish coffee mill – back in Glinka Street. Arriving in Moscow, the Soviet government installed itself temporarily at the Hotel Metropole, before moving into the Kremlin. Ransome, together with the British and American missions, took rooms at the Elite, where it seemed for a few anxious days that they would be forced to share with the German embassy. A major incident threatened, but at the last moment Evgenia – at Bruce Lockhart's request – persuaded Trotsky that the Germans should be relocated. Lockhart did not forget this favour.

Peace with Germany had opened serious rifts within the party and was followed by a Cabinet reshuffle. Trotsky, still smarting from his ordeal as a diplomat, moved to the People's Commissariat for War, taking Evgenia with him and leaving his post at the Commissariat of Foreign Affairs to be filled by Georgy Chicherin, a former aristocrat, a safe pair of hands and a devotee of English tweed. Radek remained in charge of foreign propaganda and poked fun, as always, at everybody. Only Lenin escaped his wit, and Ransome, following Radek's lead, was not slow to lay his stone at the foundation of the greatest personality cult in modern history. Arriving in Moscow he had discovered this man – whose statue would in time grace every town square from the Black Sea to Vladivostok – waiting patiently for his room at the National Hotel. The floor, Ransome noted, was littered with luggage – 'unimaginable rags', bedding rolled in blankets, frayed wicker baskets and battered trunks. 'Here was Lenin himself, the best-hated man in Russia and the man with the most influence over his followers, calm as usual, fearless as usual, without any guard whatsoever in the stronghold of Russian capitalism, which is his sworn enemy.'

Ransome's Lenin had many qualities. Before the November coup, he had spent time in hiding with a family of Finnish peasants, who discovered that he was not only eager to do his share of domestic chores, but performed them better than anybody else. Lenin was generous and humorous, so that in spite of the great weight of history resting on his shoulders, every line on his face 'was a line of laughter'. As a politician, he could be flexible as well as uncompromising. At Brest-Litovsk he had firmly insisted, at the risk of destroying his party, that submission to imperial Germany was the only way of saving the Revolution. Over the next few months, he would argue, with infallible logic, that the security of the Soviet depended on showing no quarter to the Bolsheviks' enemies on the Left. Lenin was never the slave of paradox. He always knew precisely what to do. But while Ransome marvelled that the now undisputed leader of the Revolution – who in a few short months had made a deeper impression on history than Napoleon – could silence a crowd of angry soldiers merely by raising his hand, he believed that Lenin's crowning glory was his smallness.

Ransome did not think of smallness in the sense of narrowness or weakness. As a child in Leeds, he had gathered a miniature museum in a bathroom washstand drawer, modelled the city of Leeds out of matchsticks, used a magic lantern to project glass slides onto canvas screens. England was small, but governed a vast empire. Smallness did not necessarily mean the absence of greatness; it meant the reduction of confusion, of elemental conflict, to a rational system. This smallness that Lenin possessed was that of a great thinker, spanning the infinite scale of possibility as easily as a well-told story. When Lenin argued, he did not become emotional or vindictive like Trotsky. He waited for the right time, just as he waited now in the National Hotel – a stage metaphor for the whole of Russia – while his bed was made up and his linen turned down. The Bolsheviks had enemies in Moscow on both the Right and the Left, but Ransome's idol had never been in any doubt as to how he would deal with them. Lenin preached chaos, was surrounded by chaos, but in his own person, from his tightly buttoned waistcoat to the needle-sharp pencils in his pocket, he was the quintessence of order.

As a young boy, Ransome had been taught to ice-skate by one of the anarchist leaders, Prince Kropotkin, on a little lake at the bottom of Isobella Ford's garden outside Leeds. Now, many years later, he visited the anarchists in Moscow, and as an Englishman received an unexpectedly hospitable welcome.

'Went to the Anarchist headquarters,' he wrote on 20 March,

a fine building. Black flag. Inside soldiers lolling about. In the main room I found four men. Two fairly healthy, one blind, another lame; both mad, mad as could be. The lame one was half undressed, and rose from the divan on which he lay, shattering the atmosphere with a violent smell of unwashed feet. His ideas, however, were interesting. He said that Herbert Spencer was a great anarchist, and that they (Russian anarchists) regarded themselves as successors of the Manchester school. England before the war was an almost perfect expression of an anarchist state, where all was based on good will and custom rather than on law, and the king was entirely unnecessary, except as a symbol of the authority which the natural anarchy of the British had rendered superfluous. He said they did not wish to take the government into their own hands, but did wish to become so strong that the government would become as ornamental and powerless as the King of England.

Ransome found this brief summary of anarchist principles both touching and disarming. Lenin, on the other hand, saw nothing to recommend it whatsoever. Whereas the Bolsheviks demanded total government, the anarchists proposed no government at all. Their communes had become hotbeds of political subversion. Gangs of soldiers from anarchist regiments terrorized civilians, and on one occasion, stopped the sledge of a senior Soviet official, took his wallet and his clothes, and forced him to walk home stark naked in the snow. The anarchists had stood behind Lenin when he seized power, but now that the Soviet was in Bolshevik hands, there could be no question of further cooperation. The final straw came in late March, when teenage hooligans invaded the American embassy and stole Colonel Robins' motor car, a blatant infringement of his diplomatic immunity. Incandescent with rage, he burst into Lenin's study and announced that if the Bolsheviks were incapable of enforcing order on the streets, then their government was 'bust'. Lenin warmly agreed.

The 11th of April was Evgenia's twenty-fourth birthday. That afternoon, according to Ransome's diary, he attended a celebration thrown by a few friends. In the night, the Cheka, under the command of Felix Dzerzhinsky, raided twenty-six anarchist strongholds in Moscow, including the 'House of Anarchy' – the Moscow Federation of Anarchist Groups headquarters – which Ransome had visited three weeks previously. Fifty anarchists were killed, while over five hundred were imprisoned and later executed. The following day, Ransome's diary records 'general confounding of Anarchists' and a trip with Dzerzhinsky's second-in-command, Yakov Peters, around the scenes of the raids. In his telegram to the *Daily News*, he set down the incident with a cool detachment, approving Dzerzhinsky's tactics and echoing the official line: 'Doubtless the counter-revolutionaries are making use of the Anarchists. Amongst the weapons captured is a

German machine-gun. The Soviet has finally shown itself capable of uprooting a movement which all previous governments have not dared to touch.'

Bruce Lockhart also attended Dzerzhinsky's guided tour, and recalled what he had seen in his memoirs:

The Anarchists had appropriated the finest houses in Moscow . . . The filth was indescribable. Broken bottles littered the floors; the magnificent ceilings were perforated with bullet holes. Wine stains and human excrement blotched the Aubusson carpets. Priceless pictures had been slashed to strips. The dead still lay where they had fallen. They included officers in guard's uniforms, students – young boys of twenty – and men who belonged obviously to the criminal class and whom the revolution had released from prison. In the luxurious drawing room of the House Gracheva the Anarchists had been surprised in the middle of an orgy. The long table which had supported the feast had been overturned, and broken plates, glasses, champagne bottles, made unsavoury islands in a pool of blood and spilt wine. On the floor lay a young woman, face downwards. Peters turned her over. Her hair was dishevelled. She had been shot through the neck and the blood had congealed in a sinister purple clump. She could not have been more than twenty. Peters shrugged his shoulders. 'Prostitutka,' he said, 'Perhaps it is for the best.'

The suppression of the anarchists, soon recast as the suppression of vagrant, unemployed hooligans, gave fair warning that Lenin was prepared to treat his opponents on the Left at least as harshly as his enemies on the Right. But no government could have survived the civil war with nothing more than a police force and a small militia of factory workers to enforce its authority. At the People's Commissariat of War, Trotsky was working on the formation of a new revolutionary army, trained by officers of the old regime and closely supervised by the Cheka. Very soon the soldiers' councils would disappear, just as the workers' councils in the factories would be replaced by party committees. Trotsky's army enforced rigid discipline. Recruitment was at first voluntary, then based on conscription, while deserters and mutineers were shot as counter-revolutionaries. Along with the party and the Cheka, the Red Army became the third pillar of the

Soviet state, mustered to fight the Whites and the insubordinate peasants: the 'kulaks' or 'tight fists' who withheld their grain. In three months' time, it would face Allied troops, including several battalions supplied by the British. Ransome, nevertheless, had played his own small part in its conception. In early April, he had travelled to Petrograd to speak to Captain Cromie, the British naval attaché, at the embassy, to collect a few things from Glinka Street and to ask Lola Kinel, his former research assistant, if she would hunt out some titles from the few remaining book shops: *The Mexican Rebellion*, *Partisan War* and *Guerrilla Warfare and Tactics*. Lola had been surprised and none too pleased when she found out that they were for Trotsky, but Ransome had only 'roared and chuckled', delighted by her indignation. The whole thing had been a great joke for him.

~

In the first six months of 1918, Ransome wrote over two dozen letters to various friends and relatives, complaining in equal portion of Britain's shallowness in leaving Russia to the Germans and of loneliness. England was drifting away, and as it receded, so in his imagination it became abstract and simple, separating into two worlds: the England that he attacked in his articles, and the England he longed for in quiet moments, the proper home of his childhood.

'The last four months', he told his elusive, grieving mother,

have been a complete silence from all my belongings, so that I begin to feel I haven't got any. Also, as we get no newspapers, England begins to seem a sort of Atlantis, a fantastic island of last year, that this year has sunk beneath the sea, where perhaps on clear days, when the water is smooth, travellers will be able to see it, and through special glasses inspect you and Joyce in a sub-aqueous Chapel Allerton, subaqueously feeding subaqueous hens. Writing letters to England is like writing letters to Father Christmas, and putting them in the drawing room fire to see their ashes blow hopefully up the chimney into a mysterious infinite.

In Russia, there was one other English journalist: Morgan Philips Price, who was friendly with Ransome, and by his own admission, 'up to his neck in revolution'. Price worked closely with the International Bureau, wrote fiery articles for the *Manchester Guardian* and frequently exchanged notes with his colleague from the *Daily News*. Beyond the circle of newspaper men clustered at the Commissariat of Foreign Affairs, Ransome also dined regularly with the British mission, with whom he shared a hotel, and according to Lockhart, became 'more than a visitor'. He was on good terms with Raymond Robins and Captain Jacques Sadoul, the former French military attaché, who following his conversion to Bolshevism was helping Trotsky with the army. In fact, there were at least a dozen expatriate acquaintances, each holding widely varying views on the current situation, with whom Ransome met on an almost daily basis. And yet in his letters home he mentioned none of them, as if he were the last Englishman in Moscow, as though all the other Englishmen had gone home for the holidays, leaving him alone with the natives.

'My principal friends here', he told Edith, 'are Radek and his wife, and two huge women, Bolsheviks, as tall as Grenadiers, who prefer pistols to powder puffs, and swords to parasols . . . One of them succeeded in extracting over a million poods of corn from the South under the very nose of the Germans, she at the time commanding an expedition of 300 wildly devoted sailormen.'

This was Iroida, Evgenia's sister, who had accompanied a group of Baltic sailors on a raid, a practice which had escalated into a full-scale 'bread war' against the peasants – an irony not lost on Lenin's socialist opponents. Iroida had been promoted to secretary to the chief of the Eastern Department of the Commissariat of Foreign Affairs, and had almost certainly joined the expedition as a political 'consultant': one of the party delegates or Cheka officers who kept an eye on the still unruly military. Meanwhile, Viktor, Evgenia's eldest brother, was in Irkutsk. In 1914, he had volunteered for the Tsar's army, fighting through until Kerensky's disastrous July 1917 offensive. In

Siberia he had taken up with fellow officers and would fight for the Whites against the Reds, including, within a couple of years, his brother, Roman.

Growing close to Evgenia's family, Ransome saw how revolution could scatter a group of close and like-minded people, affecting each of them in a different way. Evgenia and Iroida were trusted party officials, Viktor was lost somewhere to the east, while Evgenia's mother, Maria Alexeevna, was scraping crumbs together in famine-stricken Gatchina. Ransome, all bones and cartilage behind the red moustache and sideburns, knew what it was like to be hungry, but Maria knew what it meant to starve, with three children in hand and nothing to do but wait.

'Darling Zhenia and Ira,' she wrote in mid-April:

It was only yesterday evening that I learned your address and where you are hiding (perhaps better to say 'gone into hiding' as for almost six weeks now there has been no word or news from Evgenia and I thought she was dead) . . . About myself, I have nothing to write. Everything is the same. We are starving hard. So long as we had some rye it was possible to survive, but now, like the wolf, we have nothing. On Maslenitsa [Russian spring festival] we ate blini for a week . . . Now we do not drink tea, there is no sugar; we have forgotten the taste of butter, though it is on sale at the market for 18 roubles a pound . . . Gleb looks like a green caterpillar, and I also lay in bed all last week. Tomorrow Serafima is graduating from the gymnasium and is whimpering about white shoes, but I cannot buy them . . . We cannot go to a village, because we have no money to travel . . . Do you really not understand how hard it is for me not to know anything about you? Greetings to you from the children – Love Mum.

Thanks to Rosa Radek, Maria came down to Moscow in May, where she listened at keyholes and folded linen at the Lux Hotel. She had no choice in the matter, nor any special sympathy for the party who employed her. As to what she made of Ransome it is difficult to say. All we know is that he was shortly referring to her as 'Mother'.

~

On 25 April, Ransome dined with Colonel Raymond Robins and found him gloomy and distracted. In recent weeks, anti-Bolshevik feeling in the States had been inflamed by Edgar Sisson, who had returned to Washington with a package for the Creel Committee, a pro-war propaganda bureau responsible for such Hollywood blockbusters as *The Claws of the Hun*, *The Prussian Cur* and *The Kaiser, the Beast of Berlin*. Sisson's gift to Senator Creel and his friends was a series of letters sent between Germany and the Kremlin showing that the Bolsheviks were receiving funds directly from Berlin. The letters were forgeries, but they had caused uproar in the States. With an Allied invasion looking increasingly likely, Robins had decided to leave Russia via the Siberian railroad and put his case in person to President Wilson. Did Ransome have anything to contribute?

Ransome's *On Behalf of Russia: An Open Letter to America* was written in close collaboration with Karl Radek and went with Robins to Washington at the end of May. Thanks to Boris Reinstein at the International Bureau for Revolutionary Propaganda, it was published in July by *The New Republic* at three cents a copy. In September, it was issued in Russia with a preface by Radek describing Ransome as a man who ordinarily took no interest in politics but who on this occasion had been moved to protest by his 'warm heart', his lack of 'bourgeois prejudices', and most importantly, his 'deep love for the masses'. It opened with a quote from Ralph Waldo Emerson, intended to remind Americans of their own revolutionary origins:

> Every day brings a ship,
> Every ship brings a word;
> Well for those who have no fear,
> Looking seaward, well assured
> That the word the vessel brings
> Is the word they wish to hear.

Ransome's pamphlet brought word from Russia of more than a local movement. In the West, he said, it was easy to ignore Russia's struggles altogether or to heed the 'atheistical little minds' who declared that the Soviet was not a revolutionary government at all, but a vehicle for enemy agitation, lit up from inside by German propaganda like a 'Halloween pumpkin'. Ransome appealed to America because America had supported the French Revolution when the British condemned it. And yet he did not know if Americans, so comfortably removed from the bloody cockpit of Europe, still remembered how they had won their freedom; doubted it, in fact, when the entire American edifice was run by capitalists who fed on the workers like 'parasites on cheese'. But Ransome soon forgot about America altogether, turning instead to England, a country wrapped in 'a vast nightmare of blind folly', separated from the great events in Russia by the trenches and the sea, deprived as if by 'an angry fairy godmother' of the vision to recognize that the Soviet leaders were 'the real article, giants whose movements in the mists are of greater import to the future of the world than anything else that is happening in our day'.

'I love the Real England,' declared Ransome,

but I hate more than I hate anything on earth (except cowardice in looking at the truth) the intellectual sloth, the gross mental indolence that prevents the English from making an effort of imagination and realizing how shameful will be their portion in history when the story of this last year in the biography of democracy comes to be written . . . Shameful foolish and tragic beyond tears, for the toll will be paid in English blood. English lads will die and English lads have died, not one or two, but hundreds of thousands, because their elders listen to men who think little things, and tell them little things, which are so terribly easy to repeat.

Ransome's *On Behalf of Russia* dismissed the March 1917 Revolution as the work of a disorganized rabble exploited by monarchist reactionaries. He attacked the Constituent Assembly as a haven for counter-revolutionaries and political bankrupts, in contrast to the Soviet, who had gifted their subjects a new Russian republic. The dictatorship of the proletariat, explained Ransome, meant that every working man could cast his vote, forging laws ideally fitted to a territory so huge and culturally diverse. Allied propagandists had claimed that the exclusion of the bourgeoisie was undemocratic, but this was because the West had failed to grasp the fundamental meaning of revolution. They had forgotten, Ransome objected, that the purpose of social revolution was not to make the ruling class powerless, but to eradicate the bourgeoisie altogether. No democracy in history had provided such direct or universal suffrage to its citizens. Russia, which had once been the most backward nation in Europe, was now the most emancipated country in the world. The transition to the new society was uncomfortable, but 'once the conditions of parasitism, privilege and exploitation have been destroyed, the old divisions of the class struggle will automatically have disappeared'.

Addressing the question of Allied intervention against the Soviet, Ransome repeated that no possible government in Russia was less disposed to compromise with Germany, so opposed to all imperial ideals, so capable of uniting the Russian people against the enemy. But while he emphasized the power of the soviets in Russia, he also pleaded for the underdog. The revolutionary cause, he believed, was the cause of the weak against the strong, the lamb against the imperial lion. Indeed, so unequal was the struggle that he believed the Revolution would almost certainly fail. But if the imperialists, German or Allied, robbed Russia of its hard-won liberty, history would award the Bolsheviks the moral victory.

'These men,' he concluded,

who have made the Soviet government in Russia, if they must fail, will fail with clean shields and clean hearts, having striven for an ideal which will live beyond them. Even if they fail, they will none the less have written a page in history more daring than any other which I can remember in the history of humanity. They are writing it amid the slinging of mud from all the meaner spirits in their country, in yours and in my own. But when the thing is over, and their enemies have triumphed, the mud will vanish like black magic at noon, and that page will be as white as the snows of Russia, and the writing on it as bright as the gold domes I used to see glittering in the sun when I looked from my window in Petrograd.

As Colonel Robins left for Washington with *On Behalf of Russia* in his suitcase, Ransome abandoned his dark, chilly room at the Elite Hotel and moved into a luxurious apartment in a merchant's palace, which he shared with Evgenia, Iroida and the Radeks. As an example of the methods by which the Bolsheviks removed the 'conditions of parasitism, privilege and exploitation' in Russia, the episode makes illuminating reading: the abject terror of the cringing 'millionaire'; his gloominess as Evgenia turned down one apartment after another; Ransome's amusement when the man explained that they would not pay if only they would condescend to accept his hospitality. 'Next morning at 10am he came round with his brother and begged [Evgenia] to take his own flat, the one he lived in himself; it had a good library which would be useful to me!!!!!!'

Ransome recorded the business in his notebook, under the title 'Requisitioning a Flat'.

~

Ransome and Evgenia's love affair proceeded like a jagged cardiograph through stormy scenes and ecstatic reconciliations. Evgenia could at times be sweet-tempered; at others fiercely moody, given to 'barometric' swings that Ransome found baffling and profoundly stimulating by turns. In the first stages of the relationship, Iroida had advised him to forget the whole thing – her sister would only make him unhappy. Subsequently, there had been a great deal of encouragement: picnics in the woods outside Moscow on free days, shy confidences, sudden eruptions of rage and tears, passionate rebukes. Within days of Ransome's moving into the palace – a 'lunatic commune', as he liked to call it – violent arguments had forced him back to his bachelor room at the Elite Hotel, where he exchanged Radek's company at dinner for the crowd at the British mission: Bruce Lockhart, Captain Hicks, Captain Hill and a newcomer named Sidney Reilly. He made his peace, with a grass snake caught from a river, and was rewarded with a sunny spell – 'EP much decenter than normal' –

until the snake was lost, then found again and fed three frogs: 'EP unfriendly, v tired . . . said sick of everything. So am I!!!' On the same day, 19 June, she nevertheless agreed to run away with him to Stockholm. It may also have been the day she accepted his proposal of marriage.

Ransome's decision to quit the Revolution, or rather to remove himself to a safe haven, had been brewing ever since the evacuation of Petrograd. A Russia overrun by Germans was no place for an Englishman, but then again, an Allied intervention scarcely boded any better. Were such an invasion to take place while Ransome was still in Moscow, the cordial relations he had enjoyed with the Kremlin could not possibly continue as before. Radek had already warned him of dire consequences for British subjects should it come to open war, and Ransome had taken this into account. But there was yet another consideration. Should the Allies succeed in installing a military dictatorship in Moscow, the outlook for the present administration was grim. Speaking to Evgenia, Ransome had tried to impress on her what a thorough purge of the Soviet would mean, but she had been stubborn, weighing concerns for her own safety against her devotion to her family, her country and the wisdom of entrusting her future to a married man she had known for barely six months. Ransome, however, was both tenacious and persuasive, and eventually she caved in. She would leave 'via land' if he could arrange the trip within ten days.

On 21 June, Lord Cecil at the Foreign Office received a coded telegram from Bruce Lockhart announcing Evgenia's desire for assistance.

In case you have not received this I repeat it shortly as situation is extremely urgent. A very useful lady, who has worked here in an extremely confidential position in a government office, desires to give up her present position. She has been of the greatest service to me and is anxious to establish herself in Stockholm where she would be centre of information regarding underground agitation in Russia in the event of the Bolsheviks being overthrown by the Germans . . . Lady is not a Bolshevik but is known to all leaders of the movement. In any case she promises to take part in no practical agitation work. In order to enable her to leave secretly I wish to have authority to put her to Mr Ransome's passport as his wife and facilitate her departure via Murmansk.

In London, MI5 were against the plan, fearing that Evgenia might prove untrustworthy, but Arthur Balfour, the Foreign Secretary, saw no 'military objection' and gave the project a green light. In the event of an Allied intervention, when so little was known of the strength or deployment of Bolshevik troops, a more suitable defector – the personal secretary to the Soviet Commissar for War – could hardly have been imagined. And yet ten days passed and the couple were still in Moscow, deciding first that they would go to Stockholm, then England, then Stockholm again; wondering if it would be better to go together or by separate routes. There was no ideal course of action; it was simply a question of burning the fewest possible bridges. Meanwhile, Lockhart, dispensing with conventional diplomacy, had embraced the counter-revolution.

Between January and March 1918, Lockhart had attended Smolny on a daily basis, and according to Ransome, was rarely to be seen without a red-bound copy of Marx's *Das Kapital* clutched ostentatiously to his chest. As head of the British mission, his instructions were 'to do as much harm to the Germans as possible, to put a spoke into the wheels of the separate peace negotiations, and to stiffen, by whatever means . . . the Bolshevik resistance to German demands'. He was soon on excellent terms with Trotsky and Lenin, whom he offered guns, money and supplies. But Lockhart – an impetuous operative, mistrusted by many in Whitehall – had no guns to give, while his reports extolling the strength, integrity and high calling of the Bolsheviks only further alienated the British Foreign Office. By the time the Treaty of Brest-Litovsk was signed, any credibility remaining to him was in tatters, and with a view to salvaging his career, he effected an abrupt volte-face.

By May, Lockhart was demanding Allied intervention without

delay. The Bolsheviks, he said, were weaker than they had ever been. Rebellion was stirring in Petrograd, and in addition to the White armies, a rogue Czech legion – a defected splinter of the Hapsburg army – had clashed with regional soviets and was now advancing steadily on Moscow from Siberia. The Bolsheviks had no political allies in the capital, while in the provinces, the fledgling Red Army had its hands full fighting every class, from the dispossessed aristocracy to the rebellious peasants. It was extraordinary, he railed in his telegrams, that the opportunity had not already been taken.

Two days after Lockhart wired the British Foreign Office with news of Evgenia's proposed defection, Ransome had gone to Lenin – his first interview with the Bolshevik chairman – and discussed frankly the possibility of an attempt at regime change. Lenin had replied that in the event of Allied interference in Soviet affairs, only the Germans would benefit. 'What can take the place of the Soviet Power? The only power that can take its place is a bourgeois government. But the bourgeoisie in Russia has proved clearly enough that it can only remain in power with foreign help . . . It is easy to understand what avenues are opened up by this possibility.'

Lenin's signed statement was wired to London and appears in Lockhart's memoirs as proof that the former British Consul had always, until the very last moment, opposed the intervention which he later described as his country's 'crowning folly . . . an adventure which sent thousands of Russians to their deaths and cost the British taxpayer millions of pounds in money'. And yet Lockhart's telegrams between May and July show that he not only supported a British invasion, but was spending enormous sums in Russia on the so-called 'Moscow Centre', a loosely knit counter-revolutionary underground movement whose representatives met with increasing regularity at the Elite Hotel. Ransome, in the meantime – also living at the Elite Hotel – had become Lockhart's only direct contact with the Soviet authorities, who were preparing an unpleasant surprise.

In 1918, British espionage in Russia was a ramshackle business, poorly co-ordinated and poorly vetted. Felix Dzerzhinsky – who had long since cracked Lockhart's codes – knew that a British spy by the name of Sidney Reilly had presented himself at the Kremlin, masquerading as a British officer. He knew that the same Sidney Reilly was now gadding about Russia in a variety of disguises. In Petrograd, Ransome's friend, Captain Cromie, in company with Reilly, was handing out money to every counter-revolutionary that knocked on the embassy door. For the Cheka leader, who had devoted a lifetime to conspiracy and counter-conspiracy, it was not difficult to find suitable agents provocateurs or to ensure that their credentials withstood cursory examination. Thus, in July, when two Latvian riflemen presented themselves in Petrograd explaining that their comrades were dis-satisfied with their Bolshevik masters and wanted to return home to fight the Germans, they were greeted by Cromie with almost childish enthusiasm. Particularly interesting to Reilly, who was entrusted with the final negotiations, was the fact that the Latvians were responsible for guarding the Kremlin.

Just how much Ransome knew of the so-called 'Lockhart plot' or the extent to which he may have passed on anything he did know to Evgenia or the Kremlin is unclear, just as it is unclear whether Radek – a long-term confidant of Dzerzhinsky's – gave him any warning of the Cheka trap. Weighing his options, Ransome depended very heavily on the goodwill both of the British mission and of the Soviet, but as to how this goodwill was purchased one can only guess. What is certain is that, in the weeks running up to the Allied invasion – an invasion which Lockhart hoped to meet with a palace coup – he decided against leaving Russia under a British passport and began quite separate negotiations with Radek. Dzerzhinsky, meanwhile, left him in no doubt as to how citizens of any nationality would be treated if they were caught on the wrong side of the barricade.

'We stand for organised terror,' he had declared in June,

this must be clearly understood. Terror is an absolute necessity during times of revolution. Our aim is to fight against the enemies of the Soviet Government and the new order of life. Among such enemies are our political adversaries, as well as bandits, speculators and other criminals who undermine the foundations of the Soviet Government. To these we shall show no mercy.

~

Ransome had already used his connections at the Kremlin to effect one escape from Russia. Two months after contributing to Trotsky's Red Army library, Lola Kinel had fled Moscow with her grandmother and sister on a train packed with German prisoners of war. Thanks to Ransome, and more particularly to Karl Radek, the Kinels had been issued with fake German passports, and within days were in Poland, celebrating with a feast of white rolls and stew. Lola never forgot Ransome's kindness in evacuating her family before the Terror took off in earnest, but neither did she have any doubt as to where his political sympathies lay. He had often begged her to help the Bolsheviks, and took her refusal, she recalled, as a sign of heartlessness.

By July 1918, there was only one party that stood between Lenin and an effective monopoly of the Soviet: the Left Socialist Revolutionaries (LSRs), the party of the rural peasants, who had split from their more conservative comrades before the Bolshevik coup. In March, they had resigned their ministries in protest against Brest-Litovsk. They had condemned the bread wars. Yet they retained a substantial bloc within the Soviet Congress, and more significantly, co-directorship of the Cheka. For Lenin, the position was awkward, but on 6 July, at the Fifth All-Russian Congress, he was presented with an opportunity to remedy the situation. Ransome was present to hear the LSR leader speak.

Spiridonova, looking like a nursery governess rapt into uncontrollable frenzy, poured out a rhythmic, screaming denunciation of the Brest-Litovsk treaty. The Bolsheviks, by making peace with the Germans, had sacrificed the revolution. Better by far to have signed no treaty, have let the Germans occupy all Russia and discover for themselves that they could not hold it against an entire population determined to destroy them . . . She went on to denounce the Bolsheviks as agents of Germany, obedient servants of Mirbach, the German Ambassador in

Moscow. We Socialist Revolutionaries will not recognize the German peace . . . There was a storm of shouting, booing and cheering . . .

At 2.15 p.m., as the debate in the Hall of Nobles continued, two LSR party members serving as officers in the Cheka, Blumkin and Andreev, walked into the German embassy and asked to see the ambassador on a 'personal matter'. By way of identification, they showed a letter of introduction, supposedly bearing Dzerzhinsky's signature, to Councillor Reizling, the German chief of political affairs. During the meeting that followed, attended by Mirbach, Reizling and an interpreter, Blumkin produced a revolver and fired three times at point-blank range. Reizling and the interpreter hid under the table, but Mirbach moved towards the door and was shot in the back. The assassins leapt out of the window, dropping two grenades behind them, and disappeared into a waiting car.

Ransome, who had gone out for a bite to eat at lunchtime, heard the explosions and returned to find his old friend Vorovsky coming out of the Assembly, whistling 'Rule Britannia'. Someone, it was clear, had carried out the assassination with a view to bringing Russia back into the war against Germany, and Vorovsky assumed it was the Allies. But once the real culprits were discovered, the Bolsheviks moved with the same decision with which they had moved against the anarchists.

In the immediate aftermath of Mirbach's murder, Dzerzhinsky, acting on a tip-off, had found Blumkin and Andreev holed up in a nearby Cheka building with a group of senior LSRs. Attempting an arrest, he and his escort had been overpowered. Ransome, meanwhile, was still outside the Hall of Nobles, where he ran into Radek, who was already speaking of an LSR 'revolt' aimed not only at the Germans, but at the Soviet leadership. A battle ensued which briefly mirrored the November coup. LSR soldiers seized the Cheka headquarters at Lubianka, commandeering the telephone exchange and barricading the streets. But they had no serious plan of action and were soon overwhelmed.

Following Dzerzhinsky's release, thirteen LSRs – amongst them the vice chairman of the Cheka, V. A. Aleksandrovich –

were shot without trial (Dzerzhinsky dispatched Aleksandrovich himself), while the entire LSR Central Committee, along with all LSR delegates trapped in the Hall of Nobles, were imprisoned. Spiridonova was placed in a lunatic asylum, where Ransome hoped that she would recover her 'normality'. Meanwhile, the uprising gave the Bolsheviks a monopoly of the Cheka and provided an excuse to establish new laws for attendance at the All-Russian Assembly. Any LSR hoping to cast his vote would now have to denounce the policies of his leaders. The assassination of Mirbach had brought the Soviet 'within a hair's breadth' of renewed war with Germany, but in virtually all other respects had played directly into Bolshevik hands. Overstretched on the Western Front, the German army could not afford a serious engagement in Russia, and once this became clear, Soviet–German diplomacy was adjusted accordingly. When the new ambassador suggested that a battalion of German troops should be permitted to guard the embassy, Radek had laughed in his face. The only difficulty was that the assassination of one country's ambassador necessarily sent a disturbing message to the others, and when news of Mirbach's murder reached the Allied representatives in far away Vologda, the result was instantaneous. All of them, without exception, announced their intention to leave the country.

After months of playing the Allies against the Germans, and vice versa, the prospect of losing the diplomatic community in Vologda was unacceptable to the Kremlin. Much worse, however, was the apprehension – all too well-founded – that its evacuation prepared the way for the Allied invasion. The Bolsheviks had little hope of persuading the ambassadors by telegram, while forceful detention (an option which had been mooted) was bound to prove counterproductive. What was needed was a Bolshevik envoy who could argue the Soviet's position in person, someone well known to the foreign delegates and gifted in the art of bamboozlement. Radek volunteered immediately, taking Ransome along for the trip as 'interpreter and referee'.

Ransome's autobiography devotes an entire chapter to this

third and final trip to Vologda: the journey out, the clean and orderly stations evincing the Bolshevik miracle of remobilization, the princely reception by the Vologda soviet and the meeting with the American ambassador, David Francis, who had been horrified by Radek's sidearms, failing to understand that the outsized pistols were as integral to his uniform as his fountain pen. It was absurd, Ransome suggested, to be afraid of such a man, especially as every one of his arguments had been excellent. What would become of diplomacy if the Americans hid in the provinces? How could Francis doubt that he would be 'safer' in Moscow with the Bolsheviks close by to protect him?

Crossing town to the British legation, where Sir Francis Lindley, the British chargé d'affaires, sat at a table spread with a Union Jack, Radek merely sipped at his smoke as he regretted the damage that a hasty exit might do to Anglo-Russian relations, touching as he did so on the ramshackle nature of Britain's present operation: how troublesome it had been to have to deal with 'half-a-dozen separate, irresponsible and uncoordinated Missions, the voice of none of which could be taken for that of the British Government'. Lindley listened politely, assured Radek that his departure would in no way affect relations between Britain and the Soviet, and to Ransome admitted privately that he had no faith in the Bolsheviks whatsoever: 'You don't seem to realize that these people are our enemies.'

The adventure to Vologda was a diplomatic failure and left Ransome in little doubt that 'the game was up'. But he had not wasted his time. While Radek attended to business with the Vologda soviet, he continued his chat with Lindley, producing a letter from Lockhart establishing his good faith. The plan now, Ransome explained, was to leave Russia before his position became untenable; but he hoped to remain useful. If Lindley would furnish him with a letter to the British ambassador in Stockholm, he would maintain his Russian contacts and keep the British informed of their activities. Lindley agreed, and after dining on fifteen hard-boiled eggs apiece, Ransome and Radek returned to Moscow, pondering the second half of the equation.

With the Allies expected at Archangel so soon, there was nothing to be gained by Ransome's exiting on a British battleship, either to be shot by his own side or disowned entirely by the Soviet. Better to go through Petrograd, then on via Helsingfors to Stockholm. Furnished with both British and Soviet papers, he would leave Petrograd as an Englishman and get through the German authorities in Finland as a Bolshevik courier carrying the Soviet diplomatic bag. Under the circumstances, it was the only way he could avoid choosing sides. Evgenia would travel separately via Germany. Vorovsky was leaving shortly at the head of a mission to resume control of the Swedish legation and was pausing in Berlin. He was in need of a reliable secretary.

Ransome arrived in Moscow five days after Soviet officials, fearing their release by the advancing Czech legion, had executed the Tsar and his family in a dingy cellar in Yekaterinburg. He made no comment on the business. Stepping off his train on 22 July, he had gone straight to Lockhart and collected his dual passport. Next there were books to pack and final arrangements to make: notes on the Revolution for Evgenia to carry through Germany; discussions with Chicherin at the Commissariat of Foreign Affairs; diplomatic passes to be stamped; a last telegram to Lindley. Vorovsky's team left with Evgenia on the 27th, while Ransome – presumably to calm his nerves – went fishing in the countryside. He returned by the early train on the 29th, visited the Swedish embassy to procure a visa for his Bolshevik passport, and spent the rest of the day in a panic because Iroida could not find Evgenia's wedding ring. On 1 August, with Allied troops now poised to land at Archangel, Lockhart's mission was ordered to leave the Elite Hotel, and was out by the 2nd. By the 3rd, Ransome was in Petrograd, talking to Captain Cromie, and by the 4th, now decked out in his Soviet costume, in Helsingfors. Through his porthole he could see German gunboats in the harbour and had tried to take a photograph, but his hands were trembling too violently to focus. His disguise, nevertheless, had held, and with his bags unsearched he arrived in Stockholm on the 5th, missing the Allied invasion and a mass arrest of British citizens by twenty-four hours. It had been, to say the least, a close shave: a dramatic exit, planned on excellent intelligence, but purchased at a price. Because as Ransome sat on his bunk in Helsingfors picturing a German firing squad or worse, his suitcase had not, as he assured his London editors, contained a clutter of personal 'rubbish'. Instead, by way of earning his Soviet passport (and providing the Bolsheviks with a little leverage to ensure his continued sympathy), he had smuggled 3 million roubles in cash for the International Bureau in Sweden, an assignment that had not escaped the notice of British intelligence.

'Mr Arthur Ransome, Petrograd correspondent of the *Daily News*,' telegrammed Captain Bray to the War Office on 29 August,

is reported to be in Stockholm, having married Trotsky's secretary, with a large amount of Russian Government money, and to be travelling with a Bolshevik passport. The alleged marriage we understand to be a 'put-up' job and so the Bolshevik passport may be of little account, but the fact that he has a large amount of Russian Government money is of interest to us, and we would like to have him watched accordingly. Could you please wire out?

16

Stockholm

When Ransome arrived in Stockholm, he had received no letters from home or read any British newspaper – including the *Daily News* – since 1917. Word of his brother Geoffrey's death had possibly reached him via Sir Francis Lindley on his final trip to Vologda, but Ransome made no mention of it. For eight months, he had followed a course of his own prescription, defined by two radically opposed interests. On the one hand, a telegram in January 1918 from Balfour, the British Foreign Secretary, had encouraged him to maintain contact with the Bolshevik government, and this Ransome had done, explaining to himself all the while that he was serving king and country. On the other hand, he had allowed himself to be persuaded that the Soviet policy as described by Trotsky, Lenin and Radek was in all respects the correct one. By January 1918, he had fallen head over heels in love with Trotsky's personal secretary and become an intimate friend of her political sponsor, the Bolshevik chief of propaganda, with whom he briefly shared a house. At the same time, he had shared a hotel with the British mission, who had plotted to overthrow the Soviet government. He had fled Russia in the uniform of a Bolshevik courier, carrying money which would fund Bolshevik propaganda, but after delivering his bags to the Russian legation, had proceeded to the British embassy, where he presented Lindley's letter to the ambassador. In his pocket was a ring, intended for Evgenia when she eventually arrived from Berlin, but this ring also had a double meaning. Evgenia was described in Ransome's passport as his 'wife' – a subterfuge indulged by Balfour to supply her with cover. But Evgenia had no intention of defecting, while Ransome hoped to turn the subterfuge into an accomplished fact, to divorce Ivy and make Evgenia his legal wife. In short, in August 1918, at a time when Stockholm, as a neutral city, hosted German and British embassies, political refugees and agitators of every description – spies, mercenaries, agents provocateurs – it is difficult to imagine a single resident whose interests and national allegiance were more confused than Arthur Ransome's.

If Ransome had chosen to return to England with Evgenia in June, no obstacle would have been placed in his way, but following his arrival in Sweden his second application for a visa was turned down 'pending further investigation'. Back in Whitehall it was known that his 'official wife' was still in Berlin with Vorovsky's mission. It was known that Ransome had arrived in Sweden under highly suspicious circumstances, and that in Russia, his journalism – including his *On Behalf of Russia* – was being circulated by Soviet agents amongst Allied troops. At the beginning of August, the arrest of Bruce Lockhart, the British and French missions and over four hundred foreign nationals provided the Bolsheviks with hostages against the Allied invasion. Lockhart and his colleagues had been released when it became clear that General Frederick Poole, leading the Allied expeditionary force at Archangel, had landed with scarcely enough troops to hold his position, let alone to march on Moscow. But the propaganda war only escalated. On 18 August, Oliver Wardrop, the Moscow Consul General, who had been forced to burn confidential papers while Cheka officers beat at his door, wired London claiming that Karl Radek had 'let loose a flood of invective against Great Britain'. It was merely a matter of time, concluded Wardrop, before 'Radek's intimate friend, the sharer of his domestic hearth, Mr. Arthur Ransome, British Subject, will telegraph Radek's rhetoric to the *Daily News*'.

Under these circumstances, Ransome's most pressing concern was rehabilitation, and it was for this reason that he did not immediately condemn the Allied intervention in the press. Instead, he co-operated as fully as possible with agents of the British intelligence services in Stockholm, while insisting that his contacts with the Soviet remained indispensable to British interests. Shortly after presenting his letter of introduction to Sir Esme Howard, he was summoned for a long talk with Major

Scales, the former head of military intelligence in Russia, who found him deeply suspect politically but hugely engaging as a personality. Ransome, argued Scales, would be more useful to the Foreign Office if he were allowed to go about his business, and with a view to keeping an eye on his activities, arranged for his letters to be sent home by the diplomatic bag and his articles to be wired through the British embassy. In London, Scales's view was seconded by a Mr Gasebee of MI5, responsible for censorship at the Press Information Department, who observed:

I do not think we should contemplate for a moment the course of telling the *Daily News* that Mr. Ransome's telegrams will not be allowed through to them. That would defeat the very object which we have in view, which is to keep Mr. Ransome at his post, because by being in touch with the Bolsheviks in Russia, he will probably be a valuable source of information.

~

Ransome's diary for Stockholm is a blank until 11 August, when he sat down at his desk and typed a long letter to his editors in London, A. G. Gardiner and F. J. Hillier. Once again, his priority was rehabilitation, and after several weeks in which virtually nothing had appeared under his name in the *Daily News*, to convince his employers that he had neither wasted his time in Russia nor – a perennial failing of the English adventurer abroad – permitted himself to 'go native'. Most especially, Ransome wished to emphasize that while his intimacy with the Bolsheviks reflected no personally held political conviction, his success in penetrating this curious and occasionally savage tribe had exceeded that of any other diplomat or reporter.

'You may have guessed or heard,' he wrote,

that I have got, to an extraordinary degree, the confidence of the Soviet folk who certainly allowed me to see much more of what went on than was seen by any other foreigner, and were willing to talk straight to me when they would not do anything but put official representatives of England off with fair words.

This open-handed friendship, claimed Ransome, had been useful not only in terms of acquiring information, but of exerting real influence: 'of getting things done and of preventing other things from being done (for example of preventing the whole of the Allied representatives at Vologda being put in a saloon car and brought to Moscow by force, which Radek, whom I accompanied to Vologda, had the authority and the inclination to do)'. British officials in Russia, he explained, had seen little point in letting such a useful resource go to waste. When intervention became inevitable, Lockhart and Lindley had decided to place him in cold storage in Sweden, 'with a view to possibilities in the future'.

Ransome's network in Russia not only remained intact, but was positively strengthened by the Allied invasion. Owing to a spell in a 'small commune' with the secretary to the Commissar for War, the secretary to the Eastern Bureau of the Commissariat of Foreign Affairs and the head of the Press Bureau, his contacts were excellent. The Soviet was relying on him exclusively to tell its story candidly and clearly, and before his departure had instructed its ministers to help him in any way they could. 'All Russian Government publications, newspapers, both official and other, will be coming to Stockholm for me twice weekly. Probably, like everything that depends on Russians, it will take a little time before it works smoothly, but I think that within a week or two I should be able to keep up a better Russian news service from here than any other paper has got.'

Having established his own, virtually unlimited overview of the situation in faraway Moscow, Ransome proceeded to Britain's current policy, which left a great deal to be desired. Intervention had been a mistake, and while there was no point in 'howling over spilt milk', would do even more damage if it were to continue. Any foreign power that toppled the Soviet would have to deal with the Revolution underground, and as Trotsky had pointed out in private conversation, '. . . We may be bad organizers, but nobody will deny that we are the best disorganizers the world has ever seen.' Under the circumstances, advised

Ransome, the correct policy was to recognize the Soviet as the natural authority in Russia, to supply it with arms if possible, and to withdraw and watch the fireworks. The Bolsheviks directed all anti-imperialist resistance from Finland through Ukraine to the Middle East, where Turkey hoped to form an Islamic bloc – 'Ottoman I suppose in general character' – from Constantinople to Afghanistan. Britain was, of course, opposed to Bolshevism on principle, but why not leave the Soviet to do the dirty work? Sentiment was mere childishness at such a time, especially a sentimental prejudice in favour of the bourgeoisie, who had courted the Germans before intervention and only now spoke loudly in favour of the Allies.

'Nothing has been more interesting', observed Ransome, 'than to watch how the "bourgeois" parties veered gradually, perceiving their chance of coming to power on, as the American politicians would put it, a pro-Ally ticket.'

Looking ahead, Ransome could not promise the *Daily News* his undivided attention. Nobody would have such an excellent opportunity of watching the situation in Russia as he would in Stockholm, nor would the paper do anything but gain.

On the other hand I do not like to fix a definite length of time to my staying here, because, in the event of war continuing between the Soviet and ourselves, and of the Soviet seeming to the Germans too prickly a hedgehog to be crushed, it might be my job to use the special position which I have got to go back into the country looking for knowledge rather than news.

Ransome, in short, was prepared to continue writing for his paper just so long as he was not called back into Russia as an agent of the British government – an eventuality he looked forward to with some confidence. He felt sure the *Daily News* would understand. But in the meantime, he needed money, and over the next two weeks, his diary shows a frenzy of activity – up to nine articles a day – continuing unabated until Evgenia's arrival on 28 August. On the 29th, there is a happy silence, and on the 30th, after Ransome had hired a translator to tackle the Swedish press, an afternoon's sailing, the first of many maritime adventures together, and in Stockholm, a possible solution to an increasingly vexing problem. Shortly after reaching Sweden, Ransome had applied to the British embassy for permission to live in the Russian compound with Evgenia but had been told the arrangement would be unsuitable. Evgenia, likewise, refused to live with the British, and Ransome had hoped to acquire some sort of neutrality – and to realize a childhood dream – by living on the water. The boat in question, however, was too small, and they settled instead for a little cottage together at the mouth of the harbour.

~

Both Ransome's letter to Gardiner and a letter from Gardiner which had crossed it in the post were duly processed in Whitehall, where they appear in a bundle of 'intercepts' circulated to every branch of the intelligence services. Gardiner, under pressure from the owner of the *Daily News*, had softened his views on intervention and had grown anxious that Ransome, whose telegrams from Moscow had been in stark contrast to the opinions professed by virtually every other British correspondent, had been drawn too deeply into the Bolshevik fold. 'I am sure that you will not let your sympathy with the Soviet regime prejudice your view of events. The *Daily News* is committed, not to the theories of a party, but to the principles of the revolution . . .' Surprisingly, however, Ransome's explanation of his exploits in Moscow, and his reasons for his continued support of the Bolshevik government, had reassured his editor, who wrote again in a much more encouraging vein:

I find your letter, in spite of its very natural zig-zaggings, prodigiously illuminating. You cannot understand how befogged one gets at this end of things with all the perplexities and complexities of the Russian movement, and it is immensely valuable to get them periodically elucidated, even if the elucidation comes, as it inevitably must come, after the situation dealt with has probably ceased to exist . . .

Shortly before Ransome received this letter, the situation did change. On 30 August, Uritsky, the chairman of the Petrograd Cheka, was assassinated. Twelve hours later, Dora Kaplan, a young Socialist Revolutionary disaffected by the suppression of the Constituent Assembly, gunned down Lenin in Moscow. In both cities, the Cheka retaliated instantly and with extreme ferocity, rounding up all suspected 'counter-revolutionaries' and descending into the cells, where political and criminal prisoners alike were dragged out and shot: anarchists, LSRs, scores of 'bourgeois hostages' – noblemen, Kadets, doctors, lawyers, kulaks, merchants, priests – taken at random since the Cheka's introduction in December 1917. In Petrograd, the British embassy was invaded and Captain Cromie killed as he attempted to defend sovereign territory. In London, *The Times* reported that the British naval attaché had been murdered and mutilated: 'The British Government have demanded immediate reparation and have put M. Litvinoff [the Soviet delegate in London] and his staff under preventive arrest.' On 3 September, the British delegation in Moscow was arrested for a second time and taken into Cheka custody. Meanwhile, *Izvestia*, the official newspaper of the Soviet, revealed a foreign plot to overthrow the government:

. . . A conspiracy organised by Anglo-French diplomats at the head of which was the chief of the British Mission, Lockhart, the French Consul General Lavergne, and others was liquidated. The purpose of the conspiracy was to capture the Council of People's Commissars and the proclamation of a military dictatorship in Moscow; this was to be done by bribing Soviet troops.

Over the next few days, the full extent of Bruce Lockhart's alleged plans, co-ordinated by Sidney Reilly and involving a huge underground network of counter-revolutionary agents, was revealed: agitation in Soviet-controlled cities; the destruction of key railways and bridges leading into Moscow and Petrograd; the separation of the starving populace from vital supplies. Hoards of grain had been stockpiled by the conspirators so that when the *coup d'état* was effected, food could be rushed in to reinforce the new dictatorship. This outrageous abuse of diplomatic immunity, wholly illegal and yet so typical of imperialist tactics, had been unmasked by the Latvian guards themselves, loyal and incorruptible champions of the Revolution.

In England, the murder of Cromie on the sacred premises of the British embassy provoked universal outrage and an ultimatum from the War Cabinet threatening extreme action if any further harm came to British subjects. 'His Majesty's Government', quoted the front page of Ransome's own newspaper, 'will hold the members of the Soviet Government individually responsible, and will make every endeavour to secure that they shall be treated as outlaws by the governments of all civilized nations, and that no place of refuge shall be left to them.' Ransome himself appears to have been stunned by the news, and at first could scarcely credit it. He had liked Cromie. They had played chess together. There was no man more noble or constant. Cromie, he insisted, had been a true friend to the Soviet, one of the very few capable of inspiring trust on both sides of the ever-widening divide. His loss was a tragedy, a dreadful error, whereas the arrest of Lockhart approached farce. 'The papers here', Ransome told the *Daily News*, 'print today the story of an Entente conspiracy against the Soviet government which outdoes any sensational novel in both complexity of plan and wildness of detail. Some details are so fantastic as to cast doubt on the whole, and the whole so impracticable that I find it hard to believe it was ever seriously considered.'

On 2 September, as Lenin's life hung in the balance, Ransome wrote an obituary hailing the founder of Bolshevism as 'the greatest figure of the Russian Revolution'. Here 'for good or evil was a man who, at least for a moment, had his hand on the rudder of the world'. Common peasants who had known Lenin attested to his goodness, his extraordinary generosity to children. The workers looked up to him, 'not as an ordinary man, but as a saint'. Without Lenin, Ransome concluded, the soviets would not perish, but they would lose their vital direction.

His influence was the one constant steadying factor. He had his definite policy, and his firmness in his own position was the best curb on other, more mercurial people. In the truest sense of the word it may be said that the revolution has lost its head. Fiery Trotsky, ingenious, brilliant Radek, are alike unable to replace the cool logic of the most colossal dreamer that Russia produced in our time.

Two days later, Lenin – one bullet lodged in his shoulder, one in his lung – was showing signs of improvement, and Ransome's obituary was not used. Meanwhile, the massacre in Russia continued with the Bolshevik leader's unequivocal approval. 'Thank you,' he telegrammed Trotsky on 10 September, 'convalescence is going splendidly. I am confident that the suppression of the Kazan Czechs and White Guards, and likewise of the bloodsucking kulaks who support them, will be a model of mercilessness.'

~

In Petrograd, on 3 September, *Izvestia* announced the execution of five hundred hostages. Within the walls of the Kronstadt Fortress, a further four hundred were reported shot in a single night. Moscow, by comparison, got off lightly, with barely ninety executed in the first two days. The opening of Stalin's 'Great Terror' in 1937 would claim over 300,000 victims in a single year, eclipsing Lenin's field day on the bourgeoisie – a quarter of a million in the course of two years – by a significant margin. But the Red Terror of 1918 marked a watershed. As the Soviet press clamoured for more blood, Grigory Zinoviev, who had supervised the slaughter in Petrograd, claimed that a massive internal purge was the only possible answer to Russia's ills: 'To overcome our enemies we must have our own social militarism. We must carry along with us 90 million out of the 100 million of Soviet Russia's population. As for the rest, we have nothing to say to them. They must be annihilated.'

Ransome was in a better position than most to understand that terror was a cornerstone of Bolshevik philosophy. Between December 1917 and his exit from Russia in August, he had watched, by turns, the liquidation of the Constituent Assembly, the muzzling of the free press and the bloody suppression of political rivals. In his first political pamphlet, he had reminded complacent readers that social revolution did not mean the exclusion of bourgeois parties from government, but the absolute eradication of a class. And yet, when the full meaning of class war was revealed as a naked fact, he denied it absolutely. Mass terror, he explained, was impossible in Russia, 'because there can be no such thing unless the mass feels inclined to terrorize, which they do not'.

News of Cromie's murder, Lockhart's arrest, the attempt on Lenin's life and the resulting bloodbath reached Stockholm within four days of one another, each one challenging Ransome to reconsider his entire approach to the Bolshevik regime. But Ransome did not reconsider. Instead, his immediate reaction was to suggest that those who had not met the Bolsheviks – the British public, the hysterical pundits of the reactionary press – did not know what they were talking about. Terror, he protested, had never been intended seriously. It was simply a form of words, a rhetorical posture to scare naughty children, 'an integral part of revolutionary vocabulary, but not to be taken "*au pied de la lettre*"'. And yet the Bolsheviks themselves made no attempt to deny the Terror. Instead, they claimed that Lockhart and his cohorts, by conspiring against the people, had provoked a just retribution, visited at large on the class they championed. Dzerzhinsky had 'much valuable material in hand as to the methods of imperialism' and made his own appeal to the civilized world regarding 'the unheard of and barbarous crime going on in our country, where the English–French bourgeoisie, which boasts in democratic phrases, is now setting itself to the re-establishment of monarchy in Russia'. Radek himself had informed Ransome that the Terror was both real and 'very serious'. The only consolation he could offer was that Lockhart would not be shot, if only to deprive 'Jingo' of propaganda. The British mission in Moscow would be released in exchange for their counterparts in London. It was a great deal more than they deserved.

Unable to deny the Terror, Ransome instead explained it as a form of rational adjustment. The Soviet's hand had been forced by the prevailing anarchy, by hostile armies, by fuel shortages, by famine and disease. The Soviet, he urged, provided Russia's only viable nucleus of sanity, while politically uneducated elements within society demanded instant relief, 'seeking dimly any change although no possible change can put an immediate end to starvation or do more than change one war for another'. In the cities, he explained, 'death struts the streets so openly that for both sides he has lost his old solemnity', while in the country, peasant uprisings were not 'conscious patriotic revolts', but 'the terrific blind gestures of a starving revolution tearing at its own flesh'. As to specific atrocities, Ransome would only admit that the Bolsheviks, 'knowing that with them will go down what intellect remains', had taken 'less and less account of individual lives in what they regard as the sacred attempt of the brain to keep command of a sick body on the verge of delirium. They know their own lives are not at stake because it is impossible to stake anything whose loss is inevitable.'

Having established the Bolsheviks as martyrs, Ransome began to feel that Cromie's death was not the result of a 'fantastic misunderstanding' after all. On the contrary, the Cheka had something to go on, and it was 'highly regrettable that they should have anything to go on at all'. Under the circumstances, the only comfort he could offer was that the investigation was being undertaken by men whom Ransome knew were above any possible reproach. Yakov Peters, now supervising Lockhart's interrogation, was a man of 'scrupulous honesty', while Felix Dzerzhinsky, who as a boy had dreamed of becoming a Jesuit priest, suffered only from an excess of zeal that occasionally blinded him to the fragility of mere flesh and blood. He was a

calm cool-headed fanatic for the revolution with absolute trust in his own conscience and recognizing no higher court. He has been much in prison where he was remarkable for the urgent desire to take upon himself the unpleasant labour of other criminals, such as cleaning cells and emptying slops. He has a theory of self-sacrifice in which one man has to take on himself the unpleasantness that would otherwise be shared by many. Hence his willingness to occupy his present position. He would not act in such a case as this, nor would he allow his subordinates to act, unless he was personally convinced that such a plot actually existed.

The liquidation of the Lockhart plot went down in Soviet history as the original coup over Western intelligence. The combined might of the Allies had done its worst, but 'Iron Felix', the 'Knight of the Revolution', had slain the capitalist dragon. In Britain, by contrast, the business was largely dismissed as a Bolshevik fantasy, until half a century later records were released suggesting that even at the time the Foreign Office recognized Lockhart had vastly exceeded his authority. Cromie's death caused a national outrage, but the British government's efforts to extradite their mission, though successful, were discreet. Lockhart had been led, step by step, to perform a scenario which helped underpin Soviet nationalism under Stalin: the threat of terror from overseas used to justify terror within – a people united by fear. Meanwhile, on 8 September, Ransome sent a 'loud howl' to the *Daily News* demanding money and tobacco (he was short of both), along with a dozen plain outline maps of Russia from Stanford's of Long Acre: 'ditto six of Caucasus, Turkistan and Central Asia'.

~

In London, the Red Terror fed a horror of domestic revolution that had been building ever since the Irish Easter Rising of 1916. On New Year's Day 1918, the domestic secret service, MI5, had circulated a greetings card to its officers picturing the slouching, demonic figure of Subversion, knife in hand and exhaling wreaths of toxic smoke, creeping up on a British soldier, with only Britannia, trident in hand, to guard the hero's back. In January, rationing was introduced. In February, the Manpower Bill raised the maximum age of conscription to fifty and was preceded by what Basil Thomson, head of Special Branch, euphemistically called 'a rather sudden growth of pacifism'. Nineteen eighteen was the year of the Pemberton Billing case, otherwise known as the 'Black Book Trial', in which Noel Pemberton Billing, seconded by Ransome's old nemesis, Lord Alfred Douglas, successfully claimed in court that a black book containing the names of 47,000 British homosexuals was being used by the Germans to undermine the war effort. Recalling an illegal strike by 10,000 of London's 19,000 policemen a week before Captain Cromie's memorial service, Lloyd George claimed that Britain 'was nearer to Bolshevism that day than at any other time since'.

Most of Ransome's friends were violently opposed to Bolshevism. Robin Collingwood was working for naval intelligence. W. G. Collingwood, the ancient Skald of the Lakes, anticipated a showdown the moment Ransome set foot back in the country, while Barbara Collingwood implored him in her letters to give up dabbling in politics, which he was clearly no good at, and return as soon as possible to romances. Ransome heartily agreed. Within the literary set that he had belonged to, liberal admiration for the Revolution did not extend to mass murder, while Edith – fully aware that she now had only one son left to lose – could only concede through gritted teeth that at least he had the courage of his convictions ('my dear Maw, of course I do'). Only Ivy, of Ransome's most intimate circle, seems to have considered making contact with the Bolsheviks themselves, and this we know from a brief, intercepted correspondence with Maxim Litvinov, which Ivy conducted in mid-August: 'Stricken down by influenza, profoundly regret unable to keep appointment.'

In America, Ransome's popularity plummeted after Brest-Litovsk, and had taken a further nosedive when its ambassador, David Francis, returned from Vologda, fresh from the meeting at which Radek, accompanied by Ransome, had issued threats and neglected to leave his revolvers at the door. Raymond Robins' influence over President Wilson had proved negligible, and America's hostility to the Soviet government, notwithstanding warm words about the Revolution, had been one of the decisive factors leading to intervention. Ransome's *On Behalf of Russia* had been well received within liberal circles in the States, but the reprint immediately following the Terror, with a preface by Radek attacking the 'Allied bandits', had confirmed his reputation as a dangerous revolutionary. The *New York Times* called him 'the mouthpiece of the Bolsheviki' and stopped publishing his articles on 31 August, the day the Terror commenced.

In Russia, Ransome's abrupt departure, its manner and its timing, had made an appalling impression on the British community left behind, which deepened when Lockhart, Captain Hicks and the rest were arrested for the second time by the Cheka, interned in Lubianka 11 and told frankly by Yakov Peters that in all probability they would be shot. A memo in the British Foreign Office archive contains an anonymous telegram summarizing an interview held with Hicks by a British expatriate, profession unknown.

'I think it is my duty', runs the telegram,

to report to you that Captain Hicks of the British Mission, who is at present staying in the ex-American Consulate in Moscow, has brought to my notice the fact that there are two Englishmen whose conduct ought to be brought to the notice of the British Government, as they are exacting a not inconsiderable influence on the situation in Russia by persuading the Bolsheviks that they may count on a large measure of support from the working classes in England. The first is Mr. Arthur Ransome, who is the correspondent for the *Daily News*.

Ransome, claimed Hicks, had 'close and friendly relations' with the Bolshevik leaders throughout, but in June had promised Lockhart that if he were supplied with a British passport and obtained permission to live in Stockholm, he would cease writing propaganda and devote himself entirely to gathering information about the Revolution. The first doubts, said Hicks, had been raised when Ransome left Moscow without saying a word to members of the British mission, when he knew that their position was extremely dangerous. He had already told them that there was a party within the Soviet, headed by Radek, that wished 'to go to extreme lengths with them on account of the British landing at Archangel'. This warning was followed immediately by the first arrest of Lockhart and the British delegates. Hicks believed that Ransome was still in the country when their fate 'was as yet undecided . . .'

'His influence with the Soviets was considerable,' concluded the telegram, 'and it appears to Mr. Lockhart and Captain Hicks that, if he was too indifferent to exercise it on behalf of British subjects, he does not deserve the protection of British nationality. The Mission is further informed that he is, in spite of his definite promise, continuing his propaganda work from Stockholm.'

Concerns as to Ransome's allegiance, character and curious combination of timidity and self-importance had followed him to Stockholm, where it was reported that before fleeing Russia he had briefly visited the late Cromie at the British embassy. Overhearing a private conversation concerning outstanding loans to the Russian government and the possibility of retrieving these funds by offering bribes to Soviet officials, Ransome had burst into the room announcing: 'In the name of the Soviet I state that if you disclose the names of those willing to accept bribes, the Soviet Government will pay your debt in full . . .'

On 12 September, a British agent based in Sweden wired the Foreign Office, advising that no faith should be placed in Ransome whatsoever:

I do not know how much is known in London of Arthur Ransome's activities here, but it certainly ought to be understood how completely he is in the hands of the Bolsheviks. He seems to have persuaded the Legation that he has changed his views to some extent but this is certainly not the case. He claims, as has already been reported to you, to be the official historian of the Bolshevik movement. I suppose this is true, at all events it is true that he is living here with a lady who was previously Trotsky's private secretary, that he spends the greater part of his time in the Bolshevik Legation, where he is provided with a typewriter, and that he is very nervous as to the effect which his present attitude and activities may have upon his prospects in England. I also know that he has informed two Russians that I, personally, am an agent of the British Government, and said that he had this information from authoritative sources, both British and Bolshevik . . .

In Whitehall, these telegrams joined many others confirming a view that Ransome was an 'out-and-out Bolshevik' and showed no sign of changing his ways. There was a faction within the Foreign Office and War Office that would shortly be pushing for his arrest and prosecution under the Defence of the Realm Act.

Only one British journalist was considered as dangerous to British interests as Ransome: Morgan Philips Price, whose pamphlets, sponsored and printed by Radek's International Bureau, were currently being dropped from aeroplanes onto the heads of British troops in Murmansk. Ransome, however, was considered cleverer than Price, and much closer to the Soviet leaders themselves, and it was possibly for this reason that after two months in Stockholm, when loathing for the Bolsheviks was at its hysterical peak, he was offered a position in His Majesty's Secret Service.

~

In Ransome's diary entry for 27 September, there is a gnomic entry in tiny handwriting which reads, 'Wyatt made his proposal.' Rummaging through his papers, one finds a matching document, and a very bizarre one at that. There is no indication as to whom it was written, though one can assume it was aimed at the Foreign Office. It is an account of Ransome's meeting with a Mr Wyatt, supposedly an English accountant attached to a firm in Petrograd who claimed to speak with the full authority of the British embassy. Ransome had left the interview in a state of acute indignation.

'On September 27,' the letter begins,

I went to see Mr. Wyatt by appointment. I had previously been told by Captain Leighton that Americans from Russia had spread reports that 'in Russia I had been consistently working against the interests of the Allies', and that my position depended on my satisfying Mr. Wyatt that I was not a traitor. It appeared from this that Mr. Lindley's recommendation to Sir Esme Howard was considered of [no] value beside the gossip of chance persons, outside the British Mission, who therefore had no means of knowing how I was working, and merely formed their own opinion from the fact that I spent every moment I could talking to and listening to Bolsheviks.

Ransome's 'work', he insisted, had been of the utmost importance. So much so that he had spoken to no other Englishmen in

Russia save members of the British mission, who would not have been such fools as to 'queer' him with the Bolsheviks in order to satisfy one or two 'mutton-headed businessmen'. These niceties had been lost on Mr Wyatt, who, rudely brushing aside Ransome's claim that the ambassador himself could vouch for him, had 'come very straightforwardly to the point'. The conversation was to be an examination of Ransome's 'political soundness', which would be determined by his willingness to co-operate. Wyatt had 'pleaded, yes actually pleaded' with the ambassador on the grounds that Ransome might be useful to him, but was now doubtful. What he needed was not 'information about the state of Russia or the Bolsheviks', but only 'information that would help us to beat the Bolsheviks'.

Ransome's letter recorded his disgust at being subjected to Wyatt's bullying, along with his own stern refusal to become an Allied stool-pigeon or to transform his articles for the *Daily News* into vehicles for anti-Bolshevik propaganda.

I hinted that this would be a little difficult in view of what I had already written when I hoped that we should avoid intervention. He said I could say my change of view had been brought about by a change of circumstances. My influence, if I did so, would be very great, he said. And, as a reward, he thought he could guarantee that I should be allowed to live where I liked, while writing the desired stuff, which, of course, even if I could write it, would completely destroy the very real possibilities of usefulness which I do possess and have made use of during the last year.

All this, Ransome hoped, would make the integrity of his position as clear as possible, and yet barely a fortnight after the letter was written, he had been recruited to MI6.

There were several factors which favoured Ransome's recruitment, and the first, somewhat surprisingly, was the appearance in Sweden of Bruce Lockhart and the British mission, recently released from Cheka custody in exchange for Maxim Litvinov's legation in London. A number of meetings took place over the following days, and the upshot was that on 12 October, as Stockholm hummed with rumours that the German armies were crumbling and the Kaiser's days were numbered, Ransome dined with Lockhart and Clifford Sharp to discuss how, in the future, his talents might best be put at the disposal of British intelligence.

At present (possibly owing to the Official Secrets Act) there is no way of knowing precisely what Lockhart and Ransome's professional relationship had consisted of in Moscow, or exactly why Captain Hicks, who had so recently recommended Ransome be denied British citizenship, should have remained silent over his appointment to an organization whose sole purpose was to protect British interests. What we do know is that the failure of Lockhart's mission had deprived the Foreign Office of any direct contact with the Soviet whatsoever, so that Ransome could now claim, without exaggeration, to be the only Englishman welcomed by the Bolsheviks who was also in a position to speak to his own government. Lockhart appears to have recognized this, and groomed Ransome carefully with a view to receiving all useful news once he reached London. In return, he promised to smooth Ransome's way with Whitehall and to sort out any conflict with the *Daily News*. As for Ransome, he treated Lockhart as an ally and a friend, though, as he would shortly discover, Lockhart's friendship was of a strictly provisional kind.

Lockhart's recommendation was useful to Ransome, but his recruitment was also facilitated by the conflicted nature of the British intelligence community itself: the inter-departmental rivalries of the Home Office, the War Office and the Foreign Office, and the very marked cultural differences between the domestic and foreign branches of military intelligence, MI5 and MI6.

Officers of MI5 were institutionally disposed to loathe men like Ransome, who at a time of war, it was felt, abused their civic rights to undermine the safety of their compatriots. Looking out from their island fortress, MI5 officers were prejudiced to take a local view, considered propaganda at least as powerful as dynamite and often chafed that the laws which punished enemy spies could not be more liberally applied to gentlemen of the press. Officers of MI6, on the other hand, were devoted to furthering

British interests abroad, and were inclined, as a result, to be less inward-looking, more cosmopolitan and more pragmatic. They were usually linguists, frequently self-promoting adventurers and occasionally very reluctant civil servants indeed – accidental spies who looked forward to returning to their peacetime jobs as soon as the dust had settled. Clifford Sharp was one such man. In London, he had worked closely with Sidney and Beatrice Webb – joint leaders of the influential Fabian Society – and in 1913, had helped launch the Webbs' flagship, the radical *New Statesman*. As a fierce opponent of the war, Sharp had proved so irksome to the government that in 1917 Lloyd George personally orchestrated his conscription to the Royal Artillery. Shortly afterwards, he was extracted by the Foreign Office and sent to neutral Sweden, where he found Ransome very genial company.

Whereas Wyatt had resorted to blackmail, Sharp treated Ransome with respect. Whereas Wyatt was a 'mutton-headed businessman', Sharp was a cultured man of letters who required no sudden volte-face and later published Ransome's articles in the *New Statesman*. Ransome's recruitment to MI6 can only have been sweetened by the fact that Clifford Sharp was the son-in-law of one of his favourite children's authors, E. Nesbit, so that his election to the shadowy circles of the Secret Intelligence Service (code name 'S76') would have been flavoured with the same air of bohemian nonconformity that had once hung about the literary salons he attended in Edwardian London. Viewed practically, employment by the government offered Ransome the status he craved, a regular salary and a degree of political protection. Romantically, it placed him on the same footing as the heroes of some of his favourite novels, including Erskine Childers' *Riddle of the Sands*. Indeed, such was Ransome's exultation at finding himself at once a dignified bureaucrat and dashing sleuth that he considered quitting journalism altogether. In late October, when George Cadbury, owner of the *Daily News*, requested his presence in London for a 'short leave' and a frank discussion of his articles, Ransome declined. 'I have talked it over with Sharp,' he told Lockhart, who takes the same view as you did, that it would be foolish, merely for the sake of talking to the DN (and catching pike, seeing infant etc) to risk making my position seem so unrevolutionary in the eyes of the more rigid precisions among the Bolsheviks that it might cut off some of my at present freely flowing sources of newspapers etc. If you have not yet seen Gardiner, please be a saint, and explain with your usual tact.

Lockhart had sailed for Britain on 13 October, and over the following weeks received several letters from Ransome, each recording a fresh development. Sharp was arranging for him to be 'properly rated' in Stockholm, but on further reflection had agreed to retain the *Daily News* for the sake of cover. Plans for an observation point, or *nabliudatelny punkt*, with a view to providing intelligence on Russian affairs were already far advanced. Ransome would be one of the key players, and enclosed as proof the transcript of a long letter from Karl Radek: 'practically a general essay on the situation'. Radek had sent him an 'immense pile of stuff', and by way of advice concerning Ransome's grand history of the Revolution – a project first conceived in March 1917 – suggested a political satire. The present war, advised Radek, was coming to an end, with England and Germany already in talks to prevent world domination by America. On the other hand, it was perfectly possible that America and Germany would side against England. Peace would not end conflict between the capitalist oppressors. The strife would go on and on, pointlessly, relentlessly, until it was ended as the Soviet had long predicted it would end. 'I am convinced', Radek concluded, 'that the revolution will spoil the feast for your bankers, and that the words of Goethe's song, which I am always quoting to you, will be fulfilled, where it says that after the day of the hyena comes that of the lion.'

Ransome relayed similar correspondence to a widening circle of British agents, including – their recent difference apparently now set aside – the odious Wyatt.

~

In October, as conservative newspapers in Britain and America glutted themselves on tales of Bolshevik atrocities, maintaining an essentially sympathetic view of the Soviet apparatus proved no easy task. Lockhart had already told Ransome of his experiences as a prisoner of the Cheka: the executions he had witnessed at the Cheka headquarters in Lubianka Street; his lonely vigil inside the walls of the Kremlin; his meeting with Lenin's would-be assassin Dora Kaplan, zombie-like before she went to her death. But Lockhart's detention had provided him with only the narrowest view of the suffering experienced by ordinary citizens, Russians who lived in constant fear of arrest or the disappearance of loved ones. In October, Major Wardwell of the British Red Cross arrived in Stockholm, shaken to his roots.

'The thing that made the most terrible impact on me', he explained to Ransome,

was the indifference of the young girls in the Extraordinary Commission [the Cheka]. They seemed absolutely unaware that they were dealing with human lives. Relatives would come to enquire, one after another, the fate of the prisoners. A young girl would turn up a ledger as if consulting an account and reply 'Shot' or 'Unknown' with the utmost disregard to the effect on the unfortunate questioner. Sometimes, in the outer rooms of the Extraordinary Commission half a dozen persons would be in hysterics at once. It seemed that these girls had lost sight of humanity altogether. For them the prisoners were counter-revolutionaries, not human beings.

Ransome had not allowed Wardwell to have it all his own way. 'Terror', he had insisted, 'depends on terror in the executioner as much as terror in the executed.' But the anxiety he suffered in squaring his private circumstances with his public position was becoming increasingly difficult to bear.

Living with Evgenia in their small and by all accounts cosy cottage by the sea, Ransome received visits from former acquaintances, some of whom, as he later discovered, were 'not as friendly as they seemed'. Michael Lykiardopoulos was in Stockholm, as was Paul Dukes, a latter-day Pimpernel who smuggled out Russian aristocrats in a variety of imaginative disguises and made a fortune from his memoirs. Ransome's autobiography dismisses Dukes as a misguided, self-promoting adventurist but provides no hint as to Evgenia's reaction (if, indeed, she was told of the affair) to his own recruitment by the British Secret Intelligence Service, the discomfort she experienced as his 'official wife' in Sweden or her reluctance to seek asylum in Britain should the opportunity present itself. Prejudice against the mistress of a married man was a small thing compared to the loathing she anticipated not only from English conservatives, but also from Russian émigrés. As for Ransome, he had not yet dared mention her name in letters home. Instead, he concentrated on convincing Edith that he had not become a Bolshevik himself.

'I've only met about three likeable Bolsheviks,' he confessed,

and they were mostly likeable because of something extraneous to their Bolshevism. Radek, for example, who knows Shakespeare better than I do, and is prepared to talk brilliantly on anything under the sun, and is full of admiration for British Imperialism, which he hates at the same time. No one who knows Radek can dislike him, and certainly no Englishman could dislike him who had ever heard him describe how in Trafalgar Square he was enlightened, like Saint Paul, and, a small comic figure he must have been, looking up at the stone lions, wishing he could have been an imperialist and an English imperialist if only he had not had the misfortune to be born a Pole and a Bolshevik.

Most of the Bolsheviks, claimed Ransome, were not like Radek at all: not human figures to warm the heart. 'They are a pigheaded, narrow-minded set of energetic lunatics, energetic as if possessed by seven devils apiece, and each one of them capable of getting through the amount of work that would be done by twenty ordinary Russians.' Yet wasn't there something, even here, to admire? Did Britain not pride herself on her industry?

Ransome confessed to Edith that he had been more 'pro' than he might have been under different circumstances, but the situation in Russia was quite unique. 'In England, [the Bolsheviks] would be too much of a good thing, but in Russia, they were inevitable.' When Ransome spoke of England now, he said 'we' and 'us'. He needed his mother to understand that he had not changed, that he was still himself, that the 'revolution has not altered me personally in any way'. He boasted that no other Englishman had come closer to the Bolsheviks. Only two other foreigners on earth – Colonel Raymond Robins and Captain Jacques Sadoul (who would shortly be condemned to death *in absentia* by the French government for treason) – had the right, truly, to speak of them with any authority at all. But Ransome himself was not a Bolshevik or even a socialist. A revolutionary, perhaps; sometimes he thought so. And then sometimes not. He did not speak of his dead brother Geoffrey, or Evgenia, or of the vile letter which Ivy had sent him in September pouring scorn on his plans to divorce. Instead, he talked longingly of Tabitha ('that blessed infant') and pined for a holiday in the north country more pitifully than ever before. He was so tired, so engrossed, so utterly saturated in politics that he suspected he was finished as a real writer. But then it struck him, too, when he was at his lowest, that writing would be his only salvation.

And, oh, My Most Beloved Ancient HOW I do long to be quit of revolutions, and free to forget politics, and turn to writing the things I really want to write. I would so like to have a couple of months to spend on a new children's book. Children go on and on. The sight of them was the one thing that made me bear up when in woe these last few months. Revolts may come, revolts may go, but brats go on forever. And I would like to do a perfectly stunning brat book, and have Barbara [Collingwood] do decorations for it, or perhaps to keep Barbara for grown up fairy books, and have some rollicking impish pictures for a wild kids' book of my own.

But politics would not leave Ransome alone. On 24 October, Admiral Franz Hopper attempted to launch the imperial fleet from the German Baltic coast for a final battle against the Royal Navy, provoking a mutiny amongst his exhausted sailors. The revolt spread quickly to local workers, and on 3 November a demonstration demanding an immediate end to the war was held in Kiel under the familiar slogan 'peace and bread'. The next day, a soldiers' council was established along the lines of the Russian soviets, and as the uprising gained momentum, similar councils sprang up in every major city in the country. In Munich, a workers' and soldiers' council forced the last king of Bavaria, Louis III, to abdicate, triggering the abdication of royals in every other German state. On 9 November, the German parliament sued for peace with the Allies, while Philipp Scheidemann, deputy chairman of the German Social Democratic Party, stepped out onto the balcony of the Reichstag and announced the abdication of the Kaiser.

In Moscow, Lenin was beside himself. The longed-for international revolution was at hand. An armistice between the Allied and central powers was announced on 11 November, but Ransome did not even note it in his diary. In the first week of the month, he told the *Daily News* that conditions in Germany were precisely as they had been in Russia before the Bolshevik coup, with the only difference that in Germany the country was experiencing all the preliminary stages simultaneously. The 7th of November had marked the first anniversary of Lenin's victory over Kerensky, and the coincidence had been noted. Towards the end of the month, Ransome wired a collage of impressions from the Soviet press: great popular enthusiasm, a renewed confidence after the trials of the summer, babes in arms proudly swaddled in red. Peace, it was true, had freed the Anglo-French imperialists to concentrate their efforts on toppling the Soviet, but Lenin prophesied that the Revolution would now spread to every defeated nation. 'They [the Allies] may succeed in suppressing a single country, but they will never suppress the international proletarian revolution. They merely spread more widely the flames in which they will perish.'

In late November, Maxim Litvinov, the former Soviet delegate to London, arrived in Stockholm on a 'peace offensive'. Ransome dined with him on 29 November, and over the following weeks pressed his case both in the *Daily News* and at the British embassy. The Bolsheviks demanded immediate cessation of military intervention, and in return offered repayment in full of Russia's war debts, a return of Allied prisoners and access to

Russia's rich resources of timber, minerals and oil. Litvinov's petition, however, fell on deaf ears, and as the Allies prepared to discuss the European peace in Paris, placed pressure on Sweden to expel the Soviet legation altogether. Ransome, meanwhile, received news that back in Britain one Horatio Bottomley, Conservative MP, financial fraudster and owner of the notorious tabloid *John Bull*, was threatening to expose him as a Bolshevik spy. Ransome wrote instantly to the only man in London who knew enough of his affairs to save his reputation.

'Dear Lockhart,' he began,

I was told yesterday that Horatio Bottomley is going to start an attack on me as a 'paid agent of the Bolsheviks'.

I was also told that he is collecting affidavits from people returning from Russia supporting this beastly accusation. Of course he'll be able to get crowds of people who do not know what I was doing to say that I was continually with the Bolsheviks, as I jolly well and very rightly was.

For that the British Foreign Office is at least as responsible as I am.

From the beginning, when Sir George Buchanan showed me a telegram signed 'Balfour' suggesting that I should be used as an intermediary to ask Trotsky certain questions, my attempts to get into as close touch as possible with the Soviet people have had the full approval of the British authorities on the spot. I have never taken a single step without first getting their approval . . . As for my attitude towards [the Bolsheviks], please remember that you yourself suppressed a telegram I wrote on the grounds that its criticism of them would have put an end to my good relations with them and so have prevented my further usefulness.

Altogether, it will be very much too much of a good thing if, after having worked as I have, and been as useful as I possibly could, I am now to be attacked in such a way that I cannot defend myself except by a highly undesirable exposition (to persons who have no right to know) of what, though not officially secret service work (because I was unpaid) amounted to the same thing.

If Bottomley should make his attack, I should have to bring a libel action, and either call you, Sir George and Lindley to explain the true position, or if that for reasons of state is undesirable, be unable to prove my point, and be most unfairly blasted as an abominable low fellow.

Surely something can be done now, before it is too late, to give Bottomley a sufficient hint of the truth to prevent the attacks from being made . . .

Bottomley never published his affidavits, sparing Ransome the trouble of explaining himself in court, but in Stockholm his situation was approaching a crisis. In early December, an application to return with Evgenia to England had been approved but then withdrawn, a setback followed by confirmation that the Bolshevik legation was to be expelled from Sweden and that Ransome was to be counted as one of their number. Evgenia's repatriation to Moscow now became a certainty, and Ransome made up his mind to join her, only to be informed that the Kremlin, no longer confident of his allegiance, was refusing him entry. For a moment, it seemed as though he would find no country willing to take him at all and that he would be forced to live at sea. But the day was saved in late January by Bruce Lockhart, who either by pre-arrangement or lucky coincidence gave a lecture at King's College, Cambridge, in which he claimed (to loud objections from Mrs Macmillan) that Ransome had not visited Russia in six months and therefore could not be trusted as a reporter. Published in the *Westminster Gazette*, Lockhart's attack had been sufficient to convince the Bolsheviks to relent, and an invitation was duly issued. When the Swedes circulated the official list of Bolsheviks to be deported, Ransome's name was on it, along with a brief physical description: 'Slightly bald; hair parted on the left; narrow, shrewd eyes; large, bushy moustache; wears pince nez.'

By the end of the month, he was on an ice-breaker bound for Petrograd.

17

Six Weeks

By the morning of 30 January, the luggage of the Bolshevik legation, including Ransome's, had been examined, sealed and delivered to the quay, leaving only passports to be stamped and the
bidding of a few fond farewells. The Swedish Left Socialists, he
recalled, had turned out in force, while other 'nonpolitical
friends' such as landladies, sweethearts and laundresses wept
openly and wrung out their handkerchiefs on the dock. As the
Heimdal cast off, there was a resounding chorus of 'The
Internationale', answered by revolutionary songs from the
Bolsheviks. 'There were cheers and shouts of "Long Live Free
Russia".' Once at sea there were more songs and a chess tourna-
ment in which Ransome came second, beating Maxim Litvinov
in the semi-finals, though as he sportingly admitted, Litvinov –
known to everybody aboard as Papasha ('Papa') – was actually
the better player. In Finland, the party had been loaded onto a
special train and for the first time felt like prisoners, but any ten-
sion that might have existed between the Bolsheviks and their
guards was dispelled by little Nina, Vorovsky's eight-year-old
daughter, who flirted with everybody indiscriminately, and on
the narrow bridge that separated Soviet Russia from the West,
chatted merrily both to the Finns and to the Red Guard who
bent down to show her the hammer and sickle stitched onto his
cap. 'Crossing that bridge', wrote Ransome, 'we passed from
one philosophy to another, from one extreme of the class struggle to the other, from a dictatorship of the bourgeoisie to a dictatorship of the proletariat.'

As the Allies convened in France to discuss the terms upon
which a general peace would be agreed, the Russian Civil War
had entered its decisive phase. Since the Treaty of Brest-Litovsk,
the Allied blockade had prevented food and medicine from

reaching the major Bolshevik cities. To the east, Allied troops defended a 4,000-mile stretch of railway from Irkutsk to Vladivostok constituting the supply line of Admiral Alexander Kolchak, commander-in-chief of the White armies. The British government remained deeply divided as to the political justification for intervention, especially since the German threat had now clearly been obviated, and yet British troops remained on Russian soil, providing the Bolsheviks with an ideal platform for propaganda. In light of all this, Ransome's object was to emphasize the damage done by misguided Allied policy, while stressing the integrity and benevolence of the Bolshevik delegates who had been denied an opportunity to state their case in Paris. The result was a detailed journal kept day by day for the next six weeks, aimed squarely at the Allied peace conference and opening with the voyage of the *Heimdal*. The Soviet, Ransome suggested, was a family, and the Bolsheviks kindly parents. Nina was the spirit of internationalism that would, in time, conquer every heart in the world. Even a bourgeoise lady who had joined the party was treated kindly, though her costume left something to be desired. She was returning to her country estate in English tweed and yellow hunting boots.

~

By 1919, the whole of central Europe teetered on the verge of revolution. Berlin was already in flames. The Ottoman empire would crumble shortly, giving birth to modern Turkey. The collapse of the Hapsburg empire spawned a Soviet government in Hungary, while all along the borders of the former Russian empire newly independent countries – Finland, the Baltic States, Ukraine, Azerbaijan, Georgia, Dagestan – flailed in a violent political limbo. It was for this reason that Winston Churchill, the British Secretary for War, demanded an immediate escalation of Allied intervention in Russia: the only means, he believed, of removing the Bolshevik cancer at its root. 'Of all the tyrannies in history,' he had declared, 'the Bolshevik tyranny is the worst, the most destructive, the most degrading.' And yet even Georges Clemenceau, the French prime minister – another Bolshevik-hater – had acknowledged that decisive intervention was beyond his country's means. War had devastated France both physically and economically. His people, not to mention his troops, had no stomach for further conflict. He suggested, instead, a cordon sanitaire – a ring of client states to fence the Bolsheviks in, to starve the Revolution as one might starve a dangerous fever.

In December 1918, Lloyd George had won the general election in Britain on a wave of nationalist euphoria, but while promising that Germany would be forced to pay 'the whole cost of the war', had remained elusive on the Russian question. In the same month, President Woodrow Wilson had arrived in Paris with the firm intention of opposing a punitive peace, which he believed – correctly – would virtually ensure a second European war. But Wilson's League of Nations – a group of powerful, supervising democracies that would defend the liberty of lesser, 'self-determined' peoples – soon ran into problems of the most rudimentary kind. What was a 'people'? How should they be determined? Ethnically, politically, on the basis of religion or geography? The Bolsheviks had already considered the matter and reduced it to a working principle. The nation was a fallacy of the bourgeoisie. The 'people' were the international masses, locked into their respective countries like cattle in a field, the better to fatten them for slaughter. But neither Wilson nor his colleagues, all fervent patriots, could find a suitable definition of their own, especially with regard to Russia. Indeed, from the moment the peace conference officially opened for business on 12 January 1919, Russia, comprising one sixth of the entire solid surface of the earth, had posed the most serious challenge. Four governments claimed to speak for the whole nation, but the Whites would not speak to the Reds, and the Reds would not speak to anybody without lacing their telegrams with the most inflammatory revolutionary propaganda. It was for this reason that the Bolsheviks had not been invited to France, while a secondary conference planned for the Russians in Prinkipo had been delayed and then abandoned. Allied intervention, in any case, contradicted every principle Wilson claimed to espouse, a fact which Lenin and his comrades had not failed to turn to their advantage.

'In Paris,' the Soviet press declared,

the imperialist extortioners are trying to create their own black 'international', the so-called League of Nations. Conscious workers throughout the world know perfectly well that the so-called League of Nations is in fact a league of bourgeois robbers for the oppression of nations, for the division of the world, for the enslavement of workers, for strangling the proletarian revolution.

And so the debate continued. Wilson talked of 'the Bolshevik poison', but at the same time urged his colleagues to keep an open mind. Lloyd George, always vague on eastern European demographics – 'Who are the Slavs? I can't seem to place them' – alternated between intervention and negotiation. Likewise, in Moscow, Lenin's eagerness to exploit the chaos in Europe was mixed with a growing realization that Soviet Russia could not stand on its own. In Stockholm, Litvinov's peace offensive had pressed for a trade treaty to help rebuild the economy. At the Commissariat of Foreign Affairs, Georgy Chicherin endeavoured to choose his words more carefully. As *Izvestia* and *Pravda* turned out article after article damning the League of Nations, the Kremlin looked to Paris with regret, opening a shaky middle ground which Ransome – representing all interests in the best of all possible worlds – prepared once more to make his own.

Speaking to Litvinov, Ransome had explained that he was compiling a history of the Revolution which would, when published in England, combat the scurrilous slanders spread about by the conservative press. Speaking to Clifford Sharp, he had explained that if the Soviet fell, it would not matter: he had plenty of contacts in every party and could remain useful. Between December 1918 and his embarkation on the *Heimdal*, he had considered, at one time or another, travelling to England, France and Berlin, but at last had gone with Evgenia to Russia, framing the trip as a 'fact finding expedition' for the benefit of the Foreign Office and Lloyd George's delegation in Paris. Sharp had accepted enthusiastically, writing a strong letter to Whitehall in support of Ransome's general character.

'I would specially emphasize', he concluded,

that S76 may be regarded as absolutely honest. If you ask him any question about any of his numerous activities in Russia, you will get the exact truth. His reports about the conditions in Russia may also be relied upon absolutely with only the proviso that his views tend to be coloured by his personal sympathies with men like Litvinov and Radek. He will report what he sees but he does not see quite straight.

~

Litvinov's party arrived in Petrograd in early February, and discovered – according to Ransome's journal – a peaceful city which, in spite of Winston Churchill's claims to the contrary, was more orderly and essentially more civilized than it had been since the days of the Tsar. Where the Bolsheviks held sway, Russia was recovering its senses, a virtue that would appeal to conservatives and liberals alike. Petrograd was devoid of trouble, and while this owed chiefly to a mass migration of starving citizens to the countryside, Ransome awarded the credit without reservation to the Bolshevik leaders. The day after his arrival, he had strolled to Smolny with Litvinov and Evgenia to collect his papers and to dine with party officials. On the way he had not met a single armed patrol. Smolny, likewise, had been stripped of its defences – the dense thicket of steel that warned off the crowds when Lenin had liquidated the Constituent Assembly. The only sign of militancy was a 'horrible statue of Karl Marx' holding an enormous top hat, 'like the barrel of an eighteen inch gun'.

That evening, along with Vorovsky, Evgenia and half a dozen members of the original Swedish mission, Ransome set off for Moscow in a third-class carriage, where he succeeded in procuring a luggage rack on which he perched uncomfortably 'above the general tumult of mothers, babies and Bolsheviks'. The smell of the assembled peasants, he recalled, had been overpowering.

Ransome's first political pamphlet, *On Behalf of Russia: An Open Letter to America*, had been supervised by Karl Radek. But Radek was no longer in Russia. In December, Lenin had sent his propaganda chief into Germany to turn a 'bourgeois' revolution into a social revolution. The attempt nearly cost Radek his life. After a series of bloody street battles with pro-government troops, the German communists – the Spartacus League – had been routed and their leaders, Rosa Luxemburg and Karl Liebknecht, murdered in police custody. Radek was captured in February and placed in solitary confinement at the Moabit prison in Berlin. Things might have gone badly for him had the Soviet not wired to declare him their official ambassador. Pending the conclusion of the Paris Peace Conference, his captors preferred to keep their options open.

If Radek's absence deprived Ransome of his closest friend in the Kremlin, the departure of Morgan Philips Price, who had followed Radek to Germany, robbed him of his only English colleague at the Soviet 'press bureau'. Even the American journalists, John Reed and Louise Bryant, had returned to Washington, where they were currently facing a senatorial investigation into Bolshevik agitation in the States. Thanks to his own journalism and his trip to Vologda with Radek in July 1918, Ransome's name would be raised frequently during the inquiry. In Whitehall his loyalty remained a deeply controversial issue, while in Russia he was suspected by several Bolsheviks, including Zinoviev and Trotsky, of working as a British spy. In short, approaching Moscow with Evgenia balanced precariously on the luggage rack beside him, Ransome's challenge was to provide a sequel to his *On Behalf of Russia* which was sympathetic to his hosts without further incriminating its author. The carefully pitched compromise, drawn closely from his journal, would bear, in terms of structure and style, a more than passing resemblance to his *Bohemia in London* – a series of intimate portraits and discursive passages designed to bring the Bolsheviks into middle-class sitting rooms. And just as Ransome had once introduced his readers to the artists of Soho and Chelsea from the perspective of an enthusiastic amateur, so now he would introduce British liberals to the heroes of the Revolution, not so much as an insider, but as a curious observer. Even his chosen title – *Six Weeks in Russia* – suggested little more than a visit, a brief excursion before returning home.

~

Ransome reached Moscow on Wednesday, 5 February, 'a rare cold day' in an unusually warm winter, and was a little hurt to discover that nobody was expecting him. After a fight with the sledge drivers at the Nikolai station (1,000 per cent inflation in six months), he found no rooms at the most comfortable hotels, and for two nights, while arranging interviews with various party officials, was forced to stow his bags at the Red Fleet, an unheated flophouse for sailors. Rosa Radek, now installed at the splendid Grand Ducal apartments in the Kremlin, had supplied him with a pass but had been of no practical value with regard to accommodation. Karakhan, Chicherin's number two, found Ransome a room to work in at the Commissariat of Foreign Affairs, but the Red Fleet was so cold he could not sit still, let alone sleep. On 7 February, however, Angelina Balabanova – shortly to be appointed secretary of the Comintern – came to his rescue. He was given quarters at the National, one of two hotels reserved for Soviet officials and delegates, and shortly afterwards (thanks to Litvinov) received a letter from Lenin commanding all commissariats to lend him their assistance 'in every possible way'.

Having established himself at last in relative comfort, Ransome interviewed Boris Reinstein, who in addition to his duties supervising the International Bureau for Revolutionary Propaganda had taken charge of Allied prisoners of war. Reinstein amiably rejected any notion that British subjects had been abused. Ordinary soldiers, he insisted, were treated 'more like guests than prisoners'. In Moscow, they were issued pass-ports and visited the ballet, wandered the streets at their leisure and ate in the official canteens. Two Americans had actually broken down in tears when it was suggested they return to their comrades in Archangel. Officers, Reinstein confessed, had not fared so well, but those who complained of torture referred to the privations shared by every other Muscovite: cold, hunger, a degree of uncertainty as to their future. Ransome had confirmed this by visiting the Butyrka prison in the company of Felix Dzerzhinsky, an episode which he omitted from his journal but which was recalled by one of the British inmates in a letter to the Foreign Office.

When I was in a cell in Butirski [*sic*] Prison, Arthur Ransome visited me together with Derjinski [*sic*]. Derjinski stayed outside my cell while Ransome attempted to get me to commit myself by pretending that he was our 'secret service officer' as he said, and that I could entrust him with any message I wished to pass on to the War Office. I soon caught him out in his own game and threatened to use force if he did not leave my cell immediately.

The following day, 8 February, Yakov Peters, the man who had supervised the arrest and interrogation of Bruce Lockhart the previous summer, made room in his busy schedule. Ransome found him in his study at the Cheka headquarters in Lubianka, cleaning his gun in preparation for a shooting expedition: a weekend in the country hunting partridge. In the corner sat two secretaries, one packing wadding into cartridges, the other folding little pancakes for a picnic. Dzerzhinsky's second-in-command was 'a small man with a square forehead, very dark eyes and a quick expression. He speaks fair English [Peters had lived in England and been married to the daughter of a British banker], though he is gradually forgetting it. He knows far less now than a year ago.' Open on his desk was a copy of H. G. Wells's *Mr Britling Sees It Through*.

With no apparent prompting from Ransome, Peters declared that Lockhart was a good fellow and might not have been as guilty as he seemed, but it was a pity that his lover, Baroness Benckendorf, had since been exposed as a German spy. Peters did not hold this fact against Lockhart, for whom he felt a genuine fondness, but was disturbed by news that the young

Scotsman, who had left Russia unharmed, had now become a vehicle for anti-Bolshevik propaganda. Laid out on the desk beside *Mr Brittling* were photographs of White atrocities committed in the Baltic: the mutilated bodies of Soviet soldiers, some, Ransome noted, with their noses cut off. The war, Peters said, was draining the Soviet of good men who would be better put to work in the civil service, the factories and fields. He laughed at the Chinese torture gangs that were said to accompany every Red Army offensive, but accepted without hesitation that he had ordered civilian executions: a necessity he regretted, but which had nevertheless produced excellent results.

'For more than two months we have not had to shoot anyone until just lately when there has been an outbreak of robbery. We have now shot eight robbers, and we posted the fact at every street corner, and there will be no more robbery. I have now got such a terrible name', he added, smiling, 'that if I put up a notice that people will be dealt with severely that is enough, and there is no need to shoot anybody.'

Having gauged the treatment of British prisoners and the integrity of the Bolshevik secret police, Ransome visited Captain Jacques Sadoul, formerly of the French military mission, who asked if he would like to meet Trotsky on an armoured train bound for the north. Ransome declined, explaining that Trotsky would not have wished to speak to him. Over the next six weeks he did not leave Moscow. Instead, as Evgenia found a new post at the Commissariat for Education, he heard lectures from Chicherin on the international situation and from Lev Kamenev, president of the Moscow Soviet, on the importance of harnessing 'national unity'. By March, he had gathered anecdotes describing the Terror in the countryside (grossly exaggerated), the nationalization of the factories (highly beneficial) and the rebellious peasants, whose armies did not exist and whose representatives were driven by personal greed. Fully aware that conservatives in England would accuse him of favouritism, Ransome was careful to speak to the Bolsheviks' opponents, discovering that the Right Socialist Revolutionaries and Mensheviks now supported the party because any failure to do so would mean supporting a 'bourgeois dictatorship'. On 3 March, having amassed over a hundred pages of notes covering virtually every ministry, he attended the opening of the Third International, staged in the Moscow Court of Justice.

'The whole room,' noted Ransome,

including the floor, was decorated in red. There were banners with 'Long Live the Third International' inscribed upon them in many languages. The Presidium was on the raised dais at the end of the room, Lenin sitting in the middle behind a long red-covered table with Albrecht, a young German Spartacist, on the right and Platten, the Swiss, on the left . . . Everybody of importance was there: Trotsky [returned from the north], Zinoviev, Kamenev, Chicherin, Bukharin, Karakhan, Litvinov, Vorovsky, Steklov, Rakovsky, representing here the Balkan Socialist Party, Skripnik, representing the Ukraine. Then there were Stang (Norwegian Left Socialists), Grimlund (Swedish Left), Sadoul (France), Finberg (British Socialist Party), Reinstein (American Socialist Labour Party), a Turk, a German-Austrian, a Chinese, and so on. Business was conducted and speeches were made in all languages, though where possible German was used, because more of the foreigners knew German than knew French. This was unlucky for me.

Ransome claimed to have understood almost nothing of the proceedings, and consequently excused himself from supplying any explanation as to their function – the inauguration of the principal Bolshevik vehicle for spreading revolution abroad.

'Today,' Lenin had announced,

the workers who have remained loyal to the cause of throwing off the yoke of capital call themselves Communists. All over the world the association of Communists is growing. In a number of countries Soviet power has already triumphed. Soon we shall see the victory of communism throughout the world; we shall see the foundation of the World Federative Republic of Soviets.

~

Speaking to Nikolai Bukharin in the canteen of the Metropole, Ransome produced a magazine with a map of Europe showing actual and potential areas of revolution in red and pink. Was it surprising, he enquired, if the Bolsheviks were thought of as the new imperialists? 'Idiotism, rank idiotism!' protested Bukharin, staring at the map, although he went on to explain that the Revolution would conquer the world within fifty years. His only concern was that 'the struggle will be so bitter and long drawn out that the whole of European culture may be trampled under foot'. Quietly digesting the human cost of this, Ransome finished his tea in silence. Bukharin, he decided, was an eccentric, and he allowed him to recede into the shadows, 'fastening his coat as he went, a queer little De Quincy of the revolution, to disappear into the dusk, before, half running, half walking, as his way is, he reached the other end of the big dimly lit, smoke-filled dining room'.

Here and there, Ransome's journal hinted at the bitter under-tow of revolution: the struggle to survive; the shortages of food, of fuel; the carcass of an emaciated horse appearing and disappearing beneath a shroud of ravenous crows. He was aware that in Russia life under the Soviet offered fewer real freedoms than had been offered under the Tsar, and speaking to Sadoul, joked that within a few years men would be growing tails and climbing back into the trees. But even as he said such things, he was arguing that the suffering was temporary, that the circumstances that had produced the present situation came from outside Russia. There had been the war. Now, owing to Allied support of the Whites, there was a civil war. The Bolsheviks were not innately cruel or autocratic. As soon as the Allies withdrew their soldiers and lifted the blockade, the underlying causes of dictatorship and terror would disappear. The Bolsheviks would assume a kindlier aspect, while the soldiers of the Red Army would return peacefully to their business, whatever that might mean after so great a catastrophe.

Lenin, meanwhile, had given three interviews in as many weeks.

'More than ever, today,' Ransome wrote on 19 February,

Lenin struck me as a happy man, and, walking down from the Kremlin, I tried to think of any other great leader who had a similar, joyous, happy temperament. I could think of none. Napoleon, Caesar, did not make a deeper mark on the history of the world than this man is making: none records their cheerfulness. This little bald, wrinkled man who tilts his chair this way and that, laughing over one thing and another . . .

Lenin, mused Ransome, was the first great leader in history who utterly discounted the value of his own personality.

Not only is he without personal ambition, but, as a Marxist, believes in the movement of the masses . . . His faith in himself is the belief that he justly estimates the direction of elemental forces. He does not believe that one man can make or stop the revolution. If the revolution fails, it fails only temporarily, and because of forces beyond any man's control. He is consequently free, with a freedom no other great leader has ever had . . . He is as it were the exponent not the cause of the events that will be for ever linked with his name.

At a second meeting on 7 March, Lenin showed Ransome a note found in the American consulate following the arrest of the Allied missions in 1918. The letter denounced Ransome as a Bolshevik spy, and appears to have been offered, on this occasion, to remind him who his friends were. Ransome's journal, however, offers no comment on the business one way or the other, simply stating it as a fact before recording Lenin's views on the founding of the Third International.

'I am afraid that the Jingoes in France and England', predicted Lenin,

will make use of yesterday's doings as an excuse for further actions against us. They will say 'How can we leave them in peace when they set about setting the world on fire?' To that I would answer, 'We are at war Messieurs! And just as during the war you tried to make revolution in Germany, and Germany did make trouble in Ireland and India, so we, while we are at war with you, adopt the measures that are open to us. We have told you we are willing to make peace.'

Lenin reminded his interlocutor that 'the quickest way of restoring good conditions in Russia was, of course, peace and agreement with the Allies'. If the Allies had wanted to depose the Soviet, why had they not done so when the Red Army was in its infancy?

269

In any case, sending troops against the Soviet was like sending them to a communist university! British, French and American soldiers entering Russia believing the Bolsheviks were monsters were swiftly persuaded otherwise, especially if they had the good fortune to be captured. Yet Lenin denied that propaganda had played any significant role either in the Russian Revolution or the kindling of revolutions abroad: 'If the conditions of revolution are not there, no sort of propaganda will either hasten or impede it.'

Ransome suggested that revolution was unlikely in England, but was gently rebuked for his complacency.

We have a saying that a man may have typhoid while still on his legs. Twenty, maybe thirty years ago, I had abortive typhoid, and was going about with it, had had it some days before it knocked me over. Well, England and France and Italy have caught the disease already. England may seem to you untouched, but the microbe is already there.

~

On 28 February, Ransome had wired the British embassy in Stockholm to the effect that if he were unable to leave Russia by 3 March, then he should be sent a telegram via the Commissariat of Foreign Affairs ordering 'British Subject Ransome to come home'.

'S76', reads the relevant Foreign Office memo, 'would take the receipt of such a message to mean that the way was open for him to return, i.e., that we could help him through the Finnish frontier.'

But Ransome had not returned on 3 March, and missed a further deadline on the 9th. On 15 March, the Foreign Office considered sending one of two telegrams from the top of the Eiffel Tower. The first would read: 'Unless you are prepared immediately to return to this country passport and other facilities will cease to be granted you.' The second would come from Ivy: 'Following from Mrs Ransome. Please return as soon as possible. Am very ill. British authorities state that no difficulty will be made to your entering the UK.' Ransome left on 14 March in the company of two Americans: William Bullitt and Lincoln Steffens.

Bullitt, twenty-eight years old, ambitious and idealistic, had attached himself to Woodrow Wilson's delegation to Paris in December 1918, and as negotiations over the 'Russian question' had sunk into the sand, prevailed on Wilson's secretary to permit him to travel to Russia as an unofficial envoy. With him came Steffens, a radical journalist of the American 'muck-raking' school who, according to Bullitt, had already drafted his famous endorsement of communism on the journey out: 'I have seen the future and it works.' These two arrived in Moscow on 11 March, and according to Ransome's notes, presented themselves at the National Hotel begging for his assistance in brokering a historic peace. Ransome claimed that he had at first been sceptical. Over the past six months, he complained, every Englishman he had met, with the sole exception of Clifford Sharp, had treated him 'as a traitor', a circumstance that owed, he felt, to rumours spread about him by Americans. Bullitt, however, had hurried to reassure him. 'He said that if only I knew it, I had many who contended that America got the truth about Russia mostly from my work . . . I was very tired and perhaps more bitter than I should have been.'

Over the next three days, with Ransome at their elbow, Bullitt and Steffens enjoyed the very best the Bolsheviks had to offer: champagne, caviar, a night at the opera seated in the Tsar's royal box. By 14 March, everything had been arranged. If the Allies withdrew their troops, the Bolsheviks would end hostilities immediately and allow the rival White governments – three in total – to go about their business unmolested. In return the Allies would end all support, military or financial, for the counter-revolution. Lenin had little to lose. If the offer were accepted in Paris, so much the better. If it were refused, the Soviet would once again claim the moral high ground. Meanwhile, speaking privately to Ransome in a third and final interview, he asked him to deliver a separate offer, to be delivered to the Estonian ambassador in Finland. The Red Army had its hands full in Russia. If

Estonia would agree to a ceasefire, the Bolsheviks were prepared to honour its independence.

The only fly in the ointment, from Ransome's point of view, was Evgenia's obstinate refusal to accompany him. He was forced to leave her behind in Moscow.

~

Orders had been given by the British authorities to detain Ransome when he reached Helsingfors, but by a stroke of luck (and possibly because he had been expected to travel alone) an entirely different journalist was arrested by mistake. Unaware of his good fortune, Ransome handed the Soviet peace proposal to the Estonian embassy before travelling on via Stockholm to Norway, where he presented Lenin's letter providing him with universal access to the Soviet administration as proof of his continued usefulness to the intelligence service. On 4 April, customs in Newcastle signalled his arrival in England aboard the SS *Jupiter*. Ransome had again announced himself as an agent of His Majesty's government who had 'run considerable risks of detection at the hands of the Bolsheviks' in pursuit of information vital 'to the Authorities in this Country'. His papers were sent ahead to London, while Ransome followed on the next train, shadowed by a plain-clothes detective sergeant to ensure his safe arrival. Victor Cavendish-Bentinck, (later, 9th Duke of Portland) summed up the situation for the benefit of the Foreign Office.

I have spoken to Major Kendal of MIIc [War Office intelligence service, or MI6], Mr Farina of MI5 [domestic military intelligence], and Messers Basil Thomson and Norman Kendal of New Scotland Yard, relative to the return of Mr Ransome from Russia to this country. MIIc are not prepared to guarantee that he will not indulge in Bolshevik propaganda when in this country and merely advise that he should be interviewed by some very senior official of this Office who should inform him that it will be highly inadvisable for him to indulge in such propaganda. I venture to submit that this would be highly undesirable, for to be interviewed by a very senior official in this Office would cause

Ransome to overrate his own importance, and as he would probably, in spite of such a warning, take part in Extremist meetings in this country, he might then say that he had been warned not to do so by the senior official in question, but that he had bravely disregarded this warning and that HM Government did not dare to touch him for fear of offending the Proletariat. Also, so far as can at present be ascertained, Ransome has not committed any offence for which he could be committed for trial. (In this connection I would mention that we have received a ruling from the Director of Public Prosecution that Philips Price, who has behaved far more badly than Ransome, has not committed any offence for which he could be committed for trial). In these circumstances, I submit that there are two courses to pursue.

a). To ignore Ransome and to wait until he has committed some offence for which he can be tried. (It is highly unlikely that he will commit such an offence, as I understand that he is really rather a coward and is trying to run with the hare and hunt with the hounds).

b). For the competent Department to produce proof in some form or other (by *agent provocateur* or other means) for which Ransome could be brought to trial and given a fairly heavy sentence. He has an interview with Mr Basil Thomson this morning and will probably come up to this Office where he has been told to report himself in the same way as all other British subjects returning from Russia. Mr Basil Thomson will let me know the result of his interview with Ransome.

Stepping down onto the platform at King's Cross, Ransome was accosted by the same police officer who had escorted him – incognito – all the way from Newcastle.

'Mr Ransome?'

'Yes.'

'I must ask you to accompany me to Scotland Yard at once.'

Ransome recalled the details in his autobiography: the 'Bowler Hat' who had agreed to carry his bags, an amicable conversation in the taxi and his arrival at Scotland Yard, the fortress of British homeland security.

I was shown into Sir Basil Thomson's room and asked to sit down in the famous chair where so many criminals had sat before me. Sir Basil Thomson, extremely grim, looked very hard at me. After a moment's silence he said, 'Now, I want to know just what your politics are.'

'Fishing,' I replied.

18

No-man's-land

Basil Thomson had done well out of the war. In 1913, as the head of Special Branch, his job had been 'to look out for suspicious Irishmen'. From 1914, he included 'suspicious Germans' in his brief, and as Britain gave way to a horror of hostile infiltration, earned his *nom de guerre* 'Spycatcher Thomson' from a grateful public. Any confusion between the 'Mr' and the 'Sir' arising from Cavendish-Bentinck's internal memo and Ransome's later account arose from the fact that Thomson's knighthood, announced in the New Year's Honours list, had yet to be officially bestowed, as had his promotion to director of the whole of British civil intelligence, barring the services performed by MI5, who managed domestic counter-espionage. But a good policeman chooses his opportunities wisely. Other journalists had gone much further than Ransome. Morgan Philips Price had allegedly edited a Bolshevik newspaper – *The Call* – and caused a scandal in the Houses of Parliament which had cost him his job. In Britain, Sylvia Pankhurst, editor of the *Worker's Dreadnought*, was quite openly calling for revolution. By comparison, the correspondent for the *Daily News* seemed sane, friendly, even conservative. Ransome had explained that intervention was a waste of British resources and had offered to share his impressions with the Foreign Office. He had no intention, he assured Thomson, of stirring up trouble with the unions or of preaching fire and brimstone to the Hands Off Russia Committee. He was anxious to get off to the north country, to get on with his grand history of the Revolution, and if time permitted, to do a little fishing. It was, he explained, very close to the start of the season.

'Dear Cavendish-Bentinck,' ran Thomson's report,

I had a good hour with Ransome this morning. It is quite true that he thinks that the Bolshevik Government ought to be recognized by the

Allies, but says that this is quite consistent with refusing to allow their propaganda into this country. I am satisfied that he is not a Bolshevik in the sense that Price is; in fact he spoke quite strongly against Price. But he thinks if something is not done soon, Russia will slip into a state of anarchy, which will be far worse than the present situation. He appears to have been very closely in touch with all the Bolshevik leaders, and is perfectly frank about what they told him. I think myself that we shall be able to restrain him from bursting into print. He wants to go into the country for six months to write a book. All he wants to be allowed to put into print for the moment is a description of the ceremony of the International, which must have been very funny . . .

Thomson's view contrasted very sharply with the hostility of the Foreign Office, where Ransome was received the following day by Rex Leeper – future founder of the British Arts Council – whom he recollected coldly as a 'temporary clerk'. Anticipating a debriefing by Lord Robert Cecil, he had instead been grilled for most of the afternoon like a common criminal, and had actually been blackmailed. 'I told the young man that I had brought with me the material for a detailed report. He said that he would like to see it. Then, perhaps by mistake, he let fall an illuminating sentence. He said, 'Perhaps you do not realize that we could damn you with the Left if we let it be known that you were working for us.'

'After four hours' conversation with Ransome,' ran Leeper's report,

I believe he can do more harm in this country than even Price. Lenin would not have wasted two hours with him unless he thought he could be most useful to him here. What Lenin wants in England just now are people who will take up his policy and at the same time declare they are anti-Bolsheviks. Ransome will do this to perfection, if not by writing, then at least by talking to people.

Ransome did indeed both talk and write. Emerging from Whitehall in a state of acute indignation, he had spoken, within the space of forty-eight hours, to George Lansbury at the pro-Bolshevik *Daily Herald*, to his editors at the *Daily News* and to a young American. Her letter to her sister in New York, claiming that Ransome was sitting on a mountain of notes which he intended to publish at the earliest opportunity, was duly intercepted and passed on to the British Cabinet. 'He declares that the stuff in the papers is all lies. I could not get him to talk much because he wants to write it and sell it at a good price.' All this contrasted strongly with the assurances Ransome had given at Scotland Yard, but strangely it was Leeper who now recommended caution: 'Mr Ransome is not an agent of the Bolsheviks. He had not enough sense to see through them and for that reason takes up a sympathetic line towards them. Especially as they have always treated him well, thinking he may be useful to them.' After a second meeting with Thomson, Ransome was permitted to go about his business, and on 1 April took a train down to Kent, where Edith was staying in a substantial country house inherited by her adopted daughter, Kitty. By the 4th, he was in Hatch for his first interview with Ivy since December 1917.

Tabitha was now almost nine years old, and recalled that her parents quarrelled, that Mum-Mum was unhappy and Dor-Dor cross. Ransome had treated them all to a fishing expedition and Tabitha had been given her first rod, but she did not enjoy threading worms and caught only minnows. On the Little Nadder, her father taught her to be silent and not to cast her shadow on the water. Later, he caught an enormous pike, which the boatman had laboriously and with extreme incompetence beaten to death. These fragments survive in Tabitha's memoirs. In Ransome's there is nothing: no hint as to how he broached the subject of Evgenia, nor any clue as to his reaction when his petition for divorce – which dominated all communication between them for the next five years – was roundly rejected. On 7 April, he was back in London, speaking with Clifford Sharp (now demobbed and reinstalled at the helm of the *New Statesman*) and Stanley Unwin, who agreed to publish a pamphlet based on his recent experiences.

Six Weeks in Russia in 1919 was written in Leeds, in the old house at Chapel Allerton, where two maids prepared Ransome's meals and a stenographer took dictation. In substance, it differed only slightly from the journal he had kept in Moscow, omitting or toning down those passages which Ransome – after his brush with Thomson and Leeper – considered imprudent: his meeting with British prisoners of war; his visit with Felix Dzerzhinsky to the Butyrka jail; the signed confession which Bruce Lockhart had written for Yakov Peters and which Georgy Chicherin claimed to have in his hand. Instead, by way of a preface, he stressed his commitment to transparency, his unswerving belief that intervention was and always had been a mistake, and most of all, his complete political neutrality.

I am well aware that there is material in this book which will be misused by fools both White and Red. That is not my fault. My object has been narrowly limited. I have tried by means of a bald record of conversations and things seen, to provide material for those who wish to know what is being done and thought in Moscow at the present time, and demand something more to go upon than secondhand reports of wholly irrelevant atrocities committed by either one side or the other, and often by neither one side nor the other, but by irresponsible scoundrels who, in the natural turmoil of the greatest convulsion in the history of our civilization, escape temporarily here and there from any kind of control.

On reading the manuscript through (40,000 words in nineteen days), he confessed to finding it 'surprisingly dull'. In retrospect, he would have liked to convey some of the excitement of the Revolution, an excitement which had drawn men like Raymond Robins and himself – both 'far removed in origin and upbringing from the revolutionary and socialist movements in our own countries' – to the cause. Instead, he could only offer a modest summary of how and why an entirely unremarkable Englishman, wholly unmoved by Karl Marx or any of the more controversial orthodoxies of Lenin's government, had nevertheless found himself so deeply in sympathy with the Bolshevik regime. He had, he confessed, from the first days of Soviet power been struck by the injustices done to the Bolsheviks by the Allied press: the absurd rumours circulated by those whose ignorance of the Revolution was matched only by their hypocrisy. Yet there had been more to it than that.

There was the feeling, from which we could never escape, of the creative effort of the revolution. There was the thing that distinguishes the creative from other artists, the living, vivifying expression of something hitherto hidden in the consciousness of humanity. If this book were to be an accurate record of my own impressions, all the drudgery, gossip, quarrels, arguments, events and experiences it contains would have to be set against a background of that extraordinary vitality which obstinately persists in Moscow even in these dark days of discomfort, disillusion, pestilence, starvation and unwanted war.

In Paris, Bullitt's proposed treaty had been rejected out of hand, while on 16 April, following a revolution in Hungary, a mutiny of British soldiers at Folkestone and a rebellion by Conservative MPs execrating any rapprochement with the Bolsheviks, Lloyd George told the House of Commons that recognition of the Soviet had never been seriously considered. As Woodrow Wilson – who disowned any personal responsibility for sending Bullitt to the Kremlin and pleaded a headache when his 'envoy' begged to speak with him – mended his fences with American Republicans, the Allied Supreme Council's attitude to the Russian question hardened. In mid-April, with 30,000 Allied troops guarding his supply line, Admiral Kolchak, commander-in-chief of the Whites, pushed out of Siberia on three fronts and was soon within a couple of days' march of the Volga. Simultaneously, General Anton Denikin, scouting ahead with British planes, broke out of Rostov-on-Don and advanced north towards Tsaritsyn. As the two counter-revolutionary armies appeared to establish a pincer movement focused on Moscow, *The Times* talked jubilantly of a 'tide of victory', while Russian émigrés in London looked forward to a massacre. Ransome, however, thought only of Evgenia, whose life, he knew, would not be worth a brass farthing if the Bolsheviks were defeated. It had been a great mistake, he concluded, to have allowed her to persuade him to leave her behind.

Sometime towards the end of April, these troubles were compounded by a reshuffle at the *Daily News*. It was not a sudden decision, nor, perhaps, unexpected. George Cadbury, the paper's proprietor, was strongly in favour of British intervention and had for some time now found Ransome's articles both politically offensive and unpatriotic. The War Office had heartily agreed, but approaching Cadbury in December 1918 had been told – much to their surprise – that Ransome was in the pay of their own intelligence service. The *Daily News*, it appeared, was only employing him because 'they think the War Office and Foreign Office require the cover . . . Cadbury willing to do whatever necessary once the real desires of the WO and FO known.' Ransome's services were promptly dispensed with, along with those of his unfortunate editor, A. G. Gardiner, who went to work for Harold Williams's newspaper, the *Daily Chronicle*.

It was, from any point of view, a bitter blow, and worse because of the timing. With no newspaper to get him a visa back to Russia, Ransome's chances of retrieving Evgenia personally were slim. But he was a resourceful man and considered his options closely, beginning with Rex Leeper, whom he addressed with great courtesy on 24 April in a letter on the subject of British prisoners of war. Ransome did not know how far negotiations had gone for their extradition but under the current circumstances felt they could not go fast enough. So long as the Bolsheviks remained 'firm in the saddle' all would be well, but if Moscow were seriously threatened, he 'shuddered to think' what might happen. Defeats at the front, coupled with peasant uprisings and a loss of vital farmlands would certainly lead to a 'recrudescence of the Terror', with dire implications for British hostages. If, for whatever reason, there had been some 'hitch' in the talks, he was prepared to drop everything and leave for Russia immediately. He was entirely at Leeper's disposal.

Leeper forwarded this letter, at Ransome's request, to the 'proper quarters' and the following day received a reply from Major Herbert Selby of the Passport Control Department. 'Decline Ransome's proposal with thanks and say that negotiations are so far advanced that it would not appear that his kind invitation would be of use at present.'

Next on the list was Bruce Lockhart, whose support, over the past months, had been, to say the least, erratic. A few weeks earlier, he had told the Foreign Office that Ransome was a 'dangerous fool', a 'Bolshevist in creed and in personal activities'. And yet speaking to his old friend privately, Lockhart found himself warming to the peculiar romance of his predicament. He sent Ransome off to speak to Major Gregory, head of the Foreign Office's Northern Department, with a letter of introduction.

'This is to introduce to you Mr. Arthur Ransome of the *Daily News*. He is most anxious to see you with regard to the extraction from Russia of Miss Shelepina, a lady for whom the FO took steps in August last year . . .'

Evgenia, explained Lockhart, was now in danger on two fronts: from the Whites, who would make her suffer on account of Ransome's journalism; and from the Bolsheviks, who would certainly shoot her as a spy if they got wind of his work for the British Secret Intelligence Services. Ransome, who felt 'morally responsible' for her safety, had shown 'commendable moderation' since his return to England, resisting numerous invitations from 'the extreme Labour section in this country' and any temptation to make a nuisance of himself in print. If Evgenia were permitted to return to England, he had promised to ensure her 'political non-existence', but faced with an 'inconsiderate refusal' of his petition, might take the law into his own hands. Lockhart would not go so far as to suggest that Ransome might launch 'an open attack on His Majesty's Government', but it seemed foolish, under the circumstances, 'to drive him to desperation'.

Towards the end of May, Ransome received a letter from Basil Thomson, who had invited him round to tea, confirming that official objections to 'Miss S' entering the country had been withdrawn, and that if she wished, she could accompany a Mr Parker back to London via the usual route.

'I have at last with great difficulty', Ransome wrote to Evgenia in his best Russian, obtained permission for you to join me here in England. You will have to travel with Parker. Parker is the representative of the Red Cross in Moscow. It will be easier for you to cross the Finnish border with him.

If he has already left, you must travel to Beloostrov immediately and cross over. If the Finns do not want to let you in, you should tell them that you are travelling on to England, and that they should let you go to the English Consulate in Helsingfors. There you will be given a visa for England and all the money you will need. There you will find Mrs. Hoffer who will sort things out for you, and possibly find you somewhere to stay.

There is just one thing. Do not delay for a minute. May I remind you how dearly you paid for that one stupid act and I ask you not to do the same again. I am spending the whole time here working on my book and I am waiting for you to arrive. It is a great pity I did not take you then.

Well, Baba, I hope that this time you will not act the fool. Do not delay for a single day.

Greetings to Mama, Serafima and Gleb.

Evgenia, however, remained where she was, and Parker returned alone.

~

By May, Admiral Kolchak's army was in retreat, much to the frustration of Winston Churchill and the British hawks. General Denikin, however, continued to advance on Moscow from the south, while General Yudenich, preparing yet another White army in Estonia, had set his sights on Petrograd. Ransome, who recalled the summer as the most testing of his life, soothed his nerves as best he could. He fished for trout and pike at the weekends with Francis Hirst. He played a great deal of chess. In the Lakes, he saw the Collingwoods, and was deeply moved when the ancient Skald, who made no secret of his hatred for the Bolsheviks, crept round the table after dinner and quietly clasped his hand, 'said it was very nice to see me again or something like that . . . the words didn't matter. But the whole incident nearly made me weep.'

Nineteen nineteen was the year John Reed published his eye-witness account of the Bolshevik coup, *Ten Days that Shook the World*. In London, Virginia and Leonard Woolf hosted the 1917 Club, while the Hands Off Russia Committee demanded strikes, demonstrations, anything to prevent the travesty which was being carried out in Russia in Britain's name. But Ransome lay low, speaking privately to politicians, diplomats and fellow journalists, until finally his chance came from the most welcome of quarters.

In June, the Treaty of Versailles was published, a peace so injurious to Germany and so antithetical to the liberal fraternity promised by Wilson's great League of Nations that the Reichstag considered rekindling the war. Lenin denounced it as final proof of Allied iniquity: 'What then is the Treaty of Versailles? It is an unparalleled and predatory peace, which has made slaves of tens of millions of people, including the most civilized.' In Berlin, Radek was removed from solitary confinement to a comfortable cell, where he received visitors, collected a library and wrote articles for the socialist press. Ransome's *Six Weeks*, meanwhile, appeared in the same month, sold over 8,000 copies in a fortnight, fascinated readers who knew as much of Soviet Russia as 'the dark side of the moon' and earned a congratulatory letter from Basil Thomson. Only *The Times Literary Supplement* offered any criticism: a suggestion that Ransome, though rigorous in seeking out both Bolsheviks and their socialist opponents, had not posed a single question or queried a single answer in a way that deviated from the official Soviet line 'as set out by them for foreign consumption'. In general, however, the British press were unanimous in their approval, resulting in a sudden influx of funds, an invitation to speak before the 1917 Club, and best of all, an offer from C. P. Scott, editor-proprietor of the *Manchester Guardian*.

Charles Prestwich Scott, one of the most powerful newspaper-men in the country, was a Yorkshireman, father to Ted Scott (Ransome's contemporary at Rugby) and a close acquaintance of Ransome's godfather, Sir Arthur Acland. Many of Ransome's companions from the old bohemian days had contributed to the paper, while all of Scott's Russian correspondents had been intimate friends: Bernard Pares, Harold Williams, and most recently, Morgan Philips Price, whose public disgrace left a void just as the presence of British troops in Russia was being most hotly disputed. Scott had considered Ransome for the position as early as February, but owing to objections from his staff – he was believed to have gone over 'too completely to the Bolshevik side' – passed him over in favour of a safer pair of hands. In July, however, Price's replacement, W. T. Goode, a former elementary-school teacher, disappeared under mysterious circumstances – kidnapped, as it transpired, by British officials in Estonia and spirited to Norway. When the news came out, Scott wrote personally to the Foreign Secretary, Lord Curzon, demanding 'an explanation of this extraordinary and to all appearance wholly unjustifiable treatment of a British subject'. But Goode's misfortune was Ransome's gain. Scott offered him £1,000 a year, excluding travel expenses, and more importantly, his unswerving support in securing a visa to Russia.

'Dear Mr. Scott,' wrote a delighted Ransome on 8 July,

Here is the Memorandum. I do not see how they can refuse unless they put personal hostility above obvious public advantage.

I feel quite sure that if Hardinge [the Home Secretary] or Curzon were to talk with me for ten minutes it would be enough to dispel the bogey picture painted for them by one or two of their understrappers . . .

In the Memorandum, which I do not mind your showing to Hardinge, I have omitted two points.

(1) Except under a Trotsky regime I think I could probably be of use to British subjects in Russia, should any of them get into difficulties or want to get out.

(2) In the unlikely but possible event of Denikin reaching Moscow, it would be unwise on our part to assume that that would mean that all was over and that everybody would live happily ever after . . . The need of information would be in no way lessened, and it would be dangerous to limit its sources to Denikin's avowed supporters.

Judging from the avalanche of memos on the public record, Scott's petition, energetically seconded by Ransome, exposed every conflict within the government bureaucracy and wasted a great deal of ink. Ransome's main concern, argued Leeper, was not his country, or even the Revolution, but for 'the safety of himself and for the Jewess* of whom he is enamoured . . . Personally I have no faith in him whatsoever and could not recommend anybody with so dishonest a mind being sent to the hotbed of all lies.'

Leeper's view of Ransome's character was endorsed by Colonel Thwaites of the War Office and by Major Gregory of the Foreign Office Northern Department, who nevertheless drew the opposite conclusion. 'Mr. Ransome is a man chiefly interested in himself and the lady referred to. He is without conviction or morality. He has always sided with the winning party, and his communications will be an indication of the strength of the Bolsheviks . . . I should certainly recommend his being allowed back into Russia.'

On 21 August, it seemed that Ransome's suit would be denied, but two days later, Lord Curzon, under strong pressure from both Scott and Basil Thomson, was saying that it should be approved, so long as the *Manchester Guardian* guaranteed his good conduct.

'After all you are to be allowed to go,' wrote Scott. 'I had almost given up hope, as the War Office at first put on their veto, but Thomson has now got the thing through, as I believe he will have informed you . . .'

Further complications, however, immediately intruded. The Foreign Office had provided a passport to Russia but no transit visas from the Norwegians, the Swedes or the Finns. As Thomson – by now out of temper with the whole affair – hurried to mend the gap, Ransome approached the Estonian ambassador, Mr Piip, who greeted him with tears in his eyes on account of the peace message he had delivered from Lenin and the brave stand the *Guardian* was making on account of small countries

---

* Both Evgenia's parents were Orthodox Christians. Leeper here betrays the anti-Semitism that so often went hand in hand with anti-Bolshevism, owing to the large proportion of ethnic Jews amongst the party leadership.

such as his own. Had Ransome got his way, he would have missed out Scandinavia altogether and sailed to Reval courtesy of the Estonian merchant navy. But as Piip was recalled, Scott summoned him to Manchester to discuss the last details of his contract. Finally, just when it seemed that nothing further could go amiss, Britain was hit by a coal strike.

Frantic enquiries brought me the news that a coastal steamer was that day leaving London. I raced to the docks with a portmanteau and a typewriter. As I paid the taxi I heard the steamer whistle. I reached the quayside just as the ropes had been cast off and a gap was slowly widening between the steamer and the quay. I threw my portmanteau on board, and, with my typewriter, jumped, caught the rail and was helped over it by a smiling sailor.

Ransome crossed the North Sea on a Norwegian merchant vessel fuelled with coal dust from its ballast, and by 3 October was in Stockholm, writing a brief explanatory note to Edith: 'I am incredibly happy to be off again. It was high time. I only wish I had got away a little earlier before the summer was gone. I have arranged with Scott for six months, but I am to use my own judgment, and I should not be surprised if my own judgment brings me home by Christmas.'

Ransome did not linger, and on the following day found himself at last in the ancient harbour at Reval, where rumour had it that General Yudenich – using Estonia as a springboard for the most dangerous White offensive of the war – was within ten miles of Petrograd.

Estonia's recent history, much like Ransome's own, reflected the squabbles of far greater powers. As a province of the former Russian empire, it had gained its independence thanks to the Bolshevik coup in November 1917, only to fall prey to the German army, which restored the Baltic feudal barons a day after the inauguration of Estonia's national parliament, or 'Diet'. Following the Armistice and the withdrawal of German troops, the fledgling republic had next faced a determined onslaught from the Reds, which it weathered thanks to the intervention of the British Royal Navy and the Whites. But the favour had come at a heavy price. As Estonia continued to fend off the Reds to the east, Mr Piip had lobbied Lloyd George in the West, explaining that while his country held the British in the very highest esteem, the Whites were no more interested in Estonian democracy than the Kremlin. As soon as his business with the Bolsheviks was done, Yudenich had promised to return to Reval and repatriate the insolent 'potato-eaters' to Great Russia.

Well aware of every facet of the situation (and the recent fate of W. T. Goode), Ransome came well prepared. Back in London, orders had been sent to the British consulate and military missions to lend their assistance. About his person he carried further documentation from the *Manchester Guardian*, from Major Scales of the Secret Intelligence Service in Stockholm, and last but not least, the letter from Lenin ordering every Soviet commissariat to provide any help he might require. But Ransome had also counted on his usefulness as a peacemaker. Fitful talks had continued between the Bolsheviks and Estonians since the previous spring, and had now reached a crisis. On the Bolshevik side, a ceasefire would relieve pressure on Trotsky, who needed both hands free to cope with Yudenich. Meanwhile, the Estonians, who looked forward to Yudenich's return with mounting trepidation, lacked the resources to deal with more than one imperialist at a time.

Hurrying along to the Ministry of Foreign Affairs, Ransome found Mr Piip anxious to do business. Open diplomacy had been hindered by the presence of the British and French, who still longed for a White victory and threatened to withdraw all support if the Estonians failed to co-operate. Piip's government was reluctant to use the wireless and did not want to put anything in writing, lest it should fall into the wrong hands. Would Ransome take it upon himself to let the Soviet government know 'that any suggestion for an armistice would be accepted, and that Estonia was ready to begin peace negotiations at once?'

Ransome's version of events, set down thirty years later in his memoirs, saw him modestly accepting a proposal that might, in time, secure the future of the civilized world.

'Peace with Estonia', he recalled, 'would mean peace on the Lettish front also. It would be the first clear step towards the ending of a state of war that was damaging to both sides and a mad postponement of the recovery of Europe. I did not see how I could take any other decision than to carry the Estonian message.'

And yet a wireless message had already been sent by Ransome to Moscow, garnering a reply which suggested that his services were not as essential as he might have hoped.

'To A Ransome,' signalled Maxim Litvinov sometime before 11 October, 'crossing of the front at present presents the greatest difficulties. I advise you to wait in Estonia arrival of our Peace Delegation.'

Ransome's account of his journey into Moscow – 560 miles as the crow flies – was written up in his notebooks, rearranged for the *Manchester Guardian* in 1920 and finally, after decades of sober reflection, set down as a work of near total fiction in his autobiography. Historians will turn to the earlier versions, in which Ransome, owing to a comprehensive arsenal of visas, crossed the front with the help of General Miller (representing Estonia), was handed to the Reds by a band of Lettish peasants and passed on to Moscow, facing no greater discomfort than a hospital train, a few bumpy roads and the incessant chatter of his solitary escort. A biographer, on the other hand, might be forgiven for turning to the final draft, in which our hero, having been denied a visa by the Kremlin, scrawled a defiant note to Litvinov announcing, 'RANSOME ALREADY LEFT', jumped aboard the first available train, and twelve hours later – bidding adieu to his farmer-guide – found himself standing within yards of the Bolshevik lines with nothing but a typewriter and a small suitcase to defend himself.

I filled a pipe, lit it, and with typewriter in one hand and bag in the other, walked over the hummock behind which we had stopped and set out across the open country towards that line which might or might not be the trenches of the Russians. I puffed pretty hard at my pipe, burning my tongue but producing lots of smoke. Nobody, I reasoned, was going to shoot at a man walking across and obviously enjoying his tobacco. Certainly no Russian, whose natural curiosity was sure to be greater than any wish to let off his rifle.

For what seemed a long time nothing happened and I began to think that the farmer, merely anxious not to get into trouble with either side, had just set me to walk in a direction that would take me away from himself. Then I saw something move, as it might be a rabbit. Suddenly the line of that earth parapet was broken by several such rabbits, and I caught a glint of light on a rifle barrel. I puffed harder than ever. With my hands full I could not wave a greeting and knew that any stoppage to put down my baggage might cause a regrettable misunderstanding. So I walked on, and presently saw half a dozen men with their elbows on the parapet and their rifles pointed in a direction I deplored . . .

Arrested by the Bolsheviks, Ransome was informed that he would be shot as a spy, but succeeded in delaying his execution just long enough to be presented with a filthy brew of cherry leaves and to explain that he was no ordinary newspaper reporter. Lenin, he assured his captors, would be 'very angry' if he was shot.

'He won't be angry with me for obeying orders,' replied the platoon commander.

'Perhaps not,' agreed Ransome, quietly sipping his tea:

But here I am. I have crossed the front already, and told you that I am going to Moscow. If you shoot me and find out afterwards that it was a mistake, you won't be able to put me together again. If, on the other hand, you don't shoot me and find out afterwards that you should have shot me, that is a mistake you will easily be able to put right.

Faced with the irresistible logic of this argument, the soldiers refilled Ransome's glass, and shortly afterwards, after further friendly banter, sent him on his way. He arrived in Moscow just in time to find Litvinov, dumbfounded by his impertinence, in the very act of reading the telegram he had sent from Reval.

On 14 October, the British Consul in Helsingfors, Coleridge Kennard, wired London demanding to know if it was really true that Arthur Ransome had obtained permission to bring his mistress, Evgenia Petrovna Shelepina, out of Russia.

'I should be very grateful for a private line as to whether there is any foundation for these statements . . . I have known AR for several years and consider him to be in that most unsatisfactory of all categories of man: a literary dishonest character. As for the lady she is of course notorious, but doubtless you know this and lots besides.'

Ransome had actually told the Foreign Office relatively little about Evgenia, save that she was in immediate danger and required his assistance. Neither was this any exaggeration. By mid-October, the party administration was in uproar. On the 16th, Trotsky, marshalling every resource at his disposal – building barricades from sewage pipes, instilling confidence in his ragged troops with tanks patched together from sheets of cardboard – had mounted his last-ditch defence of Petrograd. Five days later, crack troops, on Lenin's orders, were diverted from the south, providing General Denikin with a critical window of opportunity. Every day, Moscow was expecting a flood of refugees. It was the climax of the civil war, the fatal moment for good or ill, and yet Ransome recollected nothing but the unshaken conviction, shared by every ordinary Russian, that no power on earth could remove the Soviet or shake the people's faith in their Bolshevik leaders.

Arriving on 22 October, he had checked into the National Hotel, delivered Piip's peace message and within hours had been reunited with Evgenia, celebrating with a feast of potato cakes and Horlicks Malted Milk Tablets. At night, through the walls of his room, he could hear a young father singing his baby to sleep with 'The Internationale'. The corridors of the National were full of children, boisterously taking turns to play Yudenich, Denikin or Trotsky. Moscow was quiet, with no armed patrols and no disturbances, and though the 'cheerful militarism' of the children contrasted very strongly with the gloom of the grown-ups, this was only because the grown-ups understood that they had loved ones in Petrograd to lose. In England, bourgeois refugees had 'tricked' the government into supposing that if Petrograd fell, the Soviet would also fall, but the Muscovites, insisted Ransome, were under no such illusion. 'I walked daily in the streets, in the markets, and heard much said on the subject, but not a word that suggested the least belief that there would be any change in the established social order.'

Negotiations for Evgenia's release – a significant concession in view of the trust which had once been placed in her – scarcely intrude into Ransome's description of the few days he spent in Moscow. Lenin had criticized *Six Weeks* for a lack of political orthodoxy, but withdrew his objections when Karl Radek, ensconced at the Moabit prison in Berlin, had wired in support of the pamphlet, protesting that it was the 'first thing written that had shown the Bolsheviks as human beings'. Evgenia, in the meantime, simply packed her bags. As she made her final farewells, Ransome hurried round the city visiting old friends, 'all cold, all hungry, all convinced that they had got through the worst'. Shortly before his departure, there had been a new flare-up of fighting on the Estonian front, suggesting a crossing more difficult even than before. The Kremlin had supplied papers that would see them through the Russian lines but could afford no further protection. 'Litvinov said there was such a medley of troops on the other side that we could never be sure into whose hands we should fall.'

Ransome's return to Reval is dealt with in his autobiography in a chapter titled 'The Luck of the Chess Player', and follows the pattern of a classic folk tale. At a lonely farmstead in the middle of nowhere, Evgenia had saved both their lives with the gift of a travel kettle. Next, approaching the town of Marien-heim, Ransome – dressed in his great coat and tall lambswool hat – had passed himself off as a White officer, winning a warm bed for the night and a brief cameo on the parade ground inspecting a motley brigade of Latvian irregulars armed with pitchforks and fowling irons. On the fourth day, toiling west-wards in the company of their horse, cart and a young peasant with brothers on both sides of the war, they encountered the third and most awful challenge: a long, trotting line of regular White cavalry.

No audacious shout would be any use here. We marched on . . . We marched on . . . and then there occurred the most fantastic miracle, such a miracle as had not been amongst any of the possibilities I had foreseen. I was walking along, smoking my pipe, and hoping that the moment of meeting would somehow bring the right words to my mouth, when it seemed to me that there was something familiar in the look of the young officer in command. I stared at him. He stared at me. He suddenly shot forward, pulled up his horse, and exclaimed, 'What luck! Now we can have that other game of chess! We were on the point of stopping anyhow.'

So Ransome and the young officer, whom he had first met in Galicia during Brusilov's ill-fated 1916 offensive, sat on the ground and played chess, and while field kitchens were erected and soup prepared, settled their differences as gentlemen should. Ransome was trounced, shook hands, and in return received an introduction to the local general and no further dif-ficulties.

'The rest of our journey was pure comic opera. We found the general in a railway siding. He was charming, said his own rail-way car was at our disposal, apologised to Evgenia for the cock-roaches in it and sent us on to Reval . . .'

Ransome's train to Reval was, in fact, arranged by the same General Miller who had helped him into Russia in the first place, but these particulars were forgotten in favour of a personal vic-tory to match the prevailing euphoria. In Petrograd, Trotsky, against all odds, had triumphed, driving Yudenich's forces pell-mell back to Estonia, to be evacuated by British destroyers. Yudenich himself fled to France, where he was joined before long by Denikin. For the Revolution, the darkest hour had come before the dawn, and in November, British intervention in Russia was officially renounced. Peace between Russia and

Estonia followed shortly afterwards, with Ransome's own name recorded by way of gratitude in the Estonian national archive: 'the only time', he noted ruefully, 'that anybody has ever said "Thank you" for any of my amateur meddling in public affairs'.

Immediate celebrations, however, were forestalled by a sudden nervous collapse – a combination of stomach troubles and 'brain fever' – the result of cumulative stress, possibly triggered by an affair that Ransome certainly never alluded to in the future.

Following the dissolution of the Soviet Union in 1991, a number of documents were released from the Russian classified archives to the Library of Congress in Washington, including records of goods smuggled out of the country to fund the newly established Comintern. Amongst these is 265 NKVD, filed with the Ministry of the Interior (the department supervising the Cheka), which documented the collection by Evgenia of thirty-five diamonds and three strings of pearls shortly before her departure from the country.

'Valuables received by me for England . . .' reads the inventory, before listing contents amounting to 1,039,000 roubles. 'All valuables were received in full by E Shelepina, Moscow, October 25, 1919.'

Evgenia and Ransome had left Moscow on 28 October, arriving in the Estonian capital on 5 November. Evgenia's treasure, meanwhile, handed to Soviet agents in Reval, would have found its way to England, where similar packages were being distributed to trade unions and pro-Bolshevik newspapers, including the *Daily Herald*, whose editor Ransome had met with the previous March. Whether Ransome knew of the transaction and had accepted it in advance as a condition of Evgenia's liberty or discovered it only on their arrival in Estonia is unclear. But having made a full recovery at the Golden Lion Hotel, surrounded by murals of Tsar Alexander III (who happened to have slept in the same bed), he immediately typed up an affidavit, written in both Russian and English, guaranteeing that henceforth she would desist from all activities calculated to provoke a relapse.

'Dear Arthur,' runs the note, 'I hereby promise you on my word of honour that I will undertake no political commissions in England from the Bolsheviks or any other political party, and further that I will engage in no conspiratorial work whatsoever without expressly informing you that I consider this promise no longer binding.'

19

The Anglo-Soviet Accord

Lying in state at the Golden Lion Hotel, Ransome looked back on the events of 1919 and quietly vowed never, under any circumstances, to expose himself to a similar gauntlet again. Things, nevertheless, had turned out rather well, and as British troops finally withdrew from Russia, the future, at least for two exhausted refugees, appeared to promise the beginnings of a happy ending. Yet Ransome's path back to the bosom of his family, Evgenia in tow, was far from clear. C. P. Scott did not pay his foreign correspondents £1,000 a year to fish for pike in the Lake District. Neither was Ransome free to marry simply because he wanted to, or to enter into English society – stay at any smart hotel, visit respectable friends, go down to Edith in Kent, where photographs of his father hung on the drawing-room walls and *The Times* could invariably be found on the breakfast table – hand in hand with an adulteress. Formalities regarding visas and passports were one thing, social considerations another, and if Ransome was not to forfeit the special privileges of his class, he needed a divorce.

'My Dear Ivy,' he wrote immediately on returning from Moscow,

(1) I enclose with this a cheque for £100, which I hope will be useful.

(2) You remember that I told you last year, of the lady with whom I was living in Stockholm in 1918. You have probably heard indirectly that I succeeded in rejoining her, as I told you I hoped to do. I do not intend, under any circumstances, to be parted from her again.

Now I perfectly well remember that you once, indeed more than once, told me, during the period between my first leaving you in 1913 and the winter of 1916, that you did not intend ever to divorce me.

You for your part will remember that I agreed to do without my books for example, in order that if you chose you could pretend, as it was easy to pretend during the war, that I had not really gone at all. Surely that pretence is now quite impossible.

Nor is it as if I had not up to three years ago made many attempts to take up the old existence. You know these attempts were failures and only proved absolutely that our living together meant merely that two people were wretched instead of one . . .

I know that this letter, raking up old pains, must be hurting you, and I am finding it very difficult to write. But the present undefined position is really thoroughly bad. Do you think you could, before answering this in any way, go up to London and see Stanley Unwin, my publisher, of 40 Museum Street. He will tell you exactly how things stand. When you have seen him, then perhaps if you are not going to divorce me, you will tell him what you propose to do in the event of my returning to England with the lady in question. Of course you or anybody else could make it impossible for me to bring her at all; in which case I should have no other choice but to remain in permanent exile.

Ransome's letter set out his position as plainly as he knew how. It offered money. It offered advice. It pointed out that Tabitha would not suffer any stigma, because it would be perfectly plain in the eyes of the world that it was Ivy who was divorcing Ransome and not the other way round. But Ivy proved unbending, and much to Ransome's disappointment, so did Edith. She was, by now, entirely resigned to his antics in the press, but she put her foot down when it came to inviting the Bolsheviks for Christmas.

For all these reasons, an immediate return to England with Evgenia was out of the question, and Ransome's anxiety – a dismal apprehension that his troubles were not yet over – must have contributed very materially to his 'brain fever'. But once the physical symptoms had run their course, despair gave way to his usual rugged optimism. He was, he reminded Edith, the 'same old Rapscallion' he always had been and hoped that in spite of 'domestic complications', their relationship would remain as affectionate and straightforward as ever. He had recovered, he told her, from his illness, was beating all the other correspondents at skittles and was energetic, cheerful and enjoying a clean conscience for the first time in a year. Business-wise, Scott had thought at first that he should be headquartered in Helsingfors, but Finland was teeming with White Russians, so that for the moment he preferred to remain in Estonia, where he was on excellent terms with British and local officials alike. Evgenia, meanwhile, was learning English from a translation of Hans Christian Andersen, but Ransome was keen that she should learn something of his native culture, and with this in mind requested a copy of Edith's *First History of England*, which he hoped she would inscribe 'Evgenia. Christmas 1918'. It was the very least she could do, he felt, for a woman whose nursing had practically saved his life.

In Reval, Ransome and Evgenia pranced around like puppies, admiring the tall ships and fishing boats in the harbour and the houses piled up against the walls of the ancient fortress. In the small outlying villages, cattle grazed in the street, and Ransome had on one occasion seen a flock of sheep filing out of church in single file, like the most dignified parishioners. Abandoning any notion of an immediate return to England, he began looking for more permanent quarters, which he found a little way out of the capital in Lodenzee: a discreet little *pension* where tea was served at four and became Evgenia's favourite meal. As a substitute for the north country, it lacked high hills, but boasted a forest and a lake for picnics, camping, boating and swimming – occupations which Ransome considered indispensable to happiness, and which Evgenia endured with moderate cheerfulness. Together, they were as fond of one another as two children, deeply lonely when apart and entirely conservative in their approach to wedlock. Ransome, the breadwinner, issued orders like a commodore and obeyed instantly when Evgenia's 'barometer' began to rise – a regular occurrence. They fell into the habit of pet names: she was 'Topsy', as in 'Old Top'; he was 'Charlie', as in Chaplin, owing to a similarity in gait when he was suffering from piles. In Estonia – a queer in-between place just after the war, where spies and black markets flourished – nobody knew or cared if Mr and Mrs Ransome were married or not. But though Edith sent the *First History of England* as requested, she only thawed at a distance, while Ivy – referred to now as 'Wiltshire' – remained as stubborn as ever: a selfish, cold-hearted *burzhooi*, spinning out her truant husband's purgatory from one season to the next, with each year bringing some fresh upset in Russia or some new diplomatic crisis requiring the *Guardian*'s immediate attention.

~

Over the next four years, British dealings with Russia were no longer founded on expectations of the Soviet government's sudden demise. Any lingering hopes for Allied intervention were dashed in February 1920 by the execution of Admiral Kolchak. In the same month, Lloyd George opened negotiations with the Soviet with a view to a possible trade agreement, hotly opposed by Lord Curzon and Winston Churchill but enthusiastically endorsed by the Foreign Office's Russian department. Russian wheat, it was explained, was essential to the reconstruction of the European economy, while British-made machines and technical expertise were equally vital to the development of the rich black earth of the Volga. Britain, declared Lloyd George, would kill two birds with one stone. On the one hand, there would be no need to import expensive grain from an increasingly powerful America; on the other, well-fed revolutionaries would quickly tire of the Bolsheviks. 'We have failed to restore Russia to sanity by force,' he informed the assembled representatives of British democracy. 'I believe we can save her by trade.'

Ransome had at first greeted news of a potential treaty with 'ironic amusement'. In Moscow, 'fool after fool' was being welcomed with open arms by the Kremlin, while the Russian correspondent for the *Manchester Guardian* was treated as a mere 'bourgeois observer'. Neither was it any surprise to find Lloyd George, who for years had ignored Ransome's advice on the subject, now insisting 'he had been in favour of peace all along'. He was, he told Edith, 'as sick of Russia as any man could be'.

Reflections of this kind, however, were bound to be weighed against more practical considerations. In January, Ransome had written to Scott explaining that his coverage of the Polish–Soviet war would be a distant affair owing to 'an orgy of Anti-Bolshevism and Whiteness in Poland' that made it impossible for him to cover the fighting on the spot. Finland, likewise, had proven inhospitable to gentlemen of the liberal press. Estonia, therefore, was the most sensible place to pitch camp while Russia, so close and so well known, was once again a news-worthy subject. Indeed, the only serious obstacle to Ransome resuming business was a lingering resentment over *Six Weeks*, coupled with the interminable ramblings of the Estonian–Russian peace talks. In February, however, a treaty was finally signed, opening a direct forty-eight-hour rail link to Moscow, where Radek, after lively adventures in Germany, was ready to receive visitors. Ransome was amongst the first, and after col-lecting his visa from the new Soviet legation in Reval, set out with two Norwegian journalists and Marcel Rosenberg of the Bolshevik Press Bureau. By the beginning of March, he was seated comfortably in his own office at the Commissariat of Foreign Affairs, hard at work on a new political pamphlet which would explain why Russia – the richest agricultural territory in Europe – was currently on the brink of starvation.

Ransome's first two pamphlets, *On Behalf of Russia* and *Six Weeks*, had been designed to meet a particular circumstance: a spirited critique of militant capital in the face of imminent Allied intervention; a sympathetic portrait of the Bolshevik leaders aimed at Paris in the wake of the Red Terror. Now, in the context of a possible Anglo-Soviet trade agreement, Ransome set aside politics and personality in favour of a theme which he hoped would be less controversial. *The Crisis in Russia* would focus on Russia's economic distress not as a malaise unique to the Soviet, but as part of a tide of misery sweeping virtually every nation that had participated in the war.

Nothing can be more futile than to describe conditions in Russia as a sort of divine punishment for revolution, or indeed to describe them at all without emphasizing the fact that the crisis in Russia is part of the crisis in Europe, and has been in the main brought about like the revolution itself, by the same forces that have caused, for example, the crisis in Germany or the crisis in Austria.

Ransome spoke of Moscow families huddled together like animals for warmth; the want of basic medicines; the pitiable, universal obsession with food – and warned that these things could be visited on any country, however superficially secure. England itself, isolated long enough from the outside world, would feel what it meant to revert to barbarism, to see its industries collapse, its children run naked, its dinner money rendered worthless 'because there will be no dinner to buy'. Politically, he now accepted that democracy had no place in Russia. Military conscription for the army was matched by labour conscription: those who did not work did not eat. Strikes were illegal. Political opposition had become, at best, a form of 'theatrical distraction'. But these constraints on liberty, as the workers themselves acknowledged, were trivial compared to a revival of the civil war. The overwhelming concern was to salvage what remained of Russia's industries.

'We are witnessing in Russia', he told his readers, 'the first stages of a titanic struggle, with on one side all the forces of nature leading apparently to the inevitable collapse of civilization, and on the other side nothing but the incalculable force of human will.'

As an example of this 'incalculable force', Ransome offered the Bolsheviks, but not the Cheka or 'Extraordinary Commission'. In Russia, he confessed, there was a state within a state, a group of 'Jesuitical fanatics' who struck at random like lightning 'in a particularly bad thunderstorm'. But it would be a grave mistake to suppose that the Cheka – an organization which Ransome claimed the party administration had no control over – was responsible for the almost total absence of political debate in Russia. 'I have never met a Russian', he explained, 'who could be prevented from saying whatever he liked whenever he liked, by any threats or dangers whatsoever. The only way to prevent a Russian from talking is to cut out his tongue.' In Moscow, it was simply that tongues had ceased to wag. Questions that might trouble visitors from England or America were 'brushed almost fretfully aside by men who had gone more or less hungry for two or three years'. Political ideas were no longer relevant or even welcome. What was required was political will, and in this respect the Bolsheviks, by common assent, had no rivals. While their opponents dithered, they were repairing railway wagons for the transport of grain. While well-fed Russian émigrés in London and Berlin carped on the injustices of the secret police (forgetting the horrors perpetrated by the Whites), the Bolsheviks were building hospitals. When Lenin said a thing would be done, 600,000 Communist Party members moved behind him 'as a single man', not because of Karl Marx or the excesses of misguided zealots, but to save a starving Russia. The British government and the Soviet believed in different things, but the issue in question was not the relative virtues of communism or capitalism: 'Their quarrel with each other', Ransome repeated, 'is for both parties merely a harassing accompaniment of the struggle to which Europe is committed, for the salvage of what is left of European civilization.'

In Moscow, Ransome enjoyed the company of Evgenia's family: her youngest brother, Gleb, still at school, imbibing Marx with his algebra; Roman, who had graduated from Trotsky's military academy and joined the Red Army; Maria Alexeevna, who had been so grateful to see her daughter spirited to safety that she had cried out of pure happiness. In Ransome's absence, Karl Radek had replaced Angelica Balabanova as Secretary of the Third International, or 'Comintern', headquartered at the Lux Hotel, where foreign communists lived in a bubble of tranquil security. Here Maria washed and folded sheets, while Serafima, Evgenia's youngest sister, worked as a secretary, typing up the correspondence of the Comintern's Executive Committee. Evgenia had given Ransome letters to deliver – 'Lovely Mama', 'Lovely Irka' – waiting back in Lodenzee for the smallest details of their welfare. And there would have been a great deal to tell. Viktor, who had disgraced himself by fighting for the Whites, was hiding in Irkutsk with his fellow officers. Iroida, rising rapidly through the ranks of the Soviet bureaucracy, had been posted to Tashkent as a 'diplomatic collaborator' at the propaganda school, then to Afghanistan, where the Soviet embassy was busy stirring up anti-British feeling in India. In April, Radek returned from a tour of the Caucasus and invited his old friend for an all-night chat at the Kremlin, where they shared a pipe, played with Radek's two-year-old daughter and discussed the difference between exporting Bolshevik ideas and maintaining security at home. Shortly after Radek's arrival, Ransome interviewed Lenin, who now doubted that British shop stewards would tolerate industrial conscription but quoted Hegel, whose influence on Karl Marx had been considerable, in support of his suppression of the Russian peasants: 'Hegel wrote . . . "What is the People? The people is that part of the nation which does not know what it wants."' Even Trotsky had thawed a little, and agreed to put away the egg timer which usually limited interviews to four minutes. He told Ransome that the Soviet–Polish war would inevitably be decided by the Polish workers. No bourgeois country could march on the Soviet without provoking revolution in its own backyard.

Many years later, back in London, Ransome would amuse members of the Garrick Club with stories of how in the spring of 1920 he had taken his meals in a magnificent palace across the river from the Kremlin, dining with an American millionaire, a diplomatic legation from Kabul and Enver Pasha, the former Turkish Minister for War, who had shared a sledge with him, and speeding round sharp corners, warmly embraced him, exclaiming: 'You and I are the only two imperialists in Russia. We must cling together!' Within the hallowed circle of diplomacy, men of vastly different backgrounds and beliefs shared the same salt: Enver – one of the principal architects of the Armenian genocide – seeking Soviet backing for a holy war in Persia; Afghans discussing how best to guard against British incursions on their new independence; Mr Vanderlip, looking for mining concessions in Kamchatka. Outside, the Terror continued, developing rarified tortures depending on the region: the 'glove trick' or flaying of hands; the rolling of naked bodies in barrels lined with nails; or death by fire, in which the victim was strapped to a plank and fed slowly, feet first, into a furnace. In Moscow, 1,500 'dangerous counter-revolutionaries' were executed in a single night, simply because Lenin, in an absent-minded moment, had placed a cross by their names. But very few of these colourful details found their way into *The Crisis in Russia*, which was, by its author's own admission, a dry affair. In the past, enlightened Englishmen and the Soviet had shared a common interest in resisting the Germans or in defending the freedom to dream great dreams. Now it was money, trains and food, with the hero of the hour not Trotsky or Lenin, or even the irrepressible Karl Radek, but Rykov, the Minister of Finance, struggling to balance accounts in a freezing office at the Hotel Siberia.

Back in England, the first unofficial representative of the Soviet was received at Downing Street in June, provoking lugubrious protests from *The Times* and shouts of laughter from C. P. Scott. 'The blow has fallen,' ran the *Guardian* leader. 'A Bolshevik, a real live representative of Lenin, has spoken with the British Prime Minister face to face.' Ransome, meanwhile, had left Russia in late April, stopping at his old flat in Petrograd to discover that the Cheka had been there before him.

'In Petrograd yesterday', he wrote to Edith on the train back to Reval,

between arrival and departure I rushed round to see what had become of my rooms. The infernal idiots made a search there. They found my collection of newspapers, every copy of every paper issued in Petrograd from February 1917 to February 1918, an absolutely priceless and irreplaceable collection which I had intended for the British Museum. THEY BURNT THE LOT amid the protests of my old landlady, who, however, succeeded in saving my favourite fishing rod, a few pictures and my Turkish coffee mill. Boots, felt winter boots, the files of my old telegrams, cameras, practically everything of value stolen.

It had, Ransome admitted, been a terrible shock, but he was inclined to view the business philosophically. Surveying his 'bare and ruined room' he had at first been angry, but then 'grinned a deep and solid grin'.

It is, after all, only just that I as a bourgeois should suffer like the rest, and now at least I have the necessary feeling for the chapter on that subject in my history. I had such contempt for the Russian bourgeois that I had difficulty in thinking of him without impatience, and found it hard to take him seriously when he complained of losing his piano and what not. I despise him now as much as before, but in describing his mental state after the revolution I have now the best of subjective material. Devil take it. I forgive them for stealing my boots, which were no doubt wanted for the army, but to burn that collection of papers, to destroy such material for the chronicling of their own revolution, and to BURN it . . . Forty-thousand million dancing devils with pink tails and purple stomach aches.

Back in Estonia, Ransome bought a little dinghy called *Slug*, provoked Evgenia to terrified rage by nearly drowning himself in the bay, and completed a first draft of *The Crisis in Russia*. By July, exhausted, he had succumbed to rheumatic flu, told Stanley Unwin, who was due to publish the pamphlet, that he would not be able to visit London until he was recovered, and with Evgenia to administer medicines, took to his bed until August. By October, he was in England to sign a formal agreement with Unwin, hand in a written report to the Foreign Office (an informal relationship had been resumed) and to congratulate his sister Joyce on her upcoming marriage and her 'ordered future'. He returned to Evgenia in good time for Christmas with the first British plum pudding he had eaten in years.

~

Talks with the Soviet encouraged visitors to Russia who had hitherto observed only at a distance, amongst them H. G. Wells and Bertrand Russell. Wells, arriving in Petrograd in autumn 1920, had deeply regretted the closure of every shop, the collapse of industry and the deplorable neglect of art and science. Composers could find no manuscript paper; writers had no books. Ivan

Pavlov had no laboratory, while Maxim Gorky was forced to act as a one-man charity for the preservation of Russian culture in general. Yet while such singular talents could not be expected to endure with the common herd, the blame, Wells insisted, was not with the Bolsheviks, who were energetically engaged in the reconstruction of their country. Philosophers, of course, would quibble over semantics – the definition, for example, of the 'proletariat', which as yet no Marxist scholar had convincingly supplied – but Russia had chosen Bolshevism, while the Soviet remained its only viable government. The only 'humane' course for England, therefore, was to trade with it, recognize it and to profit from whatever lessons the communist experiment could provide.

In Estonia, Ransome read Wells's *Russia in the Shadows* and approved, but had nothing to say about Russell's *The Practice and Theory of Bolshevism* (published in November 1920 by Unwin), possibly because, whereas Wells had glossed over Bolshevik ideology, Russell – the most distinguished philosopher of his generation – had taken it as his central theme.

A sweated wage, long hours, industrial conscription, prohibition of strikes, prison for slackers, diminution of the already insufficient rations where the production falls below what the authorities expect, an army of spies ready to report any tendency to political disaffection and to procure imprisonment for its promoters – this is the reality of the system.

Most disturbing to Russell, amidst the disillusion created by the Great War, was the hope that Bolshevism held out to Europe: a hope which had tempted other visitors to conceal the cause of Russia's present catastrophe. Agriculture had collapsed, not because of Allied intervention or blockade – though Russell condemned both – but because the Bolsheviks had alienated the peasants. Industry, with the sole exception of the munitions factories, had collapsed because starving workers fled to the countryside. What Russell had discovered was a systematic failure not of the universal ideals of communism, but of their over-hasty application: a failure of psychology, and worse, of philanthropy. 'Cruelty lurks in our instincts, and fanaticism is a camouflage for cruelty. Fanatics are seldom genuinely humane, and those who sincerely dread cruelty will be slow to adopt a fanatical creed.' Russell did not know if Bolshevism would triumph, but if it triumphed outside Russia he predicted the disappearance both of capitalism and of communism, and for the world, 'centuries of darkness and futile violence'.

For Ransome, the most immediate consequence of this sudden explosion of eye-witness accounts was that *The Crisis in Russia* sank like a stone. Delayed by his own corrections, and then, in March 1921, by Lloyd George's formal signature of the Anglo-Soviet Accord, it was irrelevant by the time it was published and sold less than a thousand copies. Meanwhile, in February, the *Guardian* had sent bad news. Paper, Scott explained, had become increasingly expensive thanks to a dearth of Russian timber, resulting in unavoidable cuts. He was sorry, as Ransome had done 'excellent work . . . also for personal reasons', but his hands were tied.

Ransome's contract with the *Guardian* would be renewed in a matter of weeks, but anticipating a lengthy spell without regular funds, he had looked to his resources. From Estonia he began to send articles to the *New York Herald* via their Russian correspondent, Francis McCullagh, but the relationship was vexed on both sides, with Ransome claiming McCullagh had stolen original material and McCullagh accusing Ransome of delusions of grandeur. Towards the end of February, Ransome had written to Edith announcing a 'gigantic trip' via Moscow to Persia and the Caucasus, where he hoped to investigate the 'amazing porridge pot which the Bolsheviks are stirring there', if only he could evade capture by the various local species of 'wildman'. But he had never got beyond Moscow, either because the Kremlin refused to issue the necessary visa or because his priorities had changed at the last moment. He had entered Russia in the company of Lord Leith, a British businessman appointed by Lloyd George to pave the way for a trade mission, a position which suggests that Ransome continued to enjoy the confidence of at least a portion of the British civil service. Yet on this occasion one learns of the attachment not from a Whitehall memo, but from a document in the Russian classified archives: a report originating from the INO, a branch of the Cheka established by Felix Dzerzhinsky to provide intelligence on British foreign policy in the run-up to the Anglo-Soviet Accord. Ransome, having established himself as an expert on the subject, had made a very active contribution to their research.

~

March, by any standard, was a busy month for all parties. Lloyd George had made the conclusion of Soviet peace with Poland a condition of the trade treaty, and thanks to a dramatic victory by General Pilsudski, peace had been signed. But just as the prime minister, in the face of fierce opposition within his Cabinet, committed Britain to a formal agreement, the Bolsheviks suffered a dramatic reversal. On 8 March, the Kronstadt sailors, the original heroes of Lenin's November coup – once described by Trotsky as 'the beauty and pride of the revolution' – issued a public denunciation of the regime and announced their own independent soviet. The November Revolution, declared the sailors, had been betrayed by the 'Communist usurpers'. The 'power of the monarchy' had been replaced with 'the constant fear of torture by the Cheka, the horrors of which far exceed the rule of the gendarmerie under Tsarism'.

Through the state control of the trade unions they have chained the workers to their machines so that labour is no longer a source of joy but a new form of slavery. To the protests of the peasants, expressed in spontaneous uprisings, and those of the workers, whose living conditions have compelled them to strike, they have answered with mass executions and a bloodletting that exceeds even the tsarist generals. The Russia of the toilers, the first to raise the red banner of liberation, is drenched in blood.

A more damning blow to the moral authority of the Bolsheviks can hardly be imagined, or a surer provocation. On 16 March, eight days after the proclamation was published,

Trotsky sent the Red Army across the ice to the Kronstadt Fortress and put down the rebellion without quarter, provoking an international outcry from conservatives and socialists alike. Lloyd George, however, had greeted the news with undisguised relief, signing the Anglo-Soviet Accord on the same day. 'This is purely a trading agreement', he explained to the House of Commons on the 22nd, 'recognizing the Soviet government as the *de facto* government of Russia, which undoubtedly it is . . . They have as complete control over that vast territory as any Government could possibly have under the present conditions, and therefore they have to be recognized as the *de facto* government of that Empire.'

Meanwhile, as Lenin frankly admitted that he had 'failed to convince the masses', forbidding any future political initiative outside the Party Executive Committee, the Cheka's INO, or 'Foreign Department', had submitted a report which drew heavily on Ransome's insights. British trade with Russia, ran the report, was supported chiefly by Lloyd George and fiercely opposed by Lord Curzon (former Viceroy of India) and Winston Churchill. Harold Williams, wrongly described as a 'baronet', had the most influence on the Cabinet's negative judgement of the Bolsheviks, seconded by his wife, Ariadna Tyrkova, and the MI6 agent Paul Dukes, whom Ransome despised. In general, however, the Bolshevik position was strong. 'The Soviet has a greater influence on the East,' advised Ransome, 'and [the] Muslim world is more inclined to Russian influence than it is to English.' Lloyd George, concluded the Cheka, had signed the trade treaty because he was in any case powerless to resist Soviet expansion in Persia and India. A few weeks later, Ransome was explaining that the framing of the Kronstadt uprising in the British press was evidence of 'organized pressure on English public opinion . . . Ransome considers that the time might be opportune for the Soviet Government to publish the true state of affairs.' Acknowledging receipt of this report, Lenin had written, 'In my opinion it is very important, and probably fundamentally true.'

Ransome's information – often misguided, wholly insignificant in terms of the national security either of Russia or Britain – is less arresting than his motives for giving it. His appeal to the Cheka was obvious. At one time or another he had enjoyed a personal acquaintance with every official that might have excited Dzerzhinsky's interest, from Basil Thomson at Scotland Yard, through Major Gregory of the Foreign Office's Northern Department, to Ernest Boyce, head of British intelligence in Russia – by now considered a family friend. As for Ransome's reasons for co-operating, it is possible that his concern for the safety of Evgenia's family was a factor. In 1920, Iroida had transferred from Kabul to the headquarters of the NKVD, the Commissariat for the Interior, which controlled the Cheka, and she would certainly have been expected to make herself useful. There was also Ransome's long-standing commitment to the 'Anglo-Russian friendship', which he had defended ever since the Tsar first declared war on Germany. But his most powerful motive for ingratiating himself with the Cheka was almost certainly personal advancement, a straightforward self-interest which Ransome never owned to but which explains his dealings with the British and Soviet intelligence services far more comprehensively than any other. As an agent of MI6, his recruitment had benefited nobody as materially as himself, while his admiration for the Bolsheviks was measured against no consistent ideal. Following a series of peasant revolts, workers' strikes, and most recently, the rebellion of the Kronstadt sailors, Lenin had been forced to abandon communism in favour of a limited form of capitalism, or the so-called New Economic Policy, but Ransome – weary of statistics – scarcely touched on the subject for several months. Kronstadt, meanwhile, had not shaken his commitment to the Soviet project any more than the Red Terror. Reinstalled by the *Guardian* in March, he echoed Dzerzhinsky in describing the uprising as a wholly anomalous distraction, fomented by a foreign power (the French). In Moscow, he claimed, the masses had been entirely unmoved. Stepping out from the Commissariat of Foreign Affairs, he had noticed a line of workers fishing beneath the walls of the Kremlin.

~

Ransome returned to Estonia at the end of March, played chess with the British Consul, talked fishing with the Estonian Minister for Stockholm, and occasionally dropped in to see Maxim Litvinov at the Soviet legation, where officers of the INO oversaw the transmission of funds and propaganda to Europe. Meanwhile, *Slug* was replaced with a new boat, a five-metre gaffer with a tiny cabin and a dinghy built by a local coffin-maker. *Kittiwake*, however, proved unsatisfactory, and within days of her purchase, Ransome and Evgenia had met 'and fallen in love with' the Estonian yacht designer Otto Eggers.

As an antidote to politics, boat design afforded all the excitement of state building with none of the ethical pitfalls. Very soon, Ransome, drawing on a freshly swollen bank account, was imagining a ship for the open seas, efficiently divided into water-tight compartments for the stowage of every essential. Ransome's ship would be roomy and reliable, a floating island in which a man could sleep, write and live almost as he would on land, and so colossally expensive that Evgenia promised to go without new clothes for a whole year. By July, plans were afoot to shift camp from Estonia to Latvia, where such a marvel might be built, a move to be undertaken by Evgenia as Ransome travelled to England to collect new teeth, nautical uniforms and all the hardware – sextant, compass, sidelights – so essential to a boat that was to be no mere toy but an Englishman's sea-faring castle, complete with flags, portholes and a small hand-held cannon for the firing of emergency flares. All this was revolving in his mind as he wrestled with the possibility that the Third International would bring the Revolution to Manchester 'by way of the Hindu Kush'. But his own trip to England was delayed not by ambitious Bolsheviks, but by the failure of the Volga harvest – the same harvest Lloyd George hoped would feed Europe –

leading in Russia to the loss of over 5 million lives. It was the first time Ransome had witnessed such a holocaust with his own eyes.

'We went down to the shore of the Volga,' he wrote in mid-August,

down a rough broken street, past booths where you could buy white bread, and, not a hundred yards away, found an old woman cooking horse dung in a broken saucepan. Within sight of the market was a mass of refugees, men, women, and children, with such belongings as they had retained in their flight from starvation, still starving, listlessly waiting for the wagons to move them away to more fortunate districts ... There are, of course, no latrines. The beach was black with excreta until, as an eye-witness (not a Communist) told me, the local Communists arranged a 'Saturdaying' which deserves a place in history, and themselves removed that disgusting ordure, and, for a day or two, lessened the appalling stench that is beginning once more to rise from the beach.

With an American cinematographer, Ercole, at his elbow, Ransome had visited one of the 'children's houses' providing accommodation to orphans or foundlings.

The garden, a plain courtyard with a few trees, was full of children lying in the sun under the wall, staring in silent unchildlike groups, ragged, half-naked, some with nothing whatever but a shirt. All were scratching themselves. Among these children, a man and a woman were walking about, talking quietly to them, and carrying sick children into the house, bringing others out. Ercole had hardly begun to turn the handles of his machine before some of the children saw us, and, some with fright, some with interest, all scrambled to their feet, although many of them fell again, and, too weak to get up, stayed sitting on the ground where they fell. Ercole photographed them as they were. Then he picked four little boys and photographed these alone. Wishing to reward them, he gave them some chocolate before the woman looking after them had time to stop him. 'You must not do it,' she said; 'they are too hungry.' But it was already too late. All of them who had strength to move were on top of each other, fighting for the scraps of chocolate like little animals, with small, weak, animal cries ...

Ransome had written to Edith before his departure announcing a 'very beastly job' that had been 'thrust upon' him, and over the following weeks would gladly have exchanged places with any journalist in the world. But witnessing a tragedy which had its roots in the seizure of property and grain encouraged by Lenin in the first years of the Revolution, he pointed instead to the vagrancy forced upon Russian peasants ever since the Tsar had mobilized his army in 1914.

In the siding beyond the camp was a refugee train, a sort of rolling village, inhabited by people who were for the most part in slightly better condition than the peasants flying at random from the famine. These were part of the returning wave of that flood of miserable folk who fled eastwards before the retreating army in 1915 and 1916, and are now uprooted again and flying westwards with the whip of hunger behind them . . . I walked from one end of the train to the other. It was made up of cattle trucks, but these trucks were almost like huts on wheels, for in each one was a definite group of refugees and a sort of family life. These folks had with them their belongings, beds, bedding, chests of drawers, rusty sewing machines, rag dolls. I mention just a few of the things I happened to see. In more than one of the wagons I found three or four generations of a single family – an old man and his still more ancient mother struggling back to the village which they had last seen in flames as it was set on fire by the retreating army, anxious simply, as they said, 'to die at home'. . .

In the doorway of one truck I found a little boy, thinner than any child in England shall ever be, I hope, and in his hand was a wooden cage, and in the cage a white mouse, fat, sleek, contented, better off than any other living thing in all that train. There were a man and his wife on the platform outside. I asked them where they were going. 'To Minsk,' said the man, 'those of us who live; the children are dying every day.' I looked back at the little boy, warming his mouse in the sun. The mouse, at least, would be alive at the journey's end.

20

Racundra

At a rented house in Kaiserwald, a village just outside Riga, Evgenia spent much of the winter knitting sweaters, alone with her cat, Tom, while Ransome, who had gone straight from the Volga to England and returned just before Christmas, gathered material for a special edition the *Guardian* was preparing on Anglo-Soviet affairs. In January 1922, he had been in Finland with Ernest Boyce and the Finnish Foreign Minister, Holsti. In February he was back in Moscow, speaking to Georgy Chicherin, Maxim Litvinov and Karl Radek, and to his old friend Will Peters, who had so accurately predicted two revolutions in Russia and who now returned with the British trade mission as translator and economic advisor to Sir Robert Hodgson. March saw articles by Ransome on the 'liberties, luxuries and sky-high prices' now in evidence in Moscow following the introduction of Lenin's New Economic Policy, as well as a piece on the upcoming Conference of Genoa, where Russia and Germany would for the first time sit down with twenty world powers to discuss the economic reconstruction of Europe. Very little, however, appeared under Ransome's name in the early months of the year, and even less with the coming of spring. As Evgenia roared through the house in a whirlwind of spring-cleaning, he crept from room to room clutching his sextant and his compass. After the last hard freeze of the year, he careened across the lake below Kaiserwald in an ice yacht, covering in five minutes distances that the previous year, in the diminutive *Kittiwake*, had taken well over an hour. 'It's very exciting,' he told Edith, 'but I should not care to have an ice yacht.' His own boat would be thirty foot long, twelve foot wide, with a shallow draft the better to navigate the channels and small harbours of the Baltic. She would be snub-nosed and gaff-rigged for easy handling. She would be capable of 'going anywhere', and yet as comfortable in port as a seaside cottage. Ransome's ship – her broad hull modelled on the old Estonian schooners that ferried coal and timber around the coast – would be equipped with a galley, quick-drying horse-hair mattresses, a table to eat off and write at, and a forecastle to sleep a 'boy' – in this case a septuagenarian Latvian sailor, one Captain Sehmel, as tough as a ship's biscuit. She would be so heavy in her keel it would 'take a miracle to tip her', and in case of calms (and as her sole concession to the industrial age) would be fitted with a tiny propeller 'like a little brass flower'.

Later, once the immediate frustration of the experience had faded, Ransome would claim that only Noah had ever completed a ship on time, 'because he had to'. All winter, as he studied the principles of navigation or sat bolt upright at night with an imaginary tiller squeezed beneath his elbow, he had been goading the builder, Lehtner, to greater efforts. His ship had been promised for April. She was promised again in May, and at weekly intervals thereafter. In June, Lehtner was stripped of his real name and referred to thereafter only as 'the swine'. Ransome's 'dream ship' was launched, a bare shell, in July, only to drift listlessly at anchor on the River Dvina, until Ransome kidnapped her, and in the early part of August, saw to her final fittings at the Riga Yacht Club. Two weeks later, as Evgenia swept the shavings of a new centreboard from beneath the cabin table, he presented himself at the customs office to receive his ship's papers.

'"Master and Owner of *Racundra*". Does any man need a prouder title or description? In moments of humiliation, those are the words that I shall whisper to myself for comfort. I ask for no others on my grave.'

Racundra finally weighed anchor on 20 August. Her course, carefully plotted to combine interesting sailing with an anthropological study of various remote island peoples, had taken her through the Moon Sound to Helsingfors and back again, a journey of over 700 miles, convincing Ransome that a voyage to

England the following summer could be undertaken with absolute confidence. For the moment, however, it was enough to feel that his most recent adventure had laid the foundation not only for further forays, but for a personal literary renaissance. 'In the way of writing,' he wrote to Edith in early October, 'I did pretty well, and came home with eighty photographs (sixty of which I have still to develop) and over 30,000 words written of my first little sailing book. I want to make it 60,000 altogether . . .'

~

Racundra's First Cruise, half of which was written while at sea, is the obvious precursor to *Swallows and Amazons*: episodic, anecdotal, nautical, and thanks to the prose discipline Ransome had earned through six years of journalism, shorn of all unnecessary verbal baggage. Technically, it owes a great deal to an established genre, epitomized by maritime classics such as E. F. Knight's *The Falcon on the Baltic*, just as all Ransome's experiments in writing had been grounded in established genres – the poetic essay for *Souls of the Streets*, the gothic novel for his *Elixir of Life*, or, in the case of *Old Peter's Russian Tales*, the sweetened folklore of the Victorian nursery. *Racundra* is primarily a story of adventure and discovery, appealing by virtue of the unspoken assumption that anybody with sufficient wit, daring and material resources could undertake similar adventures for themselves. Ostensibly, it is a straightforward account of a month's cruising on the Baltic, balancing the practical details of seamanship with a romantic account of exotic islands and natives, shot through with references to the favourite books of Ransome's childhood: Daniel Defoe's *Robinson Crusoe*, Robert Louis Stevenson's *Treasure Island*, James Fenimore Cooper's *The Last of the Mohicans*. Boasting to Edith that he intended 'an almost violently non-political book', Ransome took real places and people and arranged them, much to the delight of his readers, according to the prejudices of the British colonial imagination – a mixture of non-fiction and fiction, conservatism and bohemianism, insular nationalism and seagoing internationalism – where the simple act of hoisting a sail was both a revolution and the writing of a personal manifesto.

'Houses', Ransome had declared by way of an introduction,

are but badly built boats so firmly aground that you cannot think of moving them. They are definitely inferior things, belonging to the vegetable, not the animal world, rooted and stationary, incapable of gay transition. I admit, doubtfully, as exceptions, snail-shells and caravans. The desire to build a boat is the desire of youth, unwilling as yet to accept the idea of a final resting place.

Racundra's crew consisted of Ransome, the 'master and owner', Captain Sehmel, dubbed the 'Ancient Mariner' in honour of his great age and experience, and Evgenia, referred to always as 'Cook' owing to Ransome's reluctance to advertise their relationship in print and because cooking was what she did. Cameo appearances came from the island peoples, beginning with a tribe of Rousseau-esque seal hunters, early socialists ruled by a gentle lighthouse keeper who closely resembled in manner and clothing a transplanted Lenin. As *Racundra* zigzagged her way across the Baltic, each separate adventure was set down in the ship's log: a storm, a fog, a challenging passage through shoals, a midnight dash into an unlit harbour. On Runo, the 'most romantic island in Northern Europe', Ransome and his shipmates wandered through primeval forest – the dawn of history – expecting at any moment to be stung by a pygmy's poison dart. On Dago, they found a community of stubborn Estonian nationalists who refused to speak any language but their own and a Russian who kept his pigs in a sty with glass windows. Further on were the gentle milkmaids of Roogo, herding mottled cows while below them stretched the sea like a tideless china model, so diminished that 'it looked as if one could walk ankle-deep from one island to another'.

Each new port of call went down in the log, later dividing neatly into chapters: a series of tiny republics, visited briefly and then permitted to sink beneath the horizon. As an example of a

man who lived outside society altogether, Ransome presented
the ship-building hermit of Ermuiste, part man, part ocean, part
boat, viewing the modern world with lofty scorn. As a paragon
of government he offered the lighthouse keeper on Runo, and for
self-government Captain Konga, marooned on a stranded merchant vessel, happily ensconced in a cabin measured to the
length of his own body.

I have seen many cabins, but none quite like that hutch in which the
captain of the *Toledo* had his comfortable being. It was built from the
baulks of wood set up on end between the iron decks. It was six feet six
inches high, long and broad. That size, Captain Konga explained, he
had found by experiment to be the most convenient. Sitting on his
bunk, he could put wood on the stove in the corner, light his reading
lamp, take a book from the opposite shelf, eggs or bacon from his
store-cupboard, reach down his saucepan or frying pan from the hooks
on the wall, or get the boatswain's whistle, with piercing blasts of
which he summoned members of his crew. From any place in it he
could reach any other place, and that, he said, was the most labour-
saving kind of house.

In the finished book, Ransome provided, by way of an appendix, a proud description of the ship he had sailed in: the ingenious division of space, the huge cabin big enough for a dining
and writing table, the brass compass – expensive, British,
exquisitely machined – centring the universe through 360
degrees. All this was a tribute to the genius of Otto Eggers, and
also to Ransome's good sense. But the real hero of the adventure
was *Racundra* herself – 'brave little ship', 'good little ship' –
breasting thirty-foot waves in a howling equinoctial storm.
Ransome would accept no criticism of her, and acknowledged
every compliment with bashful modesty as her rightful due.
Seated at the tiller of his little wooden nation, with the pilot flag
snapping above him, he patted her sides fondly or, having discovered the delights of night-time navigation, treasured her
company in the first grey light of dawn, waiting anxiously for a
glimpse of the promised land. It was with the deepest reluctance
that he abandoned her at the end of the voyage, to be hauled up

for the winter while her master, all unwilling, was sucked back into the maelstrom of the Revolution.

~

Racundra blew into Baltic port at the end of September 1922, but Ransome, expecting to leave for England immediately, had instead been sent at short notice to Moscow, where he remained for a month, running to and fro between the Kremlin and the British trade mission. Earlier in the year, shortly after appointing Joseph Stalin General Secretary of the Central Committee (a decision he would intensely regret), Lenin had suffered a major stroke, paralysing his right side and temporarily depriving him of the power of speech. Back in London, anxiety over Soviet meddling in the East escalated, exacerbating differences between Conservatives and Liberals already inflamed by personal scandals, violent industrial strikes and an erupting civil war in Ireland. In September, a stand-off between Turkish and British troops over the Dardanelles led directly to the downfall of Lloyd George, the principal architect of the Anglo-Soviet Accord, now accused of abusing British patriotism with a view to instigating a fresh slaughter on the scale of Gallipoli. In November, the Conservatives voted to leave Britain's coalition government, and at a general election on the 15th were returned to power with a decisive majority.

Much of this, with the exception of Stalin's ascendance to General Secretary (Ransome had never mentioned him in any of his articles and appears, like most of Stalin's comrades, to have grossly underestimated his potential), found its way into the *Guardian*. Otherwise, he revised the first draft of *Racundra's First Cruise*, and with the help of Will Peters, struggled to understand the difference between a controlled and a free-market economy. Shortly before leaving Russia, he submitted a list of written questions to Lenin, wondering if the state-approved traders – the 'NEPmen' – presented a threat to Soviet power. Lenin's written answers (had not Marx himself predicted a period of capitalist adjustment?) appeared on 22 November and were republished in volume thirty-three of his posthumous *Collected Works*. They were amongst the last of his famous 'theses'.

By the close of 1922, it was clear that the leader and founder of Bolshevism was not long for the world, and that the bitter contest to succeed him had already begun. On 15 December, he suffered a second major stroke, confining him to a wheelchair and restricting his speech to words of one syllable. On 24 December, Stalin ordered him to be isolated from any political business 'for the good of his health'. Ransome, meanwhile, had returned to England, where he received a contract from Allen and Unwin for *Racundra*, and from Ivy – after ten years of marital cold war – permission at last to divorce.

~

In late January 1923, having sent off the completed manuscript, Ransome went into Russia to take the temperature of revolutionary literature, only to be recalled at the end of February by a fire at the house in Kaiserwald. Evgenia, asleep upstairs, had been saved by the cries of their cat, Tom, but in all other respects the catastrophe had been complete. Everything belonging to *Racundra*, complained Ransome to Edith, was burned to a cinder: 'sails, ropes, every single thing, all the tackle that was stored for safety! In the house, also, I gather, were all my notes for the last four years and generally [we] are left to start life over again without anything.'

The incineration of Ransome's worldly goods in Latvia was the second disaster – the Cheka's invasion of Glinka Street being the first – in which he had been deprived of vital paperwork. And yet in his personal archive at the Brotherton Library in Leeds survive half a dozen notebooks from Russia and a thick file of letters, as well as several hundred telegrams written since 1916. Missing are any letters from Ransome's mother before 1924, from Ivy before 1926, or any hint of his more controversial dealings with the secret intelligence services of both Britain and the

Soviet beyond a few names in his fragmented diary. As to the true scale of the fire or the real extent of his losses, one cannot say. What is certain is that for Ransome the incident cemented a decision, long-simmering, to draw a line under politics and to return, as soon as the divorce came through, to England and the career he had chosen before the war. In 1923, the 'Big History', which for several years now he had intended as his single most important contribution to the Revolution, was set aside, never to be spoken of again. Instead, picking the twisted remains of his cabin lamp from the ruin in Stralsunder Strasse, he acquired lodgings with neighbours, settled down to translating a novel by one of the Kremlin's pet authors – Yuri Libedinsky's *A Week* – and braced himself for one more year in exile. By May, he was back in Russia, where thanks to Lord Curzon and the Conservatives, the trade treaty was on the verge of collapse.

The so-called 'Curzon ultimatum' had been approved by the Cabinet on 25 April 1923, and was couched in the most unequivocal terms. Based on intercepted Soviet telegrams decrypted by the British Code and Cipher School (the forerunner of Bletchley Park), it rehearsed all the Foreign Office's grievances against the Bolsheviks since the treaty had been signed, concentrating specifically on their efforts to provoke revolution in Persia and India. Curzon gave the Soviet ten days to cease agitation in British territories, to cut all funds to revolutionary organizations abroad and to recall the Soviet ambassador from Afghanistan. The note had been wired to Hodgson at the British mission with strict instructions to deliver it to the Commissariat of Foreign Affairs but on no account to discuss the matter. The Soviet would either capitulate or face the consequences.

Ransome's autobiography devotes an entire chapter to the Curzon ultimatum, balancing it against the chapter in which he and Radek had visited Vologda in July 1918. In 1923, he suggested, the future of Anglo-Soviet relations was once again in his hands, but on this occasion he had been permitted to avert catastrophe. Without his timely intercession, a second war of intervention would have been inevitable.

Dropping his bags at the British mission, Ransome had gone off at once to find Litvinov and Chicherin convinced that the situation was already irretrievable. In the streets of Moscow there had been anti-British demonstrations. Curzon had been hung in effigy. Rather than diminish themselves in the eyes of the mob, the Commissariat of Foreign Affairs was already preparing a 'fighting reply'. Ransome had reminded Litvinov of Adolph Joffe, the Soviet ambassador to Berlin, who in 1918 had wired Moscow asking if a revolutionary could be expected to wear formal dress to a state function. Did he not remember Lenin's answer? 'Wear a petticoat if you can get peace by doing so!' Litvinov retorted that the British delegates were already packing their bags. Finally, perceiving a stalemate, Ransome decided that the only solution was to disregard Curzon's instructions and arrange a clandestine meeting with Hodgson. Hodgson agreed, and after hours of patient cajoling, Litvinov was also persuaded: 'I have seldom', recalled Ransome, 'drunk so much tea at the Kremlin.'

The meeting was convened outside Moscow in a country house used as a rest home for Soviet officials. Here, as Ransome played chess with the former commander-in-chief of the Red Army, Nicholas Krylenko, Hodgson and Litvinov strolled at their leisure in the woods. As the last move was made, the diplomats reached an agreement in principle. Hands were shaken all round, though Ransome remembered that Hodgson, discovering Krylenko's identity, had been appalled.

'"What? . . . And I have shaken hands with that bloody chap?"'

'"Never mind the bloodiness," said I. "You have shaken bloodier hands on the other side away in Siberia. And you may have saved a great deal of blood by being here today to shake his."'

As Curzon's demands were agreed to in every particular, Ransome, at least in his memoirs, claimed the business as a personal victory. Meanwhile, Trotsky, speaking to a joint meeting of the party, trade unions and young communists, summed up the country's present position. Post-war Europe, he declared, had hovered on the verge of revolution but was now in the grip of a violent chauvinist reaction. England was controlled by the 'extreme Right wing of the British Bourgeoisie'. Benito Mussolini's fascists controlled Italy. France, Romania, Bulgaria and Poland were all in the hands of the oppressors, leaving Russia to stand alone against the combined might of Western capital. But the Soviet was not in the least down-hearted. Curzon's ultimatum had only exposed Britain's insecurity. The Revolution was stronger for the encounter, and in the future, would be stronger still.

'We are now in Aviation Week,' Trotsky reminded his comrades,

and I think that it will be a very good thing, as I have already said at another meeting, if, after this week, we make it a regular practice to meet every attack by the Fascists . . . by building aeroplanes. They present us with an ultimatum – we build an aeroplane which we name 'Ultimatum', and so on. And since they offend us frequently and a great deal, we shall eventually read a whole stretch of history in our Soviet skies. And the more resolutely we carry out this work, the more we shall succeed in reducing the number of offences committed against us.

~

Writing to Edith in June, Ransome had dismissed the entire expedition as a waste of time:

My last trip to Russia was extremely uninteresting and I think unnecessary, however, the *Guardian* sent me, so I went. I got a lot of interesting new books there, and on two occasions went fishing in a mild way, and played two or three games of chess but generally I was most miserable there and am fairly thankful to be at home again.

Meanwhile, *Racundra*, despite the fire in Kaiserwald, was already equipped to sail, and in the company of Ernest Boyce, MI6's head of station in Russia, navigated the complicated archipelagos of the Finnish Gulf. Only minefields had prevented her sailing down the Neva as the first foreign yacht to enter

Petrograd after the war. But there would be no immediate sequel to the *First Cruise*. Instead, Ransome planned a critical biography of William Hazlitt, who had condemned Wordsworth for deserting the French Revolution. Writing to Edith in September from Estonia (*Racundra*, owing to foul weather, was put up for the winter in Reval), he asked her to fetch the relevant volumes from Sir Arthur Acland's library. 'The thing is really frantically interesting, and I feel sure that any suggestion AHDA might be moved to make would be most valuable.'

By the end of the year, he was in Moscow, but his mind was clearly in England. Ivy's solicitors had delivered her first settlement offer – shocking, Ransome felt, in its rapacity – while the Conservatives had come to grief over trade tariffs. At a forced election in December, a hung parliament led to the first Labour government in British history. The outlook for Anglo-Soviet relations had never seemed rosier, and Ransome contemplated the future with something like equanimity. In January, after Christmas in Kaiserwald, he was back in Moscow staying with Will Peters, catching rats and noting a personal anniversary. 'My fortieth birthday', he informed Evgenia, 'passed quite calmly and unnoticed, and the world looks just the same. At least I can't see any difference though I tried hard.' Three days later, Lenin died.

Ransome was at the Eleventh All-Russian Congress when Kalinin, Chairman of the Central Committee, announced the news in broken sentences. 'Almost everybody in that great theatre burst into tears and from all parts came the hysterical wailing of women. Tears were running down the faces of the Presidium. A revolutionary funeral march was played by a weeping orchestra.' Ransome's obituary, carefully prepared months earlier, appeared in the *Guardian* on the 23rd, striking a measured tone which contrasted strongly with the raw emotion he encountered on the streets. Lenin, he told his readers, had been like a lighthouse shining through a fog, obscured by the adulation of his closest followers just as much as by the vituperation of his opponents. It had never occurred to him that the Revolution rested in his hands alone, nor had he for one moment approved unnecessary killing in his name. He had been the most extreme of the extremists, but he had denounced the Terror. He would have gladly gone to the scaffold for his principles but had never allowed pride to prevent him from enforcing compromise when it was necessary. He had, at heart, been a modest person, but his 'greatness of attitude' had impressed even his enemies. 'Nobody had anything against him personally, however much they might hate the Revolution as a whole. "He at least is a genuine idealist" said people for whom the Revolution was so much brigandage and murder.'

Now this simple and in many ways domestic man, whose fame eclipsed that of Peter the Great and Napoleon, was gone, leaving his philosophy and also his body, which would become a symbol not only of unstinting service to the Revolution, but of the Revolution itself.

On 24 January, Iroida's baby daughter died, tumbling out of life weeks after she had tumbled into it – a local tragedy dwarfed by Lenin's funeral. Pausing to execrate the 'revolting self assertion' of cinematographers (a fur-clad camera was perched on the very nose of the train carrying Lenin's corpse into Saratov station), Ransome had set down his impressions of a nation in mourning: the guard of honour marching beneath a mist cast by its own breath; the crowds of workers and peasants gathered to join the three-mile procession into Moscow, tears freezing to their cheeks; the personal affection mixed with the shock of sudden desertion – 'We are suddenly fatherless.' Ransome had never witnessed such sincere and universal grief since the death of Queen Victoria, nor such bewilderment. The succession, however, was assured. Trotsky, in an oversight which many now believe determined the future of Russia, had sent his condolences from the Caucasus, and pleading illness as the reason for his absence had, according to Ransome, announced his unqualified support for the 'Council of Three': Grigory Zinoviev, Lev Kamenev and Joseph Stalin. Meanwhile, Lenin's body lay in state in the House of Trade Unions, where for four days and nights millions of pilgrims shuffled past his bier before it was carried out into Red Square. During the wake,

Ransome had listened to the cannons booming as for five minutes, across the whole of Russia, every human being, every machine, every train and turbine and steam-driven piston had frozen in its place while factory sirens howled to show that Lenin 'had been the leader of the working class'. Near the crimson catafalque stood Felix Dzerzhinsky in a brown leather coat, 'with his head bent like a Franciscan Monk', Nikolai Bukharin, editor of *Pravda*, 'still for once, like a figure carved in wax', and Stalin, with his arms folded, 'iron like his name'. Cloistered here, with the doors closed against the masses, in the company of foreign diplomats and the party, Ransome had witnessed the final ceremony.

Here and there about the hall a summer lightning of white fire for the benefit of the kinematograph operators brilliantly lit up the faces of bearded peasants in sheepskin coats, leather jacketed workmen and dull khaki uniforms. Suddenly a stir ran through the hall and all stiffened to immobility. Mrs Lenin was standing by the bier looking at Lenin's face, calm, dry eyed, as if unconscious that he and she were not alone in the room. There was absolute silence; then funeral music, a requiem followed by the Internationale, after which a revolutionary dirge was sung by all in the hall, while soldiers, even outside the hall and in the passages, stood at attention. I had a curious feeling that I was present at the founding of a new religion.

~

On 2 February 1924, James Ramsay MacDonald, Britain's new prime minister, recognized the Soviet as the *de jure* government of Russia – the end, Ransome later felt, of his service in the East, both as a journalist and a diplomat: 'My war was over.' But there was still one significant piece of business pending, and the moment the *Guardian* would let him, he was back in England to tackle it.

'My dearest Top,' he wrote to Evgenia on the 28th,

I withdraw my abuse [he had insisted she write to him daily], for I found two very nice though rather melancholy letters at Kemsing [Kent] when I got down there last night . . .

This morning I saw the solicitors, and found it was as I suspected. The other side are holding up the decree until they get me to agree to what they want in the way of money. I have put in my proposal this morning, and I suppose next week we shall get an answer to it.

If Ransome and Evgenia were to return together to England, money was an essential factor, and so Ransome fought Ivy hard, while exploring every possible alternative to continuing his work for the *Guardian* in eastern Europe. Unwin, following the success of *Racundra's First Cruise*, was demanding more yachting adventures. Francis Hirst and Molly Hamilton were planning to restart *Common Sense*. There was the Hazlitt book and freelance work, and thanks to Ransome's growing friendship with C. P. Scott's son, Ted, who now effectively controlled the day-to-day running of the *Guardian*, the prospect of 'literary editor', which Ted suggested might supply 'an arm chair in old age'. Money was one thing, and Ransome agonized about it constantly, but just as important was social rehabilitation, so that after years apologizing for the Bolshevik regime in Russia, he had now set his heart on joining the Royal Cruising Club. His only fear was that 'some swine' would blackball him for political reasons, and as the divorce negotiations progressed, this fear, coupled with Ivy's obstinacy and greed, ran through all his letters, keeping him awake at night and producing exhilarating highs when the future seemed bright and dreadful lows when the walls closed in.

Evgenia's own letters contributed very substantially to the highs, proving that after four years reading such improving books as Edith's *A First History of England* she could write like a native, and when Ivy insisted on retaining Ransome's library (a clause he had himself suggested back in 1920), how completely she understood his most vulnerable parts.

My Dear Charlie, it is too awful to think of your losing your books, and if until now I tried to believe with you that Wiltshire doesn't know what she is doing – I can't do it any longer. She knows only too well how to hurt most painfully. She is cruel. And it is most unpleasant for me, because I do not consider I am worth so much Poor Dear Charlie;

I do not think your solicitors are clever enough, nor do they have enough sympathy with you . . .

Ivy's contribution as mother to Ransome's daughter, now fourteen years old, did not figure in these letters. Indeed, Tabitha is never mentioned at all, chiefly, one suspects, because Ransome preferred to think of himself as the injured party. He missed Evgenia painfully, both to commiserate when his fortunes seemed bleak – 'I am sitting *toothless* in Chelsea' – and to share his triumphs, which amidst so much anxiety came thick and fast. In early March, he had attended an exhibition at the Cruising Club's rooms in London, and found everybody dreaming of Runo. Thanks to Edith, he was shortly speaking to a member about his admittance 'to that most exclusive gang', and shortly after that to the commodore himself, Sir Arthur Underhill, who assured him that in his own opinion *Racundra's First Cruise* was recommendation enough. On 23 March, Ransome wrote to Evgenia that 'the appalling and terrible' interview with the board of the Cruising Club was over. 'A lot of people were there and I was as shy as a very small schoolboy, ridiculously, childishly shy, I sweated all over inside my clothes.'

But everything had gone swimmingly, so that 'The Master and Owner of *Racundra*' was to be put up for membership by the commodore and a committee member of the 'very highest standing'. Ransome might have been angling for a place on the Bolshevik Politburo, an irony that was not lost on him – 'They little know' – but the upshot was that as soon as one of the older members had died, he would be in, enjoying all the privileges of that 'most Kaiserlich' of Britannic institutions. 'Then we should have the right to fly a beautiful blue ensign and generally should have very much come up in the world.'

So excited was Ransome at the prospect that his audience with Ramsay MacDonald was recounted almost as a footnote.

I spent all yesterday afternoon with the Prime Minister. I went to Downing Street at two thirty, and we talked there, and then went along to the House of Commons and continued. Then came question time in the House and I was let into the Distinguished!!!!! Strangers Gallery and watched, and afterwards continued the discussion in the Prime Minister's room. It was incredibly interesting, much the most interesting thing I have seen for years. But if anything were needed to decide me that on no account would I ever stand for Parliament, yesterday afternoon was enough.

He would, however, continue to write his reports for the Foreign Office, 'so that is alright'.

The closer Ransome came to believing he would be truly welcome back in England, the more he missed Evgenia, and the blacker Ivy seemed. If Evgenia only knew what he was suffering, she would not blame him for leaving her so cold and alone in Latvia: 'Good old Topsy. Wicked plum Topsy, who will presently get back a very thin and worn out worried Charles.' By mid-March, it looked as though within a fortnight he would be 'free to make discreet love to a certain young woman in Riga and ask her what she thinks of me as a possible husband'. Two weeks later, he had changed his mind. *Racundra* was in Reval, so of course they would have to be married in Reval. If only Wiltshire would not drag her feet.

Ivy had demanded one third of Ransome's income and full access to his annual accounts, an assumption of dishonesty he found intolerable. Henceforth, he told Evgenia, they would be forced to live like indentured servants, so that it might be worth being poor just to prove what a pittance one third of a freelance salary would be. 'I am sure', Evgenia told him, 'that you are the biggest fool in the world in your trying to treat such people like Wiltshire with so much delicacy and kindness, and I am most awfully sorry you made me believe there are good intentions on their side.'

Ransome heartily agreed. 'I have given up believing in good intentions now, and am come to think that the woman is an incarnate devil and nothing else.' Outside in the garden he noticed a thrush pecking worms to pieces, then drifted into a reverie about a novel he had in mind:

I have again got a sort of wish to write another story, and wish I could get the sort of framework I want for it. I have a vaguish idea which might get clearer, but I don't know. Anyway, I am letting it slop about in my head to give it a chance. It's very unlike anything else I know, and would mix up boats, excitement and a good deal of fun. However it may very likely just fade away into nothingness in the way fine ideas often do in lazy, stagnant minds like mine.

Ransome was by now perhaps used to expecting the worst, but equally accustomed to sudden redemption. The following day – 30 March – after a 'fine old gabble and a row', everything was arranged. Ivy would give him his father's gun and a couple of fishing rods, retaining the books he had collected since he was a child. He had acceded to all other points. Now Evgenia must go to Reval immediately, to prepare *Racundra* and to put in the three weeks residence necessary under Estonian marital law. 'It can't be me,' wrote Ransome, 'because I am still here. Therefore it must be you.' She could stay at the Golden Lion or in the old *pension* at Lodenzee. Ransome would come overland via Berlin, 'and in three weeks from the day you arrive there and Grove [the British Consul] puts the notice up, we shall be finished with all bothers about papers for ever and ever'. On 9 April, the divorce documents were exchanged, becoming absolute the following Monday. 'I am tired completely out but feel a sort of undercurrent of hope and the feeling that now at last we can make a fresh start . . . TELL SEHMEL TO VARNISH THE FISHING BOAT AND PUT IT IN THE WATER! MAKE HIM GET IT READY AT ONCE SO THAT IT HAS TIME TO DRY.'

Ransome and Evgenia were married at the British consulate in Reval on 8 May, with Grove, the British Consul, officiating and the Consul for Latvia (a close friend) on hand with champagne. On their marriage certificate Ransome described himself as 'former husband of Ivy Walker, spinster who obtained a divorce'. Evgenia was a 'spinster', daughter of Peter Shelepina, a 'Russian Civil Servant'. In July, now a British citizen, she visited her family in Moscow. She would not see them again for fifty years. By October, after a cruise inland down the River Dvina, she was taking final inventory of her belongings, and on the 19 November embraced her mother-in-law for the first time.

'My Dear Evgenia,' Edith had written shortly before she made her vows,

I send you these few lines, which I hope you will receive on your wedding day, to welcome you into the family.

You and I hold different views on certain subjects I know, but I want you to feel sure that this will not stand between us now that you are my son's wife. I send you my love, and I hope and pray that you and Arthur may have many years of peace and happiness in store. I know that you have gone through much together – that you have nursed him in sickness, stood by him in some of life's dark hours, and played with him in the bright ones – and that your influence over him has been wholly good. For all this I feel I cannot be too grateful and it fills me with the happiest hopes for the future. I do hope that when we meet we shall understand one another, and be very good friends.

21

Swallows and Amazons

The Great War, famously billed as 'the war to end all wars', was directly responsible for a greater number of future conflicts than any previous war in history. The Treaty of Versailles, intended to create a lasting peace in Europe, paved the way for Adolf Hitler. The extreme political ideologies of the post-war era, fascism and communism, gained their power to convince on the Western and Eastern Fronts. The first stones of the Cold War were laid in 1917, when Lenin disposed of Russia's fledgling democracy on the promise of 'Land, Peace and Bread', while the post-Soviet collision between Western capital and fundamentalist Islam was seeded in the ham-fisted division of the Middle East at the Quai d'Orsay. Eight and a half million soldiers lost their lives in the war; over 30 million – half the total mobilized – were wounded. For those who had lived through the catastrophe, much of the complaisance of the old world had been irretrievably shattered. There was before and there was after, and in-between, a collective trauma which marked the beginning of the modern age. One of the recurring questions arising from this trauma was why the war had been fought at all: how an assassin's bullet in Sarajevo could have caused so much damage, how so much damage could have been *permitted*. Another was how the past should now be viewed. What lessons could be learned by looking back? What was the meaning of the past at all?

One way to consider the effect of the war on the popular imagination is to think of the books that were published immediately in its aftermath: T. S. Eliot's *The Waste Land*, James Joyce's *Ulysses*, Ludwig Wittgenstein's *Tractatus Philosophicus*, revolutions in poetry, the novel and philosophy. In 1919, in Germany, Hermann Hesse produced *Demian*, in which the eponymous anti-hero declares, 'Whoever wants to be born must first destroy the world.' In England, in the same year, P. G. Wodehouse published *My Man Jeeves*, which enchanted its readers by forgetting the war altogether, or rather, by perfecting the art of ignoring what could not be forgotten. For the most influential writers of the late nineteenth and early twentieth centuries, the Great War functioned like a colossal revolving door. Some had foreshadowed it: Thomas Hardy, Rudyard Kipling, Joseph Conrad. Others, such as Ernest Hemingway and F. Scott Fitzgerald, stepped out of it fully grown. But an extraordinarily tiny number of writers were prepared to look at the actual machinery of transformation: the bombs, the gas, the disgusting, inane slaughter of the trenches. In 1929, W. B. Yeats omitted the Great War poets Siegfried Sassoon and Wilfred Owen from the first *Oxford Book of Verse*. 'Passive suffering', he famously declared, 'is not a theme for poetry.'

Historians investigating the Russian Revolution, itself a direct product of the war, will discover no shortage of passive suffering or active cruelty. In terms of grim statistics, the death toll between 1917 and 1922 might be estimated at close to 10 million. Of these, perhaps 250,000 were victims of the Cheka, while White pogroms have been blamed for the death of 150,000 Jews in Ukraine alone. Reliable figures, however, are impossible to come by. As the most dramatic political upheaval in history, the Revolution remains one of the most opaque, obscured by the very radical political differences of its commentators, the resistance of every participating faction to anything approaching candour, and the fact that it took place within a single country. More people had died in Russia during the Civil War than had died in the whole of the First World War from any country. On the internal front, atrocities committed by both sides, evidenced in grainy, archival photographs, are peepholes into an unimaginable nightmare. During the Volga famine, cannibalism was so common that in village marketplaces the bodies of butchered children were sold like so many cuts of ham. And yet the Revolution was hailed by many as the only occasion in the entire mess of the war on which mankind had asserted a truly moral authority over its destiny. If the Revolution failed, then everything had failed, and this will explain why so many writers clung to it, including Maxim Gorky, once a stern critic of Bolshevism who at the height of Allied intervention had appealed to the international masses in the voice of an evangelist:

Come and march forward with us towards a new life for the birth of which we work without thought for ourselves, sparing neither men nor things. In our wanderings and our sufferings, in the great joy of our labour, and in the passionate hope of progress, we leave all our acts to the honest judgment of history. Come with us in our fight against the old order, in our work for the creation of a new order. Forward for liberty and the splendour of life.

As for Ransome, by 1924 it is difficult to conceive of a culture more diametrically opposed to his tastes than the culture bequeathed to Russia by Lenin: a culture which despised the traditions of the old world, which condemned the individual imagination, which envisaged the development of human society in the same way that one might envisage the development of a machine. And yet Ransome did not condemn the Revolution or its principal architect – the man whose influence on history, he had declared, eclipsed that of Napoleon and Peter the Great. Instead, as Stalin continued the communist experiment in Russia, he simply withdrew to a greater distance, and in doing so constructed his own ideal community, his own particular construction of reality, so that when he sat down to write his most popular books, the past and the future merged seamlessly on the surface of a placid inland lake, as familiar and as blameless as his childhood.

~

Ransome did not escape politics by returning to England, nor was he permitted to stay there for long. Scarcely three weeks after his arrival in Kent, the *Guardian* sent him to Egypt to cover the assassination of Sir Lee Stack, the British Governor General of Sudan and commander-in-chief of the Egyptian army.

Ransome spent two months away, instantly befriending the British high commissioner in Cairo, chatting with the Egyptian prime minister and king and admiring the brass taps in the Sudanese caliph's bathtub. As a colonial excursion it was highly diverting, and it was a relief, he later recalled, to dabble in a variety of politics which suggested no urgent moral dimension, as though the participants – all equally unscrupulous – were engaged in 'a game of chess'. The only serious drawback was that Evgenia had spent her first Christmas alone with her in-laws, an experience she found trying. 'Thank you very much for looking after my much beloved old Madam,' Ransome had written to Edith from Cairo. 'I am so glad that she got on well with Cecily. And I think you realize too her solid goodness that is really only emphasized by her streaks of intolerance. I admire her tactful protest in preparing the grog by way of escaping the sermon.'

By early spring, he was home again, and within weeks, with Evgenia at his side, had found a tiny cottage perched high on the east bank of Lake Windermere with commanding views of the whole region and excellent fishing in all seasons. 'The house is called Low Ludderburn,' he told Edith,

and is marked on the Ordnance maps. It contains two rooms on the ground floor, plus scullery hole. Two rooms upstairs. A lean-to in bad repair, capable of being turned into a first rate kitchen. A huge two storey barn in first rate condition, stone built, at present with stables below, and the top part, which has a double door opening onto the road, is used to put up a Morris Cowley. Water from the Roman well just behind the house . . . A lot of apples, damsons, gooseberries, raspberries, currants, and the whole orchard white with snowdrops and daffodils just coming.

Evgenia added her postscript: 'My Dear Mother, we are so overcome by finding ourselves in possession of the loveliest spot in the whole of the Lake District.'

By August, Ransome's first fishing article appeared in the *Guardian*, the beginning of a weekly column which, thanks to Ted Scott, assured him £300 a year (not counting piecework) and a place in angling history. Collectively, 'Rod and Line' blended practical advice and discursive detail, as well as providing an ideal platform for Ransome's personal philosophy. 'We have no need to return to the Stone Age to look for barbarity,' he reminded his readers in an early article. 'We have enough and to spare. But it is true that fishing allows us to refresh ourselves by a temporary resumption of life in which a man's chief concern is not inextricably confounded with other men's activities, but is, simply, to trick a dinner out of the river.'

Reinstalled amongst his beloved Lakes, Ransome took back the life he had dreamed about since 1913. W. G. Collingwood was now old and visibly frail, but he still walked, still painted and still wrote books. Mrs Collingwood welcomed him without question as a member of the family, as did Barbara, whose first child became Ransome and Evgenia's honorary niece. Robin Collingwood read his latest philosophical treatises, which invariably made Ransome 'rather sleepy', while Dora visited in the summer holidays from faraway Syria, bringing her husband, Dr Ernest Altounyan, and her four children, Taqui, Susan, Titty and Roger.

Within weeks of moving into Low Ludderburn, work began on the barn, which was transformed into a study – quite the best study Ransome had ever had – with a large picture window onto Whitbarrow Scar. Here, surrounded by familiar totems – an antique Russian inkwell, a Russian ashtray shaped like a duck, a pocket compass, a George III penny, a miniature telescope – he wrote on every subject, from barbless hooks to Stalin's campaign against Trotsky. The old days of the Revolution, he noted, were coming to an end, its heroes replaced one by one with men he did not know and could not consider the equal of their predecessors. But Russia was paying the price of its security just as Ransome – all unwilling – was paying the price of his own. Low Ludderburn had cost £550, with 50 per cent of the capital supplied by *Racundra*, sold for two hundred guineas. In 1926, Adlard Coles took her from Riga to England, and wrote up the voyage in *Close Hauled*. Part of the deal was that she would change her name – she sailed as *Annette II* – possibly because Ransome could not bear to imagine her in a stranger's hands. It was a subject he did not like to touch on in later years.

For Evgenia, joining her husband in England meant abandoning her past altogether: her country, her language, her family. In the Lake District, she took to gardening, knitting, cooking, crossword puzzles and (with some encouragement) walking. Strangers who were rude enough to enquire into her background were greeted with a frosty silence or told that her father had been 'a very senior gardener to the Tsar'. But Ransome, who considered England not only his home, but his reward for years of nomadic roaming, found it harder, in many ways, to settle down. He relished seeing old friends again: John Masefield, Lascelles Abercrombie, Gordon Bottomley – all, like Ransome, ferocious opponents of Freud and the modern obsession with introversion and sex. Ted Scott was a regular visitor, as were Francis Hirst and Molly Hamilton. Ransome enjoyed trying for perch, pike and trout with his neighbour, Colonel Kelsall, or throwing parties for children at which – as Evgenia served up cake, sandwiches and lemonade – he entertained his guests with Anansi stories and sea shanties on his penny whistle. All this, he felt, was no more than he deserved, but life had also cheated him in ways he found hard to forgive. Over the next six years, Ransome continued to work as a journalist. He was still called on regularly by the *Guardian* to visit distant destinations, usually at Christmas. Even fishing had become, after the first couple of years of 'Rod and Line', a professional obligation which he resented. But by far his deepest grievance – the root, he came to believe, of all his other grievances – was the divorce settlement with Ivy: depriving him not only of a third of his income and the books he had collected ever since he was a boy, but, by and by, the affection of his only child.

Judging from the letters that survive amongst Ransome's papers, he made no serious effort to see Tabitha or to enquire into her affairs until her eighteenth birthday in 1928, when he sent her a bolt of white silk and wondered how life was treating her. Tabitha, it transpired, was a powerfully religious girl, a gifted seamstress and cake-baker but also fond of motorcycles, dancing by moonlight and Yeats. Given the opportunity to explain herself to a father she had not seen since she reached puberty, she was naturally effusive. She liked to walk alone. She liked to stand rapt in contemplation of the divine. She adored her mother and could not imagine ever leaving her home at Hatch or getting old. But as to Ransome, who had asked her in his letter if she thought *him* very old, she refused to be drawn.

'I cannot write', she told him,

and say to you, *no*, you are not bald, or 44, or old, or doddery, because I have not seen you for years and years – what I remember of you was a big, tall Dor-Dor who was always smoking shag, who took no end of waking up by the 'gup-clock', who 'lay down', who always had filthy puddies [fingers], who banged away at a type-writer and wrote for hours [. . .] and fished – always, and played tunes on the concertina, who wore corduroy britches and was rather hard to sit upon – but I have lots of other things besides that I remember about you.

Now for something of what you are like *now*. I imagine that you wear the same sort of hats, but grey trousers, and I think yellow boots, that perhaps you are a little bald – that your teeth are very dirty, or that perhaps you put false ones in on occasion! That you get very cross, frequently, and that you then get tired of being cross. That you have got two fat Babbas (I don't know why!) who are rather common and wild – who never remember to be quiet when you are writing and so are sent out to some cottage to amuse themselves now and then – that your new wife is untidy, with heaps of orangey red hair all over the place, and that she gets into tantrums of furiosity and nearly kills the child with a sweeping blow, but who she hugs, pets and covers with wettish kisses.

None of this was likely to pave a friendship between Tabitha and her stepmother, particularly because Evgenia, whose hair was dark and who was excessively house-proud, did not have, and never would have, any children of her own. But soon after this letter was written, Tabitha received an invitation to meet her father, alone, at Salisbury – the first time she had seen him since she was nine years old. Shortly afterwards, he invited her to sail on the Norfolk Broads with him and Evgenia, but Ivy forbade it:

'No, your father will drown you. Make an excuse and say you can't go.'

Tabitha's unfinished *Reminiscences* reveal, in the saddest possible way, an effort to understand the past from alternative points of view, an attempt which she made in the light of profound regret and much too late. Ransome, by contrast, felt his injury too keenly to perceive anything but ingratitude and wilful treachery. Wrangles over accounts and tax returns took up the majority of his correspondence with Ivy until her death in 1939. Emotionally, however, the most insurmountable obstacle to a rapprochement with his daughter was the confiscation of his books. It did not weigh with Ransome that the library he had forfeited voluntarily when he first requested a divorce might have become part of Tabitha's life. Nor did he recall his contempt for the Russian bourgeoisie as they wailed over lost pianos, the 'deep and solid grin' he had smiled when the Cheka destroyed his entire collection of revolutionary newspapers, or the library which he himself had appropriated from a trembling 'millionaire' in the spring of 1918. Instead, the loss of several thousand volumes, often inscribed by friends and gathered, for the most part, during his happy, penurious, bachelor days, became a potent symbol for everything that had been taken away from him, not just by Tabitha or his first, impetuous marriage, but by his own failure to write the stories he wanted to write. All this came to a head in 1929, when Tabitha wrote to explain why he would not see his library again:

I love the books. It is all I have got of ever having had a father (because I should have been paid for to live anyhow). You don't want them. You won't write anymore now. Mother says you say that I don't know when I hurt, and that she agreed with you. Well I have a good idea that what I've said above may make you write *one* more book, so if it does I don't mind hurting you for that, but I don't really *believe* it.

'Dear Tabitha,' Ransome retorted two years later,

In acknowledging my Christmas present to you, you seem surprised that I did not write. I will tell you why I did not.

Whenever I write a letter to you, indeed, whenever I think of you, I remember your letter to me in which you said that you thought it right that I should be deprived of my library, that you yourself believed you could make better use of my books than I could, and, finally, that you had no reason to feel any gratitude for the money that I send to your mother, although the earning of that money has meant that instead of being able to write books as I had always hoped to do, I have had to do a great deal of journalism which I have always loathed.

~

The penultimate chapter of Ransome's autobiography is headed 'Journalism versus Authorship', which might also be read as 'politics versus the imagination' or 'slavery versus freedom': Ransome's personal revolution against the oppressive circumstances which had for so long, he believed, perverted his natural judgement.

In 1924, he had spent Christmas in Egypt, covering the assassination of Lee Stack. The following year, leaving Evgenia to hold the fort in the Lake District, he was off again, this time to Russia, researching, amongst other things, a brief history of the Revolution commissioned by the *Encyclopaedia Britannica*. Shortly after Ransome's departure, Trotsky had formed a shaky alliance with Zinoviev and Kamenev against Stalin's 'Socialism in One Country', while Karl Radek – who at first remained neutral – was appointed provost of the Sun Yat-sen University in Moscow, named after the 'Father of the Chinese Revolution' and attended by a select band of Chinese communists. Before long, Radek had acquired, with his usual precocity, an extensive grasp of Chinese politics and a conviction that the interests of the nationalist Kuomintang, struggling to unite a divided China against the business interests of the West, were entirely compatible with those of the Third International. It was, therefore, unsurprising that when the *Guardian*'s reluctant correspondent was sent to China in Christmas 1926 – 'the blow has fallen!' – to cover the ensuing civil war, he should have championed the nationalists against the British-backed warlords. The last significant file on Ransome held by MI5 contains a letter from a British agent who had met him on the boat out.

I had no great difficulty in finding out what he was and why he was going to China. His name is Ransome – see *Who's Who 1927*. I soon discovered that he knew Russia well and had been in Moscow several times, where it appeared he had lived with our Trade Mission. He subsequently confided to me that he had been sent out to China by the *Manchester Guardian* to ascertain to what degree the Soviet Government was backing the Cantonese [Canton was the base of the Kuomintang], also to what extent and the amount of influence they wielded etc. He told me that he did not want this generally known. It is not difficult to get him to talk – provided one is a good listener and raises an occasional question etc – neither does he ask, or expect any return of confidence. He carried a letter of introduction to Chun, the Cantonese Minister for Foreign Affairs.

Ransome's final political pamphlet, *The Chinese Puzzle*, was published, with an introduction by David Lloyd George, in November 1927. It sold poorly, owing to the rapidity with which events had moved forward, but Ransome's heart, in any case, had never really been in it. Privately, he concluded that China was the most loathsome place he had ever visited.

'I had to learn to eat with chopsticks, and even to smack my lips when a Chinese war-lord picked a tidbit from his plate with the chop-sticks that had just left his mouth and, with polite hospitality, poked it straight into mine . . .'

Never had he found himself so graphically entangled in other men's affairs; never, in such a brief space of time, had he been so muddled or rudely reminded that civil war yields few heroes. Peking, with its illustrated Western magazines, London fashions, races and cocktail parties, disgusted him; and yet travelling south to Canton he found the nationalist army scarcely recognizable as human beings, the closest equivalent in the whole ragged gang being 'a pony and a water buffalo'. Shortly after he had visited Shanghai, the Kuomintang burst into the city and massacred the local communists, dashing all Radek's hopes for collaboration with the Third International.

'I am very gloomy about things and think it probable that the *Guardian* is very disappointed,' wrote Ransome to Edith in March:

However, that may mean that they won't send me on any more of these horrible adventures. I am too old for them. I am all for slippers and a pipe, a glass of hot rum and the quiet life. Also I hate most horribly being away from my sterling old woman. It seems such a waste. And I hate being out of England. So, perhaps, if the *Guardian* is very disappointed all may be for the best in this best of all possible worlds.

He returned to Low Ludderburn via the Siberian Express, just in time to catch the bluebells.

Christmas of 1927 passed, to Ransome's enormous relief, without incident, but in February 1928 he was off again to Moscow, affording him a profoundly unwelcome opportunity to bear witness to what he called 'the end of an epoch': the rise of 'Stalin's Sheep' and the defeat of the 'intellectuals', the so-called 'opposition' headed by Trotsky, which now included a rebellious Karl Radek.

Ransome's last trip to Russia was commissioned to cover the immediate aftermath of Stalin's first significant purge of the party leadership, and was published in the *Guardian* in nine consecutive articles. Nothing in Moscow's outward appearance, Ransome observed, would suggest that the country had just been through a crisis. It was certainly more dangerous to cross the streets, owing to an increase in motor 'taxis' and Leyland buses. The queues outside food shops had perhaps lengthened marginally. But the most serious shock had been experienced not by the masses, but by the party, which was recovering from what he called a 'bout of scarlet fever'.

Stalin's victory over Trotsky, Ransome noted sadly, was essentially a bureaucratic *coup de main*. Since 1922, the membership of the Central Committee had expanded from nineteen to over seventy members, vastly increasing the power of the General Secretary and diminishing the influence of the minority 'opposition'. It was regrettable, but in purely practical terms, inevitable. Neither was it persuasive, suggested Ransome, to protest, as

Trotsky and his allies had protested, that the new regime was the enemy of free speech. The 'old guard', after all, had never sanctioned free speech or doubted the necessity of dictatorship by a single party. Ransome did not believe that there would have been any significant difference in internal or external policy between a Soviet under Stalin and a Soviet under Trotsky. What was happening in Russia was simply a final transfer of power to the class in whose name the Revolution had been launched. Virtually all of the Central Committee were now peasants or workers. Ransome only wished they were not so 'rough'.

Trotsky and Radek had been exiled (to Alma Ata in Kazakhstan and to Siberian Tomsk, respectively) shortly before Ransome's arrival, with Radek shouting brokenly through the window of his departing train, 'Long live the genuine Leninist, Communist Revolution!' Trotsky's exit had been more carefully stage-managed, with a false date published to decoy sympathetic crowds. Scheduled to leave on a Monday, he had actually gone on a Wednesday, leaving it to Stalin's official news agency to describe the scene: the abundance and opulence of his suitcases; the 'bourgeois luxuries' in his carriage; Trotsky's insistence on taking along his shooting dog. 'Could anything be meaner', Ransome remarked bitterly in his notebook, 'to the man who made the army and won the civil war?'

Following the leadership purge of 1928, terror, once again, became the dominant method of state control, while Trotsky's family and friends were systematically deported, imprisoned or executed. Yet one of the most confusing aspects of Ransome's family history is that his in-laws not only escaped the wrath of Stalin, but adapted themselves admirably to the new regime. In 1926, Iroida, whose sister once shared a desk with Trotsky, had been promoted to deputy director of the Moscow Region Forced Labour Camp, one of the first and most populous in Russia's infamous Gulag – a position which she retained until the early thirties. Of the entire Shelepina family, only Viktor, who had fought with the Whites, was 'suppressed', but survived a brief spell in Siberia to become an engineer. Ransome gives no indication as to whether he was aware of these facts. All he recalled in his autobiography was the extreme inconvenience of his trip and the acute physical discomfort he had suffered for its duration: a raging headache and the indigestion which followed a banquet thrown in his honour by an assortment of refugee Chinese communists, including Sun Yat-sen's widow, the glamorous Soong Ching-ling. He made it back to England just in time for the daffodils and a welcome visit from Dora and Ernest Altounyan, who planned to spend a year in the Lakes with their children. The result was *Swallows and Amazons*.

~

In May 1928, Ransome had written to Tabitha to ask her how she was, walked briefly with her in Salisbury and attempted to smooth things over by feeding her strawberry cream pastries. But as his relationship with his own daughter deteriorated, he found the company of Dora's family both captivating and inspiring. They spent the summer on Coniston and Windermere, bought two boats, *Swallow* and *Mavis*, and indulged in all the activities which Ransome approved of: fishing, sailing, playing at pirates, exploring all the coves and surrounding hills, and returning exhausted in the evening to a well-earned feast.

Just as Ransome liked to date his orthodox literary life from the day W. G. Collingwood had woken him as he lay on a stone in the middle of Copper Mines Beck in 1903, so he awarded the conception of his best-known book to the January morning he was visited by the Altounyans bearing an unlooked-for birthday present. The story went like this. Ernest Altounyan had written in January 1929 – shortly before the whole family's return to Syria – asking if he might visit Ransome for tea, and Ransome, still recovering from a visit by Ted Scott's son, Dick, agreed on condition that his guest come '*alone*'. It was therefore with extreme vexation that on the day after his forty-fifth birthday (birthdays were never welcome occasions for Ransome) he viewed a car pull up outside Low Ludderburn and all four

Altounyan children disgorge themselves, while Ernest, the ring-master, was nowhere to be seen. Going down with every intention of giving them a piece of his mind, he was instead disarmed by a sudden shout of 'Many Happy Returns' and the gift of a pair of gorgeous Turkish slippers, spirited from behind Susan and Titty's back and presented as a token of their heartfelt esteem. As Ernest appeared from behind the steering wheel to wring his friend's delighted hand, Ransome experienced an epiphany. 'They were leaving for Syria,' he would soon be telling grateful readers:

They knew that henceforth I should be sailing the *Swallow*, and yet, instead of hating me, as well they might, they had brought me these slippers, which turned out to be as good as they were handsome and are my most comfortable slippers to this day. It was just then that I thought what fun it would be if I could write them a book about the *Swallow* and the lake and the island that was their playground, as it had been ours and that of our parents before us.

The Altounyans returned to Syria three days later, leaving *Mavis* in the boathouse and *Swallow* in Ransome's capable hands. In March, he received Tabitha's letter, assuring him that he would never write proper books again. But he had already begun one. The hero would be *Swallow* herself, just as the hero of his last sailing book had been *Racundra*. But this book would be a novel, his first since 1915. It would be set on a lake in the Lake District, contrived in every particular to excite the curiosity of enthusiastic explorers: a fantasy water, an inland sea, dotted with islands and navigated by four children – a captain, a mate, an able seaman, and last but not least, a ship's boy. Ransome's heroes would take the names of Dora's younger children, Susan, Titty and Roger, but the eldest child would be John, a good, solid, English name to balance the sexes, put a man at the tiller and provide Ransome with a chance to imagine himself afresh as a twelve-year-old. For Tabitha, he christened his family the 'Walkers' and gave them parents as ideal as the lake they sailed on: a father in the British navy; a mother who placed her faith absolutely in her daring crew. The stage was set at the beginning of the summer holidays. If their father agreed, Mrs Walker had promised to allow her children to camp, alone, on a Lakeland island dubbed 'Wildcat Island'. Commander Walker's telegram, wired from his destroyer on the South China Seas, would become the most famous telegram in children's literature, as well as providing a perfect example of 'telegraphese': 'BETTER DROWNED THAN DUFFERS IF NOT DUFFERS WONT DROWN.'

'"What does it mean?" asked Susan.

'"It means Yes," said Titty.'

Within two weeks, Ransome had fifty pages. Hammering away at his desk, occasionally getting up to chortle and rub his hands, the entire adventure came to him with extraordinary ease. His children would be English children playing English games. There would, of course, be pirates, a great deal of *Treasure Island* and *Robinson Crusoe*, maps, signals, navigation, daring plots and equally daring counter-plots. Halfway through the book he would introduce a rival crew – the 'Amazons', who flew the Jolly Roger – and not to miss out on the fun, he wrote himself in as 'Uncle Jim' or 'Captain Flint', a 'retired pirate' of exactly his own age, balding, filthy tempered and struggling to finish a book. These things conjured themselves so rapidly that Ransome could hardly keep up with himself. Captain Flint would be the uncle of the Amazonian Nancy and Peggy Blackett. He would fall out with Captain John. Things would go awry in all kinds of different ways, and then would be made straight again. Above all, it would be an unmistakably British novel. Distant lands would be gestured at, but Ransome, both as author and veteran of foreign affairs, had come home.

'Night after night,' he recalled, 'I used to bring it in a small attaché case from my workroom in the old barn to the cottage, so that I could reach out and lay my hand on it in the dark beside my bed.'

~

In his memoirs, Ransome described 1929 as 'a year of crisis, a hinge year [. . .] dividing two quite different lives'. In February, Ted Scott had offered him a salary of over £1,000 to go to Germany as the *Guardian*'s permanent correspondent in Berlin – an offer Ransome greeted with little enthusiasm. Meanwhile, at a party thrown by Molly Hamilton, he was approached by Jonathan Cape, the foremost publisher of the day, who asked him to put together a collection of political essays, the first of a series which Cape suggested might support him in old age. What Cape got was a selection from 'Rod and Line' and a synopsis of *The Swallows and the Amazons*, for which Ransome received £100 in advance of royalties. 'I am rather cross with him,' wrote Scott to an acquaintance, 'he has some stupid notion of a personal career.'

By May, Ransome had already completed a first draft of his manuscript, but the final draft was delayed by almost a year. In June, Scott's father, the venerable Charles Prestwich Scott, formally abdicated as editor, with the result that Ransome was awarded the 'Saturday essay': a prestigious appointment which required one column a week on any subject of his choosing – 'Dust', 'The Winding of a Clock', 'Windmills' – but proved far more taxing than anticipated. Towards the end of November, he made his last trip as a *Guardian* foreign correspondent, covering a general election in Egypt which yielded little of interest bar a flurry of novel-writing and a meeting with a young man named Malcolm Muggeridge, who joined the paper on Ransome's recommendation, made a dazzling debut and became almost as famous as a reporter as Ransome was to become as a children's author.

Ransome returned to England in February, determined to devote himself entirely to his book, but was instead faced with renewed demands by Scott to join the Manchester 'corridor' on a full-time basis as a leader writer. Ransome's refusal, after consulting with Evgenia, was frank and affectionate, the last word in a long discussion between two friends who had known each other as schoolboys.

'It means', he explained, 'that I shall have definitely turned my back on my original object, an object I still think the one which, but for the obstacles produced by my own folly in my first marriage, I am more or less capable of attaining . . .'

His only fear was that he would fail, that he was too late and that the publishers who continued to place their faith in him would soon discover he was incapable of taking a chance even if offered one: 'not a pleasant idea at all'. Ransome's correspondence with Ivy, in consequence, achieved new levels of vituperation, while by April, when the manuscript was handed to Wren Howard, his first editor at Cape, his stomach troubles had already brought him to the verge of collapse. He spent the summer alternately longing to 'hold the brute' and dreading his book's reception by the public, finally visiting a doctor on the day after *Swallows and Amazons* appeared in English bookshops.

'You will no doubt,' he wrote to Ivy, 'judging from your action in depriving me of my library, be pleased to hear that I have been to see a specialist and that I have got ulcers high up inside me, duodenal or something like that, made worse, he said, by worry and over work.'

The prescription was five weeks in bed and a strict diet of olive oil and bismuth, all of which Ransome took in London. Molly Hamilton was away in America on a lecture tour and had lent him her flat. Here he lay groaning as Evgenia (who loathed nursing) administered medication, but in early August he was somewhat cheered by a letter from the Altounyans. The greatest danger, he had decided, was that his own heroes would take offence; that they would not recognize themselves; or that they would recognize themselves and hate him because of it. So dreadful was the prospect of their displeasure that he had sent them an early proof, and lived in terror of their reply. They had been delighted.

'My Dear Arthur,' wrote Dora,

Swallows and Amazons arrived yesterday at 1pm and it is now 6am, and there have been very few hours of those 18 [*sic*] when it was not being read by somebody. I didn't ask Ernest what time it was when he came to bed – I myself read it till 11, and got to within seven chapters of the end. Well all we want to say is that we all like it *enormously* . . . *Now* I see why you think I could have illustrated it! How I wish I could!

Ransome's first reviews in the British press came towards the end of the month. Molly Hamilton wrote fulsomely in *Time and Tide*, as did Sylvia Lynd (to whom he had once proposed marriage) in the *News Chronicle*, successor to the *Daily News*. For the *Guardian* Malcolm Muggeridge surpassed himself, though retaining his habitual barb: '. . . the book is the very stuff of play. It is make-believe such as all children have indulged in: even children who have not yet been so fortunate as to have a lake and a boat and an island but only a back garden amongst the semis of suburbia.' Most gratifying of all was a review from Hugh Walpole, whom Ransome had scarcely spoken to since their argument over the Anglo-Russian Bureau in 1916.

'An olive branch?' wrote Ransome.

'A twig,' replied Walpole, and the rift was healed.

Swallows and Amazons went down well with the *Telegraph*, the *Daily Herald* and the *Church Times*, while the Altounyans demanded a sequel as soon as Ransome was fit to write one. In the meantime, he lay back on his pillows and received visitors, amongst them his childhood playmate Ric Eddison, also a noted novelist, and Lascelles Abercrombie, who read him the *Sale of St Thomas*, which he had begun before the war and only just completed – dedicated to a proud fellow author. 'He read the whole poem to me, the finest of all his dramatic poems, and then he showed me my own name at the beginning of it, and I felt like "Lawrence of virtuous father, virtuous son", endowed by Milton with immortality.'

Swallows and Amazons sold slowly at first, but was soon joined by *Swallowdale*, published the following year and received by Ransome in his own house, in company with Evgenia, just before Christmas, where he devoured his turkey in the happy knowledge that there would be no sudden call from the *Guardian* to disturb his happiness. Each sequel thereafter

22

Captain Flint's Trunk

'No, not that photograph,' Ransome wrote to his editor, Rupert Hart-Davis, when considering the layout for his posthumously published autobiography. 'Not the CID man, bootlegger or political tough and hi-jacker, but a benevolent bald-headed one, something like this.' And he enclosed a small self-portrait, just as described, with his head thrown back, his eyes closed in dignified reflection behind wire-framed spectacles, and beneath his venerable pate, the signature walrus moustache. As a final touch, he added the gown he had worn when Leeds University awarded him a doctorate in 1952, five years before the Queen made him a Commander of the British empire: the same Arthur Ransome who had so narrowly avoided prosecution under the Defence of the Realm Act, whose name remained on the Home Office blacklist of suspected Bolshevik activists until 1937, and who had introduced Trotsky's private secretary to the Royal Cruising Club. 'Mine', recalled Ransome in the epilogue to this autobiography, 'has not been a life of consistent effort towards a single end. It seems to me that I have been like a shuttlecock bandied to and fro by lunatics. I seem to have led not one life but snatches of a dozen lives. I have had a great deal of undeserved good fortune.'

Setting out to research this book, I wanted to know if Ransome had been a double agent – a man who worked for the British Secret Intelligence Service while consciously serving the interests of a hostile power. And there is a great deal of circumstantial evidence to support such a view: the addresses in his diary, smuggled diamonds, his close collaboration with Karl Radek, liaisons with senior Cheka officials and the accusations levelled at him by other British agents in the field. Ransome's success as a political journalist depended very heavily on his ability to shift not only between warring countries, but between wholly irreconcilable points of view – a facility for compromise and adroit self-transformation that made him useful to both sides. But whether he was a double agent, a peace broker or merely (to borrow Lenin's famous phrase) a 'useful idiot' is much harder to say. The First World War and the Russian Revolution tested all notions of identity to the limit: loyalty to a philosophy, to a government, to a class, to a race, to a family; to the various species of mud that each belligerent nation claimed as its birthright. Ransome's story is essentially that of a man who professed all these loyalties, often simultaneously, and it was for this reason that he is a hard subject to pin down. And yet his triumph as a children's author was the apparent modesty of his claims, his simplicity, his transparency, the appeal he made to those who, like himself, did not want the world unmade or made up but tactfully rearranged.

At the close of the twenties, English bookshops fielded a rush of belated war novels and memoirs – *All Quiet on the Western Front, A Farewell to Arms, Goodbye to All That* – most of them telling the same story: a generation betrayed by their elders, bullied and lied to, robbed of their future and later – those that survived – tormented by nightmare visions of the past. But Ransome had never fought in the war or visited the trenches of the Western Front. Neither did he have the slightest inclination to rehearse, once again, the civil war in Russia or Lenin's Terror, rekindled by Stalin at the end of the decade. *Swallows and Amazons* was, at root, a straightforward tale of innocent pleasure. Four children on holiday in the Lake District are given permission to spend the summer, beyond the prying eyes of their parents, on a Lakeland island, camping, sailing and indulging in exactly the sort of fantasies Ransome enjoyed best. In the spirit of colonial pioneers, they pitch their tents, raise their flag and do fearsome battle with the Amazon pirates, Nancy and Peggy Blackett, only to make peace and wage all-out war on the devilish Captain Flint. Ransome's heroes were the Altounyan children, blended with his own sisters and lost brother: Cecily, Joyce and Geoffrey. Mrs Walker, 'the best of all natives', was Dora Altounyan and his own mother in one person, while his father, the judgemental professor, was reborn in the uniform of a Royal Navy commander, the better to place his trust in the irreproachable Captain John. Sitting at his desk in Low Ludderburn, Ransome found no difficulty in conjuring a world which included all that was best in his life and left the worst behind, a world which expanded year on year to encompass distant continents and old friends – the ancient mariner from *Racundra's First Cruise* on a treasure hunt to the West Indies; Sun Yat-sen's widow as a Cambridge-educated pirate princess on the South China Seas. Ransome's adventures became famous for their carefully drawn detail, the authority which convinced so many young readers that his heroes could be addressed in letters as real people. But for those who had lived through the war, it was the promise Ransome made to himself that appealed most deeply: the promise of a world in which the rules had not been broken; in which parents loved and trusted their children; in which children, secure in that knowledge and in the excellent character of their guardians, set out on their own to discover new lands, engage in mock battles, and when the excitement was over, to return to warm beds, roaring fires, familiar faces and the prospect of repeating the adventure year after year, without fear of interruption or irretrievable tragedy, as though the real war had not been fought at all.

Swallows and Amazons was a book about recovery, and it was for this reason, perhaps, that Ransome's admirers have spent so much of their time unearthing the originals of cherished places or characters: Octopus Lagoon, Squashy Hat, the Death and Glories, the real identity of the Dixons, the Jacksons, or the Swainsons who so closely resemble the Swainson family that hosted Ransome's first childhood holidays in Nibthwaite. When Ransome fans gather together for walks, they follow the paths walked by Ransome's heroes. They compare maps of the Walkers' lake and maps of Windermere and Coniston, with each landmark carefully cross-referenced or appended with a question mark to indicate an ongoing dispute. Meetings of The Arthur Ransome Society are cheerfully competitive affairs at which lectures are given on every aspect of Ransome's life that might help illuminate his books: genealogy, fly tying, coastal navigation, a slide show depicting the flora and fauna of the Norfolk Broads. And yet while Ransome offered his readers an ideal return, he could scarcely have been satisfied if he had not made it clear who that return truly belonged to, whose character was most at stake, who had most to hope for from his redemption and who, ultimately, would set a limit to the curiosity of strangers. Thus, in the opening pages of *Swallows and Amazons*, the Walkers encounter Uncle Jim Turner, anchored halfway between the land of adults and the children's island colony, sitting on his houseboat and struggling to write his memoirs.

"'I knew he was a retired pirate,' said Titty. 'He has a secret. They all have. Either it's dark deeds or else it's treasure.'"

Anybody who has read *Swallows and Amazons* will recall that Uncle Jim was not at first a pleasant man, that he shakes his fist at *Swallow*'s crew, that he callously rejects the company of his Blackett nieces, that his villainy runs so deep that at one point he even accuses Captain John of lying. Closeted in his cabin, Ransome's alter ego is the enemy of all happiness, and remains so until his autobiography, locked in an old travel trunk, is mistaken for valuables, stolen by out-of-towners and hidden on a nearby island for later retrieval. Released from the malevolent spell, Jim wakes as if from a dream, and having apologized handsomely to Captain John, promises the Blackett girls that he will never write another book again. Free now to join the fun, he adopts his *nom de guerre*, Captain Flint, fights a terrible sea battle, obligingly walks the plank, serves the victors a magnificent tea aboard his houseboat (preserved for posterity at the Windermere Steamboat Museum) and is justly rewarded. Titty, who had witnessed the theft quite by coincidence and who now views Captain Flint with an almost maternal eye, leads her rehabilitated pirate to the place where his past is buried. Here, secreted on Cormorant Island beneath the roots of a dead tree, sealed with locks and reinforced with stout iron bars, is Flint's battered sea chest, plastered with exotic travel labels and containing (to the vast disappointment of his playmates) nothing but a typewriter, an assortment of canvas-bound diaries and a dog-eared stack of paper.

'That's all right,' said Captain Flint, fingering the bundle as if he loved it.

'It's very dull,' said Roger. 'Titty said it was treasure.'

'There's treasure and treasure,' said Captain Flint. 'It takes all sorts to make a world. You know Able seaman, I can never say thank you enough to you. If I'd lost this as I thought I had, I'd have lost all the secrets of my pirate past, and I've put the best of my life into this book. It would have gone forever if it hadn't been for you.'

~

Swallows and Amazons would not have been complete without a formal absolution, a gesture of forgiveness towards Ransome's more carefully guarded self, extended by the ideal children of his imagination. But while Titty Walker, so game and imaginative, was content to return Captain Flint's past in exchange for the gift of a trained parrot, Ransome's daughter did not relent so easily. In 1930, Tabitha had written to thank her father for a copy of his book, but found it 'tired' and 'churned out'. She regretted that she could not get further than Chapter Twelve.

Ransome's reply came just before her twenty-first birthday, along with a set of Chinese silver bracelets. All the old grievances were brought up again: the library, the alimony, the demands placed upon him owing to her mother's profligacy and increasingly, he suggested, to Tabitha's own. Setting aside her insufferable ingratitude, he nevertheless, as her father, had some things to say to her, and the first was that 'THERE IS NO SUCH THING AS UNEARNED MONEY.'

It was bad, Ransome explained, to lend out money at interest (Ivy had received a small annual endowment in her father's will), but to spend money one did not have was theft, 'STEALING'.

'Your share of the affair in such a case is no better than that of a bug or a flea that sucks blood and gives nothing. It is a shameful part, not worthy of a decent human being.' Neither was a twenty-first birthday party any particular occasion for rejoicing. There was no call for expensive parties or ballgowns or cakes. It was a mere 'division of time'. Unless, of course, one took the opportunity to reflect on what it meant to become a responsible adult, which led Ransome to a treatise on marriage.

Indirectly, not from you, I hear that you have several times promised to marry people and then decided not to. On that, too, I have something to say.

Remember that for some inscrutable reason you are more likely to come to care for a man after you are married to him than he is to come to care more for you after he has married you. So, whatever other mistake you make, DO NOT MAKE THE COLOSSAL AND IRREVOCABLE MISTAKE of marrying a man if he has shown even the slightest sign of suspecting that he is not quite sure whether he wants you. To do that is to ask for trouble for yourself, besides being wickedly unfair to him. Of course you can make him marry you if you like. Any woman can. It's nothing to be proud of. But, if you do, that first little doubt will come up again and grow and grow, and things will end either in a long bicker over who of two unhappy people is to have the affection of your children, or (and this is better for any child than to be witness of a long civil war in the house) in his running desperately away. If he does run away, let him. I can imagine nothing worse for a child than to watch a father and a mother fight for its affection. Much better that it should have one or the other. But I hope there will never be any need for you to consider such things. Only, be sure at the start, not only that you love him but that he loves you. And be sure that you love HIM and not the imaginary person that you think you will be able to make of him. If you go and try any of the remodelling business he will either submit, when you will know that he is not worth having, or not submit, when you will quarrel or he will bolt and anyway you will lose him.

This was the only explanation Ransome ever offered his daughter as to why his first marriage had collapsed, though in casting himself as the real victim of the piece, he succeeded in ignoring Tabitha's feelings altogether. Finally, he wished her 'many happy returns of the day', hoped that in the course of her life she would make a lot of other people happy as well as herself, 'and that from one end of it to the other you will never ask people to pretend an affection for you which they do not feel'. If Tabitha wished, she could come and visit him at Low Ludderburn and 'see the sort of life that is lived here, and the country that has been the background of people of your race for a very long time indeed'. But in the meantime, he had worked himself round to a sort of fondness for her again, so that 'Writing this I somehow forget your letters and remember only a round woolly Babba of long ago, and it's odd to think that today you will have to stoop to get in through the cottage door, and that you won't be able to cross the parlour without ducking your head so as not to crack it on the beams.'

~

Tabitha was not the only person Ransome argued with in the immediate aftermath of *Swallows and Amazons*. In 1931, Bernard Pares – the man who had initially introduced him to Harold Williams, who had collaborated in establishing the Anglo-Russian Bureau and who had intervened on his behalf with the British ambassador to save him from the trenches – published his memoirs, which included, by way of comic relief, a note sent to him by Ransome at the height of British intervention in Russia. The note read, 'If I am a Bolshevik, I am also the man who tells the Nancy stories.'

More than half of Ransome's review of this book – printed with extreme reluctance by Ted Scott in the *Guardian* – was devoted to denying such a note had ever existed, while the debate with Pares spilled over into a dozen furious letters. There had never been any 'Nancy' stories. There had only been 'Anansi' stories. And yet Pares, who claimed to recall every detail of the affair, had said that Ransome's favourite Jamaican folk tales had always begun 'Dear Nancy'.

'Would it surprise you to learn,' thundered Ransome,

that NOT ONE OF THESE STORIES begins in this way? Would it surprise you to learn that no little white girl called Nancy is concerned in the stories or mentioned in them at all? Would it surprise you to learn that instead they all begin with a reference to Queen Victoria? Would it surprise you to learn that your little white 'Nancy' is really 'a big black fat hairy spider'?

As to the suggestion that Ransome had ever announced himself a Bolshevik, it was both offensive and ridiculous.

I begin to doubt whether you realize just what it is to which I object. If a man describes a biologist as a beetle, because he writes about beetles, the biologist may remain quite indifferent. After all it is a question of opinion. The man may honestly think that a biologist is a beetle. What I object to is something quite different, and that is the statement that the biologist in question *mistook himself for a beetle.*

Ransome's anxiety as to precisely how, or by whom, his former adventures in Russia might be construed never left him, but were somewhat eased by the success of his new career. Two years after the fall-out with Pares, he was already well on his way to becoming a wealthy man, and thanks to Evgenia's ruthless eradication of aluminium cookware from the kitchen (and to a great deal of milk), made a respectable recovery from his gastric complaints, achieving the rosy corpulence prescribed by his doctor. Gone was the gaunt and angular Ransome of the Revolution, staring wolfishly at the camera in his press-corps uniform or dismounting a Soviet train in his greatcoat and tall astrakhan hat. By the mid-thirties, he rarely weighed less than sixteen stone, wore three-piece tweed suits by preference and was usually photographed surrounded by manuscript pages, tying flies or helming one of his many boats. Ransome and Evgenia moved often over the next thirty years – to Suffolk, back to the Lakes, to London, to the Lakes again – always seeking the perfect combination of gardening, fishing and sailing, or the convenient proximity to friends and shops offered by the city. *Racundra* was succeeded by the *Nancy Blackett*, then *Selina King*, who after a couple of years was laid up for the course of the war. In 1946, she was sold, as all Ransome's boats and houses were sold, for a painful loss and replaced by *Peter Duck*, which was returned to the boat builder in disgust, then repurchased and treasured for three seasons, before it was replaced by Ransome's last two boats, each of which was called *Lottie Blossom*. Ransome's quest for the 'quiet life', in short, remained as restless and as circular as ever, punctuated by sudden accesses of generosity (two children would find their first novel, *The Far Distant Oxus*, personally supervised and brought to publication by their hero) and violent rows with those who dared to intrude on his privacy or presumed to question his opinions. But as Cape placed him in the hands of Rupert Hart-Davis, an editor who specialized in 'difficult authors', he continued to charm far more often than he alienated, while the popularity of *Swallows and Amazons* and its sequels ensured his reputation as a model Englishman.

Amongst Ransome's readers were the young Princess Elizabeth; W. G. Collingwood, who survived just long enough to confess that the second in the series, *Swallowdale*, had pleased him just as much as the first ('and I can't say fairer than that!'); J. R. R. Tolkien, whose children owned the whole set; likewise A. A. Milne; and the American Junior Literary Guild, who ensured his market across the Atlantic. Ransome's novels have been read in Spanish, Czech, Polish and Slovak, in Chinese, Japanese and Korean. In Britain, his name became so identified with patriotic post-war nostalgia that to suggest, even today, that he had ever been a journalist during the Revolution is to provoke murmurs of surprise, while to add that he had worked for MI6, offered information to the Cheka and had married Trotsky's secretary ensures amazed hilarity of outright disbelief. Ransome's rehabilitation was so complete that he became a national treasure, a sort of grade-one-listed author, part of the British heritage, so that only the most eccentric or mean-spirited of his critics dared voice any criticism whatsoever: David Garnett, who mourned Ransome's betrayal of his rebellious past; Malcolm Muggeridge, who wondered if Ransome spoke to *all* English children; William Trevor, who joked that if two departments of the civil service had lain abed together for long enough, 'they would have produced the magnificently right-minded *Swallows and Amazons*'. But Ransome's fiercest critic was Evgenia, who deplored almost every book as it was written, only to praise it as his greatest effort to date when it was published. Her letter condemning the *Picts and the Martyrs*, the eleventh and penultimate novel in the series, is often blamed for prematurely ending his career.

'My Dear Darling,' she wrote in August 1942, as Hitler's troops advanced on Stalingrad,

I am very sorry I am going to hurt you very much – but I don't believe in Fool's Paradise or in beating about the bush.

I finished reading your book and I think it is hopeless. It is the best manuscript you produce – it can be sent to the printers as it stands – but the book as a whole is dead.

If the Swallows are not allowed to grow up, if they are put back into the same background with the same means of enjoying themselves as they have done holiday after holidays – they can't help repeating themselves – so that the arrival at Rio, the setting up of camp, taking possession of their new boat, are no longer things done for the first time – fresh and exciting – but pale imitations of something that happened many times before. This feeling of imitation and rehash is continually forced on one by references to previous adventures in the same places . . .

After *Peter Duck*, *We Didn't Mean to Go to Sea* and especially after *Misses Lee* I think that even your faithful readers who always ask for the same characters doing the same things in the same places would find it dull. Your rivals would be very happy and well justified in saying that you 'missed the bus' . . .

You don't know how awfully sorry I am not to be able to say: 'it is your best yet.'

Written across the top of this letter – crumpled, then smoothed, as though it had been hurled away in a fury, then rescued from the waste-paper basket – is Ransome's explanation: 'I stopped it for a year but in the end let Cape have it.'

And Cape were glad to get it.

~

For Evgenia, the frustration of reading one story after another in which the Swallows stood still may have been aggravated by Uncle Jim's credentials as a confirmed bachelor. And yet there is no suggestion in her surviving correspondence that she urged a book recounting Captain Flint's adventures in the Soviet. *Swallows and Amazons*, coincidentally, was begun in January 1929, weeks before Leon Trotsky was finally exiled from Russia, but neither Ransome nor his wife had anything to say on the subject. If one examines the Walkers' first adventure closely, one will find, it is true, faint traces of the Bolsheviks: a pair of young female pirates who might well have wielded 'pistols instead of powder puffs' during the Revolution; an insular committee establishing the rules and regulations of an ideal society; a tendency on the part of the author quietly to erase any challenge to the happiness and purity of the world he created. In general, however, it is easy to understand why scholars of Ransome's fiction rarely feel the need to examine his time in Russia at all. Thus, in 1936, nobody wondered why the man who produced *Coot Club* and *Pigeon Post* had contributed a brace of obituaries to the *Guardian* following the execution of Grigory Zinoviev and Lev Kamenev. When the Walkers' most intrepid adventure, *We Didn't Mean to Go to Sea*, was published in 1937, nobody saw any explicit irony in the title, or noted that in the same year Ransome's old friend Karl Radek had been the star witness in Stalin's second show trial. Confessing himself a slave to Trotsky, Radek had provided evidence against a dozen former comrades and received a sentence of ten years' hard labour in the Gulag. In 1939, on Stalin's orders, he was beaten to death in his cell. Owing to the secrecy of the execution, Ransome's obituary, recalling Radek's wit and courage, was never published.

In his autobiography, Ransome recorded a list of Bolshevik friends who had lost their lives since 1924, noting that 'Those who rewrite history must see to it that no contradictory witnesses survive.' In the meantime, his attitude to bereavement closer to home was curiously erratic. Geoffrey's death in 1917 was mentioned briefly, while Edith's, in 1944, was not mentioned at all.

The death of his father when Ransome was thirteen years old (about Captain John's age) was described in unusually grisly detail, from the moment Professor Ransome's ankle was broken, through each stage of amputation, to the spectacle of the lurching coffin at his funeral. But the tragedy he felt most keenly was the loss of Ted Scott, who drowned in Lake Windermere in 1932. Ransome was visiting the Altounyans in Aleppo when the accident happened, and returning to hear the news, could not forgive himself. He had introduced Ted to sailing. He had chosen his boat. He had written to him from Syria ordering him not to drown before he, Ransome, was there to fish him out. 'It was as if our world had come to an end. I have never had such a close friend as Ted. We had no secrets from each other . . . I felt now that I ought to have joined him in Manchester instead of sticking to my books. Worse, I could not rid myself of the thought that I had killed him.'

Nowhere else in his memoirs did Ransome come close to such a candid confession of regret. His grief over Ted Scott's death was overwhelming, compounded by a conviction that he had betrayed a sacred trust, placed his own interests before the interests of his friend, failed to understand, at the crucial moment, where his responsibilities lay. And yet, when one considers how frequently Ransome provoked censure for precisely these reasons, his guilt, on this occasion, feels like a proxy guilt, inviting the very sensible reassurance that he had nothing to feel guilty about. Ted, who had died of a heart attack in chilly April water, suffered owing to circumstances entirely beyond Ransome's control. Tabitha was a different matter.

In 1939, Ivy died, but Ransome's relations with Tabitha never recovered. In her early twenties, shortly after receiving his coming-of-age letter, she married a dockworker, John Lewis, and gave birth to two children, neither of whom her father showed any inclination to meet. In 1942, the couple moved to Falmouth, where Tabitha wrote to Ransome complaining of penury and offering to sell him his library. Deeply offended at the suggestion, he never replied, and in consequence had the pleasure, some months later, of hearing that a London bookseller had purchased the entire collection – over 10,000 volumes – for £25. He succeeded in salvaging some notebooks and a few first editions signed by personal friends; the rest were sold in blocks at public auction.

Tabitha left her first husband just after the war, and in 1953 wrote to her father again, this time from Taunton in Somerset, confessing that she had a new man in her life and would like to seek his advice. Ransome, expecting to meet his future son-in-law, hurried down and was ushered into the drawing room, where, sipping his tea, he was confronted by an eighteen-year-old girl, Hazel Lewis, who wondered shyly if she might say hello to her grandfather. So horrified was Ransome by this deception that he made immediately for the train station, pushing Tabitha roughly aside when she offered to give him a lift. It was, he told her coldly, 'the same old lunatic asylum'. Their correspondence ends abruptly in the same year.

Ransome and Evgenia had no children of their own but made do for many years with two beloved cats, Polly and Podge, the children of family and friends, and the surrogate children of Ransome's books, whom he grew so close to that he found it increasingly difficult to relate to them in any other guise. Thus, in Syria, though he had enjoyed the Altounyans' company, and had written the greater part of *Peter Duck* under their roof, he could not shake a feeling that Dora's brood of heroes were not quite the genuine article. 'Ernest and Dora are in good form,' he had written to Edith in February,

but I must say it seems a little queer now, after two years of living with them all in *Swallows and Amazons* and *Swallowdale*, to meet them all as actual human beings running about. My lot seem to me the solider, but Ernest's are very nice, and eager to know 'what is going to happen to us next?' They have, of course, adopted Genia completely.

Sadly, over the following years, it struck Ransome that Ernest's children, and more particularly Ernest himself, were not so nice at all. Shortly after the run-away success of *Peter Duck*, Taqui and Susan came over from Syria to attend school near by,

where they were constantly quizzed (much to their embarrassment) over their role in the books. Articles appeared in newspapers on the subject, while letters written to Ransome demanding
to meet the 'real' Swallows assumed a sinister subtext. Little by
little, he convinced himself that Ernest and his 'Armenian brats'
were stealing credit away from him, undermining his effort, and
worst of all – though Titty assured him on numerous occasions
that her family were heartily fed up with the whole business –
misunderstanding the creative process itself. As he grew older,
Ransome insisted, with increasing urgency, on the literal truth
that great writers did not write stories *for* children or for anyone
else, but for themselves, so that their readers were privileged not
to receive, but to 'overhear' a tale which emerged, quite spontaneously, from the depths of the author's imagination. To suggest
that he had simply lifted the identities of four existing children
was tantamount to accusing him of plagiarism, and for Ransome
the charge of dishonesty or fraudulence struck deep and painful
chords. In 1958, he demanded that Cape suppress *Swallows*'
famous dedication: 'To the six for whom it was written in
exchange for a pair of slippers.' When Ernest died in 1962,
Ransome read his obituary in *The Times* with disgust, underlin-
ing all references to *Swallows and Amazons* in angry red ink. In
1947, following the publication of the last in the series, *Great
Northern?*, he sat down to write his autobiography, with a view
to countering the 'stupid lies' that had been circulated about his
time in Russia and to thanking W. G. Collingwood for his kindness. But Ransome's memoirs contained no mention of the debt
he owed Collingwood's grandchildren, while Tabitha makes her
final appearance at the age of five. In the postscript, he dedicated
all his happiness to Evgenia:

The weakness that made possible my first marriage and so cost me my
library and all else that I possessed at that time might have ended in my
final shipwreck. Instead, to set against the misery that came from it, I
can look back on more than thirty years of unclouded happiness with
my second wife. In all that time I have felt firm ground under my feet
instead of quicksands. But for her I should have been dead and unable

to write this book. And but for her resolute courage in taking the risk of extreme poverty I should never have dared to take the step that gave me, towards the end of my life, the twenty years in which I have been able to write those books that may seem to some children an excuse for my existence. Further, but for her relentlessly honest criticism, they would be worse books than they are.

~

In the Brotherton Library at Leeds University, along with Ransome's papers, is Evgenia's own, heavily vetted description of the Revolution – the first days of the Bolshevik coup, her employment by the Commissar of Foreign Affairs, the time she accidentally put a bullet through Trotsky's window – with a note supplied by Ransome recommending 'a very good account of what it looked like to a young honest Russian'. Further contributions by Evgenia include a brief correspondence with Iroida and some photographs, including a picture of her with Iroida and Serafima in 1972. The most remarkable thing about this photograph is how English Evgenia appears beside her sisters. After an absence of almost fifty years, having forgotten almost all her Russian, she had visited her family in Moscow, where she presented her eleven-year-old grand-nephew with a toy car. Gleb Drapkin recalls little of the encounter. Evgenia had hardly spoken to him, though she had talked to Iroida, Serafima and Serafima's husband, Athanasius, about cats. These three lived together in the same apartment, while Gleb had come with his mother to visit. No doubt they chatted over his head and felt free to compare – albeit cautiously – the domestic details of their lives. But Gleb had thought his present a marvellous thing: 'Truth to tell, I was more amazed with the English toy than the English *babushka*. It was the first time I had seen a toy car of this kind.'

It was only in the nineties, after the collapse of the Soviet Union, that Gleb discovered, thanks to the internet, that his great-uncle was not merely a 'British journalist', but a famous children's author. Subsequently, he read Ransome's political

pamphlets and then his autobiography, which he thought entertaining because of its humour and the way Ransome spoke of
historic figures as familiar, likeable human beings. But the novelty of the relationship, as well as Ransome's amiable detachment, had lost some of its charm on closer inspection. Gleb's
eponymous grandfather (Evgenia's youngest brother) had been
killed during the siege of Leningrad. Life had been hard for his
mother. He wondered if it was typical in England to live an
adventurous youth and then return home to digest the experience at leisure: 'to research the amusing life of foreign natives,
to excavate their treasures, and in the quiet of old age to contemplate a favourite English garden, live a quiet life behind a
desk, or set out with fishing tackle for the river'.

Ransome was not without helpers in tailoring his official history. Rupert Hart-Davis, later knighted for his contributions to
literature, became a close friend, and as Ransome's literary
executor, supervised a final purge of his archive, a condition of
his appointment agreed to in 1951. Evgenia, who had
denounced each of Ransome's books as it was written, encouraged him in all his vendettas as an expression both of love and of
ownership, continuing, when he was gone, to resist any attempt,
real or imagined, to usurp, distort or exploit his reputation, of
which she was immensely proud. But for Ransome, the chief difficulty in composing his memoirs – the reason, perhaps, why
they were left to be pieced together by Evgenia and Hart-Davis
after his death – was the difficulty of knowing where to place
himself. Was he the romantic hero of his adventures or was he,
on the contrary, a helpless prisoner of fortune? Was he responsible for his life or was he innocent? Active or passive? Energetically engaged with the great events he had witnessed or the
blameless pawn of lunatic powers? In Ransome's hands, the
story of his life became a protracted exercise in self-justification,
the last utterance of a man who, like the hero of *The Fool of the
World and the Flying Ship*, had become so clever that 'all the
court repeated everything he said'. And yet, after paying off
every naysayer who had stood in his way, from the baleful spirit

of his father to Lord Crawford of the Ministry of Agriculture and Fisheries, the most powerful impression left by Ransome is that he struggled constantly to believe in himself, that the reason for so much retrospective reshuffling was not his romantic conviction in an elusive ideal, but the absence of conviction; a querulous, judgemental void, planted in childhood and shared by so many of his contemporaries – the so-called 'lost generation'. The world had changed a great deal in his lifetime, and almost never because he had willed it.

Ransome died in 1967, two years before Neil Armstrong set foot on the moon. Had he lived to see it, he might (recalling Defoe) have been enchanted, or possibly deeply offended, just as he was deeply offended by the invention of television. As a patriot, he had played his part in the Second World War by selling as many books as he could, convinced that his taxes would make a significant contribution to Britain's struggle against Hitler. In the opening years of the Cold War, he read every article in the British press with indignation. 'He was in Russia,' wrote Hart-Davis to a friend, '. . . and nobody else is right, bless him.' Ransome's last home, from 1961, was Hill Top cottage in the Lake District, but he had little strength left to enjoy it. He had fallen and been confined to bed. In 1962, his back was operated on, and he made a poor recovery, enjoying a brief respite for his eightieth birthday in 1964, when the papers were full of congratulatory articles and the post office jammed with letters. In 1965, he went to Cheadle Royal Hospital, near Manchester, where, besides Evgenia, his regular visitors included Dick Kelsall, son of Colonel Kelsall, who talked to him quietly after a series of strokes had rendered him semi-comatose and incapable of speech. Ransome, Dick recalled, was unmoved by contemporary news of any kind, but reminiscences of the pleasure given by his stories excited him. He struggled to express himself. He slapped his sheets.

He was buried at Rusland Church, halfway between Windermere and Coniston Water. Eight years later he was joined by Evgenia, who, after extended feuds with the grown-up Altounyan children, the BBC and finally with fellow guests at a retirement home for well-to-do ladies in Oxfordshire, succumbed to a heart attack and was laid in the same grave. In 2003, I visited them there and found fresh flowers in a jam jar and a conch, painted with a tall ship under sail – gifts from grateful readers. Rusland is a quiet place and pilgrims tend to be reverent and peaceful, though controversy occasionally divides them. At the Windermere steamboat museum, for example, *Esperance* is advertised as the original model for Captain Flint's houseboat, while over on Coniston, the *Gondola* has staked a rival claim. Each candidate has excellent credentials – an illustration in *Winter Holiday*, a postcard Ransome once sent a friend – so that the quarrel will last as long as it remains enjoyable. Ransome, meanwhile, sits on the fence, choosing neither one side nor the other, keeping his counsel in the best of all possible worlds. Indeed, it struck me then that if his fantasy had come true – if Windermere and Coniston had burst their banks and flowed together – then he and Evgenia would lie at the deepest part of his dream, where far above the Walkers had launched their *Swallow* and had all their adventures.

Note on Sources

The majority of Ransome's papers can be found in the Brotherton Library at Leeds University, where Ann Farr, one of the talented few capable of deciphering his handwriting, began to catalogue them in the 1980s. The archive is extensive, and in many ways quite candidly revealing, comprising Ransome's correspondence, diaries, telegrams, photographs, a collection of notebooks and drawings, and the drafts of his many books and stories, both published and unpublished. Notable omissions are any letters from Edith before 1924, Ivy before 1926, or Tabitha before 1928. Ransome's first surviving letter to Evgenia was written in 1919, begging her to leave Russia in the company of Mr Parker of the Red Cross. There is no indication in the Brotherton archive of Ransome's recruitment to MI6, or of his co-operation with the Cheka. Evgenia's own career within the Bolshevik administration is covered by her notes, which were dictated to Ransome shortly before or after she joined him in Stockholm in 1918.

In England, I have looked at several collections of Ransome's papers outside Leeds. Reading University houses the Jonathan Cape correspondence, which concerns the business end of Ransome's literary affairs. The *Guardian* archive at Manchester University holds many letters shedding light on his career as a journalist. In the Lake District, the Museum of Lakeland Life in Kendal holds Dora Collingwood's diaries, some letters and diaries of W. G. Collingwood, and a number of Ransome's possessions donated by Evgenia: a typescript of *Swallows and Amazons*, a portion of his library, his desk, his typewriter and a cross-section of the miscellanea he liked to keep about him when writing. No serious biography of Ransome would be possible without Wayne G. Hammond's excellent bibliography, which was at my elbow during the weeks I spent at the British Library's newspaper archive in Colindale.

The British National Archive holds the official correspondence regarding Ransome between 1915 and 1937, and also the War Office's file on Geoffrey Ransome, including his medical notes, the telegram informing Edith of his death, and a letter requiring her to reimburse the Treasury for a small sum Geoffrey had been overpaid in error during the last months of his life. Documents relating to Ransome are scattered through the various departments of the administration, with the highest concentration to be found with the Foreign Office. In 2005, a bundle of papers was declassified by MI5 which proved beyond doubt that he had worked for the British Secret Intelligence Service and that he was suspected at the highest level of working for the Bolsheviks. Whether this bundle constitutes everything that remains on the official record remains to be seen.

In Russia I found a very helpful and experienced advisor in Liuba Vinogradova, and a brilliant research assistant in Dasha Lotareva. Dasha was responsible for finding Comintern files on Evgenia, her mother and siblings, as well as introducing me to a colleague in St Petersburg who produced everything available on her father and immediate forebears. Thanks to Dasha, I was able to understand Evgenia's peasant ancestry, her reasons for joining the Soviet civil service, and the part she and Iroida played in the Bolshevik administration. Before I wrote this book, almost nothing was known about Evgenia's background, and very little about Evgenia herself, yet her story is quite as remarkable as Ransome's own. Indeed, as Dasha pointed out to me, the history of the Shelepina family, taken as a whole, reads like a miniature history of the Revolution.

With Dasha, I looked through the Russian state archives, which opened to Western researchers following the collapse of the Soviet Union in 1991. The archives of the FSB (the latest incarnation of the KGB), the Ministry of Foreign Affairs and the War Ministry remain classified, but in recent years historians have benefited from the work of Professor Christopher Andrew and two former high-ranking FSB officers, Oleg Gordievsky and Vasili Mitrokhin. The resulting books, *KGB, The Inside Story* and *The Sword and the Shield*, afford the most comprehensive histories of Soviet intelligence yet published, with Ransome emerging as one of Dzerzhinsky's earliest inside sources on British foreign policy. In a letter to me, Professor Andrew warned against overestimating Ransome's impact on Anglo-Soviet affairs as an informant of the Cheka (he had no sensitive state secrets to betray), but emphasized how unusual his position had been. 'It is difficult to think of any British writer who has ever been acquainted with quite so much of the leadership of a major, hostile intelligence agency: including Dzerzhinsky, his two deputies and the first resident in London [Nicholas Klishko].'

In the United States, the University of Indiana holds Bruce Lockhart's papers, including a brief but illuminating correspondence with Ransome in 1918. The file contains Ransome's description of his work for Clifford Sharp, his reaction to news that Horatio Bottomley was threatening to expose him as a paid Bolshevik agent, and a transcription of a letter from Karl Radek. There are other Ransome papers held in America, notably 5,000 volumes from his personal library which California State University purchased at the time of his death.

Finally, returning to England, Ted Alexander and Margaret Ratcliffe both possess private collections of papers, and both have been exceptionally generous to me. Ted Alexander's pioneering research, detailed in his *Ransome in Russia*, has been an invaluable resource throughout this project, as has Hugh Brogan's biography, *The Life of Arthur Ransome*, published in 1984 to celebrate his centenary.

Bibliography

Aitkin, Jonathon, *A War of Individuals: Bloomsbury Attitudes to the Great War*, Manchester University Press, 2002

Alexander, Ted, *Ransome in Russia*, Portchester Publishing, 2003

Altounyan, Taqui, *In Aleppo Once*, John Murray, 1969

Andrew, Christopher, *KGB, The Inside Story of its Foreign Operations from Lenin to Gorbachev*, HarperCollins, 1990

Andrew, Christopher, *Secret Service: The Making of the British Intelligence Community*, Heinemann, 1985

Andrew, Christopher, and Mitrokhin, Vasili, *The Mitrokhin Archive and the Secret History of the KGB*, Basic Books, 2001

Ayerst, David, *The Guardian: Portrait of a Newspaper*, Collins, 1971

Brogan, Hugh, *The Life of Arthur Ransome*, Jonathan Cape, 1984

Bromwich, David, *Hazlitt, the Mind of a Critic*, Oxford University Press, 1983

Brownell, Will, and Billings, Richard N., *So Close to Greatness: A Biography of William C. Bullitt*, Macmillan, 1987

Bryant, Louise, *Six Red Months in Russia*, Arno Press, 1970

Callaghan, John, *Socialism in Britain*, Basil Blackwell Ltd, 1990

Christman, Henry M. (Ed.), *Essential Works of Lenin: 'What Is to Be Done?' and Other Writings*, Dover, 1987

Collingwood, R. G., *Autobiography*, Oxford University Press, 1939

Collingwood, W. G., *Thorstein of the Mere*, Edward Arnold, 1895

Cowden, Morton H., *Russian Bolshevism and British Labor*, Columbia University Press, 1984

Cowley, John, *The Victorian Encounter with Marx*, British Academic Press, 1992

Dukes, Paul, *The Story of 'ST 23': Adventure and Romance in the Secret Intelligence Service in Red Russia*, Cassell, 1930

Everitt, Nicholas, *British Secret Service During the Great War*, Hutchinson, 1920

Figes, Orlando, *A People's Tragedy: The Russian Revolution, 1891–1924*, Jonathan Cape, 1996

Graves, Robert, *Goodbye to All That*, Anchor, 1929

Hall, David, *Far Headingley: Weetwood and West Park*, Far Headingley Village Society, 2000

Hammond, Wayne, G., *Arthur Ransome: A Bibliography*, Oak Knoll Press, 2000

Hard, William, *Raymond Robins' Own Story*, Harper, 1920

Hardyment, Christina, *Arthur Ransome and Captain Flint's Trunk*, Frances Lincoln, 2006

Hattersley, Roy, *The Edwardians*, Little Brown, 2004

Hobsbawm, Eric, *Age of Extremes: A Short History of the Twentieth Century 1914–1991*, Abacus, 1995

Keach, William (Ed.), *Literature and Revolution: Leon Trotsky*, translated by Rose Strunsky, Haymarket Books, 2004

Keegan, John, *The First World War*, Pimlico, 1999

Keep, John L. H. (Ed.), *The Debate on Soviet Power: Minutes of the All-Russian Central Committee of Soviets*, translated by John L. H. Keep, Clarendon Press, 1979

Kennan, George, *The Decision to Intervene*, Faber & Faber, 1957

Kennan, George, *Russia and the West*, Hutchinson, 1961

Kennan, George, *Russia Leaves the War*, Faber & Faber, 1956

Kettle, Michael, *The Allies and the Russian Collapse*, André Deutsch, 1981

Kinel, Lola, *Under Five Eagles*, Putnam, 1937

Knox, Major-General Sir Alfred, *With the Russian Army, 1914–1917*, Hutchinson & Co., London, 1921

Laybourn, Keith, and Murphy, Dylan, *Under the Red Flag: A History of Communism in Britain, c.1849–1991*, Sutton, 1999

Leggett, George, *The Cheka: Lenin's Political Police*, Oxford University Press, 1981

Lensch, Paul, *Three Years of World Revolution*, Constable & Co., 1918

Lerner, Warner, *Karl Radek: The Last Internationalist*, Stanford University Press, 1970

Lloyd George, David, *War Memoirs*, Vol. III, Ivor Nicholson and Watson, 1933

Lockhart, R. H. Bruce, *Diary*, Vol. I, Macmillan, 1973

Lockhart, R. H. Bruce, *Memoirs of a British Agent*, Putnam, 1934

Lockhart, R. H. Bruce, *Retreat from Glory*, Putnam, 1934

MacMillan, Margaret, *Peacemakers: Six Months that Changed the World*, John Murray, 2001

Marx, Karl, and Engels, Friedrich, *The Communist Manifesto*, Penguin, 1967

Masefield, John, *The Old Front Line*, Macmillan, 1917

Muggeridge, Malcolm, *The Green Stick*, Fontana, 1975

Pares, Bernard, *Day by Day with the Russian Army, 1914–1915*, Constable & Co., 1915

Pares, Bernard, *My Russian Memoirs*, Jonathan Cape, 1931

Pipes, Richard, *The Formation of the Soviet Union, Communism and Nationalism, 1917–1923*, Harvard University Press, 1964

Pipes, Richard, *The Russian Revolution, 1899–1919*, HarperCollins, 1990

Price, M. Philips, *My Three Revolutions*, Allen and Unwin, 1969

Ralston, W. R. S., *Russian Folk Tales*, Smith, Elder, 1873

Reed John, *Ten Days that Shook the World*, Penguin, 1977

Remarque, Erich Maria, *All Quiet on the Western Front*, Ballantine, 1982

Rothstein, Andrew, *When Britain Invaded Soviet Russia: The Consul who Rebelled*, Journeyman Press, 1978

Russell, Bertrand, *The Practice and Theory of Bolshevism*, George Allen & Unwin, 1920

Sandle, Mark, *A Short History of Soviet Socialism*, UCL Press, 1999

Service, Robert, *Lenin: A Biography*, Macmillan, 2000

Silkin, Jon (Ed.), *The Penguin Book of First World War Poetry*, Penguin, 1979

Sisson, Edgar, *One Hundred Red Days*, Yale University Press, 1931

Stevens, E. S., *'– and what happened', being an account of some romantic meals*, Mills & Boon, 1916

Stone, Norman, *The Eastern Front*, Penguin, 1975

Thomas, R. George, *Edward Thomas: A Portrait*, Oxford University Press, 1987

Thomas, R. George (Ed.), *Letters from Edward Thomas to Gordon Bottomley*, Oxford University Press, 1968

Thomson, Sir Basil, *The Story of Scotland Yard*, The Literary Guild, 1936

Thomson, John M., *Russia, Bolshevism and the Versailles Peace*, Princeton University Press, 1966

Trotsky, Leon, *The Bolsheviki and World Peace*, Boni and Liveright, 1918

Trotsky, Leon, *The History of the Russian Revolution*, Sphere, 1970

Tyrkova-Williams, Ariadna, *Cheerful Giver: The Life of Harold Williams*, Peter Davies, 1935

Tyrkova-Williams, Ariadna, *From Liberty to Brest-Litovsk*, Macmillan, 1919

Ulman, Richard H., *Anglo-Soviet Relations 1917–1921*, Princeton University Press, 1972

Volkogonov, Dmitri, *Trotsky, The Eternal Revolutionary*, The Free Press, 1996

Wallace, Stuart, *War and the Image of Germany*, John Donald, 1988

Wells, H. G., *Russia in the Shadows*, Hodder and Stoughton, 1920

White, Stephen, *Britain and the Bolshevik Revolution: A Study in the Politics of Diplomacy, 1920–24*, Macmillan, 1979

Wilson, A. N., *The Victorians*, Hutchinson, 2002

Wilson, A. N., *After the Victorians*, Hutchinson, 2005

Wyndham, Francis, and King, David, *Trotsky: A Documentary*, Penguin, 1972

ARTICLES IN JOURNALS

Andrew, Christopher, 'The British Secret Service and Anglo-Soviet Relations in the 1920s Part I: From the Trade Negotiations to the Zinoviev Letter', *The Historical Journal*, Vol. 20, No. 3 (Sept. 1977), pp. 673–706

Borman, Arkady, 'Harold Williams: A British Journalist and Linguist in Russia', *Russian Review*, Vol. 28, No. 3 (July 1969), pp. 327–37

Buzinkai, Donald I., 'The Bolsheviks, the League of Nations and the Paris Peace Conference, 1919', *Soviet Studies*, Vol. 19, No. 2 (Oct. 1967), pp. 257–63

Carr, E. H., Radek, Karl, and Price, M. Philips, 'Radek's "Political Salon" in Berlin 1919', *Soviet Studies*, Vol. 3, No. 4 (April 1952), pp. 411–30

Daniels, Robert V., 'The Kronstadt Revolt of 1921: A Study in the Dynamics of Revolution', *American Slavic and East European Review*, Vol. 10, No. 4 (Dec. 1951), pp. 241–54

Debo, Richard K., 'Lockhart Plot or Dzerhinskii Plot?', *The Journal of Modern History*, Vol. 43, No. 3 (Sept. 1971), pp. 413–39

Gankin, Olga Hess, 'The Bolsheviks and the Founding of the Third

International', *Slavonic Year-Book. American Series*, Vol. 1 (1941), pp. 88–101

Hafner, Lutz, 'The Assassination of Count Mirbach and the "July Uprising" of the Left Socialist Revolutionaries in Moscow, 1918', *Russian Review*, Vol. 50, No. 3 (July 1991), pp. 324–44

Mandel, William M., 'Arthur Ransome: Eyewitness in Russia 1919', *Slavic Review*, Vol. 27, No. 2 (June 1968), pp. 290–95

Neilson, Keith, '"Joy Rides"?: British Intelligence and Propaganda in Russia, 1914–1917', *The Historical Journal*, Vol. 24, No. 4 (Dec. 1981), pp. 885–906

Woodward, David R., 'British Intervention in Russia During the First World War', *Military Affairs*, Vol. 41, No. 4 (Dec. 1977), pp. 171–75

BOOKS BY RANSOME

ABC of Physical Culture, Henry J. Drane, 1904
The Souls of the Streets, Brown and Langham, 1904
The Stone Lady, Brown and Langham, 1905
The Child's Book of the Seasons, Anthony Treherne & Co., 1906
Highways and Byways in Fairyland, Alston Rivers, 1906
Pond and Stream, Anthony Treherne & Co., 1906
The Things in Our Garden, Anthony Treherne & Co., 1906
Bohemia in London, Chapman & Hall, 1907
A History of Storytelling, T. C. & E. C. Jack, 1909
Edgar Allan Poe: A Critical Study, Martin Secker, 1910
The Hoofmarks of the Faun, Martin Secker, 1911
Oscar Wilde: A Critical Study, Martin Secker, 1912
Portraits and Speculations, Macmillan & Co., 1913
The Elixir of Life, Methuen & Co. Ltd, 1915
Old Peter's Russian Tales, T. C. & E. C. Jack, 1916
On Behalf of Russia, The New Republic, 1918
Aladdin and his Wonderful Lamp, Nisbet & Co., 1919
Six Weeks in Russia, George Allen & Unwin, 1919
The Soldier and Death: A Russian Folktale told in English, John G. Wilson, 1920
The Crisis in Russia, George Allen & Unwin, 1921
Racundra's First Cruise, George Allen & Unwin, 1923
The Chinese Puzzle, George Allen & Unwin, 1927
Rod and Line, Jonathan Cape, 1929
Swallows and Amazons, Jonathan Cape, 1930
Swallowdale, Jonathan Cape, 1931
Peter Duck, Jonathan Cape, 1932
Winter Holiday, Jonathan Cape, 1933
Coot Club, Jonathan Cape, 1934
Pigeon Post, Jonathan Cape, 1936
We Didn't Mean to Go to Sea, Jonathan Cape, 1937
Secret Water, Jonathan Cape, 1939
The Big Six, Jonathan Cape, 1940
Missee Lee, Jonathan Cape, 1941

The Picts and the Martyrs, Jonathan Cape, 1943
Great Northern?, Jonathan Cape, 1947
Fishing, The National Book League at the University Press, Cambridge, 1955
Mainly About Fishing, Adam & Charles Black, 1959

PUBLISHED AFTER RANSOME'S DEATH

The Autobiography of Arthur Ransome, edited with prologue and epilogue by
Rupert Hart-Davis, Jonathan Cape, 1976
The War of the Birds and Beasts and Other Russian Tales, edited and intro-
duced by Hugh Brogan, Jonathan Cape, 1984
Coots in the North and Other Stories, edited with introduction and notes by
Hugh Brogan, Jonathan Cape, 1988
The Blue Treacle, The Story of an Escape, with an afterword by Christina
Hardyment, Amazon Publications, 1993
Arthur Ransome on Fishing, Jonathan Cape, 1994
Signalling from Mars, a collection of Ransome's letters, edited and with an
introduction by Hugh Brogan, Jonathan Cape, 1997

BOOKS EDITED, TRANSLATED OR WITH CONTRIBUTIONS BY RANSOME

The Dream Garden: A Children's Annual, edited by Netta Syrett, John Baillie,
1904
The Book of the Open Air (British Country Life in Autumn and Winter),
edited by Edward Thomas, Hodder and Stoughton, 1908
Stories by Edgar Allan Poe: The World's Story Tellers, edited by Arthur
Ransome, T. C. & E. C. Jack, 1908
Stories by Ernest Theodor Wilhelm Hoffman: The World's Story Tellers,
edited by Arthur Ransome, T. C. & E. C. Jack, 1908
Stories by Nathaniel Hawthorne: The World's Story Tellers, edited by Arthur
Ransome, T. C. & E. C. Jack, 1908
Stories by Prosper Mérimée: The World's Story Tellers, edited by Arthur
Ransome, T. C. & E. C. Jack, 1908
Stories by Théophile Gautier: The World's Story Tellers, edited by Arthur
Ransome, T. C. & E. C. Jack, 1908
The Book of Friendship, arranged by Arthur Ransome, T. C. & E. C. Jack,
1909
Stories by Cervantes: The World's Story Tellers, edited by Arthur Ransome, T.
C. & E. C. Jack, 1909
Stories by Chateaubriand: The World's Story Tellers, edited by Arthur
Ransome, T. C. & E. C. Jack, 1909
Stories by the Essayists: The World's Story Tellers, edited by Arthur Ransome,
T. C. & E. C. Jack, 1909
Stories by Honoré de Balzac: The World's Story Tellers, edited by Arthur
Ransome, T. C. & E. C. Jack, 1909
The Book of Love, arranged by Arthur Ransome, T. C. & E. C. Jack, 1910
Stories by Gustave Flaubert: The World's Story Tellers, edited by Arthur
Ransome, T. C. & E. C. Jack, 1910
A Night in the Luxembourg, Remy de Gourmont, translated, and with a pref-
ace and appendix by Arthur Ransome, 1912

BIBLIOGRAPHY

The Odd Volume: Literary and Artistic, edited by John G. Wilson, The Musson Book Co., 1912

A Week, Iury Libedinsky, translated, and with an introduction by Arthur Ransome, 1923

Encyclopaedia Britannica, 1926 (Ransome's contribution comprises four essays: 'Brest Litovsk, Treaty of', Vol. 1, pp. 432–3; 'The Revolution and After' and 'The Constitution', under the general heading 'Russia', Vol. 3, pp. 408–28; and 'Trotsky, Lev Davidovitch', Vol. 3, pp. 829–30)

The Kuomintang and the Future of the Chinese Revolution, George Allen & Unwin, 1928 (with an unsigned 'publisher's note' by Arthur Ransome)

The Book of the Fly-Rod, edited by Hugh Sherringham and John Moore, Eyre & Spottiswoode, 1931

Down Channel, R. T. McMullen, with an introduction by Dixon Kemp and a biographical foreword by Arthur Ransome, George Allen & Unwin, 1931

The Cruise of the Teddy, Erling Tambs, with an introduction by Arthur Ransome, Jonathan Cape, 1933

The Junior Book of Authors, edited by Wilbur C. Hadden and Julia E. Johnsen, The H. W. Wilson Company, 1934

The Far Distant Oxus, Katherine Hull and Pamela Whitlock, introduction by Arthur Ransome, Jonathan Cape, 1937

The 'Falcon' on the Baltic, E. F. Knight, with an introduction by Arthur Ransome, Rupert Hart-Davis, 1951

The Cruise of the 'Alerte', E. F. Knight, with an introduction by Arthur Ransome, Rupert Hart-Davis, 1952

The Cruise of the 'Kate', Empson Edward Middleton, with an introduction by Arthur Ransome, Rupert Hart-Davis, 1953

The Voyage Alone in the Yawl 'Rob Roy', John Macgregor, edited with an introduction by Arthur Ransome, Rupert Hart-Davis, 1954

The Constant Fisherman, Major H. E. Morritt, foreword by Arthur Ransome, Adam & Charles Black, 1957

F. W. Hirst by his Friends, Oxford University Press, 1958

Acknowledgements

In 2004, I received a Royal Society of Literature Jerwood Award for Non-Fiction, and in 2007, an Authors' Foundation Grant from the Society of Authors. Each supplied liquidity and badly needed confidence at vital moments, along with a very welcome sense that writers, despite all evidence to the contrary, belong to a community. I am extremely grateful to both foundations, and to Paula Johnson, who has been such a friendly and encouraging presence throughout.

This book would certainly not have been written if I'd been left to my own devices. Six years ago, Claire Paterson, now my agent, phoned and asked if I would like to write a biography of Arthur Ransome. She must have wished many times since that she had never proposed it, but I'm delighted she did, and more delighted still to be able to say – 'Look, Claire, it's done!'

My editor, Neil Belton, who has read every chapter several times, reminded me early on, and to my great relief, that a book is just a pile of paper. Few people could have understood with greater imagination or generosity what I was doing, where I was succeeding and where I was most likely to take a fall. Over the years I've benefited so much from his friendship, and from the friendship of his family. I would also like to thank Ian Bahrami and Anne Owen for making the last few months of this project so much more pleasant than they might otherwise have been.

At the start of all this I spent a great deal of time up in Leeds, where I stayed with Professor Francis R. Bridge, cycled to the Brotherton Library every day along the canal, and returned to drink whiskey, collaborate on the crossword or saunter across to the Barge. Thank you, Roy. Many thanks also to the staff at the Brotherton Library, to Ann Farr, who was responsible for cataloguing Ransome's papers, to Christina Hardyment, the executor of his literary estate, to Arthur Lupton and Dick Kelsall for supplying first-hand accounts, and to Margaret Ratcliffe and Ted Alexander for exceeding the call of duty. In Russia, Dasha Lotareva and Liuba Vinogradova guided me through the labyrinth. Later, Gleb Drapkin, Evgenia's great-nephew, sent me long emails describing his family, as well as many photographs. Imagining the past in a foreign country is no easy business, and without these three I would have been lost entirely.

Several people have been generous enough to read through various drafts, amongst them Ted Alexander, Bert Patenaude, Lev Grossman, Sophie Gee, Alistair Breach, Emily Irwin, Philip Marsden, Jemima Lewis and Christina Hardyment. Will Hobson, whose intuitive understanding of language and the shape of ideas always staggers me, has read it in so many drafts I hesitate to remind him of it.

Finally, I would like to thank Susan Chambers, who almost five years ago recoiled as I did a handstand in Hyde Park. She was there when I finished the first chapter. She has studied every sentence. She has listened to me grumble over it in four countries and nine houses and has only rarely told me to shut up. Incredibly, in May 2008, she married me.

Index

Robins, Colonel Raymond, 182,
189, 200, 204, 216, 218, 254
Rodzianko, Mikhail, 103, 112,
132-3
Roman (Evgenia's brother), 300
Rosenberg, Marcel, 298
Ross, Robert, 56, 57, 58, 62, 78
Rothstein, Theodore, 29-30, 172-3,
176, 199
Rouse, W. H. D., 25, 26
Rowlandson, Maurice, 5
Royal Cruising Club, 325, 326
Rugby School, 21, 23-6
Russell, Bertrand, 303, 304-5; *The
Practice and Theory of
Bolshevism*, 304

Russia, 76-8, 103, 125; 'Bloody
Sunday' massacre (St Petersburg),
45, 127, 196; bread riots and
demonstrations, 123, 128-9; creation of Anglo-Russian Bureau,
114-15, 119, 138, 188, 347, 355;
crisis in, 298-9, 304-5; evacuation of Bolshevik government to
Moscow, 203, 204, 210; famine,
309-11, 331; and First World
War, 111, 113, 118-19, 121,
148-50, 151; growth in dissatisfaction with Romanovs and calls
for revolution, 103-4, 111-12,
125, 126-7; hostility from United
States towards Soviet government,
244; and Lenin's New Economic
Policy, 308, 312; and March
Revolution, 123, 128-32; and
murder of Rasputin, 125, 126;
peace negotiations and treaty
signed with Estonia, 271-2,
286-7, 291-2, 298; peace talks
with Germany at Brest-Litovsk
and treaty signed, 171, 178, 182,
183, 191-207, 210, 211, 223,
226, 258; recognition of Soviet as
de jure government by Britain,
324; ruling of by Soviet Petrograd
and Duma after March
Revolution, 135-6; scandals, 120;
third centenary of Romanov

dynasty celebrations, 76; trade
agreement with Britain *see* Anglo-
Soviet Accord; war with Germany
and Galician offensive, 86-7,
87-8, 89-90, 103; withdrawal of
British troops, 291, 294
Russian Civil War, 6, 159-60, 176,
258-9, 278, 281, 285, 289, 291;
Allied intervention in, 223-4,
230-1, 233, 235-6, 258-60, 277,
278; death toll, 331
Russian Revolution, 331-2 *see also*
November Revolution
Russian Social Democratic Labour
Party, 91, 141
Rykov, 302

Sackville-West, Vita, 60
Sadoul, Captain Jacques, 216, 254,
266
St Petersburg, 73, 76, 84-5, 86, 88
Sassoon, Siegfried, 46
Scales, Major, 233-4
Scott, Charles Prestwich (C. P.), 24,
282-3, 294, 295-6, 302, 345
Scott, Ted, 24, 325, 335, 345, 360
Secker, Martin, 53, 54, 58-60, 61-2
Second World War, 365
Selby, Major Herbert, 279
Serbia, 87
Sharp, Clifford, 250, 261-2, 276
Shatov, Bill, 163
Shelepina, Evgenia Petrovna *see*
Ransome, Evgenia
Shelepina, Iroida (Evgenia's sister),
216, 221, 300-1, 308, 323, 341,
363
Shelepina, Pyotr Ivanovitch
(Evgenia's father), 186
Shelepina, Serafima (Evgenia's sister),
300, 363
Shiel, M. P. (Matthew Phipps), 32-3;
The House of Sounds, 33
Shlyapnikov, Alexander, 142
Sichel, Edith, 42
Sisson, Edgar, 182, 218
Smith, Pixie Coleman, 44
Smolny Institute, 180